Praise for *Rapid Web Applications with T...*

"Dear PHP,

It's over between us. You can keep the kitchen sink, but I wan[...]

With TurboGears, I was able to shed the most heinous FileMaker Pro legacy 'solution' imaginable. It has relationships based on fields that change frequently, causing 'disappearing data.' I replaced it with an easy to maintain TurboGears application. Defunkifying and normalizing many years worth of munged data took twice as long as developing the TurboGears's application itself. TurboGears's excellent set of tools and best-of-breed approach makes it so easy to build applications quickly."

—**Isaac Csandl**, Manager of Information Technology, Chicago Legal Search, Ltd.

"TurboGears has resulted in significant time savings for rPath. Before it was released, we expected to spend significant time building a Web framework for our rPath Appliance Agent product. TurboGears sharpens our focus on building a quality application; it allows us to provide more value to our customers, rather than reinventing the Web wheel."

—**Michael K. Johnson**, rPath Founding Engineer and Coauthor of
Linux Application Development, Second Edition

"I think this is the first time that a Web framework's functionality has been so obvious."

—**Bruce Eckel**, Author of *Thinking in Java* and *Thinking in C++*

"TurboGears helped me build more complex Web applications more quickly and with fewer headaches than any other framework I've used. Just like Python itself, it made me more productive with a minimal learning curve."

—**Quentin Hartman**, System Administrator

"TurboGears has changed the way I develop Web applications, from model, to view, to controller. Thanks to the power of TurboGears, I was able to develop the first version of WhatWhat in less than a week of my spare time."

—**Jonathan LaCour**, Development Team Lead, Optio

"TurboGears has provided a way for me to greatly enhance my productivity by realizing the potential of Web-based agile development with Python."

—**Brandon Goldfedder**, Vice President of Engineering, Information Extraction and
Transport (IET Inc.), and Author of *The Joy of Patterns*

"TurboGears really changed the way I schedule project releases: It allows me to deliver them faster and with better quality than when I used to use GUI toolkits."

—**Jorge Godoy**, Owner of G2C Tech Consultoria in Brazil, former Lead Developer for Conectiva documentation team

"With TurboGears, I was able to transition my Python projects into Web applications as easily as possible."

—**Benjamin T. Hamilton**, Software Engineer

"Norwegian-based company Scanmine AS makes extensive use of Python and Turbo-Gears in all parts of its operation. TurboGears makes it a breeze to build highly sophisticated Web 2.0 applications with out-of-the-box features for multiple languages with full Unicode, REST, AJAX, RSS/Atom, and more. This enables Scanmine to put a face on their technology development in a minimal amount of time.

"It has been said that there are as many Web frameworks as there are Python Web programmers. This apparent Web framework fragmentation has long been perceived as a weakness, until TurboGears came along and turned weakness into strength."

—**Rune Hansen**, Senior Systems Designer, Scanmine AS

"TurboGears is a well thought-out framework; the design choices it has made will help you be more productive. TurboGears will give you confidence with its foundation of stable best-of-breed Python components. If you are coming from other languages, consider working in TurboGears and Python to bring fun back into your Web development work."

—**Jeff Marshall**, Partner with FrozenBear

"When we started developing Oprius Foundations with TurboGears, we weren't sure if it really would help us develop quicker and higher-quality code. After two months, we had a task manager to rival Tada List. After seven months, we had an entire contact management system to compete with the big boys."

—**Jason Chu**, Lead Developer, Oprius Software Inc.

"Conventional programming wisdom states that rewriting any working project from scratch is a bad idea. TurboGears was good enough to convince me to do this anyway, and I have been nothing but thrilled with the results. With TurboGears, I was able to implement an AJAX-based Web site with a nice Web API more easily than I ever thought possible. If you are trying to do either of those in Python, you owe it to yourself to look at this project. Using TurboGears was one of the few times in my programming career where a task was significantly less complicated than I thought possible."

—**Adam Jones**, Lead Programmer, RecursiveThought Software

Rapid Web Applications with TurboGears

Prentice Hall
Open Source Software Development Series

Arnold Robbins, Series Editor

"Real world code from real world applications"

Open Source technology has revolutionized the computing world. Many large-scale projects are in production use worldwide, such as Apache, MySQL, and Postgres, with programmers writing applications in a variety of languages including Perl, Python, and PHP. These technologies are in use on many different systems, ranging from proprietary systems, to Linux systems, to traditional UNIX systems, to mainframes.

The **Prentice Hall Open Source Software Development Series** is designed to bring you the best of these Open Source technologies. Not only will you learn how to use them for your projects, but you will learn *from* them. By seeing real code from real applications, you will learn the best practices of Open Source developers the world over.

Titles currently in the series include:

Linux® Debugging and Performance Tuning: Tips and Techniques
Steve Best
0131492470, Paper, ©2006

Understanding AJAX: Using JavaScript to Create Rich Internet Applications
Joshua Eichorn
0132216353, Paper, ©2007

Embedded Linux Primer
Christopher Hallinan
0131679848, Paper, ©2007

SELinux by Example
Frank Mayer, David Caplan, Karl MacMillan
0131963694, Paper, ©2007

UNIX to Linux® Porting
Alfredo Mendoza, Chakarat Skawratananond, Artis Walker
0131871099, Paper, ©2006

Linux Programming by Example: The Fundamentals
Arnold Robbins
0131429647, Paper, ©2004

The Linux® Kernel Primer: A Top-Down Approach for x86 and PowerPC Architectures
Claudia Salzberg, Gordon Fischer, Steven Smolski
0131181637, Paper, ©2006

Rapid Web Applications with TurboGears

Using Python to Create Ajax-Powered Sites

Mark Ramm

KevinDangoor

Gigi Sayfan

PRENTICE
HALL

Prentice Hall

An imprint of Pearson Education

Upper Saddle River, NJ · Boston · Indianapolis · San Francisco

New York · Toronto · Montreal · London · Munich · Paris · Madrid

Cape Town · Sydney · Tokyo · Singapore · Mexico City

Many of the designations used by manufacturers and sellers to distinguish their products are claimed as trademarks. Where those designations appear in this book, and the publisher was aware of a trademark claim, the designations have been printed with initial capital letters or in all capitals.

The authors and publisher have taken care in the preparation of this book, but make no expressed or implied warranty of any kind and assume no responsibility for errors or omissions. No liability is assumed for incidental or consequential damages in connection with or arising out of the use of the information or programs contained herein.

The publisher offers excellent discounts on this book when ordered in quantity for bulk purchases or special sales, which may include electronic versions and/or custom covers and content particular to your business, training goals, marketing focus, and branding interests. For more information, please contact:

U.S. Corporate and Government Sales
(800) 382-3419
corpsales@pearsontechgroup.com

For sales outside the United States please contact:

International Sales
international@pearsoned.com

 This Book Is Safari Enabled

The Safari® Enabled icon on the cover of your favorite technology book means the book is available through Safari Bookshelf. When you buy this book, you get free access to the online edition for 45 days. Safari Bookshelf is an electronic reference library that lets you easily search thousands of technical books, find code samples, download chapters, and access technical information whenever and wherever you need it.

To gain 45-day Safari Enabled access to this book:

- Go to http://www.prenhallprofessional.com/safarienabled
- Complete the brief registration form
- Enter the coupon code 1MLQ-R4QN-MBVS-33N6-EHJM

If you have difficulty registering on Safari Bookshelf or accessing the online edition, please e-mail customer-service@safaribooksonline.com.

Visit us on the Web: www.prenhallprofessional.com

ISBN 0-13-243388-5
Text printed in the United States on recycled paper at R.R. Donnelley and Sons in Crawfordsville, Indiana.
First printing, November 2006

Library of Congress Cataloging-in-Publication Data

Ramm, Mark.

Rapid Web applications with TurboGears : using Python to create Ajax-powered sites / Mark Ramm, Kevin Dangoor, Gigi Sayfan.

p. cm.

ISBN 0-13-243388-5 (pbk. : alk. paper) 1. Web site development. 2. Python (Computer program language) 3. TurboGears (Computer file) 4. Ajax (Web site development technology) I. Dangoor, Kevin. II. Sayfan, Gigi. III. Title.

TK5105.888.R355 2006

006.7'6--dc22

2006032304

For all the developers and users that have made TurboGears what it is today, and for all of you —the readers—who will go on to use TurboGears to build something insanely great.

Contents

Part III: Exploring a Real World TurboGears Application

Part V: TurboGears View Technologies

Part VIII: Appendix

Preface

Rapid Web Applications with TurboGears is designed to help you learn to develop web applications faster by using the full set of features included in TurboGears.

To that end, we've divided this book up into several parts: First we'll get an overview of TurboGears and how everything fits together. Then we'll dive right in and create a simple application, and get an overview of how TurboGears works. Then we'll jump into a real world project management application that takes advantage of many of TurboGears's more advanced features. These first three sections are designed to introduce the commonly used features of all the main TurboGears components, to provide you with some insight into the TurboGears philosophy, and to help you build web applications faster. When you're done with the first three sections, you ought to be able to use TurboGears to write reasonably complex applications.

When you're ready to take it up a notch, we also have several more sections that go in depth on each of the various technologies that TurboGears uses to make your life easier.

We'll delve more deeply into MochiKit, SQLObject, Kid, and CherryPy. We'll also explore the TurboGears specific pieces, widgets, and decorators in much greater depth. We'll talk about scaling and performance. We'll show you more advanced patterns, and generally help you take your TurboGears programming ability to the next level.

Along the way you may want to download example code, ask questions, or get more information about a particular subject. We've created www.turbogearsbook.com so that there is a living and changing repository for all kinds of extra stuff that we couldn't fit in the book, or which is simply too new to have been included here.

This book assumes you have a basic understanding of web technologies like XHT-ML, CSS, and Javascript along with an understanding of Python, and the basics of Relational Databases. We've tried not to assume too much, and we intentionally picked reviewers who were new to one or more of these areas in an attempt to make the learning curve as smooth as possible. But if you are new to any of these technologies, we've got some articles, links, and book recommendations on our website.

The goal for TurboGears, and for this book, is to make easy things easy, and hard things possible. After the first couple sections you should feel comfortable making basic database driven sites, and after the next few sections you'll have the tools you need to create complex Ajax enabled sites with dynamic user interfaces.

Acknowledgments

This book would not have been possible without help from dozens of members of the TurboGears community who answered questions on the mailing list, contributed code snippets, documented features on the wiki, and otherwise supported us as we wrote this book. Thank you all. This book came into being because of Mark Taub's belief in the project and initial encouragement. We are equally indebted to Debra Williams Cauley and Arnold Robbins, whose experience and editorial guidance made every step of the way a little bit easier, and whose contributions definitely make this a better book.

We also need to thank a huge array of people. It's been said that it takes a village to raise a child but it sure seems to us that it also takes a village to write a book.

Writing this book has at times felt like living at the center of a whirlwind of activity from dozens of people. We want to say thank you to everyone who helped out. Many helped directly by reviewing chapters, providing sample code snippets, and even writing for us. Others provided help by organizing things so we would have time to work on the book. The community support has been amazing, as has the personal support from coworkers, friends, and family.

We'd especially like to thank the kind people who helped us out by writing for us. Max Ischenko, wrote Chapter 20, "Internationalization," Simon Belak wrote about his work with TurboGears decorators in Chapter 17, "CherryPy and TurboGears Decorators," Remi Dellon (founder of the CherryPy project) wrote much of Chapter 18, "Deployment," and Alberto Valverde provided sample code and lots of helpful input in Chapter 16, "TurboGears Widgets: Bringing CSS, XHTML, and JavaScript Together in Reusable Components."

In addition, it seems that a thousand people offered advice, suggestions, pointed out typos, and otherwise helped us to craft a better book. I'm sure we're missing a few of you, but thank you: Artem Marchenko, Ben Hamilton, Bill Zingler, Bram Vandoren, Charles Ulrich, Fredrik Lundh, Humberto Diógenes, Jeff Marshall, Jorge Godoy, Jorge Vargas, Max Ischenko, Michele Cella, Mike Coyle, Neil Blakey-Milner, Neil Tiften, Peter Russell, Roger Demetrescu, Tim Crawford, Tim Lesher, Jim Yorkshire, and Yves-Eric Martin.

Mark

I couldn't possibly have written this book without the help of my wife, Laura. She pitched in and worked on layout, copy editing, organizing reviewer feedback, copying chapters, researching various topics, and everything else I couldn't do because of schedule pressure. She also provided a willing sounding board for my crazy ideas and handled the consequences of my absurd schedule with patience and grace. Without her support, this book would not have been possible, without her help it would not have been nearly as good, and without her I would not be who I am. Thank you!

Kevin

My wife, Surekha, has been amazingly supportive of me running off to start another business (Blazing Things) even though we now have a daughter to worry about as well. Without Surekha's support and encouragement, we wouldn't have TurboGears today. I also need to thank my daughter, Crysania, for being a wonderful two-year-old and for letting daddy get his work done.

TurboGears

Thank you to all the TurboGears project leaders and developers who have made the project successful and vibrant. CherryPy is led by Remi Delon. Kid was originally created by Ryan Tomayko and has been carried forward by David Stanek. SQLObject is led by Ian Bicking. MochiKit development is led by Bob Ippolito. `setuptools` and `RuleDispatch` are the work of Phillip Eby. Jason Pellerin gave us the Nose testing package. Ondrej Zara's JavaScript code for WWW SQL Designer is an integral part of TurboGears's Model Designer. And, of course, TurboGears wouldn't be possible without Guido van Rossum.

The primary contributors to TurboGears 1.0 itself are: Elvelind Grandin, Ronald Jaramillo, Alberto Valverde Gonzalez, Michele Cella, Richard Standbrook, Simon Belak, Max Ischenko, Jeff Watkins, Dan Jacob, Karl Guertin, Jorge Godoy, and Lee McFadden.

TurboGears has benefited tremendously from the efforts of hundreds of talented developers within the Python open source community, and we are proud to be a part of that community of intelligent, dedicated, open-hearted, and friendly developers. We've learned a lot from the community, and hope that in this book we can give back some small measure of what has been given to us.

PART I

TurboGears Fundamentals

Chapter 1

Introduction to TurboGears

In This Chapter

This book is for people who have clients, managers, and co-workers always asking them for more. It's a book for people who need to write better web applications faster. My guess is that includes most of you.

Your boss, your customers, your co-workers want more software than you can write, and they want it *now*. On the other hand, you have enough trouble trying to get the SQL right for each of those 30 new forms Jane asked you for last week.

1.1 Why TurboGears?

The good news is that many, perhaps most, of your problems don't stem from what Fred Brooks (in his famous essay *No Silver Bullet*) called the "essential complexity" of the task. Instead, many of your problems are imposed on you by your programming language, your database tools, the nature of web development, and the framework/tools you are currently using.

That might not seem like that's good news to you. But it is! Nobody can solve the essential problems of your application for you. Those problems are unique to the application you want to write, and there's no way around solving them yourself. Fortunately, lots of people are working on TurboGears to move all the accidental complexity of your application into the TurboGears framework so that you don't have to write that code any more. They do this because all of that accidental complexity applies to their projects, too.

Because you'll write less code using TurboGears, learning the ins and outs of TurboGears programming has the potential to make you significantly more productive and can give you the tools and free time you need to make your applications sexier and more responsive.

In other words, better tools such as TurboGears can solve a lot of your problems and make programming complex web applications a lot easier.

1.1.1 Making Easy Things Easy

TurboGears brings together a number of the best tools available in Python for writing maintainable, database-driven, Ajax-enabled web applications.

Every web application is composed mostly of code that does the following:

- Gathers user requests and processes them appropriately (flow-control)
- Organizes and stores all kinds of data in a database (object relational mapping)
- Generates pages (hopefully nice looking pages) to present back to the user (presentation)

TurboGears brings together best-of-breed tools that make these three things "drop-dead easy."

CherryPy enables you to create new URLs simply by creating a class or function with the right name in the root controller class.

SQLObject enables you to define a class for a particular set of data and have it map automatically to a relational database. In fact, as soon as you've defined your data classes, you can generate the database itself with the simple command: `tg-admin sql create`.

Kid, a templating engine, enables you to create templates that can be viewed in a browser without any preprocessing, which can be handed off to a designer, who can tweak the look in her favorite WYSIWYG editor.

1.1.2 Making It Easy to Maintain

If you look at a typical PHP, ColdFusion, ASP, or JSP application, you'll see that nearly every page includes sections devoted to user presentations, database access, and flow control, and that all of this code is jumbled up together in one tangled mess.

For small applications, this works fine; but when things start to grow a bit, it gets pretty hard to maintain. When your boss asks you to make a simple change in one place, you can easily break things in code in another file; and if you aren't careful, you might not discover the breakage until a week later when one of the VPs calls to tell you about how he made a fool of himself when he did a demo of your application for a client and everything fell apart.

Eventually, you start cringing inside every time a user comes to you with a change request—and that's no way to live! You start coming up with excuses, customer requests get ignored, and your application starts to suffer from neglect. Finally, your users move on to something that works better, and your application dies an unnecessary death.

TurboGears helps you to solve the maintainability problem in a couple of ways:

- It pushes (but does not force) you to structure your code to maintain what "enterprise software architects," whoever they are, call the model-view-controller (MVC) paradigm.
- TurboGears has compartments for presentation code (templates or views), flow-control code (controllers), and data-persistence code (models).

We talk more about MVC in Chapter 3, "The Architecture of a TurboGears Application," but for now you can think of TurboGears as one of those metal dinner plates you always see in war movies. You know the ones with separate compartments for potatoes, vegetables, and your main dish.

Beyond the basic MVC program, TurboGears is written in Python, which is designed with as much emphasis on readability as ease of programming. This means that when you come back to old code after a couple of weeks or months, Python is designed to help you understand what is going on as quickly as possible, and TurboGears is similarly designed to make your code as easy to reread as possible.

1.2   The History of TurboGears

Python has a wealth of freely available tools for doing just about anything: serving up web pages, accessing your database, putting content into templates, bathing the cat, and so on. (Okay, the cat-bathing library hasn't been released yet, but we hear it's coming real soon now.) This leaves just one problem then: How do you know which is the "best?"

Ultimately, what's "best" varies from application to application and programmer to programmer. It's often a matter of taste: Choice is good. On the other hand, as of early 2005, if you needed to make a web application, you had to make a choice about how to access the database, another choice about how to handle web requests, and yet another about how to generate finished pages. If there were five viable options for each of those, that meant you needed to evaluate 15 different packages! Not only that, you had to look at how they worked together, giving you dozens of options to evaluate! When confronted by this, many people just make their own packages (which just increases the number of choices available to the next coder in line).

But suppose you avoided the temptation to "roll your own"; after you've finished sorting through the available packages and choosing the ones that were right for you, you still need to wire them up to work well together. They're all working toward the same goal:

making data or functionality available on the web. But, each part focuses on a narrow piece of the puzzle. It becomes your job to look out for the whole of your project.

When working on the Zesty News product, Kevin Dangoor, the creator of Turbo-Gears, had to make these choices and wire them up. He even changed those choices a couple of times midstream as the differences in approaches became more apparent. In June 2005, he decided that it made sense for his business to release these tools in a convenient, bundled package. In July, he had settled on a good set of tools that worked well together. They all felt "Pythonic," and it didn't seem like a big mental leap to use the different parts of the package.

With Kevin's glue code, documentation, and packaging in place, TurboGears was presented at the first Michigan Python Users Group meeting on September 14, 2005, with the software's public release three days later.

Historical fun fact: TurboGears was originally called Rapido. Because of possible trademark concerns, Kevin changed the name to TurboGears the day before the Michi-PUG meeting.

Within three weeks, Kevin's 20 Minute Wiki screencast had been downloaded more than 15,000 times, and people were driving 4+ hours to attend a day-long developer session to work on new TurboGears features.

Kevin had no idea that his little project was going to get that kind of reception. But, it seems that there was a lot of pent-up demand for a full-stack framework that reused some of the high-quality components already available in Python.

1.3   TurboGears, Ajax, and Web 2.0

Recently, there has been a lot of hype about web 2.0 applications and Ajax. In a lot of cases, the hype has passed out of the realm of technical discussion into pure marketing jargon. There are a lot of people selling pretty animations as though they were revolutionary. But, underneath it all, there is a real revolution happening. On the technological side, JavaScript now works reliably to send and retrieve data from the server and to add it to an existing page in real time.

Ajax is shorthand for Asyncronous JavaScript and XML, but it has come to be used to describe a variety of techniques that allow the JavaScript to talk to your server and dynamically update your page in real time. Sometimes, XML is not involved; the server response can be plain HTML or serialized JavaScript objects—it doesn't matter, we still call it Ajax.

Technology aside, Ajax's real impact is that it is enabling a revolution in user interface design for the web. For more than 10 years, the dominant paradigm of web development has been this: "Serve up a series of dynamically generated pages." Now we're starting to see that user interaction does not need to be chunked up into whole page sections. Ajax-enabled pages have code to send requests for dynamic updates to the server, receive live responses, and update themselves automatically. This really is a revolution in user interface design, and TurboGears includes MochiKit JavaScript library, and a variety of prebuilt widgets to help you take advantage of everything that Ajax can bring to your application.

Unfortunately, revolutions take work, and this one is no different. Hopefully, nobody has to die, or go without food, or take 40-hour guard shifts, or do any of the stuff that real revolutionaries do. But, you will have to write JavaScript, debug it on different browsers, and understand a little bit about the Document Object Model (DOM).

Fortunately, the MochiKit makes all of this easier. So, your personal revolutionary statement won't end up costing your life—or even a good night's sleep.

1.4   Why TurboGears Values Being "Pythonic"

When reading Python-related sites, the word *Pythonic* comes up fairly often. If you use Python a lot, you tend to find a commonality in how libraries approach their use. This coding style, or development philosophy, extends beyond the standard library and into many third-party libraries that you can download.

Tim Peters, one of the core Python developers, summed it up probably better than anybody. And now his words are imortalized in the Python interpreter. If you pull up a Python prompt, and type `import this`, you will see *The Zen of Python*. It's possibly the best definition of *Pythonic* that you'll find.

```
>>>import this
The Zen of Python, by Tim Peters
Beautiful is better than ugly.
Explicit is better than implicit.
Simple is better than complex.
Complex is better than complicated.
Flat is better than nested.
Sparse is better than dense.
Readability counts.
Special cases aren't special enough to break the rules.
Although practicality beats purity.
```

```
Errors should never pass silently.
Unless explicitly silenced.
In the face of ambiguity, refuse the temptation to guess.
There should be one-- and preferably only one --obvious way to do it.
Although that way may not be obvious at first unless you're Dutch.
Now is better than never.
Although never is often better than *right* now.
If the implementation is hard to explain, it's a bad idea.
If the implementation is easy to explain, it may be a good idea.
Namespaces are one honking great idea -- let's do more of those!
```

With TurboGears, we try to adhere to these principles as much as possible. In addition, we seek to use standard Python language constructs as much as possible. Requests coming in from the web become standard method calls when they reach your code. Expressions in the templates are standard Python expressions. Even MochiKit, which is written in JavaScript, provides a number of functions that are part of the Python standard library, but missing from JavaScript.

All of these things add up to a programming environment that seeks to ensure that you're not surprised. Or, if you are, you're pleasantly surprised that the environment did exactly what you expected it to do.

1.5   What Can You Do with TurboGears?

TurboGears is designed to help you write web applications. You can write wikis; Flickr-like photo-sharing sites; or a new database-driven, Ajax-enabled, dynamic, web 2.0 fan site for Charlize Theron. Whatever you want, you can do it with TurboGears.

TurboGears is not a content management system, nor is it a giant enterprise application framework. But, you can use it to build a content management application, as somebody already has, or to build enterprise applications, if that's what you need.

TurboGears is currently best suited to those who can control their database structure, but it is rapidly becoming the best "agile language" web framework for those of you who have large, complex databases.

The TurboGears team is integrating SQLAlchemy to bring the ease of Turbo Gears-style development to people who need more flexibility and power in the way they deal with relational databases. (See Appendix A, "SQLAlchemy," for an introduction to SQLAlchemy.)

As of this writing, people are using TurboGears to build blogs, project management tools, wikis, tag-handling mini-applications, RSS aggregators, content management systems, customer relationship management systems, web front ends for large scientific data processing applications, Java servlet monitoring systems, web-based interfaces for managing virtual servers, community event-planning tools, and dozens of other web applications.

You can think of TurboGears as a super-charged web application complexity-reduction engine, which makes developing all of these kinds of applications easier by automating many of the things you used to have to do by hand.

1.6   Coming Soon to a TurboGears Near You

Open-source software development is different from that of the commercial software world. When you're paying people to develop software for you, you can hold them accountable to get what you need done in a reasonable time frame. With open-source software, you have no such assurances. You can't require anyone to do what you think needs to be done, and you certainly can't hold someone to a time frame.

Open-source software gets built up either because people need something for projects they're doing for their work or because they find it fun or interesting to create some cool bit of software.

When you lead an open-source project, you can't count on things getting done unless you know that someone is working on it for a specific project with a deadline. To balance this out on the plus side, however, you'll get all kinds of unexpected contributions from all over. Features you never would've imagined yourself suddenly show up in your inbox.

With those things in mind, here are some clues about things planned for TurboGears.

As mentioned earlier in this chapter, integration of the SQLAlchemy object-relational mapper (ORM) is an important part of our plans for the future! Right now, SQLAlchemy requires a bit more code than SQLObject for many types of applications. But, it also makes it possible to create a whole new set of applications that otherwise would have been prohibitively difficult with SQLObject. When some higher-level application programming interfaces (APIs) are created for SQLAlchemy, it will easily be among the best ORMs for any language.

The big theme for the first major release after 1.0 is "application reuse." We want to make it possible to easily install a blog or a wiki, customize it for your site, and integrate it in no time. This feature would equally apply to your own applications. You'll be able to easily install and extend the same basic product for each customer that comes along.

We also plan to extend the authentication/authorization system to handle many more requirements "out of the box." Right now, it offers a super-simple API that meets a great many needs, but doesn't provide a smooth or obvious upgrade path if your needs go beyond what's included. We want to provide that path.

1.7   Summary

- TurboGears is designed to abstract away the common complexities of developing web applications, so that you can focus on the particular needs of your application.
- TurboGears and Python are intended to help you create code that is easy to read and easy to maintain.
- Kevin Dangoor built the first version of TurboGears reusing existing Python projects including SQLObject, CherryPy, Kid, and MochiKit.
- Ajax and web 2.0 concepts weren't grafted on to TurboGears—they were built in from the beginning.
- The design philosophy behind Python encapsulated in The Zen of Python is important to Kevin and the rest of the TurboGears team, and you'll often hear qoutes from The Zen of Python in mailing list discussions.
- TurboGears is continuing to grow into a framework that can be used by even larger and more-complex projects. SQLAlchemy, in particular, promises to make TurboGears the best dynamic language framework for people who have to work with large, complex, or legacy databases.

Chapter 2

Getting Started with TurboGears

In This Chapter

In this short chapter, we cover the basics of installing TurboGears and setting up a simple database to use with your web applications. Then we create a super-easy Hello World application and take a first brief glimpse at how you can use something called MVC to help structure your application to make the code clearer and easier to maintain.

2.1 Installing TurboGears and SQLite

Before you can start writing cool new TurboGears applications, you have to install it and all of its component pieces on your computer. The good news is that thanks to Phillip Eby, Python Eggs, and Easy Install, this is now amazingly easy to do for anybody running Windows, Linux, or Mac OS X.

With Philip Eby's Easy Install package, installing TurboGears is now as easy as this:

1. Install Python 2.4 or 2.5, if not already installed. You certainly can use TurboGears with 2.3, but unless you have a compelling reason to do that, your experience is going to be *significantly better* if you use a newer Python release. If you do choose to use Python 2.3, you must do some things differently than we do here in this book because TurboGears makes heavy use of function/method decorators to save you time and to make your code easier to read. So, although you can use TurboGears with 2.3, the examples in this book are specifically designed to work with Python 2.4 or later. See the sidebar "Decorators in Python 2.3" for more information.

2. Install TurboGears by downloading the setuptools/EasyInstall bootstrap script (ez_setup) and running it. You can find the script, along with detailed platform-specific instructions, at www.turbogears.org/download.

3. Install and configure whatever database back end you need.

The easiest way to get a SQL database is to install SQLite 3 and pysqlite 2. On Windows, this is as easy as `easy-install pysqlite`. If you use Ubuntu or another Debian-based Linux version, you can `apt-get install sqlite`, and then `apt-get install pysqlite2`. Red Hat and SUSE have RPM Packet Managers (RPMs) in their repository.

What Are Python Eggs?

In addition to a robust standard library, Python has a huge selection of freely available and usable add-on libraries. These libraries do everything from providing cross-platform graphical user interfaces to complex mathematics. The Python Cheeseshop, formerly the Python Package Index (PyPI), provides an index to many of these packages.

Before the Eggs, installing one of these packages meant doing this: following the links from the Cheeseshop until you can download it, downloading the package, and running `python setup.py install`.

On some Linux systems, you can `apt-get <somepackage>` and have the package installed. On the Mac, you can get something similar from Fink or DarwinPorts. Things get more complicated when you bring Windows into the picture.

To make matters worse, some packages depend on other packages to function. Sometimes it's harder than it should be to install an applicaiton and all its dependencies.

This is where Python "eggs" come in. Phillip Eby's `setuptools` package enables your Python to handle eggs, and the convenient `easy_install` command makes installing Python packages consistent and easy on every platform.

Thanks to `setuptools`, you can type `easy_install TurboGears` to get Turbo Gears and the correct versions of many packages that TurboGears uses, all in the correct formats for your platform.

The egg format provides a plug-in extension mechanism that packages such as TurboGears can use. For example, TurboGears supports plug-in packages of widgets. After you install an egg containing widgets, those widgets automatically appear in tools such as the TurboGears Widget Browser.

Unlike traditional Python packages, eggs also have the advantage of allowing you to install multiple versions of a package and choose the correct one at runtime. This multiple install enables you to test out code with both development and stable versions of a library to ensure that your application runs well with both versions.

You can find more detailed install instructions at www.turbogears.org. The Turbo-Gears site always contains the most up-to-date platform-specific instructions. It also has instructions on how to do a rootless install on Linux and some tricks to help make your install experience on Windows as easy as possible.

If you already have MySQL or postgres 8 installed, however, you can just use that.

> NOTE: We assume your familiarity with using the command line on your platform of choice. Some Windows and Mac OS X users seem not to have discovered the power of the command line. If you're one of those people, take a few minutes and make friends with the command line. I promise she's a great friend to have and can definitely bail you out of a lot of trouble. You can find lots of links to more information about using the command line at www.turbogearsbook.com/command-line.

2.2 Creating a Hello World Application

Okay, now that you have TurboGears and SQLite installed (or another database if you chose that route), you are ready to start your first TurboGears application. This is easier than it looks.

TurboGears provides a command-line administrative interface to help you with common development tasks, from creating a new project to opening up a database and creating all the tables necessary to hold your data. But more about all of that later, for now let's just use the `tg-admin` command to create a new application.

This couldn't be simpler, you just open up a command prompt window and type the following:

```
tg-admin quickstart
```

You are then asked for the name of your project. For this first project, just call it `hello`. The next thing you must provide is your package name. TurboGears does its best to turn your project name into a reasonable package name, omitting spaces and other characters that are illegal in package names. So, in this case, you can just press Enter to accept the default package name, which will also be hello. You also want to answer no to the next question because we do not plan to password protect this little "hello world" application.

```
Enter project name: hello
Enter package name: [hello]
```

Then it spits out a bunch of text like this:

```
Enter project name: hello
Enter package name [hello]:
Do you need Identity (usernames/passwords) in this project? [no]
Selected and implied templates:
   TurboGears#tgbase        tg base template
   TurboGears#turbogears   web framework


Variables:
   identity:   none
   package:    hello
   project:    hello
Creating template tgbase
Creating directory .\hello
  Recursing into +einame+.egg-info
    Creating .\hello\hello.egg-info/
    Copying PKG-INFO to .\hello\hello.egg-info\PKG-INFO
    Copying paster_plugins.txt to .\hello\hello.egg-info\paster_plugins.txt
    Copying sqlobject.txt_tmpl to .\hello\hello.egg-info\sqlobject.txt
  Recursing into +package+
    Creating .\hello\hello/
    Copying __init__.py_tmpl to .\hello\hello\__init__.py
    Copying release.py_tmpl to .\hello\hello\release.py
    Recursing into static
      Creating .\hello\hello\static/
      Recursing into css
        Creating .\hello\hello\static\css/
        Copying empty to .\hello\hello\static\css\empty
      Recursing into images
        Creating .\hello\hello\static\images/
        Copying favicon.ico to .\hello\hello\static\images\favicon.ico
        Copying tg_under_the_hood.png to .\hello\hello\static\images\tg_under_the_
➥hood.png
      Recursing into javascript
        Creating .\hello\hello\static\javascript/
        Copying empty to .\hello\hello\static\javascript\empty
    Recursing into templates
      Creating .\hello\hello\templates/
      Copying __init__.py_tmpl to .\hello\hello\templates\__init__.py
Creating template turbogears
  Recursing into +package+
    Recursing into config
```

```
    Creating .\hello\hello\config/
    Copying __init__.py_tmpl to .\hello\hello\config\__init__.py
    Copying app.cfg_tmpl to .\hello\hello\config\app.cfg
    Copying log.cfg_tmpl to .\hello\hello\config\log.cfg
  Copying controllers.py_tmpl to .\hello\hello\controllers.py
  Copying json.py_tmpl to .\hello\hello\json.py
  Copying model.py_tmpl to .\hello\hello\model.py
  Recursing into sqlobject-history
    Creating .\hello\hello\sqlobject-history/
    Copying empty to .\hello\hello\sqlobject-history\empty
  Recursing into templates
    Copying login.kid to .\hello\hello\templates\login.kid
    Copying master.kid to .\hello\hello\templates\master.kid
    Copying welcome.kid to .\hello\hello\templates\welcome.kid
  Recursing into tests
    Creating .\hello\hello\tests/
    Copying __init__.py_tmpl to .\hello\hello\tests\__init__.py
    Copying test_controllers.py_tmpl to .\hello\hello\tests\test_controllers.py
    Copying test_model.py_tmpl to .\hello\hello\tests\test_model.py
  Copying README.txt_tmpl to .\hello\README.txt
  Copying dev.cfg_tmpl to .\hello\dev.cfg
  Copying sample-prod.cfg_tmpl to .\hello\sample-prod.cfg
  Copying setup.py_tmpl to .\hello\setup.py
  Copying start-+package+.py_tmpl to .\hello\start-hello.py
Running C:\Python24\python.exe setup.py egg_info
Adding TurboGears to paster_plugins.txt
running egg_info
writing requirements to hello.egg-info\requires.txt
writing hello.egg-info\PKG-INFO
writing top-level names to hello.egg-info\top_level.txt
reading manifest file 'hello.egg-info\SOURCES.txt'
writing manifest file 'hello.egg-info\SOURCES.txt'
```

This `quickstart` command creates a directory structure, and a couple of template files for you to put your code into. Don't worry about the details just yet, however; we come back to it. For now, we just want to get started doing something that works!

You can now navigate into the `hello` directory that we just created. In it you will find `start-hello.py`. Run this by entering the following:

```
python start-hello.py
```

You should then see this:

```
mark@ubuntu:~/tg0.9/hello$ python start-hello.py
2005/12/26 13:03:58 CONFIG INFO Server parameters:
2005/12/26 13:03:58 CONFIG INFO     server.environment: development
2005/12/26 13:03:58 CONFIG INFO     server.logToScreen: True
2005/12/26 13:03:58 CONFIG INFO     server.logFile:
2005/12/26 13:03:58 CONFIG INFO     server.protocolVersion: HTTP/1.0
2005/12/26 13:03:58 CONFIG INFO     server.socketHost:
2005/12/26 13:03:58 CONFIG INFO     server.socketPort: 8080
2005/12/26 13:03:58 CONFIG INFO     server.socketFile:
2005/12/26 13:03:58 CONFIG INFO     server.reverseDNS: False
2005/12/26 13:03:58 CONFIG INFO     server.socketQueueSize: 5
2005/12/26 13:03:58 CONFIG INFO     server.threadPool: 0
2005/12/26 13:03:58 HTTP INFO Serving HTTP on http://localhost:8080/
```

If you get an error, the most likely cause is that you already have a service running on port 8080. You can fix this easily by running TurboGears on another port. To change the port your TurboGears application runs on, just open `dev.cfg` in the root directory of your application and change the line that reads

```
# server.socket_port=8080
```

to

```
server.socket_port=3000
```

(Remember to remove the # sign!!!)

At this point, you should be able to run the `start-hello.py` program.

If everything works, you should next be able to open a browser and go to `http://localhost:8080/` and see the "Are you ready to Gear Up?" page (as shown in Figure 2.1). Of course, if you are running on another port, you must put that in the URL!!

If this worked, your application is up and running.

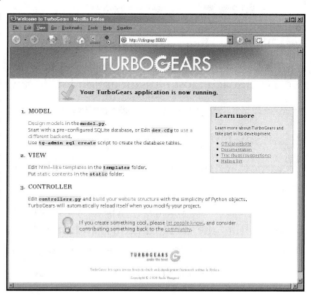

FIGURE 2.1 TurboGears welcome page

Decorators in Python 2.3

TurboGears makes extensive use of "decorators." Decorators are discussed in more detail later. The examples in this book are written in this form:

```
@expose()
def some_method(self, someval):
    return "Hi"
```

The `@expose()` is a decorator, and the `@` syntax was introduced in Python 2.4. Luckily, the `@` is just syntax sugar. If you're using Python 2.3, you can translate the above into the following:

```
def some_method(self, someval):
    return "Hi"
some_method = expose()(some_method)
```

That is the standard way to do decoration in Python 2.3. It's more verbose, but it works. Lucky for us, however, TurboGears offers a special convenience syntax for decoration:

```
[expose()]
def some_method(self, someval):
    return "Hi"
```

The preceding code works in both Python 2.3 and 2.4. We don't use this syntax in the book examples because it is nonstandard. However, it is definitely the easiest and most pleasant option for Python 2.3 users.

2.3   Say Hi! (Simple Template)

Okay, now for the obligatory Hello World example. It is really easy, so it won't take more than 30 seconds.

Go to the `hello` directory within your application path, and to the `templates` directory within the `hello` directory, and find the `welcome.kid` file. Open it up in a text editor (or whatever programming editor you use).

Replace everything inside the `<body></body>` tags with `<h1>Hello World</h1>`.

Your `welcome.kid` file should now look like this:

```
<!DOCTYPE html PUBLIC "-//W3C//DTD XHTML 1.0 Transitional//EN" "http://www.w3.org/
➥TR/xhtml1/DTD/xhtml1-transitional.dtd">
<html xmlns="http://www.w3.org/1999/xhtml" xmlns:py="http://purl.org/kid/ns#"
    py:extends="'master.kid'">

<head>
    <meta content="text/html; charset=UTF-8" http-equiv="content-type"
➥py:replace="''"/>
    <title>Welcome to TurboGears</title>
</head>
<body>

<h1>Hello World</h1>

</body>
</html>
```

And when you browse back to `http://localhost:8080`, you should now see this:

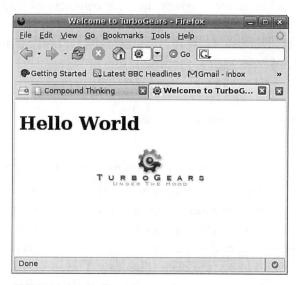

FIGURE 2.2 Hello from the template

That's it for our basic Hello World program, but let's add a bit of dynamic content to make this more like a real web application.

2.4   Custom Greetings (Hello from the Controller)

Sure, that wasn't much code, but it looks an awful lot like a static HTML page, and you probably want to see something more *dynamic*; so let's take a look at how this simple application works and add a bit of dynamic content, which is generated in another Python file called the controller, to our page before we display it to the user.

In the `hello` project is a `hello` folder that contains the file `controllers.py`. This file is what gets called when you browse to your web application. When you open that file in a text editor, something like this displays:

```
import turbogears
from turbogears import controllers, expose


class Root(controllers.RootController):
    @expose(template="hello.templates.welcome")
    def index(self):
        import time
        return dict(now=time.ctime())
```

This file defines what happens when the user connects to a specific URL. Each method in the Root class defines another URL, so if you want to have a `http://local-host:8080/hello` URL, you can easily do so: Just define a new method called `hello` to handle the request and send back a response to the browser.

Let's do that now. Just add this to the bottom of the file:

```
    @expose(template="hello.templates.hello")
    def hello(self):
        import time
            return dict(greeting="Greetings from the Controller")
```

Notice a couple of important things about this code. Don't worry if parts of it do not make sense yet; we cover the details soon. For now, it's enough to know that every time you go to `http:/localhost:8080/hello`, this method is called; and when it has finished processing, it calls the `hello.kid template` (which is processed by the Kid templating engine) found in our templates directory. The `dict` returned by this method is automatically available in our template, so we can use it to create dynamic content in the final web page that will be sent out to the browser.

The next thing we need to do is to make a copy of `welcome.kid` and call it `hello.kid`. Then you can open this file in your favorite text editor and add this line directly below `<h1>Hello World<h1>`:

```
<span py:replace="greeting">message from the controller goes here</span>
```

Save this file, and you are ready to go to your new `hello` method, which will create a dynamic message from the controller at `http://localhost:8080/hello`. You don't even have to restart your TurboGears application, if you're in development mode. It watches to see whether anything changed and automatically restarts, so you can make a change and then test it right away in your browser.

The displayed page should have both the Hello World heading, which we saw in Section 2.3, and the new message we passed in from the controller. This case isn't all that interesting because we just passed in a simple string, but you can use this technique to create much more complex web pages with simple and easy-to-understand templates.

You can change this message at any time in your controller file, along with the layout in `hello.kid`. Then when you click reload on the Hello page, the controller and the template automatically reload in your application, enabling you to see the effects of your change right away.

That's it, your first TurboGears application (see Figure 2.3).

FIGURE 2.3 Hello from the controller

2.5   Summary

- The TurboGears command `tg-admin quickstart` can create a brand new Turbo-Gears project for you, complete with all the files you need to get started.

- TurboGears publishes the methods defined in the root controller (which you can find in `controllers.py`).

- TurboGears templates are standard XHTML documents, with a few extra processing directives.

- TurboGears uses decorators such as `@expose(template="hello.template.welcome")` to determine which methods can be called directly from the web, and to define which template can be used to render the final page.

- When your controller returns a `dict`, the contents of that dictionary are automatically available as local variables in your template.

- If you're running Python 2.3, you can use decorators to define which objects are published, but with a slightly different syntax. All examples in this book use the standard Python 2.4 syntax, but there are Python 2.3 versions of some of the example code available at www.turbogearsbook.com.

Chapter 3

The Architecture of a TurboGears Application

In This Chapter

TurboGears is built around the model-viewer-controller (MVC) paradigm. MVC is a system for breaking up applications into three different main sets of components: models, views, and controllers (see Figure 3.1). This is good because the model helps you to write applications faster and makes them easier to understand and maintain.

3.1 What Is MVC?

Let's start out with a high-level overview of the MVC architecture. Don't worry if this makes your head hurt—we explain in more detail in the next few pages.

1. The models represent various pieces of domain data, such as a person's name, or the total sales for the day so far at your local Victoria's Secret branch, or the current status of your build tests.
2. The views present that data to the user in some way. They might display a list of users on a web page, show a running sales total on an LED display, or power on a red lava lamp when the builds fail.
3. Controllers listen for input (actions), provide the logic necessary to parse those actions, send update requests to the model, and sometimes invoke new views for display.

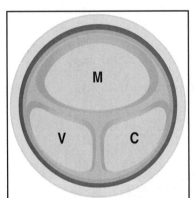

FIGURE 3.1 Keep your code separated with MVC

One benefit of MVC is that it helps you keep different parts of your application separated and isolate potential changes to one area of your code.

So, to bring it all together, suppose you've hacked together an automated build system for the team of developers you are getting together to work on your new Ajax-enabled web 2.0 start-up that you think is going to revolutionize the way we buy organically grown toe lint on the Internet.

If you use MVC for this automated build system, when you check in your code and one of your unit tests fails, the automated build test program will send a message to your application's controller object.

Purity, Pragmatism, MVC, and the Web

Before we lose all 11 of you who actually remember MVC from Smalltalk-80, we thought we'd mention that this isn't the way the original MVC worked. Back then, controllers listened for key presses and mouse clicks, and then interpreted those things and sent messages over to the model to change its state. Every view object was responsible for paying attention to the model and updating itself whenever there was a change.

In the meantime, WebObjects, Struts, and Cocoa have redefined MVC to include a tighter relationship between view and controllers. In a way, this was inevitable because modern window managers and web programming have abstracted away most of the "user event interpretation," which used to be the controller's main job. There's plenty of room to move some view functionality over into the controller, which helps keep views simple enough that designers have a fighting chance to be able to edit views on their own.

So, nearly all modern MVC-based web frameworks use the controller as a place to put some of the glue code and to provide (at least potentially) a layer of abstraction between models and views.

The controller object in turn publishes that information to the model, which changes its state to Tests="Failing."

Meanwhile, you have a view class that's polling the model regularly to see whether it has changed, and when it does, it starts playing an endless loop of Homer Simpson saying "D'oh!" (at least until somebody fixes that darned failing test). That, in turn, sends a message to the controller, which updates the model, at which point the view sees that the model has changed so that the tests are no longer failing and stops playing that annoying MP3.

3.2 Design Patterns and Object-Oriented MVC

In a fully MVC framework, views are observers of controllers and models, and models are observers of the controller. Okay, so you might be asking us, "What exactly does it mean for a view to be an 'observer of the model?'" Well, this is "design pattern speak" for saying that the view either subscribes to the model so that it can be updated whenever the model is changed, or that it polls the model periodically for updates and changes when that happens.

Perhaps you are asking yourself why all this stuff about MVC is important. Will it help me build better applications or help me impress Jenny from marketing?

It might. You'll be able to build more-robust applications, with better separation of concerns, so that when Jenny asks you to make a change to the layout on one of your pages, you'll be able to do it without fear that you might screw up your database.

When we say that a view is an observer of the model, it means that your models don't have to know anything about the views and how they work. So, they are totally disconnected from any change in the way the data is presented to the user. This is important in web applications because the "look and feel" is more likely to change than the underlying domain model, and so it is easy to update the things that you are most likely to update. Therefore, you can easily respond to the new girl in marketing's request to make the web interface look more appealing (all while you are totally relaxed with absolutely no worries that you are going to break your mission-critical model code on the back end).

Likewise, the controller gets called when a user clicks a link or a submit button on one of the views. This action causes an HTTP Post or HTTP Get message to be sent to the server. That message is then trapped by TurboGears, which in turn calls a controller method. That method takes the input that it is given, publishes a change to the necessary model objects, and then passes everything to a view, which displays a new page for the user.

One of the keys to making this architecture work is that models, views, and controllers have a "look but don't touch" rule; views aren't allowed to change models, controllers aren't allowed to change views, and models don't know anything about controllers or views and are merely changed by the various controller objects and published to views. This means that the scope of any given change is limited by the MVC pattern:

- With MVC, you can change which data is presented in a view and the way that it is presented without the need to rewrite any model or controller code.

- With MVC, you can change the way you react to a specific user action, without the need to rewrite any model or view code.

A Brief History of MVC

Web application development has come a long way in the past 10 years. It used to be that we used standard CGI and wrote a separate program to process every form. Most of our application code involved parsing request strings and using string concatenation to spit HTML output back to the user. This took forever to write, and ran slowly because we had to start up a new process for every request!

Then came ASP, PHP, and ColdFusion, which allowed us to have a single server process that took client requests to a specific URL and grabbed the corresponding file with HTML and embedded code, processed the code, and returned the resulting HTML. This was easier to write because generally there was more HTML than code, so it was easier to embed the code in the HTML rather than the HTML in the code. And it performed a lot better because everything ran in a single process, and you could cache database connections.

Then along came JSP, with Java servlets, which allowed "business logic" to be separated from "presentation logic" so that JSP pages could focus just on presentation and servlets could do everything else. This was a lot more maintainable, although people still tended to put too much code into the JSP presentation side of things, because it was a lot easier than writing a new servlet.

Then somebody remembered that this kind of problem had already showed up in the 1970s when people from Xerox Parc were inventing the modern GUI. In 1978, Trygve Reenskaug, along with a number of others at Parc, designed something called model-viewer-controller into the first object-oriented Smalltalk GUI. The theory behind MVC eventually made its way into Objective-C by 1986. Then, just after the original Macintosh computer was released, and the GUI was starting to take off, MVC received its first in-depth coverage in the book *Object-Oriented Programming: An Evolutionary Approach* by Brad J. Cox and Andrew J. Novobilski (Addison-Wesley, 1986).

Finally, MVC made its way to the Internet via WebObjects, and was popularized by Java Struts. You don't need to know all this history to use TurboGears; but if you lived through some or all of this, you should know that TurboGears strips away a lot of the verbosity and configuration requirements of web frameworks such as Struts, to make the MVC architecture easy to use.

- With MVC, you might have to update one or more views when you change a model, because as an observer, views are still users of the model application programming interface (API).

- But with MVC, you probably won't have to create new controller code unless that model change is connected to new or changed user actions.

3.3   Understanding SQLObject and TurboGears Models

At the core of an MVC style application is your domain model, which in TurboGears is usually connected to a relational database through SQLObject. As mentioned in Chapter 1, "Introduction to TurboGears," SQLObject makes database rows into objects and the data they contain into attributes.

This means you can write simple commands like these:

```
> User(first_name="Jane", last_name="Goodall")
> users_named_jane = UserTable.selectBy(first_name="Jane")
```

FIGURE 3.2 SQLObjects are automatically stored in table rows.

For now, we'll assume that the User class is already created. So, the first command creates a User object for Jane Goodall and inserts it into the database in a new row. The second returns an iterator of all the user objects (all the rows in the user table) that have a first_name of "Jane."

As you can see from the example, you don't need to write SQL to update or do simple queries to the database. Not only that, you can create whole new databases from SQLObject after you've defined your model objects (or create model objects from your database!). That way you don't have to duplicate the database definition in both your model objects and SQL files.

This also has the side effect of making it incredibly easy to change database back ends midstream if you determine that your initial choice isn't cutting it.

Okay, enough generic SQLObject stuff. How does this all fit into the MVC paradigm?

With SQLObject, it is incredibly easy to define a simple API for your views to see your model data, without having to know anything about the database.

Let's create a simple SQLObject class and play with it:

```
mark@ubuntu:~/tg0.9$ tg-admin quickstart
Enter project name: SQL Playground
Enter package name [sqlplayground]:
Do you need Identity (usernames/passwords) in this project? [no]
```

Now you can navigate into the SQL-Playground directory and edit the dev.cfg file to tell it where your database is. Because we are using SQLite, you need to find the line that looks like this:

```
# sqlobject.dburi="sqlite:///file_name_and_path"
```

You must change it to include the full path to your database file and remove the # sign from the front of the line so that it will no longer be commented out.

For Linux and Mac OS X users, that might look something like this:

```
sqlobject.dburi="sqlite:///home/mark/turbogears/SQL-playground/sqlplayground.db"
```

For Windows users, it will look something like this:

```
sqlobject.dburi="sqlite:///c|/turbogears/SQL-playground/sqlplayground.db"
```

Now we are going to make our data model, generate our database, and fire up an interactive model so that we can play with the SQLObject API. And we are going to do all of this in less than a dozen lines of code!

Here goes:

The first step is to cd into the sqlplayground directory inside your project directory, SQL-Playground, and edit the model.py file. Just add something like this:

```
class User(SQLObject):
    user_name = StringCol(alternateID=True, length = 20)
    first_name = StringCol()
    middle_initial = StringCol(length=1, default=None)
    last_name = StringCol()
```

When you save this file, you can run `tg-admin sql create` from the SQL-Playground directory to automatically generate and run the SQL commands necessary to create the tables to go along with the model you just described! If you aren't following along and using SQLlite, you might need to create your database manually, before SQLObject can create your tables for you.

Your final step is to run `tg-admin shell` and start playing with the interactive shell. Now you use SQLObject to create, delete, and use objects. For example, you can create a new user with this command:

```
>>> User(user_name="fwray", first_name="fay", last_name="wray")
<User 1 userName='fwray' first_name='fay' middle_initial=None last_name='wray'>
```

If you add another user, that user is automatically added to the next row:

```
>>> User(user_name="bigfish", first_name="carl", last_name="Blankenmeyer")
<User 2 user_name='bigfish' first_name='carl' middle_initial=None last_
➥ name='Blankenmeyer'>
```

You can retrieve a user from the database like this:

```
>>>User.get(2)
<User 2 user_name='bigfish' first_name='carl' middle_initial=None last_
➥ name='Blankenmeyer'>
```

Or you can get a set of users with a key like this:

```
>>>u = User.selectBy(user_name="fwray")
>>>list(u)
```

And you can update a user with simple Python commands like this:

```
>>> u=User.get(2)
>>> u
<User 2 user_name='bigfish' first_name='carl' middle_initial=None last_
➥ name='Blankenmeyer'>
>>> u.first_name="Carl"
>>> u
<User 2 user_name='bigfish' first_name='Carl' middle_initial=None last_
➥ name='Blankenmeyer'>
```

SQLObject also makes it easy to do fancier things such as add foreign key relationships and many-to-many relationships with join tables, but we come back later to explore more of the SQLObject APIs as we go through the tutorials.

The key thing for right now is to have some some idea about how model objects work in TurboGears, which will help you to understand SQLObject's part in TurboGears's MVC implementation.

If you don't need to keep your information in a relational database, you can also save and retrieve model data to standard Python objects, flat files, or wherever your application requires. You can even have model objects that grab and parse information from external services.

You can also build model objects that combine several SQLObject operations within a single method, or combine SQLObject updates with XML-RPC updates, file system changes, and so forth, so that you can present your views with the cleanest possible API.

You should never change your model directly from the view. Instead, the view should allow the user to generate actions that are run by the controller, and if necessary the controller will update the model.

3.4   Understanding CherryPy and TurboGears Controllers

At the center of a TurboGears application is CherryPy, responding to every user action and sending changes to the model and view.

In other words, CherryPy provides the controller part of the MVC paradigm in TurboGears, and that means that it is responsible for parsing user actions and passing state-change requests to your model objects. It also calls the view template and can pass it whatever data it needs to present to the user.

It sounds like a lot, but actually TurboGears makes writing controllers easy.

Although views can pull data from the model, many people prefer to gather up whatever the view needs and pass it into the view as a dictionary.

There are legitimate reasons to move this kind of logic from the view into the controller. For one thing, the less code you have in your view, the easier it is to get a designer to work with you on those pages. Also, you may need to package the same data for several different output formats (HTML, XML-RPC, JSON, and so on), and it helps to keep the data access logic centralized in a single controller.

By default, TurboGears creates a file `controllers.py` for your controller classes in the application sub-directory whenever you use `tg-admin quickstart` to create a new project.

Because a web-based application encapsulates every single user action into an HTTP Get or HTTP Post request, our controller layer needs to listen for those requests, interpret them, and call the appropriate method, passing in the appropriate parameters.

The good news is that CherryPy and the TurboGears framework take care of most of this work for you.

For example, CherryPy takes every incoming request, tries to match it up to the object hierarchy in your controller classes, and calls the appropriate method. Oh, and for good measure, it passes in any parameters that were embedded in the HTTP request.

We saw this in Chapter 2, "Getting Started with TurboGears," when we created the "hello" method. We requested http://localhost:8080/hello, and the hello method was called. If you created the goodbye method, the same thing happened there.

Let's take a look at some sample code that bypasses Kid templates and sends output directly to the browser:

```
class Root(controllers.RootController):
    @expose()
    def index(self, name="John Carter"):
        return "I am %s, of Virginia" % name
```

Okay, so there's one more thing you have to understand to effectively use controllers in TurboGears, and that's the @expose() decorator. If you are new to Python, or just haven't used decorators before, this is easy.

TurboGears provides several decorators for controller methods. We talk about Turbo-Gears Decorators in depth in Chapter 17, "CherryPy and TurboGears Decorators," but we can get going with just @expose.

@expose provides a quick and easy method for you to use to say whether that particular method is public or private. You can also provide a view template that can be used to display the data your controller returns.

The syntax is simple, enabling you to expose a controller method to the web with one line:

```
@expose()
def index(self):
    pass
```

And if you want to send that to the index.kid template, you can do it by adding the name and location (in standard Python dotted notation) to the .expose decorator like this:

What Is a Decorator?

A decorator is a way to tell Python to do some extra stuff automatically whenever a function is called. This means you can use a decorator to easily add similar functionality to a whole bunch of methods—without repeating code. This is particularly useful for "cross-cutting" concerns such as security that would otherwise end up "infecting" all of your classes with a bunch of similar code.

In Python, functions are "first-class objects," which means you can pass a function around just like any other object. So, if we wanted to log any access to a function, we could write a `logging_decorator()` that takes care of the logging.

Before the advent of decorators in Python 2.4, we could write code like this to ensure that our `logging_decorator()` is always called before the `fun()` function:

```
def fun(x):
    ...
fun = logging_decorator(fun)
```

The last line replaces the original `fun()` object with a brand new function object created by calling the `logging_decorator` function, and passing in our original `fun` object as a parameter. The new `fun` object we've created will run the logging decorator, and when that's done it will run the original `fun()` function, which then gets to do its thing, without any knowledge of the logging that just happened.

Python 2.4 decorator syntax makes this process even easier:

```
@logging_decorator
def fun(x):
    ...
```

The `@logging_decorator` is semantically equivalant to `fun = logging_decorator(fun)`. It wraps `fun()` with a call to `logging_decorator`, without the need to repeat the name of the original function three times.

TurboGears and CherryPy provide several decorators in addition to `@expose()` that you can use in your controllers to make your life easier. We explore those decorators in depth in Chapter 17.

```
@expose(template="project_name.templates.index")
def index():
    pass
```

Where `project_name` is the name of your project!

3.5   Understanding Kid and TurboGears Views

TurboGears uses the Kid templating system to do all the formatting and display logic work that comprises the view section of the MVC paradigm. If you are used to PHP, Cheetah, JSP, or ASP, you'll quickly notice that Kid has its own way of doing things. But if you stick around long enough, you'll notice several important advantages to the Kid way.

First of all, if you work with a designer, she'll fall in love with you right away when you show her how she can open up Kid templates easily in Firefox or Dreamweaver.

On the other hand, if you're not lucky enough to work with a great designer, perhaps you'd like to use Dreamweaver, Nvu, or some other WYSIWYG tool to edit your designs yourself (in which case, you'll be the one falling in love with Kid).

I'm sure plenty of you are the hard-core programmers who write a half dozen well-formed 200KB XHTML+CSS and XML configuration files from memory before breakfast. Kid has a lot for you to love, too.

Basically, Kid templates are XML documents with special namespace attributes that tell the Kid processor how to process the template. Most of the time, this means your Kid templates will be valid XHTML documents before they are processed, and valid HTML documents after they are processed and sent out to the user's browser.

The fact that Kid can guarantee that your documents will be well formed has lots of benifits. For example, as discussed in Chapter 8, "RSS, Cookies, and Dynamic Views in Fast Track," the JavaScript function `innerHTML()` works great (as long as you give it valid HTML, and Kid output is always valid).

Of course, if you want to, you can use Kid to output all kinds of other XML documents, from XHTML to RSS feeds, XML-RPC, or whatever you happen to need.

But that's probably getting ahead of things. Right now, you just want to see some basic Kid templates so that you can get your mind around how this all works:

```
<?python
some_text = "SomeText is in the title now!"
?>
<html xmlns:py="http://purl.org/kid/ns#">
```

```
<head>
  <title py:content="some_text">This is replaced.</title>
</head>
<body>
  If you loaded this in Firefox directly the title is "This is Replaced" But
  if you opened through TurboGears the title will be " SomeText is in the title
now!"
</body>
</html>
```

If you save this snippet of code as `welcome.kid` and throw it in the `templates` directory of a freshly quick-started project, you can open up the Kid file directly in your browser, or you can start up your server and see the brand new title.

The preceding example shows how you can use the `<?python ?>` processing instruction to embed pure Python code in your template. But beware, you are *not* allowed to return strings to the template from a `<?python ?>` processing instruction. This might seem like a pain at first, but it really helps to maintain the designer friendliness of Kid. Another even more important benefit of this restriction is that it helps you to avoid the kind of ugly spaghetti code mess of application logic mixed in with the markup code that you often see in PHP, ASP, or JSP code.

The example also shows how you use the `py:content` tag on an attribute to replace the content of that attribute with the value returned by some Python expression. This is one of the keys to making your templates work well in Nvu and Dreamweaver.

If you want to take a shortcut, you can replace the `<title>` attribute described previously with the following:

```
<title>${SomeText}</title>
```

This will have the same result when you run it from within TurboGears. But if you open it in Firefox, Nvu, or Dreamweaver, the title will just be `${SomeText}`, which isn't all that pretty, and because it's not hidden in an attribute, it is much easier for a designer to accidentally change, and therefore break, your application. Nobody wants that!

3.6 MVC Meets Ajax

Recently, there has been a dramatic shift in web development paradigms. Ajax seems to be taking the world by storm, so now it is no longer a given that a user action is going to create an HTTP Post (or HTTP Get) that will then return a brand new page.

Instead, user actions can be picked up by JavaScript on the page and turned into requests that go to the server and get a value back, which is then passed back to the in-page JavaScript by the browser.

Even with more JavaScript view logic, and dynamic updates on the same page, the MVC paradigm still works; you still use views to generate user actions, which are handled by the controller and returned to the browser. You don't have to generate a new page every time something changes. This can be a huge win in terms of improved user experience, and decreased bandwidth. Not only that, Ajax also enables another common MVC idiom that previously had been impossible to implement on the web. As mentioned earlier, in the olden days of GUI MVC, views were often designed to poll the model so that they could automatically update themselves whenever something changed. Without Ajax, there was no good way to do this effectively through the web, but now you can have tickers that show alerts when stock prices drop below a certain threshold, or that let you know when your friend has logged in to the same site you are using, and so on.

Unfortunately, writing Ajax-enabled applications isn't as easy as it should be. Different browsers have different request objects that communicate back to your server, and depending on which browser your user has, you'll need to pick the "right" kind of request object and code to it. Perhaps even worse is that even though JavaScript, and the Document Object Model, has been standardized for years, XML manipulation in JavaScript isn't the same for all browsers. The list of cross-browser differences is large enough that without help you could easily try it and determine that all this talk about new user experiences isn't worth the hassle.

But don't let all that get you down. Writing cross-browser Ajax applications doesn't have to be a brain bending experience. TurboGears comes with a built-in answer to many of the problems that make the JavaScript development experience painful. Turbo-Gears includes a fantastic library of helper functions called MochiKit. MochiKit is great because it has tests that run against all the major browser platforms; so when it says that it handles browser incompatibilities for you, you can actually trust that it works!

With MochiKit, you can use the MochiKit request object to talk to the server, and be confident that your request will work in IE6, Firefox, and Safari. You don't have to use MochiKit or Ajax to build TurboGears applications, if your application just returns static pages—you can skip past all of this new-fangled Ajax stuff and get right down to business. But, if you have a basic understanding of JavaScript syntax, and a desire to build highly interactive web applications, TurboGears includes MochiKit,

SimpleJSON, and Widgets, which all work together with the standard TurboGears components to make building ultra-dynamic Ajax-enabled web applications a lot easier.

3.7   Summary

TurboGears automates much of the work of building web applications using the MVC architecture.

- SQLObject makes it easy to store data in a relational database; and to get, update, and use that data like regular Python objects.
- CherryPy handles user actions (represented by HTTP Get or Post requests).
- The methods in your controller classes map directly to URLs.
- Kid templates are valid XML files, and they are guaranteed to produce valid HTML.
- Kid templates can be opened and manipulated in WYSIWYG tools such as Dreamweaver and Nvu.
- JavaScript (and by extension Ajax) programming isn't always easy because of differences in browser implementation, but MochiKit has extensive tests and will help make creating dynamic applications that work in IE, Firefox, and Safari easier.

PART II

Building a Simple TurboGears Application

Chapter 4

Creating a Simple Application

In This Chapter

Now that we have an idea of how each piece works, let's walk through a simple application that uses everything we know about CherryPy, Kid, and SQLObject.

4.1 Building a Simple Bookmark Collection Site

We'll build a small program to save and categorize links. If you want to imagine a user for this, you can think of the tourist association of a small town such as Mars, Pennsylvania, which needs a central place to aggregate links for restaurants, bed-and-breakfasts, and tourist attractions.

Before we get started on any project, no matter how small, there are a couple of things we always do. First we set up a version control repository. All the code for this book lives in a Subversion repository. In that repository we already have a sample code folder for each chapter, so all we have to do is check out that folder, cd into it, and add our new project like this:

```
cd code/4/
tg-admin quickstart
...
svn ci
```

Everybody makes mistakes, so we're big believers in version control for everything. In fact, we used Subversion to store every revision of every chapter of this book! You can use CVS or Perforce, Bazaar-NG, or whatever version control system you want. You can even skip this step and just start writing code, but we've learned the hard way that something always happens that makes you wish you had used some kind of version control so that you can go back and fix whatever broke. For more information about Subversion, check out the Resources page on our website (www.turbogearsbook.com). Even though we're not going to mention it every time we finish a section, you can bet that we finish every major edit with a quick `svn ci`.

After you've created your bookmarker project, the first thing you'll probably want to do is to check to make sure everything works: `python start-bookmarker.py`. As before, we test this by browsing to `http://localhost:8080/`.

Just like in Chapter 3, "The Architecture of a TurboGears Application," the first step after generating a new project is to set up our SQLite database connection URI: If you're running on Linux or Mac OS X and using SQLite, you can edit the `dev.cfg` file to change the SQLite configuration line to look something like this:

```
sqlobject.dburi= "sqlite:///var/testdatabases/bookmarker.py"
```

This assumes that you'll want to keep your databases in `/var/testdatabases/`, but you can easily edit that to keep your database file wherever you want.

If you're on Windows, you edit the same file with a URI that includes the drive letter:

```
sqlobject.dburi = "sqlite:///d|databases/bookmarker.db"
```

This puts your database in a `databases` folder on your `D:` drive.

At this point in the process, we know we want a list of bookmarks with a name, a URL, and some descriptive text.

So we'll just use the SQLObject column definition syntax (Table 4.1) to define a simple model in `model.py`:

```
from sqlobject import *

from turbogears.database import PackageHub

hub = PackageHub("bookmarker")
__connection__ = hub

class Bookmark(SQLObject):
    name=UnicodeCol(alternateID=True, length=100)
    link=UnicodeCol()
    description=UnicodeCol()
```

After we've got our `Bookmark` class defined, we can use `tg-admin sql create` to have SQLObject generate the database. Hoorah! There isn't a need to keep a separate SQL data definition language file synchronized with your application!

All three of our database columns contain Unicode strings, but SQLObject provides column classes for most data types; we've listed them all in Table 4.1.

TABLE 4.1   Model Classes SQLObject Column Types

SQLObject Column Types	Description
`BLOBCol`	Blob of binary data—jpeg's, word files, etc. (Works with MySql, Postgres, and SQLlite only)
`BoolCol`	Stores true/false data, works (differently) on all back ends
`CurrencyCol`	Equivalent to `DecimalCol(size=10, precision=2)`
`DateCol`	Stores date returned as `datetime`
`DateTimeCol`	Stores date and time—returned as `datetime`
`DecimalCol`	Stores a `decimal` (`size=`(Number of digits), `precision=`(after the decimal)
`FloatCol`	Stores a floating-point number
`PickleCol`	Can store any Python object (It is an extension of `BLOBCol`, which uses the pickle module from the Python standard library to store serialized objects.)
`StringCol`	Stores a `string` (If length is defined, that's the length; if not, a TEXT col is used.)
`UnicodeCol`	Special `string` column that encodes in UTF-8 by default
Model Classes SQLObject Column Parameters	
`dbName`	Name of Column in database (If none is specified, Pythonic name is converted from MixedCase to underscore_separated; for example, UserName becomes user_name.)
`default`	Defines the default value for the column (If not set, the column is required.)
`alternateID`	If true, 1) makes column value unique, 2) creates a "byUsername like method" to your class
`unique`	If true, makes column value unique
`notNone`	If true, null not allowed for the column

Okay, so now we've got a model class and a database back end. The next thing we're going to do is fire up a Python shell where we can play with our model and add some initial data. To do this, type `tg-admin shell`, and you'll be greeted with a standard >>> Python prompt with your model objects already imported for you. So we can add new `Bookmark` objects like this:

```
$>tg-admin shell

>>> Bookmark(name="Google", link="http://www.google.com", description="The one
➥ link to rule them all.")
<Bookmark 1 name='Google' link="'http://www.googl...'">
>>> from turbogears import database
>>> database.commit_all()
>>> Bookmark(name="Compound Thinking", link="http://compoundthinking.com",
➥ description="A blog.")
<Bookmark 2 name='Compound Thinking' link="'http://compoundt...'"
```

```
>>> from turbogears import database
>>> hub.commit()
```

Now we've got a couple of bookmark objects defined and mapped to rows in our database. All we need to do is create a controller method that handles a list request and sends a set of all the bookmarks to the template. Remember that CherryPy (and therefore TurboGears) handles all the incoming HTTP/request stuff for you, and calls the first method that matches the URL in your controller's class hierarchy.

So, let's open up controllers.py and edit it to look like this:

```
import logging
import cherrypy
import turbogears
from turbogears import controllers, expose, validate, redirect

from bookmarker import json

log = logging.getLogger("bookmarker.controllers")

class Root(controllers.RootController):
    @expose(template="bookmarker.templates.welcome")
    def index(self):
        import time
        log.debug("Happy TurboGears Controller Responding For Duty")
        return dict(now=time.ctime())

    @expose(template="bookmark.templates.list")
    def list(self):
        from model import Bookmark
        b=Bookmark.select()
        return dict(bookmark=b)
```

We have now accomplished the following:

1. Decided to expose this using the bookmark/templates/list.kid template (using Python dotted notation to locate the template within our project)
2. Pulled in an iterator with every Bookmark object (that is, every row from our bookmark table)
3. Passed that iterator over to our view in a dictionary as a bookmark

Now the only thing left to do before we have running code is to create the list.kid template. Make a copy of welcome.kid and rename it to list.kid.

Why Do Controllers Return a Dictionary?

Something that often jumps out at new TurboGears users is how controller methods return a dictionary. In other frameworks, you either return a string representing the output to send to the user, write the output via a response object, or possibly return some object that can directly render the output.

By returning a dictionary rather than rendered output, you're able to leave the decision of how to render the output to TurboGears. The first advantage to this is that it saves you some code. If you're using CherryPy alone, you have to call your template engine to render out your template and then return the string that you get back. This gives you complete control over the template engine used, but it also makes you do all the work.

The next advantage to the TurboGears approach is that it enables you to return multiple forms of output from a single method. This makes it possible to conveniently use one set of logic to generate output that can be used in different ways. One example of this that comes up often is the ability to generate an HTML page if a user comes directly to that URL, or to generate JavaScript Object Notation (JSON-formatted data for Ajax requests.

But, you're not limited to HTML and JSON. You can also output XML or plain text from the same method. We talk more about how to configure all these options in Chapter 19, "The TurboGears Toolbox and Other Tools."

A third advantage to returning a dictionary rather than the direct output is in testing. TurboGears provides a way for your test code to call your controller methods and just get the dictionary back, instead of rendering it out to HTML. This gives you an easy way to test your controller's logic without worrying about how the view is working. It's also a lot easier to inspect the values in a dictionary than it is to inspect generated HTML.

If for some reason the dictionary return values can't properly express what you need the method to return, you can always return a string, just like you can with plain CherryPy.

Table 4.2 provides a quick view of each major Kid construct you'll use in your template.

TABLE 4.2   Kid Template Basics

Kid Construct	Description

`<?python`
`x = 0`
`?>`
	Embed larger chunks of Python in Kid with `<?python ?>` syntax.

`${Variable}`	Replaces this expression with the value of Variable.
`py:for`	Repeats this tag once per item in the set provided.
`py:if`	This element (and all its descendants) should be rendered only if the `py:if` =value is true.
`py:content`	Replaces the contents of an XHTML element with the value of the `py:content` tag.
`py:replace`	Replaces the entire attribute with the value of the `py:replace` tag.
`py:strip`	If the expression is true, eliminate the tag but keep everything under the tag.

After you've got a new `list.kid` file, delete the contents of the body and replace it with the following:

```
<!DOCTYPE html PUBLIC "-//W3C//DTD XHTML 1.0 Transitional//EN" "http://www.w3.org/
TR/xhtml1/DTD/xhtml1-transitional.dtd">
<html xmlns="http://www.w3.org/1999/xhtml" xmlns:py="http://purl.org/kid/ns#"
    py:extends="'master.kid'">

<head>
    <meta content="text/html; charset=UTF-8" http-equiv="content-type" py:
➥replace="''"/>
    <title>Boomarker</title>
</head>

<body>
  <ul>
    <li py:for="bookmark in bookmarks">
      <a href="${bookmark.link}">
        <span py:content="bookmark.name">Link to Bookmark</span>
      </a>
    </li>
  </ul>
</body>
</html>
```

Okay, all done! Now you can browse over to `http://localhost:8080/list` and see what you've done.

Before we move on, let's take a deeper look at template code. There are three different ways that you can put dynamic text into your Kid templates, and we've intentionally used all three in this example. The most conceptually simple is the `${bookmark.link}` style, where you put a reference to a Python object that you want to be placed into the final string. If you've used PHP, ASP, or JSP, this will be familiar to you. The `${whatever}` is replaced by the contents of the `whatever` variable, which you probably passed in from the controller that called this template.

The main limitation of this style of variable replacment is that it's not particularly designer friendly, or at least is not WYSIWYG tool friendly. When you open up this kind of code directly in a browser (rather than running TurboGears), you see that the `${}` content shows up in the output. Because the actual data is likely to be longer than its variable name, this can throw off your whole design. Not only that, but it's easy for a designer to accidentally replace `bookmark.name` with `Bookmark name` when running a spell checker (or whatever), and thus break your final output.

That's why we have `py:content`. When you put this inside of a tag, the entire contents of that tag are replaced by the value assigned to the `py:content` directive. In our example, we're replacing `Link to Bookmark` with the value of the name attribute of our `bookmark` object (`bookmark.name`). The other nice thing about this is that Dreamweaver, Nvu, and other WYSIWYG tools generally ignore XML tag attributes that they don't understand. This makes it less likely that a designer will accidentally break your template code.

The third major way to insert text into our template is to use `py:replace`. This works almost like `py:content` except that it replaces the entire XHTML tag with the value we assign to it. So in our example, we replace the entire `meta content` tag with ' ', because we are extending `master.kid` and therefore pulling in its header information. But we still need header content so that our page will display correctly when you open it in Firefox, Nvu, or Dreamweaver.

There's one other feature of Kid in this example that warrants mentioning. We use the `py:for` attribute as a processing directive to iterate over all the items in our set of `Bookmark`.

The `py:for` directive has the same syntax as a regular `for` loop would in Python. Except instead of relying on indentation to mark the end of the loop, it just iterates over the XHTML tag it is attached to, along with all its subnodes. When you close the tag, you are signaling the end of the loop.

We use the `${VariableName}` replacement method to put the link information into the anchor tag's `href` value because this isn't displayed, and the links don't have to work when our designer is playing around with the template.

But then when it comes to the name of the bookmark, we used `py:replace` inside a span tag to replace `Link to Bookmark` with the name of the bookmark. This means that when we (or a designer) view this page in Firefox we'll see that friendly text rather than the cryptic looking `${bookmark.name}` text.

We don't use it in this simple example, but `py:if` works just like Python `if` statements. Kid also has lots of other tools to help you compose pages from smaller chunks. For example, Kid has tag attributes such as `py:match` and `py:def` as well as functions such as `xml()` and `document()`. (We get back to these in Chapter 5, "Enhancing Our Bookmark Application.")

We can still do a lot to improve this little application. We can add an administrative interface for adding new links and the ability to save categories for our links. We walk through most of these things in the rest of this chapter and in Chapter 5. But before we move on to those projects, let's modify the `list.kid` template to display the descriptive text that's in the database.

Go ahead and try it on your own.

As always, this code (including the solution to the earlier exercise) is available on our website at www.turbogearsbook.com/code.

4.2 Testing TurboGears Applications

So now we have a working page, and it was easy enough to make. But before we go on adding more and more functionality to our page, let's take a quick break and look at how you write tests for TurboGears applications. It's never too early to start writing tests. In fact, TurboGears is designed to suport Test Driven Development, in which you write your tests first, and code second.

We don't have time to go over all the valuable information that has been written in support of writing unit and functional tests. If you're not convinced already, we're not going to force you to change the way you write code. For those who are convinced that writing tests early and often will save time on every change you make later, however, we're going to cover testing right up front.

TurboGears provides simple integration with Nose (http://somethingaboutorange.com/mrl/projects/nose/). With a simple `nosetests` command, you can run `unittest.TestCase` objects, doctests, or simple test functions in a module.

To run your tests, just type `nosetests` in the top-level directory of your project. Nose will then look through your project's directories to find whatever tests it can and run

them all. Nose isn't magic; it just looks for files with test in the name, and methods/
functions with test in the name, and runs those.

Before we start writing tests, we should take a look at the `turbogears.testutil` helper functions that we can use to make writing tests easier. The first function is `testutil.`
`call`, which calls one of your controller methods and returns the dictionary directly
without applying the Kid template to it. That makes it really easy to double check that
your method does the right thing without worrying about how the result is presented
to the user.

TurboGears quickstart automatically creates a couple of sample tests that will pass
if you run `nosetests` on a freshly quickstarted project. You can see those tests in the
`test_controllers.py` file in your `/tests` directory.

When you understand them, you can erase them and add a new test that does a
simple check on the controller we just created, by using the `testutil.call` function:

```
from turbogears import testutil
from bookmark.controllers import Root
import cherrypy

def test_list_controller():
    """list method should return a set of bookmark objects called bookmarks."""
    cherrypy.root = Root()
    output = testutil.call(cherrypy.root.list)
    assert output.has_key('bookmarks')
```

This test is simple; but if you try to expand it to test the value associated with the
`bookmarks` key, your tests will start failing. This is because we haven't set up any database
configuration for our tests.

Generally, you don't want to run your tests against your actual database; you want
a test database. Luckily, `testutils` has a class `DBTest`, which makes writing tests that
interact with the database remarkably easy.

Here's a sample of a simple test that connects to a separate test database:

```
from turbogears import database, testutil
from bookmarker.model import Bookmark
import cherrypy

database.set_db_uri("sqlite:///:memory:")

class test_full_stack(testutil.DBTest):
    def get_model(self):
```

```
      return Bookmark

  def test_list_template(self):
      """Checks to see that our template is applied"""
      testutil.createRequest("/list")
      assert '<TITLE>Boomarker</TITLE>' in cherrypy.response.body[0]
```

We have a few extra imports in this test module. From TurboGears, we need `tes-tutil` again, as well as `database`. And of course, if we're going to use our `Bookmark` class, we'll have to import that from our `bookmarker.model` module, too.

The first thing this module does is set up the database connection URI. The `set_db_uri()` method is pretty self-explanatory, but it's worth noticing that we can : `memory` to indicate that our SQLite database ought to exist only in memory. This is great for tests because it's fast and transitory.

The actual `test_list_template` test is pretty simple. But it uses another `testutil` function, `createRequest()`. This function calls through the whole stack for whatever URL you pass it. In this case, it's calling the list method, and rendering the results through the template. The final results are stored in the `cherrypy.response.body` list, so we can easily check that the expected results are present there.

Looking at this test, it's not immediately clear exactly how it uses the database. This test is using basic string functionality to make sure that particular text is present in the response. This is more of a functional test than a unit test because it examines the final, rendered output. Because this renders a template that iterates through all the bookmarks in the database, it won't work unless it can find a database connection.

This test adds a record to the database, and then checks the response to ensure that the proper link shows up in the final template.

Given all of this, you can easily write tests that do more interesting functional tests. For example, it's probably worthwhile to write a quick test that adds a record to the database and then checks the /list page to see that the proper link shows up in the final output. That way, if anything goes wrong in the middle, we should get a failing test. Here's a simple functional test that does exactly that:

```
  def test_list_contents(self):
      """If we add a record to the model, it should
         show up in the final page text"""
      Bookmark(name="Compound Thinking",
               link="http://www.CompoundThinking.com",
               description="A {not so} random link.")
      testutil.createRequest("/list")
```

```
       assert '<A HREF="http://www.CompoundThinking.com">' in cherrypy.response.
➥ body[0]
```

> NOTE: If you use Python's doctest functionality to embed texts in docstrings, Nose will find and run these tests, too. But you should be aware that doctests don't provide output in a way that Nose can record; so you'll only get pass/fail information on these tests. This isn't a big hurdle, because you can always run the doctests on that particular module manually and get more detailed information on why that particular test failed.

4.3 A Simple Form to Add Bookmark

TurboGears has lots of tools to help you build, validate, and process form data. There's a web-based data editing tool in the TurboGears toolbox, and even an experimental FastData class to automate form creation for your model classes.

We cover each of these tools, but for now let's create a new method to our controller to add new bookmarks and feed data to it from a simple web form. Rather than do this all in one big step, let's start by creating a save_bookmark method in our controller that adds a predefined bookmark to the database. We set up some variables, and then create a new Bookmark object with the exact same syntax we used earlier in the chapter when we created our first bookmark through tg-admin shell.

By now, the code to do this should look familiar to you:

```
@expose()
def save_bookmark(self):
    name="Blue Sky on Mars"
    link="http://blueskyonmars.com"
    description="Another not so random link."
    Bookmark(name=name, link=link, description=description)
    raise redirect("/list")
```

This method sets up a few variables, and then creates a new Bookmark object using the exact same syntax we used earlier in the chapter when we created our first bookmark through tg-admin shell. When our new record is added to the database, the user will be sent the results of the /list page.

After you add this method, you can check to see that this works by browsing to http://localhost:8080/save_bookmark, and you should see the new bookmark in the list.

Of course, we don't really want to hard-code bookmarks to be added, so we can adjust the code to do something like this:

```
@expose(template="bookmarker.templates.add")
def save_bookmark(self, name, link, description):
    b=Bookmark(name=name, link=link, description=description)
    raise redirect("/list")
```

This saves a new bookmark into the database, and then redirects the user to the standard list view. But now we need to get the name, link, and description variables from somewhere. Remember from Chapter 3 that CherryPy turns HTTP Post names and values directly into named parameters that will be passed into your exposed object? So, all you need to do is create a form that submits a name, link, and description to the /save_bookmark URL and everything will work.

You can copy list.kid to form.kid and edit the body to add a form. Here's the basic HTML you need in the body of form.kid:

```
<body>
<form NAME="Add Bookmark" METHOD="post" ACTION="/save_bookmark">
  <p>Name: <input name="name"></input></p>
  <p>Link: <input name="link"></input></p>
  <p>Description:<textarea name="description" rows="4" cols="30"></textarea></p>
  <p><input type="submit" value="submit"></input></p>
</form>
</body>
```

This form submits its contents to the server, and CherryPy calls save_bookmark with the form inputs as named parameters, and save_bookmark adds the bookmark to the database and then redirects the user to /list.

To publish form.kid, we need one final step. We add a new method to our controller that looks like this:

```
@expose(template="bookmarker.templates.form")
def bookmark(self):
    return dict()
```

Now, if you browse to http://localhost:8080/bookmark, you'll get a form, and when you fill out that form, a new bookmark will be added to the database.

That's about all it takes to build a basic user input mechanism with TurboGears. Of course, there's a lot more that could be done. Our form and list pages aren't attractive, so some HTML/CSS magic would help a lot. But more important, there's no code to edit existing forms, delete unwanted bookmarks, or handle data validation. We cover all of that in the next chapter.

Why `raise redirect`?

At first glance, raising an exception to redirect the user to a new URL seems a bit odd. After all, aren't exceptions supposed to indicate errors in the program?

It turns out that exceptions aren't always about errors. In fact, Python has an `Exception` base class and another base class for errors (`standardError`). An exception really just signals a change in control flow. Python's iterators take advantage of this by raising `stopIteration` when the iterator is exhausted.

What makes `raise redirect` nice is that it's an unambiguous signal that the code that follows is not going to execute. After you've stated you want to redirect the user, further processing doesn't make sense. If `redirect` was a normal function call, it would be possible to call it and then proceed to produce output that you expect to go to the browser, which is confusing. `raise redirect` neatly eliminates the possibility.

4.4   Summary

- You can define the columns and tables in your database easily in Python classes, and SQLObject will automatically generate them whenever you run `tg-adin sql create`.

- You can use `tg_admin shell` to add new records to your database easily. You create new records in the database by instantiating new objects.

- We used the Kid processing directive `py:for` for the first time to loop over all the bookmarks in the database. Kid's `py:for` and `py:if` functions work just like the standard Python constructs.

- TurboGears provides a set of utility functions to help you write unit and functional tests. Unit tests for controller objects can be easily written using `testutil.call()`, which should first be passed a controller method (in our example `cherrypy.root.list`) that you want to call. Functional tests can use `testutil.createRequest()`, which takes the URL you want to test and runs through the full CherryPy stack, renders the output through your template, and makes it avalable in `cherrypy.response.body[0]`.

- When you post a form, it's easy to use those values in your controller methods because CherryPy passes them into the method as named parameters.

Chapter 5

Enhancing Our Bookmark Application

In This Chapter

Now that we've got a basic bookmark application, there are a thousand ways to improve it and make it more useful. I'm sure you've already thought of some, so let's get started by creating a way to list our bookmarks by category. This will help us delve deeper into SQLObject and how it handles more-complex data relationships.

5.1   Updating Our Model

Before we start, let's think for a second about the result we want. We're going to have a bunch of links and a bunch of categories; that much is easy, and it's pretty obvious that categories are going to have more than one link, otherwise there's not much point in categories!

But are we ever going to have to have multiple categories for one link? I think the answer is yes. There will be some hotels that are also restaurants, some bed and breakfasts that are also historical landmarks, and so on. With that information in hand, we probably need to bite the bullet and create a join table to manage this many-to-many relationship.

Lucky for us, SQLObject's `RelatedJoin` functionality makes this amazingly easy:

```
class Categories(SQLObject):
    categoryName    = StringCol(alternateID=True, length=100)
    categoryItems   = RelatedJoin('Bookmarks')

class Bookmarks(SQLObject):
    bookmarkName    = StringCol(alternateID=True, length=100)
    link            = StringCol()
    description     = StringCol()
    categories      = RelatedJoin('Categories')hhh
```

When SQLObject sees that categories and `categoryItems` are `RelatedJoin` column types, it automatically creates a join table for us, as well as a couple of simple methods to help manage the relations contained in that table. In this case, it will create `addCategories` and `deleteCategories` methods and add them to the `Bookmark` class, and an `addBookmarks` method, which it adds to the `Categories` class.

We should also be able to get a "list" (actually it's a SQLObject `selectResults` iterator, but it acts like a list) of all the categories related to that bookmark with `Categories.select()`, and then get a list of bookmarks per category by accessing its `categoryItems` property.

But before we get to that, we have a few things to clean up. Just because we changed our model schema doesn't mean that we can start using it—because we already have an existing database that doesn't match the schema in our database! Right now, the easiest way to get everything back into sync is to delete our bookmarks database and re-create it using `tg-admin sql create`.

Even after we do that, if we fire up our application now, we'll still get errors. Why? Because I changed the bookmark attribute `name` to `bookmarkName` to make reading some of the examples clearer, but that application programming interface (API) change almost certainly broke something.

Luckily, we have some unit tests to help us find what broke, so we can just run `nosetests` and get some errors. After we've fixed the errors, we can feel comfortable adding new functionality.

Here's the first relevant bit:

```
======================================================================
ERROR: the list page should contain a link to Google
----------------------------------------------------------------------
Traceback (most recent call last):
  File "C:\turbogears\class\bookmarker\bookmarker\tests\test_functional.py", line
14, in test_list_contents
    description="A {not so} random link.")
  File "c:\turbogears\tg-dev\thirdparty\sqlobject\sqlobject\declarative.py", line
92, in _wrapper
    return_value = fn(self, *args, **kwargs)
  File "c:\turbogears\tg-dev\thirdparty\sqlobject\sqlobject\main.py", line 1197,
in __init__
    self._create(id, **kw)
  File "c:\turbogears\tg-dev\thirdparty\sqlobject\sqlobject\main.py", line 1216,
in _create
    raise TypeError, "%s() did not get expected keyword argument %s" % (self.__
class__.__name__, column.name)
TypeError: Bookmarks() did not get expected keyword argument bookmarkName
```

So, it looks like our tests are not passing `bookmarkNames` when they create new bookmarks. This is easy to fix: We just change `.name` to `bookmark.bookmarkName` in our tests and rerun them.

Oops, now we get a different error:

```
FAIL: If we add a record to the model, it should show up in the final page text
------------------------------------------------------------------
Traceback (most recent call last):
  File "C:\Documents and Settings\Mark\My Documents\book\code\5\bookmarker\book-
marker\tests\test_functional.py", line 17
, in test_list_contents
    assert '<A HREF="http://www.CompoundThinking.com">' in cherrypy.response.
body[0]
AssertionError:
```

This tells us there is something wrong with our template; it's not returning what we expect. We can then either add

```
    print cherrypy.response.body[0]
```

to our `test_list_contents` method right before the failing assert (so that we can see the template output and determine what's wrong), or we can fire up our application and browse to `/list` and see the offending page ourselves.

Either way, we'll find that TurboGears gives us a long stack trace showing that the rename of `name` to `bookmarkName` has created yet another problem. The whole stack trace is there, but the only thing we need to know to find the source of our problem is the last line:

```
AttributeError: 'Bookmarks' object has no attribute 'name'
```

It looks like our `list` template is still looking for a `bookmark.name`. We can fix that quickly by opening up `list.kid` and changing `bookmark.name` to `bookmark.bookmarkName`; and then our test passes!

We could continue to track down places where our code needs to be updated this way. However, the only remaining place where you'll have to update the code is the controller method that handles updating the database. So, go ahead and go over there and change `name` to `bookmarkName`:

```
@expose(template="bookmarker.templates.add")
def save_bookmark(self, name, link, description):
    b=Bookmarks(bookmarkName=name, link=link, description=description)
    raise redirect("/list")
```

Now we can start adding a page that lists all the bookmarks by category, and perhaps another page that lets us look up the bookmarks in the category we want to see.

So, let's change our `list` controller to return all the categories from the database, and then we'll iterate over that in the template. Even though we'll continue to test our code, we aren't always going to show all of our tests in this book. Nonetheless, we'll be writing them for our examples, which you can always download from www.turbo-gearsbook.com/code.

5.2 Listing by Category

Let's change our `list` controller to return all the categories from the database, and then we'll iterate over that in the template. First, however, we need some data in our database so that we'll have something to see when we get this code written.

We could easily add more sample data from the command line. But it's time to introduce another set of tools that come with TurboGears. If you run `tg-admin toolbox`, a special TurboGears application called the Toolbox starts.

The Toolbox contains the easiest way to add data to your application during development. The CatWalk tool works with all the databases that TurboGears supports, including SQLite, MySQL, and PostgreSQL. If you start the Toolbox from the root of your project directory, it will pick up your database configuration from your TurboGears config file and work with your existing database with no configuration.

The `tg-admin toolbox` command should automatically open a browser; if it doesn't, you can just browse to `http://localhost:7654` and click CatWalk to start editing your data.

CatWalk is powerful and easy to use, but there are a couple of tips that will make adding join relationships easier.

Although it's pretty obvious how you can add information to your tables with CatWalk, the interface to create relationships for many-to-many joins isn't immediately apparent. But it's simple: Add the information you want to both tables normally, and then when the things you want to link together exist, go back and browse the category you want to add bookmarks to, and then click Manage Relationships.

Feel free to use it whenever you need to add data to your model while in development. In fact, as we are finishing up this book, work is underway to make a CatWalk-style admin interface that you can easily use and extend right within your application. So, it's possible that by the time this book comes out in print, CatWalk will make creating CRUD (Create, Read, Update, Destroy) interfaces in TurboGears even easier.

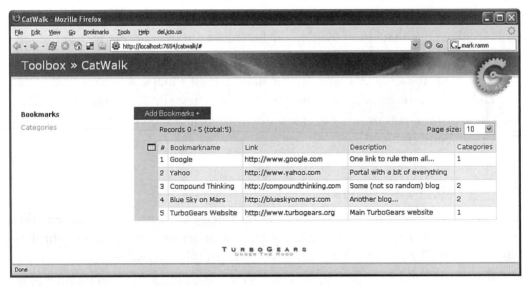

FIGURE 5.1   Using CatWalk to add data

As previously mentioned, you can also add categories and bookmarks from the command line. And even though we can add all the data with CatWalk with less typing, let's explore the command-line interface, because that's the same syntax we need when we want to relate bookmarks and categories in our code later on.

TurboGears, `tg-admin shell`, and SQLObject make this easy to do from the command line or a script. SQLObject automatically creates `addCategories` and `removeCategories` methods for our `Bookmark` objects. It also creates `addBookmarks` and `removeBookmarks` methods for our `Categories` objects. These methods are based on the name of the class on the other end of your multiple join. If we fire up `tg-admin shell`, we can add a new category with the following:

```
a=Categories(categoryName="Search")
```

This is the same thing we did earlier, so it ought to be familiar now. We can also grab a bookmark like this:

```
>>> b=Bookmarks.get(1)
```

Then we join them together by passing `a` to the `addCategories` method of `b`, or by passing `b` to the `addBookmarks` method of `a`:

```
>>> b.addCategories(a)
>>> a.addBookmarks(b)
```

Either of these commands sets up a relationship between these two rows by generating a new row in the join table that SQLObject created to hold information about the relationships between bookmarks and categories.

After you've added some data, the next order of business is to add a controller that passes our categories in to a Kid template.

You'll want to update your import at the top of the file to pull in both bookmarks and categories from the model, and then you can create a new method in controllers that returns a SQLObject `selectResult` object with all the categories in the database. This is all we need because SQLObject makes it easy to iterate over all the bookmarks in a particular category:

```
@expose(template="bookmarker.templates.categorylist")
def list_by_category(self):
    c=Categories.select()
    return dict(categories=c)
```

This controller method looks almost exactly the same as the `list` method. The only difference is that now we're selecting everything in the `Categories` table and sending that SQL `selectResults` object to our template, while `list` uses the `Bookmarks` table instead.

So, we could create a `categorylist.kid` template file that looks like this:

```
<body>
  <span py:for="category in categories">
    <h3 py:content="category.categoryName">Category</h3>
  </span>
</body>
```

This template just lists all of our categories, but that's not exactly what we want. We really want to loop over all our categories, and then for each category loop over the bookmarks in that category and display them, too. Fortunately that's easy, too:

```
<span py:for="category in categories">
  <h3 py:content="category.categoryName">Category</h3>
  <ul>
    <li py:for="bookmark in category.categoryItems">
      <a href="${bookmark.link}">
        <span py:replace="bookmark.bookmarkName">Link to Bookmark</span>
      </a>
      --  <span py:replace="bookmark.description">
          Description of the Bookmark goes here.
          </span>
    </li>
  </ul>
</span>
```

This shows a couple pieces of Kid and SQLObject that you haven't seen yet, so let's take a closer look at how it works. This template uses a span tag as the top level of its py:for loop to iterate over the contents of the category object. Inside that is a list item (li) tag that loops over each of the bookmarks in that category and creates the same link format we used in our original list page. It does this by calling the categoryItems method on our category object—and if you remember, category is a SQLObject selectResults iterator that automatically gets the categoryItems method because categoryItems is defined as a relatedJoin.

Remember: The py:for directive in a tag repeats that tag *and all subtags* for each item in the list (or whatever iterable object you give it).

Other than that, we are just using the same code we previously used to print the list of all bookmarks to list only those links that are members of our current category.

5.3   Updating Our Form

Now that we have bookmarks and categories, however, we notice that there's no easy way to add the categories for a bookmark when we create them through our form. We could approach this problem in several ways. We could try to do this with CatWalk by mounting it inside our application; or we could write a standard HTML form, parse the post results in our controller, do whatever validation we need, and have our controller pass the data on to our SQLObject class, which will automatically inject it into the database. But the current manifestation of CatWalk isn't easy to modify to do what we want, and handling validation, displaying error messages, and all of that seems like a lot of work.

So, let's explore a third option that uses a TurboGears feature you haven't seen yet: widgets. You can always do things by hand when you need to, just like we did in Chapter 4, "Creating a Simple Application," but most of the time widgets are going to make life a lot easier. The form widget definitely makes it easier to handle data input and validation in your application. Previous web-based widget interfaces have tended to be either too complex for the simple cases or impossible to use for the complex cases. But TurboGears widgets have been designed to make easy things easy, and complex things possible.

So, now for a whirlwind tour of widgets.

On the simplest level, you can think of widgets as an easy way to reuse "packages" of HTML, JavaScript, and CSS on your pages in a smart way. So, for example, if you reuse a form widget that has associated JavaScript functions and CSS styles 100 times on one of your pages, TurboGears is "smart" enough to only inject those JavaScript and CSS chunks to your page header one time. We talk about writing your own widgets in Chapter 16, "TurboGears Widgets: Bringing CSS, XHTML, and JavaScript Together in Reusable Components," but for now let's take a look at some of the widgets that come prebuilt in TurboGears.

There's a widget for every kind of standard form element from simple text areas to multiple select boxes. For now, we'll explore simple form element widgets. We cover more-complex widgets with more JavaScript and CSS later in this book. By the time we're done, you'll be able to build your own widgets that can encapsulate large swaths of complex and dynamic view code.

Fundamentally, there are two types of widgets: simple and compound. A compound widget is one that contains any number of member widgets. In this chapter, we use a few of the simple form element widgets to build a compound form widget.

Before we get started, we need to import a few more `turbogears` modules for this next section.

Because we're using widgets, we want the `turbogears.widgets` module, and because we want validation and we want to handle our own errors, we also want to import `validators` and `error_handler` from the `TurboGears` module. Although it might add a bit of convenience if we automatically imported all these modules into our controller, TurboGears avoids that kind of thing. In Chapter 1, "Introduction to TurboGears," we mentioned the Zen of Python—in Python and TurboGears we value "explicit over implicit." We want you to be able to understand and control your namespace; after all, you might be importing other modules from other projects or other frameworks. Also, generally we think you should be the one in control of your life and your application.

Anyway, now our imports look something like this:

```
import logging
import cherrypy

import turbogears
from turbogears import controllers, expose, validate, redirect, \
                       widgets, validators, error_handler

from bookmarker import json
from model import Bookmarks, Categories
```

A form widget is a way to automatically create forms by bundling together a bunch of widgets and validators into something easy to inject into the Kid template. So, the first thing we do is create a list of the widgets we'll be using to build our form. Before we tackle the project of moving a newly created form that handles the relationship between Bookmarks and Categories, we'll just replace the existing form with a new widget-based form that validates the URL we send in and ensures that the name and description are filled out before we save anything to the database.

To do that, we create a new BookmarkFields class, which subclasses WidgetsList, and then use that class to set up a bookmark_form object:

```
class BookmarkFields(widgets.WidgetsList):
    bookmarkname = widgets.TextField(validator=validators.NotEmpty)
    link = widgets.TextField(validator=validators.URL)
    description = widgets.TextArea(validator=validators.NotEmpty)

bookmark_form = widgets.TableForm(fields=bookmark_fields(),
                                  submit_text="Save Bookmark")
```

There's a lot of new stuff going on in this little piece of code. We create a class BookmarkFields that subclasses WidgetsList and contains several individual widgets. Each of these widgets is defined with a reference to the validator that will govern the use of that widget. Even if you aren't requiring a particular field or validating its contents, you might still want to use a validator because that's what converts the raw strings passed back from the browser into the appropriate Python type. Of course, if what you *want* is a string, you don't need a validator at all.

Following the standard TurboGears philosophy of reusing existing Python libraries wherever possible, TurboGears incorporates Ian Bicking's FormEncode validators here;

so, if you have experience with FormEncode, all the same things apply. In Chapter 16, we talk about some of the more complex things you can do with validators that interact with more than one field, or that return custom object types.

If you don't know FormEncode, the only thing you need to know for now is that passing a validator to a form field widget is all you need to do to convert the string received from the browser into the proper Python type. All three of our fields are text strings, and we want to force the user to fill out all three; however, one of them is supposed to contain a URL, so we set that validator equal to `validators.URL`, and the other two to `NotEmpty`.

The last thing we did in the sample code snippet was to define our form widget. Forms require that we define a `fields` parameter with a list of widgets or a `WidgetsList` object, and they can also accept a `submit_text` variable, which will be turned into a label for the Submit button. In this example, we set the fields equal to our `bookmark_form` WidgetsList.

We can then send this form out to a template from one of our controllers:

```
@expose(template="bookmarker.templates.form")
def bookmark(self, parameter_1, tg_errors=None):
    b = model.Bookmarks.get(parameter_1)
    submit_action = "/save_bookmark/%s" %parameter_1
    return dict(form=bookmark_form, values=b, action=submit_action)
```

We're mounting this `bookmark` method under the root class, and using CherryPy's positional parameter handling to let us handle requests such as `/bookmark/1`. The 1 is loaded into the `parameter_1` variable, which we use to retrieve the bookmark row with an ID of 1. Then, we set up a values dictionary where we set the names of each of the widgets in our phone equal to the values we get from the database. We're going to need this values dictionary in our template so that we can prepopulate the form with data.

We also want to pass a `submit` action into our form, so we're setting that up here, too; and then, as usual, we return a dictionary to our template.

Now that we've got our data set up, all the hard work is done, and all we need to do is create a new template by copying one of the existing templates and replacing the body text with something that looks like the following:

```
<body>
    ${form(value=values, action=action)}
</body>
```

That's pretty simple.

Not only do we have less code, our new form is better. If we pass it an existing book-mark, it will display the fields properly and allow you to edit them.

Of course, in a lot of cases you want to have control over exactly how your form layout works. We get to that in good time, but for now I'll just say that the form widget provides hooks to get very customizable (and designer-friendly) forms exactly the way you want them to look. The default format for the form can be seen in Figure 5.2, and you can learn more about customizing your forms in Chapter 16.

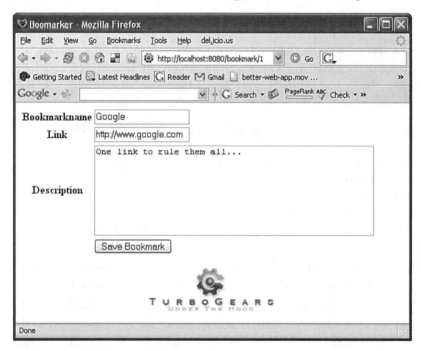

FIGURE 5.2   Edit bookmark form

This code instantiates a form widget and sets the values for each of the member widgets. We also configure the post button with the action we want it to take when the form is submitted. Widgets are stateless and can be reused at any time (even on the same page). This allows for all kinds of cool things such as repeating widgets—so we could have a bunch of bookmark forms on one page. But, it also means that you shouldn't try to store your data in a widget.

If you remember, we set up our `submit_action` as `/save_bookmark/` followed by the ID number of the bookmark we're editing. This means we need to update the `save_bookmark` method to handle this:

```
@expose()
@error_handler(bookmark)
@validate(form=bookmark_form)
def save_bookmark(self, parameter_1, **kwargs):
    return "Bookmark ID = (" + parameter_1 + "
                       ".join(["%s : %s " %item
                       for item in kwargs.iteritems())]))
```

This is just a mockup of the save form, but it's useful if you want to check to make sure everything is working before moving on.

If you test this code in your browser by going to `http://localhost:8080/bookmark/1`, you should get a form with data from the first bookmark you have defined in the database.

If you edit it, but leave the name blank, you should get the same page back—with an error message next to your name field. The same goes for your link (which not only has to exist, but is required to be a valid URL) and description fields. You can see this in action in Figure 5.3.

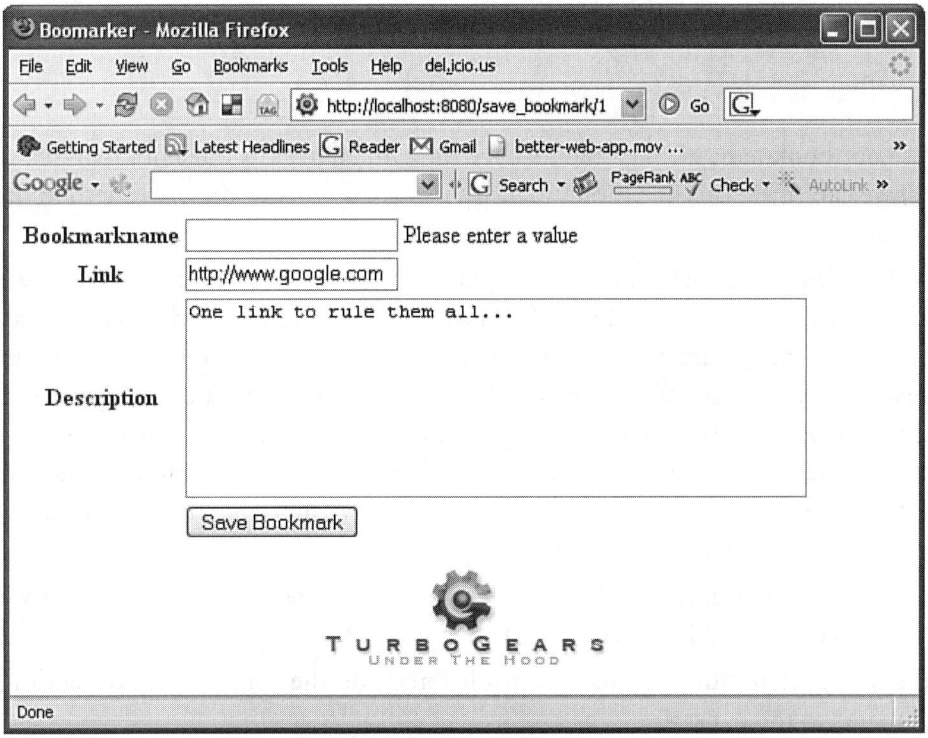

FIGURE 5.3   Edit bookmark form with Failing Validator

This might seem like magic, but it's actually not hard to understand what's going on here. We used the `@turbogears.validate` decorator to declare that the `save_bookmark` method validates a `bookmark_form`, and the `@turbogears.error_handler` decorator to tell our method where to send our form errors to. This means that when there is a validation error, everything gets sent back to the same method that created the form. However, one thing we didn't tell you about form element widgets comes into play here: When they render themselves to HTML, they check to see whether the failing validators have attached an error message, and they inject that message into HTML they create, in addition to the form elements they originally injected.

So, now that we know our form works, with validation and everything, we can think about saving data into the database. This is as easy as updating our model objects with the values from the form:

```
@expose()
@error_handler(bookmark)
@validate(form=bookmark_form)
def save_bookmark(self, *args, **kwargs):
    b=Bookmarks.get(*args[0])
    b.set(**kwargs)
    raise redirect("/index")
```

Because our bookmark form elements have the same names as our bookmark class attributes, we can make things simple by just passing `**kwargs` to the `.set` method on our bookmark.

We're also using positional parameters to grab the rest of the URL, but this time we are catching them with `*args`. For those of you who are new to Python, the `*name` syntax grabs all the positional parameters and puts them into a list. This is an incredibly useful Python feature, because you can use it to handle any number of positional parameters. In this case, it would be easy to use named parameters, but using `*args` makes it easy for our code to handle the case where no `index` value is being passed into our method without blowing up. This is going to be important soon when we use the `edit_bookmark` controller to handle adds as well as updates.

When the form is submitted, the user is sent back to the index page (which we haven't created yet, but we'll get back to that in a minute).

First, let's go back to our bookmark controller and add the ability to handle adding new bookmarks to the database:

```
def bookmark(self, *args, **kwargs):
    if args and args[0] == "add":
        values = ""
        submit_action= "/save_bookmark/"
        b="
    if args and args[0] == "edit":
        from sqlobject import SQLObjectNotFound
        try:
            b = Bookmarks.get(args[1])
            values = kwargs
        except SQLObjectNotFound:
            values = ""
            flash("That's not a valid Bookmark, do you want to add one now?")
        submit_action = "/save_bookmark/edit/%s" %args[1]
    return dict(form=bookmark_form, values=b, action=submit_action)
```

This isn't that much different from what we had before, but we're now checking for either an `add` or a `save` parameter in the URL. We also converted to just grabbing the keyword arguments via `**kwargs`.

So, now if the user enters a URL such as `bookmark/edit/3`, `arg[0]` will be `edit` and `arg[1]` will be `3`. Our function will then try to get `Bookmark` with the ID of `3` from the database, and assign the form `values` to the `values` dictionary. If the `Bookmarks.get()` method fails, SQLObject will raise an `SQLObjectNotFound` exception, which we catch, and create `values` as an empty string, set the flash message to an error message, and call the form.

We haven't discussed `turbogears.flash` yet, but it's useful for letting the user know the results of their actions. If you extend `master.kid` in all your templates (as we do in a quickstarted project by default), the TurboGears flash message will always show up on the next page rendered. In this case, our error message will show up at the top of the next form.

Now, if we add a new bookmark, our `save_bookmark` function is going to break, because it only handles adding new bookmarks to the database and has no means to edit existing bookmarks. So, let's add that:

```
def save_bookmark(self, ID, **kwargs):
    from sqlobject import SQLObjectNotFound
    try:
        b=Bookmarks.get(ID)
        b.set(**kwargs)
    except SQLObjectNotFound:
```

```
            Bookmarks(**kwargs)
        raise redirect("/index")
```

We just added another `try/except` block to mirror the one in our form-creation method. If the bookmark ID passed in isn't found in the database (because it doesn't exist yet), our `except` block creates a new `Bookmarks` object.

5.4   Tying Everything Together

Because we're redirecting everybody to the `index` method, we probably ought to create one. So, here goes:

```
<body>
    <h2><a href="/list_by_category">Bookmarks by Category</a></h2>
    <h2><a href="/list">All Bookmarks</a></h2>
    <h2><a href="/bookmarks/add">Add New Link</a></h2>
</body>
```

This is just plain HTML, but it uses the `bookmark`, `list`, and `list_by_categories` URLs that we defined earlier. Before we finish things off, we really need to add a link to each of our bookmarks in the `/list` page that will allow a user to edit that bookmark:

```
<body>
  <ul>
    <li py:for="bookmark in bookmarks">
        <a href="${bookmark.link}">
          <span py:replace="bookmark.bookmarkName">Link to Bookmark</span>
        </a>
          -- <span py:replace="bookmark.description">Description of the Bookmark
             goes here. </span>
          <br />
          <a href="${'/bookmark/edit/'+str(bookmark.id)}">edit</a> --
          <b> Categories: </b>
          <span py:for="cat in bookmark.categories">
           ${cat.categoryName}
          </span>
          <hr width="300" align="left"/>
      </li>

  </ul>
</body>
```

In this little template, we have a loop for each bookmark in the database, and an inner loop for each category attached to that bookmark. This gives us a nice listing of the bookmark name and description, along with a link to the edit page for that specific bookmark. All of this is followed by a list of the categories that bookmark is related to.

5.5   Selecting Categories

It's not complicated to add another widget to our form which displays and updates categories for us. There are several ways to do this: We can use a list of check boxes, a series of clickable links, or some kind of Ajaxified Web 2.0 drag-and-drop interface. But, our users probably already know how to use a multiple select field, and it's easy to add, so let's start with that.

We'll do this in two phases. The first is the easiest; we wire up the widget into our form and make it display the existing categories for each of the bookmarks in our database. The second part, which is really not difficult either, is to update the contents of our database based on the user's selection.

So far, the only thing we've used is text fields, so we didn't have to define any user options; but we want our select widget to contain a list of all the categories in the database, so we must get those category options and then feed it into the widget somehow.

We have several ways to do this:

- We can define the options at widget instantiation time (and the widget will use the same options every time it's displayed).
- We can pass in the options at widget rendering time (so that the widget can dynamically hand an options list to our widget).
- We can assign a callable, which the widget will use to get the options dynamically.

All three of these methods can be incredibly useful. For instance, if I have a widget that's always going to display a static list of options, I just pass it in at instantiation time, and then I never have to worry about it; and it's incredibly easy to just reuse that widget in another form. On the other hand, if I want my list of options dynamically updated based on current database values, it makes a lot of sense to encapsulate the logic for getting the options list in a single function that the widget can call to get the list when it needs it. With either of these two methods, I don't even have to think about building the options list when I'm displaying my form; they're just there automatically.

But there are also times, particularly when I have complex context-sensitive logic to determine the options needed, when the second method is easiest.

Whereas Python has the "one (and preferably only one) obvious way to do it" philosophy, there are important use cases for each of these three widget option definition methods.

In our case, we want a list of options, but we want it to be updated whenever a new option is added to our application. So, this is an obvious time to use a callable to define our options list:

```
def get_category_options():
    categories = model.Categories.select()
    options = []
    for category in categories:
        options.append(category.ID, category.categoryName)
    return options
```

A `MultipleSelectField` widget expects to receive a list of two value tuples, one tuple for each item you could select. The tuples should be in the format `(1, "First Option")`, where the first item in the tuple defines the value returned when that option is selected, and the second option, the string, defines the value that is displayed for that option. So, the preceding code just gets a list of categories from the database and iterates over that list appending a tuple with the `id` and `categoryName` of each record.

We could also use Python's list comprehension syntax to make this even simpler:

```
def get_category_options():
    categories = [(category.ID, category.categoryName)
                    for category in model.Categories.select()]
    return categories
```

Next, we update our `bookmark_fields` list with a categories widget:

```
class bookmark_fields(widgets.WidgetsList):
    bookmark_name = widgets.TextField(validator=validators.NotEmpty)
    link = widgets.TextField(validator=validators.URL)
    description = widgets.TextArea(validator=validators.NotEmpty)
    categories = widgets.MultipleSelectField(options=get_category_options)h
```

If you're defining the options at render time, the `MultipleSelect` field won't be able to guess what kind of elements you're going to pass it (and expect to get back out of it)! Rather than guess, it will warn you that you need to define a validator. Remember, validators don't exist just to enforce validation rules; they also convert the HTTP POST string results into valid Python variables of the type you expect—so if the widget can't figure out what you'll be expecting at the end, it's not going to be able to convert it for you. And rather than make some bad guess that gives you an error way down the road, the widget sensibly decides to fail early, right at instantiation time.

Okay, so now we have a MultipleSelect field in our form, and you can fire up your browser and go to http://localhost:8080/bookmarks/edit/1 to see it in action.

But what we really want is to have existing categories preselected for our users so that they can see what's in the database and update it. Widgets make this easy, too; as you've already seen in the earlier example, we can pass in a value at render time. In this case, all we need is a list of the index fields for each category that this bookmark belongs to.

Actually, you can define the display value for a widget at instantiation time, with a callable, or at render time—just like the options list. So, you have total flexibility, and all the widget parameters work the same way. More often than not, however, you are going to want to define the default values at render time.

Here's the new controller code for our bookmark editing form:

```
@expose(template="bookmarker.templates.form")
    def bookmark(self, *args, **kwargs):
        from sqlobject import SQLObject NotFound
        if args and args[0] == "add":
            values = ""
            submit_action= "/save_bookmark/"
        if args and args[0] == "edit":
            try:
                b = Bookmarks.get(args[1])
                default_options = []
                for a in b.categories:
                    default_options.append(a.id)

            values = {"bookmarkName" : b.bookmarkName,

                        "link": b.link,

                        "description" : b.description,

                        "categories": default_options}
        except SQLObjectNotFound
            values = ""
            turbogears.flash = ("That's not a valid Bookmark, " +
                            "do you want to add one now?")
```

```
submit_action = "/save_bookmark/edit/%s" %args[1]
return dict(form=bookmark_form, values=values, action=submit_action)
```

The new code here is in lines 10-13, and all we're doing is creating a list of the ID values of each of the `categories` associated with the `Bookmarks` object that we're editing. We then just put the `default_options` into our `values` dictionary under the `select_categories` key. We don't even have to edit our template—just fire up your browser and take a look; it should "just work."

But we don't just want to *look at* the category values, we want to *edit* them. So, let's make a couple of simple changes to our `save_bookmark` method:

```
@expose()
@turbogears.error_handler(bookmark)
@turbogears.validate(form=bookmark_form)
def save_bookmark(self, *args, **kwargs):
    try:
        b=Bookmarks.get(args[1])
        b.bookmarkName=kwargs["bookmark_name"]
        b.link = kwargs["link"]
        b.description = kwargs["description"]
        Bookmarks.updateCategories(b,kwargs["select_categories"])
    except:
        b=Bookmarks(bookmarkName=kwargs["bookmark_name"],
                    link = kwargs["link"],
                    description = kwargs["description"])
        for item in kwargs["select_categories"]:
            b.addCategories(Categories.get(item))
    raise redirect("/index")
```

In the `try` clause, we're updating an existing object, so we have to delete existing relationships as well as add new ones. In the `except` clause, we know the bookmark doesn't exist yet, so our job is simpler; we're just adding new relationships. To do that, we iterate over the list of integer values we got back from our `select_categories` widget, and then use the automatically generated SQLObject `addCagetories` method to add these relationships to the database.

Is `updateCategories` another automatically generated method created for us by SQLObject? No; instead of adding a bunch of functionality to our controller to check for existing relationships and adding or deleting when necessary, we're creating an `updateCategories` method in the `Bookmarks` class.

The ability to move complex logic out of the controller and into the model is critical to maintaining a clean model-view-controller (MVC) design.

SQLObject makes this easy. Our Bookmarks class is just a plain old Python class that can take new methods whenever you need them. So, now that we've added updateCategories the Bookmarks class in our model looks like this:

```
class Bookmarks(SQLObject):
    bookmarkName    = StringCol(alternateID=True, length=100)
    link            = StringCol()
    description     = StringCol()
    categories      = RelatedJoin('Categories')

    def updateCategories(some_bookmark, new_categories):
        for existing_category in some_bookmark.categories:
            some_bookmark.removeCategories(existing_category)
        for each_category in new_categories:
            some_bookmark.addCategories(each_category)
```

The updateCategories method takes a Bookmark object and a list of integers. It removes all the existing category relationships from the database for that bookmark and adds a new Category for each integer in the new_categories list. Because we passed our select object the ID values of our category records, and we got back a list of the ID values that were selected, there's nothing special we need to do here. We can add the relationship by passing the ID value in to the addCategories method. Before we do that, we remove all the preexisting relationships so that what we're left with is just the new values returned from the form.

5.6   Summary

- SQLObject creates join tables for you when you use RelatedJoin column types.
- SQLObject dynamically creates add and remove methods for managing the relationships contained in those join tables
- When you write unit tests, you can use them to make sure changes don't break your application.
- Each of the HTML form elements has a matching TurboGears widget, and you can bundle those widgets together and have TurboGears create forms for you dynamically.

- TurboGears form widgets know how to display validation errors on the same form where they are rendered. And, all of this can be done automatically for you when you use widgets.
- CherryPy turns additional URL pieces after a matching method into positional parameters. You can then use these parameters in your code and use URL structures as part of your controller object's public API.

PART III

Exploring a Real World TurboGears Application

Chapter 6

Exploring More Complex Models in WhatWhat Status

In This Chapter

With the Bookmarker application under our belt, it's time to move on and look at a real-world application. In the next three chapters, we explore one of the first open-source TurboGears applications to be released: WhatWhat Status.

There's a lot to learn from the WhatWhat Status application, and we start out by exploring some features of SQLObject and TurboGears models that didn't come up in the Bookmarker application. We also look at the Identity framework, which is TurboGears's built-in mechanism for doing authentication/authorization. Along the way, we deal with some of the issues that come up while building a real-world application in TurboGears. Particularly, we talk about how to build model objects that keep your controllers from becoming a jumbled mess.

6.1 What Is WhatWhat Status?

WhatWhat Status is a project management application, but it's not your average project management application. Rather than focusing on creating Gannt charts, work breakdown structures, and calculating project costs, it focuses on helping the people involved in a project better communicate what they are working on, the risks they face, and the overall status of the project.

Before we embark on our code walk through of the WhatWhat Status application, it's a good idea to get a big-picture overview of how WhatWhat Status is designed to work and what problems it tries to solve.

Here is how Jonathan LeCour, creator of WhatWhat Status, described the purpose of his application: "WhatWhat Status is less of a project management application, and more of a communication tool. We found that all of the things that are associated with 'project management tools' were MS Word templates, charts, graphs, and other complexities. When we started moving toward agile processes and were still using these kinds of things, it didn't make any sense!"

The new agile methodologies (Scrum, XP, and so on) create a different kind of project process. It's one that involves the developers much more directly in the selection of when and how to do the various project tasks. Rather than create a huge work breakdown structure with complex dependency charts, and then start assigning work, dividing up responsibility and creating a gigantic project plan with associated Gannt charts, an agile team breaks the project down into shorter iterations, and then asks the customer to help them decide which features to implement in each iteration.

Agile teams need to be populated with enough people with the right skills to finish the expected features in that iteration, and it is the team's responsibility to keep track of what is happening and get those features completed within the iteration.

This means that the problem of communication is much more important than the problem of dependency tracking. (Actually, I think this is true of any project team of more than five people, but it is particularly true when you use agile methodologies!)

You have group code ownership, and you work on delivering features one user story at a time, and you expect people from the team to choose which stories from this week's work to do next on their own. Traditional tools require daily updates just to stay in sync with what's really going on, so they slow you down.

However, there's still a need to track and manage project status and project risks, and that's where WhatWhat Status comes along. WhatWhat Status was the first major open-source project built in TurboGears, and it provides an ideal way for us to see how you can build larger applications in TurboGears.

6.2   Logging In and Using WhatWhat Status

To follow along with the code in the next few chapters, download and install What-What Status. Although you can download the latest version from the WhatWhat Status website (www.cleverdevil.org/whatwhat/), you're better off downloading the exact version we're using from our website: www.TurboGearsBook.com/code/whatwhat.

WhatWhat Status has four main screens: Dashboard, Project, Recent Changes, and People. And the vast majority of the action takes place on the Project page, where individual projects are managed. There's one more screen in WhatWhat Status, for logging in to the application, but that isn't so much a WhatWhat Status feature as a module that we haven't had a chance to look at yet: TurboGears Identity.

The Identity module provides an easy way for you to restrict access to various parts of our application based on the user's login ID and whatever group membership or permissions you define. If you remember back to when we quickstarted our Bookmarker application, the quickstart script asked if we wanted to use Identity, and we said no.

If we had said yes, quickstart would have included some additional code on our newly created project. The `model.py` file would have included `Users`, `Groups`, and `Permissions` classes, where we could store information for what users exist in the system and what permissions they ought to have. Quickstart would also have updated our `controllers.py` file to include `login` and `logout` methods, and have thrown the necessary Kid templates into our `templates` directory for good measure.

Every page in WhatWhat Status checks to see that you are logged in before allowing you to access it; if you aren't logged in, you are redirected to the login page, as shown in Figure 6.1.

After you've logged in, you are redirected to the page you originally tried to get to. In most cases, this is the Dashboard; if you received an e-mail link to

FIGURE 6.1   WhatWhat Status login

a particular project page, and you came into WhatWhat Status by clicking on that link, however, you are redirected there.

The Dashboard page shows a list of all the active projects in the system with a quick summary of the various elements of each project (Figure 6.2). Projects can contain any number of Risks, Issues, Notes, Files, Questions, and Answers. Another critical piece of any project is its current Status, which displays prominently in red if the status indicates that some additional attention is required. The Dashboard is intended as a way for developers to

FIGURE 6.2   Project Dashboard

quickly communicate this information to each other and to other important stakeholders in the project.

If you click any of the projects on the Dashboard, you are taken directly to the project's page (as seen in Figure 6.3). As discussed in Chapter 8, "RSS, Cookies, and Dynamic Views in WhatWhat Status," the Project page relies on Ajax features to make creating and updating Risk, Notes, Issues, and so forth, simple and quick. Click Add Risk, and a new form appears right there in the page, allowing you to quickly update that piece of the project. When you click Save, the page is automatically updated, and you can go on adding more Risks, Questions, Files, or doing whatever other updates you need to do.

FIGURE 6.3 WhatWhat Status Project page

This highlights one of the key use cases for Ajax. If a process isn't efficient and easy to use, developers aren't going to waste their time "filling out paperwork." WhatWhat Status's use of a few well-placed Ajax forms means that updating a project status involves no page reloads and no waiting on the server.

And that brings us to another important feature of WhatWhat Status. Developers will see a project tracking system as a waste of time if they don't see people reading and responding to the information that goes into the system. So, WhatWhat Status steals a page from the wiki playbook and includes a Recent Changes page, which can be used to see all the new or updated Projects, Issues, Risks, Files, Questions, and Answers. The thing that makes this page most useful, however, is the RSS feed generator, which means that project team members, managers, and other stakeholders can just subscribe to the feed and see the changes in their favorite feed reader in near real time.

6.3   Exploring the WhatWhat Status Model

Now that you have a picture of how WhatWhat Status works, let's take a look at the code. The authors of WhatWhat Status have built a significantly more complicated database structure than our Bookmarker application, and although there should be plenty of familiar looking code, we also find quite a few new TurboGears features. In general, I find that if I start my code reviews by trying to understand the data model and working my way up through the controllers to the front end templates, I understand everything better. Here's a picture of the WhatWhat Status data model:

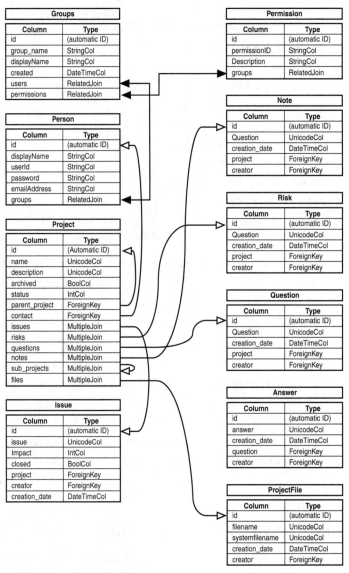

FIGURE 6.4 WhatWhat Status data diagram

As you can see, there's actually quite a bit going on in the WhatWhat Status model, and that's not the half of it because the WhatWhat Status authors have created a number of methods in the SQLObject classes that map to each of the fields in the database. Unfortunately, that means that we won't have the time or the space to cover every single class or method in depth, but we highlight all the interesting parts so that you can easily go over the rest of the model code at your leisure and understand everything that is happening.

There are quite a few imports at the top of the WhatWhat Status `model.py` file, which pull in all of SQLObject's column type classes:

```
from sqlobject                    import (SQLObject, UnicodeCol, StringCol,
                                          ForeignKey, MultipleJoin, IntCol,
                                          DateTimeCol, BoolCol, RelatedJoin,
                                          DatabaseIndex)
from turbogears.database          import PackageHub
from datetime                     import datetime, timedelta
```

There are a few constants defined, but let's skip on down to the first table object, which defines the `Person` class, which is used to store information about WhatWhat Status users.

```
class Person(SQLObject):
    displayName    = StringCol(length=255, alternateID=True)
    userId         = StringCol(length=32, alternateID=True)
    password       = StringCol()
    emailAddress   = StringCol()

    groups = RelatedJoin("Groups",
                         intermediateTable="tg_user_group",
                         joinColumn="user_id",
                         otherColumn="group_id")

    def _get_permissions( self ):
        perms = set()
        for g in self.groups:
            perms = perms | set(g.permissions)
        return perms
```

The `Person` class is pretty simple, but there are a couple of new things worth mentioning here.

The first is that SQLObject provides easy ways for you to customize the way your column objects are mapped to database tables, right in your model class definition.

The authors of WhatWhat Status are using this SQLObject feature to customize the groups column class, by defining the name of the intermediate table that they want created, as well as the column names they want included in that table.

Remember, SQLObject enables you to define properties for a column. And we've already seen that the most important property on a RelatedJoin class is the first, which tells SQLObject which SQLObject class this RelatedJoin connects to (in this case) Groups.

You might think it's easier to just pass the Groups class in here, rather than a string, but it's possible that this class is going to have a circular reference to the Groups class, and that can create ugly problems at instantiation time. Passing a string allows SQLObject a fighting chance to resolve this for you.

There are other SQLObject class properties; WhatWhat Status uses the intermediateTable, joinColumn, and otherColumn properties to override the default names for the join table and its columns.

This is particularly useful when you want to connect to a legacy database, where you don't want your Python objects to be named after the existing column names.

The second thing to notice is the _get_ syntax; this is a SQLObject shortcut that can look like magic until you understand it. Any time you create a _get_something method, SQLObject automatically creates a something attribute for your class. When you try to retrieve the something attribute, _get_something is called, and the results are returned. This can be used to override attribute access for existing table rows or to create entirely new attributes (in this case, def _get_permissions).

This is required because Person replaces TurboGears.identity's User table and needs to provide the API that Identity is looking for in a user type object. We return to this method and delve into the details of identity, custom identity providers, and how WhatWhat Status user authentication/authorization works in Chapter 22, "TurboGears Identity and Security."

```
class Groups(SQLObject):
    groupId     = StringCol(length=16, alternateID=True)
    displayName = StringCol(length=255)
    created     = DateTimeCol(default=datetime.now)

    # collection of all users belonging to this group
    users       = RelatedJoin("Person",
                              intermediateTable="tg_user_group",
                              joinColumn="group_id",
                              otherColumn="user_id")
```

```
# collection of all permissions for this group
permissions = RelatedJoin("Permission",
                          joinColumn="group_id",
                          intermediateTable="tg_group_permission",
                          otherColumn="permission_id")
```

This code does a lot of the same things we've seen before, but there are a couple things worth looking at in a bit more depth in the Groups class.

In line 4, notice that we can use standard Python expressions when setting the default value for a particular column. Not only that, but the DateTimeCol knows enough to take a Python datetime object.

In line 7, we see the RelatedJoin that matches the one we saw earlier in the Person table. This allows our Identity system to use the group() method on any Person object to find all the groups that user is a member of, or the users method of any Group object to find all the people who are in that group.

The next class we are going to look at is by far the largest and most complex in our model. But don't worry, we've seen a lot of it before, and we'll go slowly and highlight each of the pieces that are new.

```
class Project(SQLObject):
    name            = UnicodeCol(length=255, alternateID=True)
    description     = UnicodeCol()
    archived        = BoolCol(default=False)
    status          = IntCol(default=STATUS_NOT_STARTED)
    parent_project  = ForeignKey('Project')
    contact         = ForeignKey('Person')
    issues          = MultipleJoin('Issue', orderBy=['-impact', '-creation_date'])
    risks           = MultipleJoin('Risk', orderBy=['-impact', '-creation_date'])
    questions       = MultipleJoin('Question')
    notes           = MultipleJoin('Note', orderBy='-creation_date')
    sub_projects    = MultipleJoin('Project', joinColumn='parent_project_id')
    files           = MultipleJoin('ProjectFile', orderBy='creation_date')

    idx_project     = DatabaseIndex('parent_project')
    idx_contact     = DatabaseIndex('contact')
```

A couple of new features here can save you a lot of time and hassle if you learn them:

- orderBy

The orderBy property works for any kind of column, and it can reduce the need to pass special sort-order information in when you call a select object. For example,

WhatWhat Status always lists the issues for a particular project sorted first by impact and then by date. So, they add an `orderBy` property to the `issues` column to create a default order for the SQLObject result set that is returned through that join.

Because WhatWhat Status defines `orderBy` to be `['-impact', '-creation_date']`, the results of a call to a `Project` object's issues method will return a set of issues sorted first by impact, in reverse (high to low) order, and then by creation date (again in reverse order).

- `idx_project`

The `idx_project = DatabaseIndex('parent_project')` line is useful only if you are using `tg-admin sql create` to generate your tables automatically from your SQLObject model classes. When you create a new database using `sql create`, this line adds an index for the `parent_project` column to the `Project` table, which can drastically increase performance on some `select` queries.

We look at this in more detail in Chapter 12, "Customizing SQLObject Behavior," but it's worth mentioning a couple of additional features of the `DatabaseIndex` syntax here. You can pass multiple columns to the `DatabaseIndex` method, and even to SQLObject's special `sqlbuilder` expressions, to make multicolumn indexes, or other "special" indexes. You can also require that the index (even a multicolumn index) be unique by adding a `unique = True` parameter.

The WhatWhat Status developers have added more than 20 additional methods to the `Project` class that will make common actions they want to take easier to handle in the controller. Here are a couple of examples:

```
def _get_recent_notes(self):
    now = datetime.now()
    delta = timedelta(15)
    return [note for note in self.notes
            if (now - note.creation_date <= delta) or
               (note.last_edit_date is not None and
                now - note.last_edit_date <= delta)]

def _get_open_risks(self):
    return [risk for risk in self.risks if not risk.closed]

def _get_closed_risks(self):
    return [risk for risk in self.risks if risk.closed]
```

By using `_get_recent_notes`, the controller can get back a list of all notes added or edited in the past 15 days for a particular project. Remember, SQLObject automatically generates a recent_notes attribute from the _get_recent_notes method, which always returns only the notes created or modified within the past 15 days. This returns a list of notes for each note in self.notes, which fits the filter criteria. Notice how using SQLObject's multiple join feature makes the call to the database totally transparent. You just have a project object and you call its notes method to get an iterator back, no SQL trickery needed.

If you aren't familiar with list comprehensions, here's what they do: They enable you to create a new list by filtering the contents of an existing list based on the expression that comes after the list.

The basic syntax of a list comprehension is: for item in iterable if expression. So you could write something like the following one liner to get a new list of all the items with a value greater than 1 in a list_or_iterator.

new_list for item in list_or_iterator if item > 1

Of course, using list comprehensions to filter a SQLObject results iterator is not the most high-performance way to go about getting a result set back from the database. It'll go to the database and retrieve all the members of that SQLObject result set, create a copy in memory, and only then run the list comprehension to filter the results down to what you want.

In general, the fastest way to get a list that contains only the notes related to this project added or edited in the past 15 days is to use SQLObject's query builder syntax to do this same query, using database-independent code to build a SQL query that only returns the rows you need. SQLObject's query builder enables you to create arbitrarily complex queries that perform similarly to native SQL, but also have database independence and give you the easy SQLSelect result set access methods that we've come to expect from our model objects.

In this case, there are unlikely to be more than a few dozen notes per project, so it's quite unlikely that this operation is going to be a bottleneck. So, it's better to do this the easy way in standard Python. However, if we were to profile WhatWhat Status later (as you learn about in Chapter 21, "Testing a TurboGears Application"), and discover that this method actually is a bottleneck, we could easily replace the contents of this method with an optimized version that uses the SQLObject query builder (without having to change a line of controller or view code).

In some cases, you might find that SQLObject's caching behavior works in your favor, particularly if you are doing a series of list comprehensions on the same results, because you avoid the round-trip overhead of another database call. (For more information on the theory behind this, see Martin Fowler's excellent book *Patterns of Enterprise Application Architecture*; for more information about SQLObject and performance, see Chapter 11, "Mastering SQLObject," and Chapter 12, "Customizing SQLObject Behavior").

Skipping over a few methods that don't do anything new, we find _total_questions has a slight twist on the same list-comprehension-as-results-filter idiom we've been discussing:

```
def _total_questions(self):
    list1 = [question for question in self.questions]
    list2 = [question for sub_project in self.sub_projects
            for question in sub_project.questions]
    return list1 + list2
```

At first glance, this seems to be exactly the same thing we've already seen; and for the most part, it is. However, the call to self.sub_project bears mentioning because sub_project is a multiple join against projects, so we aren't looking to another database table to find our sub_projects. Every sub_project is itself a project with all the same fields as any other project. So, we are now selecting all the sub_projects related to this project and iterating over them to get a list of questions, returning both lists, so _total_questions is actually returning all the questions associated with this project and with all of its sub_projects.

6.4   Writing Better Model Classes

Before we move on to looking at WhatWhat Status's controller code, here are a few tips for creating better models.

6.4.1   Keep All Model Logic in Model Methods

The first critical thing to remember is that even though you are using a SQLObject to wrap a database that just stores your data, your model objects are not just data-containing blobs. They are full-fledged objects with methods as well as attributes. So, in addition to storing your data, they can contain program logic. Perhaps this goes without saying, but somehow people don't seem to be used to treating their object relational mapper (ORM) classes like regular classes.

The critical thing to remember about model-viewer-controller (MVC) is that all the data, and all the rules and logic about how the data can be manipulated, ought to live in the model. The controller's job is just to tell the model about a user action and to start the methods by which the model will update itself.

The classic example of this is a checking account object with a withdrawal method. You probably want to verify that there is enough money in the account, and if there isn't, abort the transaction. But even if there is enough money in the account, you still want to update several tables:

- You want the withdrawal logged in an account history table.
- You want the withdrawal amount deducted from the current balance value in the appropriate table.
- You want the ATM machine's current cash balance updated in another table.

The list could go on and on, but the point is that your model objects ought to be responsible for updating themselves, so that your controller can just say `try_withdrawal(300)` and not have to know about everything that needs to be done for a valid withdrawal transaction.

6.4.2   Create New Classes to Encapsulate Complex Relational Logic

Feel free to create your own classes when you need to go beyond what SQLObject gives you for free.

Another general rule: Don't have your controller check for some model state and then, depending on what you find, do any of a variety of things. When you design your code so that you can just call a method in your model, which checks whatever state needs checking and updates itself, you're much better off.

It's important that your model objects act like objects rather than just state-containing blobs.

If your model objects have methods that encapsulate the whole state+logic that is associated with your model, your controllers will be free to do what they are designed to do: handle user actions.

6.5   Summary

- WhatWhat Status is a real-world project management application developed in TurboGears by Optio Software to track internal projects.

- WhatWhat Status uses a special feature of SQLObject that automatically creates a `some_property` attribute for a model object whenever you define a `_get_some_property` method that returns the value of the `some_property` attribute.

- The TurboGears Identity module makes it easy to require that users log in to a site before accessing protected resources.

- SQLObject join columns can take an `orderBy` parameter, which will define the default order in which the records from the adjoining table will be returned.

- The MVC paradigm asks that you put all model-related behavior into your model objects. And SQLObject makes database records into model objects for you. But there's nothing keeping you from wrapping SQLObjects and other data objects in a new class that provides your controllers with a nice model API.

Chapter 7

Controllers, Views, and JavaScript in the WhatWhat Status

In This Chapter

N ow that we've seen the WhatWhat model, let's move one step up the stack to look at some of the WhatWhat controller methods. In the process, you will learn about the TurboGears built-in authentication and authorization methods and how to build URL hierarchies by mounting classes within the `root` controller.

7.1 Dashboard Controller

If you keep adding more and more methods to the same `controllers.py` file, it's going to get out of hand pretty quickly. Luckily, it's easy to handle this growing complexity by moving some pieces out to separate modules. WhatWhat has separate controller modules for the Dashboard, Project, People, Recent Changes, and Feed features. We won't have time to look at each of these in depth, but we do take a look at a few of them to see what we can learn.

Remember that everything in CherryPy is built up off of the `root` controller. To mount classes from other modules, you just import the controller you're keeping in a separate file and mount it within your root controller. Here's how WhatWhat does it:

```
import turbogears    as tg
import cherrypy      as http

from turbogears                   import identity, controllers, flash
from subcontrollers.dashboard     import DashboardController
from subcontrollers.project       import ProjectController
from subcontrollers.people        import PeopleController
from subcontrollers.recentchanges import RecentChangesController
from subcontrollers.trackfeed     import WhatWhatFeed

class Root(controllers.RootController):

    @tg.expose()
    def index(self, *args, **kw):
        raise tg.redirect('/dashboard')
    <<<Login controller removed...>>>
```

*The site-wide index just redirects the user to the **DashboardController** index method.*

```
dashboard        = DashboardController()
project          = ProjectController()
people           = PeopleController()
recentchanges    = RecentChangesController()
feed             = WhatWhatFeed()
```

root.dashboard points to the DashbardController class. So, browsing to /dashboard will call DashboardContrller's index method

Note that the method in the root controller is using `raise tg.redirect('/dashboard')` to take anybody who comes to a WhatWhat website and send them directly on to /dashboard. And, this generates a call to the dashboard class, which is an alias for DashboardControler. Then, because there is no specific method name called within DashboardController, the index method is triggered.

If we take a look into dashboard.py in the subcontrollers subdirectory, we can see what happens when the index method is called:

(There's also a new_project method, but we come back to that later.)

```
Whatwhat dashboard.py
import turbogears          as tg
from turbogears            import identity, validators
from fasttrack.model       import Person, Project, status_codes


class DashboardController(identity.SecureResource):
    require = identity.not_anonymous()

    @tg.expose(template="fasttrack.templates.dashboard.index")
    def index(self):
        all_projects = Project.select("parent_project_id is Null " +
                                "order by upper(name)")

        projects = [project for project in all_projects if not project.archived]

        archived_projects = [project for project in all_projects
                        if project.archived]

        people = Person.select(orderBy='displayName')

        return dict(active_section='dashboard',
                    projects=projects,
                    archived_projects=archived_projects,
                    people=people,
                    status_codes=status_codes)
```

7.1.1   WhatWhat Security and Identity

Before we start looking inside of the `index` method, there's another import TurboGears feature at use here that deserves a closer look. Jeff Watkins created an authentication and authorization framework that allows TurboGears applications to define users, groups, and permissions and makes it easy to secure particular resources in your website to specific users or those who are members of a particular group. Jeff Watkins created TurboGears identity with a remarkably simple application programming interface (API).

You can decorate any controller with the `require` method from the `turbogears.identity`, with whatever restrictions you need. To restrict access to the `DashboardController` `index` method to only logged-in users, you could just write something like this:

```
@tg.expose(template="whatwhat.templates.dashboard.index")
@require(identity.not_anonymous)
def index(self):
    pass
```

The `require` decorator checks to see whether the current request is coming from a logged-in user, and redirects the user to the login page if necessary. Of course, if all the `identity` module did was give you the ability to require that a user be logged in, it wouldn't be all that helpful. The TurboGears `identity` module has a simple but powerful developer interface. You can restrict access to pages to particular users or groups, you can set up specific permissions for your page, and you can associate that permission with groups. And you can check things such as `in_any_group`, `in_all_group`, or `has_all_permissions`. You can also access the identity information from within your controller, allowing you to write code like this:

```
from turbogears import identity
if "editor" in identity.current.groups:
    value = "Do something interesting here"
else:
    value = "Do something less interesting here"
```

If you pass the `identity` objects into your template (or import them using a Python block `<? from turbogears import identity ?>`), you can easily use check particular permissions with `py:if` to hide specific page sections or administrative links from regular users.

Although the decorator syntax makes TurboGears `identity` easy to use, it's also a bit cumbersome when you want to restrict access to an entire directory tree. But Turbo-Gears makes that easy, too.

The `identity` module provides a class for you to subclass whenever you want to protect a whole swath of your site all at once. The class that does this for you is called `SecureResources`. All you have to do is create a controller class, which inherits from `SecureResources`, and override the `require` method with whatever restrictions you need.

This is exactly how WhatWhat uses the `identity` module here. Because WhatWhat restricts access to all the `dashboard` methods to logged-in users, the `DashboardController` class subclasses `identity.SecureResource` and assigns `require` to `identity.not_anonymous`.

Therefore, all the methods of the `DashboardController` class will only be accessible to logged-in users. Behind the scenes, the `SecureResource` class contains code that prevents any user who browses to any of the protected methods in the `DashboardController` subclass without logging in first from accessing any of the subpages of `/dashboard`.

Any class that subclasses `SecureResources` automatically redirects users who fail to meet the required criteria to either a login page, with a flag that lets the login page know where to send the user when the login is complete, or to a page that tells users that their user account does not have sufficient permission to view that resource. Of course, if the would-be user does not have an account, and can't authenticate, that user won't be able to get in at all.

If this seems a bit simplistic to you, it is; but it's all that WhatWhat requires. As you've briefly seen, the `identity` framework does allow for much more complex authorization logic, but WhatWhat is designed to help project teams and company managers communicate their experiences more widely. So, it isn't designed to keep data secret from any of the managers or project members.

If you have different needs, however, it is simple to modify it and thus create a much more complex permissions structure. If you create users and add them to the admin group (using CatWalk or `tg-admin shell`), you could replace `identity.not_anonymous` with `identity.in_group('admin')`.

And if you have several groups that ought to have access to the Dashboard view, you can create a `view_dashboard` and grant the `admin`, `manager`, `project_managers`, and `team_leads` group the `view_dashboard` permission. By default, `identity` stores these permissions in your database using a many-to-many relationship between groups and permissions—just like there was between bookmarks and categories. So, adding new permissions uses the same syntax: `TG_Group.addTG_Permission("view-dashboard")`.

Instead of covering all of that right now, however, we devote much of Chapter 22, "TurboGears Identity and Security," to covering the TurboGears `identity` framework.

7.1.2   Exploring the Dashboard Index

After the user has been authenticated, the main body of the `index` method is evaluated:

```
@tg.expose(template="whatwhat.templates.dashboard.index")
def index(self):
    all_projects = Project.select("parent_project_id is Null " +
                                  "order by upper(name)")

    projects = [project for project in all_projects if not project.archived]

    archived_projects = [project for project in all_projects
                         if project.archived]

    people = Person.select(orderBy='displayName')

    return dict(active_section='dashboard',
                projects=projects,
                archived_projects=archived_projects,
                people=people,
                status_codes=status_codes)
```

`DashboardController`'s `index` method is concerned with getting each of the top-level projects from the `Projects` table and sorting them into archived and current projects.

Probably the biggest new thing we are seeing here is the `Project.select` (`parent_project`ID...) method call. If you remember our model had a one-to-many relationship between projects and subprojects. In effect, this creates a column with the ID value of the parent project of each of our projects. Only the projects with a `Null` value in this column are top-level projects, and for now we want just the top-level projects.

Of course, `Project.select()` itself isn't new if you've been following along. We first used the `select` method by passing it no arguments at all, as in `Project.select()`, in which case we got back the contents of every column for every single row in the database, just as if we had written a SQL query such as this:

```
SELECT * FROM person
```

Then we took a quick look at how you can pass a Python expression such as the following:

```
person.select(firstName = "Carl")
```

This statement returns a set of all the objects with a first name value of firstName== "Carl"—just as if we had written a SQL query such as this:

```
SELECT * from Person where first_name="Carl".
```

When you use an SQLObject's `select` method, SQLObject determines what SQL to send to the database for you, which is nice. But even more important, it helps you avoid SQL injection attacks by automatically escaping everything. If you use your own string stuff to build a `where` clause, you can easily get hit by a SQL injection attack if you're not careful.

SQL injection attacks are created when users "inject" some SQL commands into the form they are filling out. If you then use that string in a SQL query (like an insert that is intended to put the contents of that file into the database), you can end up running the code that the users wrote directly against your database.

You can also create much more complex Select queries using SQLObject's query-builder syntax, which you learn more about in Chapter 12, "Customizing SQLObject Behavior." That's generally the way we recommend creating queries in TurboGears.

But, because Python and SQLObject both have an attitude that says "We're all consenting adults here," there is nothing to stop you from writing your `where` clauses by hand. We respect your right to evaluate the options and make rational choices about what you do in the privacy of your own controller module (even if that means doing something some programmers think is wrong).

And that's just what WhatWhat is doing.

```
all_projects = Project.select("parent_project_id is Null order by upper(name)")
```

Considering the state of SQLObject's documentation, the WhatWhat authors indicated that it was easier to just write the query by hand than to figure out how SQLObject's query builder works, particularly when checking against values such as `Null`. We hope we have fixed that problem in Chapter 14, "Creating Better JavaScript with Mochikit," where we take an in-depth look at query builder.

But as long as you're careful, there's nothing wrong with writing `where` clauses by hand like this. And in this example from WhatWhat, there is absolutely no chance of an SQL injection attack because the code just passes a plain string with no string substitution at all.

If you look closely at the preceding code, you'll notice one other gotcha for writing your SQL by hand this way. The WhatWhat Project class defines

```
parent_project = ForeignKey('Project')
```

Notice that this `select` query looks for `parent_project_id` rather than `parent_project`. This is because SQLObject automatically creates column names for you based on some internal rules. Of course, you can modify these rules, and we tell you how in Chapter 12. But for now, all you need to know is that whenever you create a query by hand in SQLObject, you have to use the actual name of the column in the table. You can do this by either memorizing the SQLObject rules for creating table names or looking them up in your database whenever you want to use them.

After `index` has an SQLObject result set with all the top-level projects in it, it uses two list comprehensions to split that into a list of current projects and a list of archived projects. It also pulls down a SQLObject `selectResults` object for all the people in the database.

This is another good place to think about what belongs in the controller and what belongs in the model. In all of WhatWhat, the `dashboard` controller is the only place that needs a list of top-level projects sorted into archived and current projects. So, it is probably fine to leave this logic here. But if ever there are other places where this same data is required somewhere else, it makes a lot of sense to move this into the model. The model-viewer-controller (MVC) puritans among us might even say that this kind of thing should always go in the model; but because this often grows up organically in the controller over time, it might not be worth moving it to the model until you find yourself needing that same data somewhere else. The key principle is to avoid repeating the same code in multiple places.

So, after everything is said and done, the `index` method passes a dictionary to our Kid template (`whatwhat.templates.dashboard.index`). In that dictionary, we have an `active_session` marker, a list of current projects (called projects), a list of `archived_projects`, a "list" of people, and a list of possible status codes (which we imported from our model).

7.2   Dashboard Templates

The next logical place to go in our WhatWhat code walkthrough is the template code that displays the Dashboard. You can see a sample of this template's output in Figure 7.1.

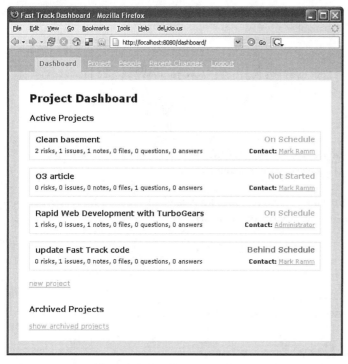

FIGURE 7.1   Dashboard Listing of open projects

This is by far the largest Kid template we've seen, so it should help you to see how to put everything together in a more complex page.

The first thing the `whatwhat.templates.dashboard.index` template does is use Kid's `<?python ?>` syntax to embed a brief snippet of Python into the template:

```
<?python
     from whatwhat.model import STATUS_BEHIND_SCHEDULE
?>
```

In general, it's a good idea to use `<?python ?>` directly at the top of your template whenever you need it. Unlike ASP, JSP, or PHP, you can't return results directly to your rendered template from a `<?python ?>` statement, and it makes this difference, and your code in general, a lot clearer if you don't start mixing Python code segments into the middle of your XHTML.

Here are the contents of the `dashboard.kid` file:

```
<body>

  <h2>Project Dashboard</h2>
  <h3>Active Projects</h3>

  <div class="project"
       onclick="document.location.href='${tg.url('/project/%s' % project.id)}'"
       py:for="project in projects">

    <div class="top">
      <h3 py:content="project.name" />
      <span py:if="project.status != STATUS_BEHIND_SCHEDULE" class="status good"
      py:content="status_codes.get(project.status)" />

        <span py:if="project.status == STATUS_BEHIND_SCHEDULE" class="status bad"
         py:content="status_codes.get(project.status)" />
      </div>

    <div class="bottom">
      <span class="contact">
        <span class="label">Contact:</span>
        <a href="mailto:$project.contact.emailAddress" py:content="project.contact.
displayName" />
      </span>
      <span class="info">
        <span py:replace="len(project._total_risks())">some</span> risks,
         <span py:replace="len(project._total_issues())">some</span> issues,
        <span py:replace="len(project._total_notes())">some</span> notes,
        <span py:replace="len(project._total_files())">some</span> files,
        <span py:replace="len(project._total_questions())">some</span> questions,
        <span py:replace="len(project._total_answers())">some</span> answers
        <br/>
          <span py:if="len(project.delayed_subprojects) > 0">
          and <span py:replace="len(project.delayed_subprojects)" /> delayed sub-
projects
          (<a py:for="i, sub_project in enumerate(project.delayed_subprojects)"
href="/project/$sub_project.id" title="$sub_project.name">${i+1} </a>)
        </span>
      </span>
    </div>
  </div>
  <br/>
```

This chunk of code creates a couple of static headings, and then goes into a giant loop that iterates over every project in the projects list that was passed into our template by the `index` method in `dashboard.py`. Each project has two display sections, which are organized into two different `div` tags. The first `div` contains a header with the `Project` name and the status. This is where they are using the `STATUS_BEHIND_SCHEDULE` variable from our `<?python ?>` statement at the top of the template. This keeps project status encoding information in one place (our model), so that if for any reason it ever changes (say we need to create a "pending approval" status), we only have to update our code in one place. The `py:if` statements allow WhatWhat to set the class attribute to "good" for all projects that are not behind schedule, and bad for the projects that are behind schedule. This allows WhatWhat to color code these items through standard CSS.

Here's what the relevant portion of the `dashboard.css` file looks like:

```
div.project h3 { float: left; font-size: 14px; margin: 1px; }
div.project span.status { float: right; font-weight: bold; font-size: 14px; }
div.project span.good { color: #85c034; }
div.project span.bad { color: #ee0000; }
div.project span.archived { color: #666; }
div.project span.label { font-weight: bold; }
div.project div.bottom { margin-top: 24px; }
div.project span.contact {float: right;}
```

*This is what makes projects with **span.good** green and **span.bad** red.*

As you can see, all span elements in `div.project` are styled here. If you aren't familiar with CSS, you might want to check out the references on our website. But, in brief, this CSS file contains the visual display information for the HTML created by the `dashboard.kid` template. It looks for class attributes on the various HTML elements in our page and applies the correct styling. In this case, the `h3` tags will be aligned on the left, have a 14px font, and so forth. Status information will be on the right and will be color coded based on whether it's good or bad. The great thing about using Kid templates and CSS is that it makes it easy to get help from a designer when you need to work out the details of how everything should look. They can open up your templates in their tool of choice and play with the CSS.

Now we come to the bottom div (inside the project div). There's not much new here, but it's worth a second look because it's a bit more complicated than anything you've seen before. The first attribute creates a mailto: link to the contact for the current project. This is immediately followed by a section that shows how many risks, notes, issues, files, questions, and answers are in the database for this project.

Remember: All of this is still happening inside the big project loop that iterates over the top-level projects. Every subelement of original project `div`, where `py:for "project in projects"` was called, is part of that loop. So, this whole thing is going to be repeated for all the top-level projects in the database.

Which brings us to the next section of code. WhatWhat creates another loop inside the main loop, which gets each of the subprojects for the current top-level project and displays the information for that subproject.

7.3   Adding a New Project

The Dashboard isn't just a place to display existing projects, it also provides a way to quickly add a new project to your database.

Rather than have a form for adding a new project always sitting there taking up space in the `dashboard` form, the WhatWhat developers created a JavaScript function that toggles the form between hidden (its default state) and visible.

Here's the code in `dashboard.kid` to display the form:

```
<a href="#" onclick="toggle('new_project');
 clr('ta_new_project');fcs('tf_desc'); return false;">new project</a>
<div id="new_project" style="display: none;">
  <form id="form_new_project" action="new_project" method="post">
    <table>
      <tr>
        <td width="120"><b>Project Name:</b></td>
        <td><input id="tf_desc" type="text" name="name" size="50" /></td>
      </tr>
      <tr>
        <td><b>Contact:</b></td>
        <td>
          <select name="contact_id">
            <option py:for="person in people" value="$person.id">
              ${person.displayName}
            </option>
          </select>
        </td>
      </tr>
      <tr>
        <td><b>Create Sub-projects</b></td>
        <td><input type="checkbox" name="subprojects" /></td>
      </tr>
      <tr>
```

This form is normally hidden unless the user clicks to create a new project.

```
          <td colspan="2"><b>Project Description</b></td>
        </tr>
        <tr>
          <td colspan="2">
            <textarea id="ta_new_project"
                      rows="4"
                      name="description"
                      cols="72">
          </textarea>
          </td>
        </tr>
      </table>
    <a href="#" onclick="submit('form_new_project'); return false;">add</a>
    <a href="#" onclick="toggle('new_project'); return false;">cancel</a>
  </form>
</div>
```

*This JavaScript submits the form to the **new_project** method in our controller. The next line hides the form if you hit cancel.*

The sample bookmarker application uses the TurboGears form widget to automatically generate our forms, but the WhatWhat project takes another approach and creates the form by hand. The authors of WhatWhat create a table and the input fields, and handle the form action themselves. The `action` attribute tells us that this is going to be posted to our web server, to `new_project`, which will call that method in our `dashboard` controller. (I told you we'd get back to it!) If you've ever written an HTML form before, this is going to look pretty familiar to you. The only TurboGears-specific stuff in here is the `py:for` loop that generates the list of options in the `contact_id` field.

There is a middle way, between accepting the restriction of automatic form rendering on your page and doing things by hand the way WhatWhat does. And in most cases, this middle way is the most efficient method to manage forms because you get all the power of widgets to handle their own validation errors along with total control of the placement of the fields on the page.

Chapter 20, "Internationalization," covers this in detail. For now, however, we content ourselves with a quick example.

Suppose you create a new Project form from a controller that looks like this:

```
class ProjectFields(widgets.WidgetsList):
    title = TextField(label="Project", validator=validators.NotEmpty())
    client_revenue = widgets.TextField(validator=validators.Number())
    project_form = widgets.TableForm(fields=ProjectFields(),
                                     action="save_project_test")
```

You could then write code such as this in your template:

```
<div py:content="form.display_field_for('title', value=product.title)" />
    <div py:content="form.display_field_for('Client Revenue', value=product.
client_revenue)" />
```

You might have to work a little bit to wrap your mind around widgets. When you get used to using them, however, you will quickly see their benefits. Widgets do a lot of the hard work for you, including the following:

- Automatically render the right kind of field in your form
- Enable you to use widgets such as the AutoComplete widget that require special JavaScript components
- Render validation error messages for each field on their own

That said, TurboGears widgets are never required, and you can always do what WhatWhat does and roll your own forms. For example, if you are showing a bunch of PHP programmers how to write TurboGears applications, this way of doing forms is going to seem a lot more familiar to them and will make the first step of the transition easier.

The final section of the `dashboard.kid` template is pretty simple:

```
<h3>Archived Projects</h3>

<a href="#" id="show_archived" onclick="toggle('archived_projects');toggle('show_
archived');toggle('hide_archived'); return false;">show archived projects</a>
<a href="#" style="display: none" id="hide_archived" onclick="toggle('archived_
projects');toggle('show_archived');toggle('hide_archived'); return false;">hide
archived projects</a>

<div style="display: none" id="archived_projects">
  <div class="project archived" onclick="document.location.href='${tg.url('/
project/%s' % project.id)}'" py:for="project in archived_projects">
    <div class="top">
      <h3 py:content="project.name" />
      <span class="status archived">Archived</span>
    </div>
  </div>
</div>
</body>
</html>
```

Its job is to create a list of all the archived projects in the database, and display it only if the user clicks the Show Archived Projects link. In Section 7.4, we look at the JavaScript helper libraries used in WhatWhat, and how they are called on this page to dynamically show and hide page sections.

7.4   Dashboard Controller `new_project`

WhatWhat uses a few common JavaScript functions in its pages, and our `dashboard` template imports this set of `master.js` functions.

The major use of JavaScript in `dashboard.kid` is to dynamically display the `new_project` form.

```
<a href="#" onclick="toggle('new_project'); clr('ta_new_project');fcs('tf_desc');
return false;">new project</a>
```

This line defines an `onclick` event that does three important things:

- It toggles the visibility of the `new_project` element.
- It clears the text in the `new_project` text area field, which contains a description of the new project.
- It clears the `desc` text field, which contains the project name, and moves the focus to it so that the user can just start typing.

These things are actually done by three different functions from `master.js`:

```
function fcs(element_id) {
        var element = document.getElementById(element_id);
        element.defaultValue = '';
        element.value = '';
        element.focus();
}
function clr(element_id) {
        var element = document.getElementById(element_id);
        element.defaultValue = '';
        element.value = '';
}

function toggle(element_id) {
        var element = document.getElementById(element_id);
        if (element !== null) {
```

clr clears value property of a form element.

toggle checks to see whether an element is displayed. If the element is displayed, toggle hides it. When it's hidden, toggle displays it.

```
                if (element.style.display == "none") element.style.display =
"block";
                else element.style.display = "none";
        }
}
```

The `toggle` function takes an `element_id`, which in this case is the named div `new_project` and contains our whole form. It then checks to see that the `element_id` it received actually exists. Then it checks the `style.display` property of that element. If it's `none`, the function updates it to `block`, otherwise it changes the display property to `none`—effectively telling the browser to hide that element.

But the `toggle` function doesn't remove the values in any of the elements in the form, so the WhatWhat `onclick` event also fires up the `clr` function passing it the "`ta_new_project`" `element_id`. This function is simple; it just looks up the element in question and replaces its value and `defaultvalue` with an empty string. The `fcs` function does the same thing as `clr`, but it also sets the focus to the element.

After a user fills out the form, a couple of simple JavaScript statements in our template either cancel (and toggle off) or submit the form:

```
<a href="#" onclick="submit('form_new_project'); return false;">add</a>
<a href="#" onclick="toggle('new_project'); return false;">cancel</a>
```

The `submit` function takes an `element_id`, looks up the form, and calls its `submit` method (which posts the results to the URL defined in the `action` attribute of the form itself):

```
function submit(form_id) {
        document.getElementById(form_id).submit();
}
```

In this case, it sends the results to the relative URL `/new_project`, and that calls the `new_project` method on our `dashboard` controller. We said we'd come back to that method later, and here we are, so let's take a look at `new_project` to see how these form results are processed:

```
@expose()
@validate(validators=dict(contact_id=validators.Int(),
                        subprojects=validators.Bool()))

def new_project(self, name, description, contact_id, subprojects=False):
    contact = Person.get(contact_id)
    main_project = Project(name=name,
                        description=description,
```

```
                          contact=contact,
                          parent_project=None)
    if subprojects:
        dev_project = Project(name=name + ' - Development',
                              contact=contact,
                              description='Development sub-project for ' + name,
                              parent_project=main_project)
        doc_project = Project(name=name + ' - Documentation',
                              contact=contact,
                              description='Documentation sub-project for ' + name,
                              parent_project=main_project)
        qa_project  = Project(name=name + ' - QA',
                              contact=contact,
                              description='QA sub-project for ' + name,
                              parent_project=main_project)


    raise tg.redirect('/dashboard')
```

The post data for this form is passed into the `new_project` method as parameters. The `@validate` decorator processes some of the incoming form data. You might remember from before, validators function not only to confirm that incoming data is valid, but also to convert that data into the correct Python data type. This means that `contact_id` and `subprojects` will be turned into an `int` and a Boolean before the main body of the `new_project` method is executed.

The first thing this method does is look up the person in the database to be the primary contact for the project. The next thing it does is create a new project with the data from the form. The next thing it does is determine whether subprojects ought to be created for this project; if so, it creates three subprojects, one for development, one for documentation, and one for testing and quality assurance.

7.5   Summary

- TurboGears provides the `identity` module for easy authentication/authorization in your web applications.

- You can restrict access to a particular method with `@require(identity.not_anonymous)` or any combination of the identity checks.

- Identity also provides a special controller class (`SecureResource`) that enables you to protect that class and all its methods with a single `require=identity.not_anonymous`.

- You don't have to rely on your controller to provide all the variables in your Kid templates—you can import anything you need using the `<?python ?>` syntax Kid provides.

- It's easy to create pop-up forms with a little bit of JavaScript. But unless you submit them to the server asyncronously, this isn't quite Ajax yet. We get to Ajax more in Chapter 9, "Ajax and WhatWhat Projects."

- If you want to use validators without widgets, you can use the `@validate` decorator and set up a dictionary of validators to match the names of the fields that are coming in from the form.

Chapter 8

RSS, Cookies, and Dynamic Views in WhatWhat Status

In This Chapter

The WhatWhat Status RecentChanges page provides real-world examples of several important new TurboGears features. The RecentChanges sub-controllers uses cookies and RSS feeds. So, we take a look at those, but most important, this is where we see the first appearance of user-defined widgets. If you remember, we said that widgets bundle up HTML, CSS, and JavaScript in a reusable way, and the authors of WhatWhat Status took advantage of this to reduce code duplication in the "recent changes" template.

8.1   Cookies and RecentChanges

One critical feature of the WhatWhat Status software is the recent changes page, which enables users to see anything new on any of the projects in the system. And Recent- Changes is also worth a look because it uses a number of new TurboGears features, which can make your life easier.

In particular, we look at how to use CherryPy's `response` object to set cookies, how to define your own widgets, and how to use Kid template non-XHTML XML formats (in this case, RSS and Atom).

The `cherrypy.response` object enables you to add special information to the response that CherryPy will pipe out to the user. The response object has `headerMap`, `SimpleCookie`, `body`, `sendResponse`, and `wfile` attributes; and we discuss each of these in more detail in Chapter 17, "CherryPy and TurboGears Decorators." But for now, we focus on cookies because they are the most commonly used component.

For those of you familiar with the `cookie` module from the Python Standard Library, this explanation is going to be short: `cherrypy.response.simple_cookie` is just an instance of the `SimpleCookie` class in the standard library's `cookie` module.

For the rest of us, a `simple_cookie` just stores a cookie name and value, and sends it to a user's browser. The browser then sends that same name value pair back to the web server on every subsequent request.

Cookies are easy to use in TurboGears. You normally already have CherryPy imported, but if not, you must `import cherrypy` in your controller and then you can write code like this in your controller methods:

```
cherrypy.response.simple_cookie['user_name'] = 'Billy Bob Thorton-Wilder'
```

As long as you create different names for your cookies, you can set several different cookies, which will all be returned by the web browser on the next page request.

Cookies commonly store user state information. The main advantages of using cookies to maintain user state are as follows:

- Cookies are the HTTP standard way to maintain user state.
- Even if you are load balancing your site across multiple servers, the state information is always packaged up with a user's request.

The disadvantages of using cookies are as follows:

- If users bookmark a page and come back to it after the cookie expires, they won't get what they expect.
- Cookie data is sent back and forth as clear text, so it's not secure. (Never, ever, ever store a credit card number in a cookie!)
- The data in the cookie is stored on that particular client computer; so, if the same user comes back to your site from another machine, the cookie won't be available.
- A small minority of users turn off cookie support when browsing the web, and they may not like you if you use cookies.

If you are writing a web application targeted to web security experts, or hard-core privacy activists, you will definitely want to avoid cookies. But, if you take reasonable precautions, they can be an incredibly useful tool.

WhatWhat Status sets a cookie to remember how much "new" project information to display for a particular user session:

```
@tg.expose()
def change_time(self, change_hours):
    http.response.simple_cookie['time_frame_id'] = change_hours
    http.response.simple_cookie['time_frame_id']['path'] = '/'

    raise tg.redirect('/recentchanges')
def _timeframe(self):
    if http.request.simple_cookie.has_key('time_frame_id'):
        return int(http.request.simpleCookie['time_frame_id'].value)
    return 24
```

In addition to name value pairs, (sometimes called morsels) a `simple_cookie` can take several optional attributes. The most important attributes are `['domain']`, `['path']`, and, ['expires']. Because these are optional, and WhatWhat Status has no particular reason to restrict access to this cookie information, the only one they are setting is the path, which ensures that every user request to the WhatWhat Status server gets access to this cookie's information. This function takes a number that is passed in change_hours and puts it in the cookie.

After the cherrypy.response.simple_cookie object has been set, this function calls raise tg.redirect, which stops the execution of the function and sends the user on to the link indicated (in this case, to the index method of RecentChangesController).

But before we move on to the meat of the Recent Changes page, let's take a look at the _timeframe method, which accesses the cookie information we set in change_time. In the same way you set the cookie using CherryPy's response object, you can check it via CherryPy's request object. The .value method of simple_cookie returns the string bound to the key you give it. And in this case, the WhatWhat Status authors are converting that string into an int and returning it. If the cookie does not exist, they just return 24 hours (1 day).

With all that cookie stuff out of the way, let's delve into the controller code:

```
import turbogears          as tg
import cherrypy            as http

from turbogears            import identity
from whatwhat.model        import Project, status_codes, impact_codes, chance_
codes
from whatwhat.utils        import getRecentChanges
from whatwhat              import utils, widgets

class RecentChangesController(identity.SecureResource):
    require = identity.not_anonymous()

    @tg.expose(template="whatwhat.templates.recentchanges.index")
    def index(self):
        utils.checkIdentity(http.request.identity.user)
        all_projects = Project.select("parent_project_id is NULL " +
                                "order by upper(name)")

        projects = [project for project in all_projects if not project.archived]

        recent_proj = getRecentChanges(projects, self._timeframe())
```

```
    return dict(active_section='recentchanges',
                recent_proj=recent_proj,
                status_codes=status_codes,
                chance_codes=chance_codes,
                impact_codes=impact_codes,
                time_hours=self._timeframe(),
                questions_widget=widgets.questions_widget,
                issues_widget=widgets.issues_widget,
                risks_widget=widgets.risks_widget,
                notes_widget=widgets.notes_widget)
```

The nice thing at this point in our journey through TurboGears and WhatWhat Status is that there's not going to be much new going on in the controller.

Calling the `index` method will return a page based on the `templates.recentchanges.index` Kid template (which we look at in a second), and again we construct a dictionary to pass into the template. The only difference here from what we've seen before is that the authors of WhatWhat Status moved a couple of functions into `whatwhat.utils`, and they are importing a bunch of widgets of their own design from the WhatWhat Status `widgets` module.

We'll get back to widgets in a minute, but for now let's take a look at the `utils` function `getRecentChanges`. This particular function takes a list of projects and the number of hours into the past that the user wants to see. In this case, the number of hours is pulled out of a cookie or set to a default value by the `_timeframe()` function.

The `getRecentChanges` method call goes through all the projects in the database and creates a list of projects that have recent updates to their issues, risks, notes, files, or questions, and returns a list of project objects.

The code for all of that looks like this:

```
def getRecentChanges(projects, hours):

    recent_proj = []
    recent_issues = []
    recent_risks  = []
    recent_notes  = []
    recent_files  = []
    recent_questions = []
    recent_answers = []

    for project in projects:
        if len(project._new_issues(hours)) > 0:
```

```
        for issue in project._new_issues(hours):
            recent_issues.append(issue)
    if len(project._new_risks(hours)) > 0:
        for risk in project._new_risks(hours):
            recent_risks.append(risk)
    if len(project._new_notes(hours)) > 0:
        for note in project._new_notes(hours):
            recent_notes.append(note)
    if len(project._new_files(hours)) > 0:
        for file in project._new_files(hours):
            recent_files.append(file)
    if len(project._new_questions(hours)) > 0:
        for question in project._new_questions(hours):
            recent_questions.append(question)

    new_proj = RecentProj(project.name, project.id,
                    recent_notes, recent_issues,
                    recent_risks, recent_files, recent_questions)

    recent_proj.append(new_proj)
    recent_issues = []
    recent_risks = []
    recent_notes = []
    recent_files = []
    recent_questions = []

return recent_proj
```

RecentProj takes these elements and creates a new object with attributes for issues, risks, notes, files, and questions, which we add to the recent_proj list and pass to the template.

As the method iterates over each of the projects, it calls all of those model methods that we looked at in Chapter 6, "Exploring More Complex Models in WhatWhat Status." If there are new issues, notes, or whatever, it appends them to the appropriate list. Notice that new_proj is assigned by another method call to RecentProj, which constructs project objects. It is these project objects that are going to be passed into the template.

RecentProj takes the project name, id, and the lists of recent notes, issues, risks, files, and questions, and creates attributes for each of them:

```
class RecentProj(object):

    def __init__(self, proj_name, proj_id,
                    recent_notes, recent_issues,
                    recent_risks, recent_files,
                    recent_questions):
```

```
self.proj_name          =   proj_name
self.proj_id            =   proj_id
self.recent_notes       =   recent_notes
self.recent_issues      =   recent_issues
self.recent_risks       =   recent_risks
self.recent_files       =   recent_files
self.recent_questions   =   recent_questions
```

The `getRecentProjects` method in our controller returns a list of these `RecentProj` objects. This list gets passed on to the Template as the list `recent_proj`. You can see the results of all this in Figure 8.1.

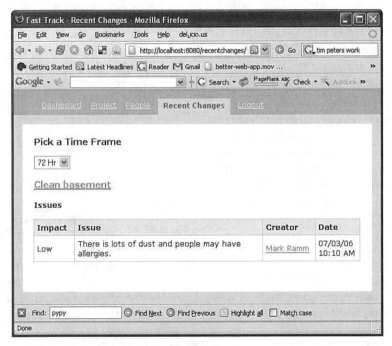

FIGURE 8.1 Recent Changes example

8.2   The Recent Changes Template

Let's take a quick look at the template that displays the Recent Changes page. Much of this template should be familiar to you by now, but there are several new things on display here. First, there's the use of `textilize`. Next, there's the first appearance of TurboGears internationalization features. Not only that, the WhatWhat Status folks created a couple of application-specific widgets, which are used in the following code.

```
<?python
    from whatwhat.model import STATUS_BEHIND_SCHEDULE, status_codes, impact_codes,
chance_codes
    from whatwhat.utils import textilize
    from turbogears.i18n.format import format_date
    from cgi import escape
?>


<!DOCTYPE html PUBLIC "-//W3C//DTD XHTML 1.0 Transitional//EN" "http://www.w3.org/TR/
xhtml1/DTD/xhtml1-transitional.dtd">
<html xmlns="http://www.w3.org/1999/xhtml" xmlns:py="http://purl.org/kid/ns#"
    py:extends="'../master.kid'">


<head>
    <meta content="text/html; charset=UTF-8" http-equiv="content-type"
py:replace="'''"/>
    <title>WhatWhat Status - Recent Changes</title>
        <script src="/static/javascript/master.js" type="text/javascript"></script>
        <link href="/static/css/master.css" media="screen"
            rel="Stylesheet" type="text/css" />
        <link href="/static/css/project.css" media="screen"
            rel="Stylesheet" type="text/css" />
        <link rel="alternate" type="application/rss+xml"
            href="${tg.url('/feed/rss2.0')}" title="RSS Feed" />
        <link rel="alternate" type="application/atom+xml"
            href="${tg.url('/feed/atom1.0')}" title="Atom Feed" />
</head>


<body>
  <h3>Pick a Time Frame</h3>
```

Whenever a user changes the drop-down list, the form will be automatically submitted, and the page reloaded.

```
  <form id="pick_time" name="pick_time" action="change_time" method="post">
      <select name="change_hours" onchange="document.pick_time.submit()">
          <option value="24"
                selected="${(None, '')[int(time_hours) == 24]}">24 Hr
          </option>
          <option value="48"
                selected="${(None, '')[int(time_hours) == 48]}">48 Hr
          </option>
          <option value="72"
                selected="${(None, '')[int(time_hours) == 72]}">72 Hr
          </option>
      </select>
  </form>
```

```
<div py:for="proj in recent_proj">
    <h3 py:if="len(proj.recent_issues) > 0 or len(proj.recent_risks) > 0 or
➥ len(proj.recent_notes) >0 or len(proj.recent_questions) >0">
      <a href="${tg.url('/project/%s' % proj.proj_id)}">${proj.proj_name}</a>
    </h3>

    <h4 py:if="len(proj.recent_issues) > 0">Issues</h4>
    <div py:if="len(proj.recent_issues) > 0">
       ${issues_widget.display(issues=proj.recent_issues,
       ➥ read_only=True, show_closed=False)}
    </div>

    <h4 py:if="len(proj.recent_risks) > 0">Risks</h4>
    <div py:if="len(proj.recent_risks) > 0">
        ${risks_widget.display(risks=proj.recent_risks,
        ➥ read_only=True, show_closed=False)}
    </div>


    <h4 py:if="len(proj.recent_notes) > 0">Progress Notes</h4>
    <div id="project_notes">
        ${notes_widget.display(notes=proj.recent_notes, read_only=True)}
    </div>

    <h4 py:if="len(proj.recent_questions) > 0">Questions</h4>
    <div id="project_questions">
        ${questions_widget(questions=proj.recent_questions, read_only=True)}
    </div>

    <h4 py:if="len(proj.recent_files) > 0">Files</h4>

    <ul py:if="len(proj.recent_files) > 0" id="files">
      <li class="file" py:for="file in proj.recent_files">
        <div class="file_content">
          <div>
            <a href="javascript:void(0)"
              onclick="javascript:window.open('/static/files/$file.systemfilename', '
              ➥ ', 'fullscreen=no,toolbar=yes,menubar=no,
              ➥ scrollbars=yes,resizable=yes,directories=no,location=no')">
                   ${file.filename}</a>
            </div>
            <br/>
            <div class="file_info">
                <span>
```

```
                    Posted by
                      <a class="file_creator"
                         href="mailto:$file.creator.emailAddress">
                       ${note.creator.displayName}</a>
                      on ${format_date(file.creation_date,
               ➥    time_format=' %I:%M %p')}
                    </span>
                  </div>
                </div>
              </li>
          </ul>

       </div>
   </body>
   </html>
```

Right at the top of the template is code that allows a user to select a different time frame for this page. It submits a predefined number (24, 48, or 72) to the `change_time` method of the `RecentChangesController`, which sets a cookie that tells the controller how far back in time to go when preparing the list of recent projects.

The big section of code starting with `<div py:for="proj in recent_proj">` iterates through each of the project objects in the `recent_proj` list, checks to see whether any of its elements have recent activity, and if so prints each of those elements one by one, by calling its particular widget.

8.3   WhatWhat Status Widgets

In the widgets directory, you'll find `widgets.py`, which defines each of the widgets that WhatWhat Status uses in the Recent Changes page.

Each of these widgets inherits from the `turbogears.widgets.widget` base class, which provides methods such as the `display` method used to display each widget in the recent changes template:

```
from turbogears.widgets import Widget

class NoteWidget(Widget):
    template        = 'whatwhat.widgets.templates.note'
    template_vars   = ['note', 'read_only']
    read_only       = False
```

```
note_widget = NoteWidget()


class NotesWidget(Widget):
    template        = 'whatwhat.widgets.templates.notes'
    template_vars   = ['notes', 'read_only', 'note_widget']
    note_widget     = note_widget
    read_only       = False

notes_widget = NotesWidget()
```

There are widgets for Questions, Risks, Projects, etc. But when you understand the NotesWidget, the others will all be trivial to figure out. To render properly to the browser, every widget needs a template. This can either be a .kid file, or it can be placed right inside the widget. For anything more complex than a simple text area, you are better off creating a .kid file for the template and referencing it—the way the WhatWhat Status authors do here.

Widgets also have special variables that can only be set at widget instantiation or at render time, called params. The NotesWidget has two params: note and read_only, which are assigned at render time. The note param will be the actual text of the note that is passed into the widget at render time in the recent changes template. The other thing that happens at render time is that read_only is being set to True.

Let's take a look at the note widget template:

```
<?python

    from whatwhat.utils import textilize, getGroups
    from turbogears.i18n.format import format_date
    from turbogears import identity

    groupids = getGroups()
?>
<li xmlns:py="http://purl.org/kid/ns#" id="note_$note.id" class="note"
    onmouseover="show_inline('remove_note_link_$note.id');show_inline('edit_note_
link_$note.id')"
    onmouseout="hide('remove_note_link_$note.id'); hide('edit_note_link_$note.
id');">
    <div class="note_content" id="note_content_$note.id">
      <div>${XML(textilize(note.note))}</div>
        <div py:if="note.last_edit_date != None">
          <i>Last edited:
            ${format_date(note.last_edit_date, time_format=' %I:%M %p')}
```

```
        </i>
      </div>
    <br/>
    <div class="note_info">
      <span>  Posted by
        <a class="note_creator"
           href="mailto:$note.creator.emailAddress">
        ${note.creator.displayName}</a>
        on ${format_date(note.creation_date, time_format=' %I:%M %p')}
      </span>
      <a py:if="(identity.current.user == note.creator or 'admin' in groupids)
and not read_only"
         style="display: none" id="edit_note_link_$note.id" href="#"
         class="edit_note_link" onclick="request_note_content($note.id); return
false;">edit
      </a>
      <a py:if="(identity.current.user == note.creator or 'admin' in groupids)
and not read_only"
         style="display: none" id="remove_note_link_$note.id" href="#"
         class="remove_note_link" onclick="remove_note($note.id); return
false;">remove
      </a>
    </div>
  </div>
  <div py:if="not read_only" class="note_content" id="edit_note_$note.id"
style="display: none;">
    <textarea style="display: block; width: 540px; height: 275px;"
             id="ta_edit_note_$note.id" name="content" rows="16" cols="74">
    </textarea><br/>
    <a href="#" onclick="edit_note($note.id); return false;">save</a>
    <a href="#" onclick="cancel_edit($note.id); return false;">cancel</a>
    <br/>
  </div>
</li>
```

By moving all this code out of the RecentChanges template and the projects page, the authors of WhatWhat Status are reducing code duplication. There's a lot of JavaScript in this widget (which we look at in more depth in Chapter 9, "Ajax and What-What Status Projects"): but in this case, the template passed in `read_only=true`, so most of the dynamic sections of this widget are not executed. Either way, the most important piece of this widget is this little bit of code: `<div>${XML(textilize(note.note))}</div>`. It takes a note instance from the database, processes it, and then renders the resulting XHTML out to the page.

The authors of WhatWhat Status wanted to enable users to use italics, bold, and other markup in their text. So, they are providing access to the textual markup language to their users. Lucky for us, there is an easy-to-use Python language interpreter for textile already built, so theoretically all that is needed is to import the proper module and pass our note text through the textile function. Because there's a little bit of added complexity to make sure that the results of `textilize` are encoded in UTF-8 (to match the default encoding of our Kid template), the authors of WhatWhat Status wrapped textile up in a helper function, which they keep in the `whatwhat.utils` module:

```
def textilize(unicodeStr):
    return textile(escape(unicodeStr).encode('utf-8'), encoding='utf-8',
output='utf-8')
```

Note that if you just pass the result of `textalize` into Kid using `${textilize(someString)}`, you probably won't like the results you get.

Normally, Kid takes whatever strings you pass it and escapes them into proper HTML, so special charaters such as < and & become `&lt;` and `&amp;` which are then recognized by the browser and turned back into the < and & characters for display to your user.

If Kid didn't escape these characters from the strings you pass in, it would create invalid XML, and broken HTML, and things would start to look pretty darned funny in the browser. But sometimes you already have the XHTML and you just want it displayed, and that's where Kid's XML function comes in. XML(value) bypasses Kid's escaping mechanism, and slides your XHTML right into Kid. By default, Kid then turns it into HTML from XML the same way that it processes any other XHTML to produce the final page output.

Beyond inserting the text for the note, the note (when in read-only mode) will just display the author's name with a link to her e-mail address, along with that note's creation date:

```
<span>  Posted by
   <a class="note_creator"
      href="mailto:$note.creator.emailAddress">
   ${note.creator.displayName}</a>
  on ${format_date(note.creation_date, time_format=' %I:%M %p')}
</span>
```

Everything else is inside a `py:if` block, which will not be executed if `read_only = true`. But don't worry, we aren't going to skip over this stuff for long; it features prominently in Chapter 9, where we discuss the details of how WhatWhat Status's project page works and peer a little bit more deeply into WhatWhat Status's use of JavaScript and Ajax.

8.4 Easy RSS with FeedController

More and more applications are including RSS and Atom feeds so that updates can be monitored in people's RSS aggregator of choice. Because this need is expressed so often, TurboGears includes a FeedController class that makes it easy to create RSS feeds for your application. And WhatWhat Status takes advantage of the FeedController, which automatically produces valid RSS and Atom feeds when you pass in a properly structured dictionary, with a title, subtitle, author, link, ID (all of which are strings), and an entries list that contains elements for each entry in the feed.

Each item in the entry's list is required to have several fields (updated, title, summary, link, and so on), which are used to create the necessary RSS feeds. The actual construction of the feeds is handled by WhatWhatFeed's superclass, the `FeedController`, which has exposed `rss2_0`, `atom0_3`, and `Atom1_0` methods that use their respective Kid templates to generate the feed. But, each of these three methods for the standard feed formats gets its data by calling the `get_feed_data` method. So, creating your own feeds is as simple as subclassing `FeedController` and overriding the `get_feed_element`:

```
class WhatWhatFeed(FeedController):
    entrys = []


    def _feed_item(self, item, title, item_body):
        entry= {}
        entry["updated"] = item.creation_date
        entry["title"] = title + " " + item.project.name
        entry["published"] = item.creation_date
        entry["author"] = item.creator.displayName
        entry["link"] = cherrypy.config.get('whatwhat.recentchangesurl')
        entry["summary"] = textilize(item_body[:30])
        self.entrys.append(entry)
        entry = {}

    def get_feed_data(self):
        self.entrys = []
        all_projects = Project.select("parent_project_id is NULL " +
                    "order by upper(name)")
        projects = [project for project in all_projects if not project.archived]
```

```
print self._timeframe()
recent_proj = getRecentChanges(projects, self._timeframe())

for proj in recent_proj:
    self.entry = {}
    if len(proj.recent_issues) > 0:
        for issue in proj.recent_issues:
            self._feed_item(issue, "Issue:", issue.issue)

    if len(proj.recent_risks) > 0:
        for risk in proj.recent_risks:
            self._feed_item(risk, "risk:", risk.description)

    if len(proj.recent_notes) > 0:
        for note in proj.recent_notes:
            self._feed_item(note, "note:", note.note)

    if len(proj.recent_questions) > 0:
        for question in proj.recent_questions:
            self._feed_item(question, "Question:", question.question)
            if len(question.answers) > 0:
                for answer in question.answers:
                    entry = {}
                    entry["updated"] = answer.creation_date
                    entry["title"] = "Question:Answer %s:%s" % (
                                        question. question[:30],
                                        question.project.name)
                    entry["published"] = answer.creation_date
                    entry["author"] = answer.creator.displayName
                    entry["link"] = cherrypy.config.get(
                            ➥ 'whatwhat.recentchangesurl')
                    entry["summary"] = textilize(answer.answer[:30])
                    self.entrys.append(entry)
                    entry = {}

return dict(
        title="whatwhat recent changes",
        link="http://10.0.0.1/dashboard",
        author={ "name" : "Your Name Here",
                 "email" : "YourEmail@email.com" },
        id="http://10.0.0.1/dashboard",
        subtitle="recent changes feed",
        entrys=self.entrys
    )
```

```
def _timeframe(self):
        if cherrypy.request.simpleCookie.has_key('time_frame_id'):
            return int(cherrypy.request.simpleCookie['time_frame_id'].value)
        return 24
```

For each of the key items in a project (issues, risks, notes, questions, and answers), the `get_feed_data` loops over each item and creates an entry dictionary. This entry has several required keys, which contain all the information needed to create the various feeds. The required keys are as follows:

- `updated`—Should contain a `datetime` object indicating when the element was last updated
- `title`—Should contain a string containing the feed item's title
- `published`—Should contain a `datetime` object indicating when the feed element was originally published
- `author`—Should contain a string with the author's name
- `link`—Should contain a link back to the canonical location of the feed element
- `summary`—Should contain a summary of the feed item's contents

With the exception of answers (which have a slightly different entry format) the creation of individual entries is done by the `_feed_item()` method, which simply appends each new entry to an overall `entries` list.

The WhatWhat Status feed controller is only complicated because several different types of objects need to be included in the feed. In general, creating your own feed is as simple as defining what goes in the entries you want to include in the feed and creating a list of entries. The FeedController takes care of everything else.

8.5 Summary

- You can use `cherrypy.request.simple_cookie` to get access to any cookie information that came along with the request. Although CherryPy gives you easy access, the `simple_cookie` is a part of Python's built in cookies module.
- You can create your own widgets by subclassing the `widget` base class and defining `template`, `template_vars`, and whatever `params` you need.
- Your widgets can encapsulate JavaScript and CSS, so you can reuse them on multiple pages. The widget will automatically include the right links in the page header for you.

- TurboGears includes a FeedController module that makes it easy to create new RSS and Atom feeds. You just create a list of dictionaries containing the required elements, and FeedController creates properly formatted feeds for you.

## Chapter 9

Ajax and WhatWhat Status Projects

In This Chapter

You want to do dynamic Ajax-enabled web 2.0 projects, do you?

Well, we've got them. If you've been living under a rock for the past 18 months, you might not have heard of Ajax. No technology is perfect, but Ajax has definitely become an important technology to know and use. It can make your web applications faster and more responsive.

Ajax is most useful when it enables you to create more responsive user-friendly applications by using asynchronous requests from within a page. This can make your applications easier to use. But it can be kind of disconcerting when things on your page start magically appearing or disappearing. And that's where one of the most user visible parts of the whole Ajax world comes in: visual effects.

In this chapter, we explore the way that WhatWhat Status uses visual effects to make the project's pages more dynamic and easier to use.

9.1 Handling Ajax Requests

The first thing to think about when dealing with Ajax is the way the browser and server communicate. From the server side, everything still comes in as an HTTP request and gets passed to the first object to match in the CherryPy controller hierarchy. So, the first thing you generally want to do is set up a controller method that handles an HTTP request and returns the data you eventually want your JavaScript to see.

In general, you will return one of three things to the browser: HTML, XML, or JSON.

9.1.1 Ajax Requests/HTML Responses

An HTML request is definitely the easiest to understand. Your browser makes a request to the server, you return HTML, and the browser hands it back to some JavaScript that will render that HTML at some point in your page. Because it is so simple, and most of the HTML construction work is done on the server, it's often the easiest way to go.

For example, the WhatWhat Status people have methods in the ProjectController that send back an HTML fragment. `create_note` takes a string as a parameter from the Ajax request that calls it. It then gets the current user ID from the identity object, uses the `_active_project_id()` function to get the current project ID from a cookie, and saves all of this to the database as a new note. When it's done, it just returns the HTML output that you get when you render a `note_widget`:

```
@tg.expose(fragment=True)
@tg.validate(validators=dict(note=validators.String()))
def create_note(self, note):
    creator = Person.get(identity.current.user.id)
    project = Project.get(self._active_project_id())
    note = Note(creator=creator, project=project, note=note)
    return widgets.note_widget.render(note=note, read_only=False)
```

The resulting HTML is then returned to the browser, which places it in the page using an ultra-simple JavaScript that modifies the DOM (Document Object Model). If you're new to the DOM, don't worry; we talk about it more in the next section. For now, all you need to know is it can write JavaScript that replaces an element of your page with the HTML returned by an Ajax request.

This is often the easiest and cleanest way to do things because it enables you to create HTML from Python using Kid templates, which is something you already have to know how to do. And, although DOM scripting has come a long way since the massive incompatibilities of IE and Netscape 4, it'll probably never be as straightforward as Kid templates.

9.1.2 Ajax Requests/JSON Responses

But sometimes you need to update several different portions of the page, or you want to trigger some kind of visual effect, or you just want to pass a value in to your JavaScript from the server, where you can process it in any way you like.

By far, the easiest way to do this is to use JSON. JSON stands for JavaScript Object Notation, which is just a fancy way of saying that what you pass back is a collection of JavaScript objects in the form of a string. JSON is a subset of JavaScript, so you can `eval` a JSON response from the server and get an object or set of objects back.

MochiKit provides an easy way to get JSON from the server via `loadJSONDoc()`, and WhatWhat Status uses this kind of thing, too. For example, you can click Close to close any open risk; that triggers an asynchronous request to delete that risk from the database. Then, when the risk is closed, the server sends back a JSON object with a single Boolean value:

```
@tg.expose(allow_json=True)
@tg.validate(validators=dict(risk_id=validators.Int()))
def close_risk(self, risk_id):
    risk = Risk.get(risk_id)
    risk.closed = True
    return dict(success=True)
```

When the JavaScript in your page receives this value from the browser, it can then update the page to remove that risk. This delayed feedback helps the user know that the element was actually removed from the server (especially when it is coupled with a visual effect, as it will be on this page).

9.1.3   Ajax and XML Responses

You can also return XML to the browser from TurboGears. From the controller side, all you do is define a Kid template, which creates the XML file you'll send back to the browser. In the controller, the only difference between sending a dictionary to a Kid template, which will be rendered into XML for an Ajax request, and sending a dictionary to a Kid template, which will be rendered as an HTML web page, is the content type you choose in the `@expose()` decorator. The only difference is the content of the Kid template, which will render to some non-XHTML doc type.

This is easy as pie; and if that's all there was to it, you would be just as well off using XML as JSON as your standard communication protocol in your Ajax requests. The problem is what happens at the browser when the XML request is parsed. You have to parse the XML in your JavaScript, which is no problem (unless you want cross-browser support). Several differences between Firefox, Safari, Opera, and Internet Explorer can easily create headaches for you.

For example, Internet Explorer skips whitespace text nodes, whereas Firefox and others maintain the text node, even if it contains only whitespace. Because many XML generators, including Kid, maintain whitespace between elements to nest the emitted code and make it readable, you'll get different results from IE vs. Firefox when you check to see how many child nodes a particular XML element has. But that's probably getting ahead of ourselves a bit; we really haven't talked about the DOM yet. So, if you don't know exactly what the difference between an element and a node is, don't worry about it. Unless you have a specific reason, you'll proably be better off using JSON to send data structures back to your browser.

And for those of you who do have a compelling need to use XML as a transport mechanism, I promise we'll come back to DOM manipulation in JavaScript in a little bit.

9.2 Digging Into the Project Controller Methods

In the next section, we take a deeper look at how we can use MochiKit to make sending Ajax requests to the browser easier. Before we get there, let's take a look at the WhatWhat Status project controller and how it handles these Ajax requests, and what it sends back to the browser:

```
import turbogears          as tg
import cherrypy            as http
import commands
import socket
import md5
import time
import random
import os


from turbogears           import identity, flash, validators
from datetime             import datetime
from whatwhat             import utils
from textile               import textile
from whatwhat.widgets     import widgets

from whatwhat.model       import (Person, Project, Risk, Note, Question,
                                  Answer, Issue, chance_codes, impact_codes,
                                  status_codes, ProjectFile)

class ProjectController(identity.SecureResource):
    require = identity.not_anonymous()

    @tg.expose()
    def default(self, *args, **kwargs):
        parts = http.request.path.rsplit('/')
        if len(parts) == 3 and parts[-1].isdigit():
            return self.project(parts[-1])


    @tg.expose()
```

```
def index(self, *args, **kwargs):
    project_id = self._active_project_id()
    if project_id:
        raise tg.redirect('/project/%s' % project_id)
    return self.locate()


@tg.expose(template="whatwhat.templates.project.locate")
def locate(self):
    all_projects = Project.select("parent_project_id is NULL order by
➡ upper(name)")
    projects = [project for project in all_projects if not project.archived]

    return dict(active_section='project',
                projects=projects)
```

Right at the top, notice again that we are requiring that every access to this controller or any of its methods will require that Identity knows who you are, and that you're properly logged in to the system.

The default, index, and expose methods in the preceding code provide ways for the project controller to find the right project in the database and ensure that the `project` method gets passed the correct values. We've already talked about how the default method works, but here's a quick reminder in case you skipped ahead: The `default` method is what you get if none of the other exposed methods are called directly. In other words, if your URL is `http://localhost:8080/project/project`, the `project` method is called; but if the URL doesn't match `locate`, `project`, `toggle_closed_risks`, or any of the other methods in this controller, the default method is called.

In this case, the default method grabs the URL string from CherryPy, splits it around the / character, and checks to see whether the last element in the parts list is a number. If it is, it assumes that number is the project you want to see and passes you on to the project's file with the correct ID.

The `index` method is what is called if you use a URL such as `localhost:8080/project/`.

WhatWhat Status uses cookies to remember which project you were looking at, and automatically brings you back to the right project page. To do this, the `index` method calls `_active_project_id` to check to see whether there is a cookie value set for the active project ID, and if so it sends the request along to the project controller with the value it got from the cookie. The code for the function that gets the cookie should be familiar by now, but here it is:

```
def _active_project_id(self):
    if http.request.simpleCookie.has_key('active_project_id'):
        return int(http.request.simpleCookie['active_project_id'].value)
    return None
```

If `_active_project_id` can't retrieve an active project value from the cookie, it returns `None`, and the `index` method passes the user along to `locate`, which grabs a list of all the current projects and sends the user to `whatwhat.templates.project.locate`, which then displays a page with a drop-down list of projects. When the user selects a project from that page, the user gets sent to `/projects/7` (or whatever project ID the user selected). Because there is no `7` method in the project controller, the default method gets called, and the user gets passed to the project with the correct number.

All of this might seem unnecessary, but it gives WhatWhat Status nice and pretty URLs for the project page, which are easy to use in our templates, and which also have the property of being RESTful. REST stands for REpresentational State Transfer, and it's a term used to describe a particular way of organizing resources on the web. We talk more about REST in Chapter 17, "CherryPy and TurboGears Decorators," but for now, it's probably enough to say that REST is an application design pattern that emphasizes URLs that are universal (every object in the system is represented by a unique URL), stateless (the URL is all that is needed to define that particular resource), and have a well-defined set of operations that can be performed on them.

In this case, FastTrack has a unique URL for every project in the system, and each element in the URL has a specific, well-defined meaning. `/project/` indicates that we are looking at a project, and the `/7` indicates that we are looking at the project with the ID of 7. If the WhatWhat Status authors implemented a delete mechanism for projects that answered to `/project/7/delete`, which deleted project 7, that would indicate a fully RESTFul interface.

The simpler alternative to defining these methods is to present WhatWhat Status users with links such as `/project/project/7`. Not only is this URL redundant, it could also be confusing to the user, and we'll constantly have to type that `/project/` into all of our links, which is no fun either.

All of this brings us to the central method of the project controller `project()`:

```
@tg.expose(template="whatwhat.templates.project.project")
@tg.validate(validators=dict(project_id=validators.Int()))
def project(self, project_id):
```

```
project = Project.get(project_id)
user_person = Person.get(identity.current.user.id)
groupids = utils.getGroups()

http.response.simpleCookie['active_project_id'] = project_id
http.response.simpleCookie['active_project_id']['path'] = '/'

people = Person.select(orderBy='displayName')

return dict(active_section='project',
            project=project,
            chance_codes=chance_codes,
            impact_codes=impact_codes,
            status_codes=status_codes,
            show_closed_risks=bool(self._show_closed_risks()),
            show_closed_issues=bool(self._show_closed_issues()),
            show_all_notes=bool(self._show_all_notes()),
            people=people,
            user_person=user_person,
            groupids=groupids,
            risks_widget=widgets.risks_widget,
            issues_widget=widgets.issues_widget,
            questions_widget=widgets.questions_widget,
            notes_widget=widgets.notes_widget)
```

Even though this method is a bit longer than most of the ones we've seen so far, it is still conceptually simple. It gets the project object from the database, and assigns the project_id value to a cookie. Then it gets the current user's ID, and the groups they are a member of, and passes this data to the template in a dictionary. It also passes some codes from the model (which we've already seen), several Boolean values (which will determine whether closed Risks, Issues, and Notes will display), and a few widgets for good measure to the template.

This might seem like a lot of information to pass to one template; as you will see, however, the project template is totally dynamic and has the potential to display a lot of different information.

If you look at the project controller, you'll see a dozen or so additonal methods, most of which are going to be called by JavaScript functions on the project.kid template. So, rather than wade through these all at once, without understanding the context in which they are called, we'll circle back around and cover some of them as we look at the JavaScript that calls them.

9.3   A First Look at `project.kid`

Let's take a look at `project.kid`. This is certainly the longest bit of code we've seen so far, and there's lots of new stuff in here.

We'll take a multipass approach where we run through the whole template at rather high speed to get a lay of the land, and then we'll take a slightly deeper look at scripting the DOM, using lots of examples from this template and `master.js` and `project.js`, and then we'll circle back around a third time to look at how you can meld server calls with simple DOM manipulation to achieve that "dynamic Ajax-driven" website effect that everybody seems to want these days.

9.3.1   Laying the Groundwork for Our Project Page

The first thing you should see in the `project.kid` file is a `<?python>` tag:

```
<?python
        from whatwhat.model import STATUS_BEHIND_SCHEDULE
        from whatwhat.utils import textilize

        def get_display_notes(project, show_all_notes):
                if show_all_notes:
                        return project.notes
                return project.recent_notes
?>
```

This should look familiar to you. The `project.kid` template starts out with a quick bit of Python that imports the `textilize` function (which we explored in Chapter 8, "RSS, Cookies, and Dynamic Views in WhatWhat Status"), and the behind-schedule status identifier. The `get_display_notes` function is new, but it should be pretty easy to see what it does. If the `show_all_notes` value is true, it returns a list of all the notes; otherwise, it returns just a list of recent notes.

Next we see the header, which shows a bunch of JavaScript imports. In addition to what we see here, there is a "hidden" import at work. TurboGears includes an option to import MochiKit on every page of your application. That way you don't have to bother to manually import it in your template, and WhatWhat Status makes use of that option to get MochiKit on every page.

In addition to the basic JavaScript improvements and Ajax helpers that MochiKit provides, WhatWhat Status uses some third-party visual effects to provide users with feedback as Ajax things happen. So, they import prototype, and scriptaculous, along with several scriptaculous libraries.

As I write this there is a functional port of the scriptaculous visual effects libraries sitting in the trunk of MochiKit's subversion repository, so there is an extremely high probability that you won't have to import all of this into your projects. You can just use MochiKit's visual effects library.

Here's the section of `project.kid` that does all the JavaScript library imports:

```
<head>
    <meta content="text/html; charset=UTF-8" http-equiv="content-type" py:re-
place="'''" />
    <title>WhatWhat Status - Project Details for ${project.name}</title>
    <script src="/static/javascript/master.js"
     type="text/javascript"></script>
    <script src="/static/javascript/project.js"
     type="text/javascript"></script>
    <script src="/static/javascript/thirdparty/prototype.js"
     type="text/javascript"></script>
    <script src="/static/javascript/thirdparty/scriptaculous.js"
     type="text/javascript"></script>
    <script src="/static/javascript/thirdparty/effects.js"
     type="text/javascript"></script>
    <script src="/static/javascript/thirdparty/slider.js"
     type="text/javascript"></script>
    <script src="/static/javascript/thirdparty/builder.js"
     type="text/javascript"></script>
    <script src="/static/javascript/thirdparty/controls.js"
     type="text/javascript"></script>
```

In addition to importing JavaScript libraries, you can always define page-specific functions right there in your page header. If for some reason you need to use dynamically generated JavaScript, this is probably the easiest place to do it. Fortunately, WhatWhat Status just needs to prevent huge notes from being added to the database, so they created a `check_note_length` function to ensure that notes are always fewer than 1500 characters.

```
<script type="text/javascript">
//<![CDATA[
    function check_note_length(note) {
        var note = document.getElementById(note);

        if (note.value.length >= 1500) {
            alert('Please use separate notes for lengthy posts');
            note.focus();
```

```
                              return false;
                    }
            return true;
        }
    //]]>
    </script>

    <link href="/static/css/master.css" media="screen" rel="Stylesheet"
    type="text/css" />
    <link href="/static/css/project.css" media="screen" rel="Stylesheet"
    type="text/css" />
</head>
```

And the head portion of our template is rounded out by a couple of links to the stylesheets that make things look nice on our page.

9.3.2   Using Ajax to Update Project Status and Descriptions

Right at the top of our template body, we see the project name, description, and project status edit box.

These are created with the following code from the template:

Only displayed if logged in user is the project contact, or an administrator

```
<body>
  <h2 id="project_name" py:content="project.name">Project Name</h2>
  <div
   py:if="project.contact == user_person or 'admin' in groupids" id="status">

      <select id="project_status" py:if="not project.archived" name="status"
      onchange="update_project(); return false;">


        <option py:for="status in status_codes.keys()" value="$status"
        selected="${(none, '')[status == project.status]}">
          ${status_codes[status]}
        </option>

      </select>
      <span py:if="project.archived">Archived</span>
      <br />
  </div>
```

```
<div class="bad"
        py:if="(project.contact != user_person
        and (not 'admin' in groupids))
        and (project.status == STATUS_BEHIND_SCHEDULE)"
 id="status">
  ${status_codes[project.status]}
</div>

<div class="good"
        py:if="(project.contact != user_person
        and (not 'admin' in groupids))
        and (project.status != STATUS_BEHIND_SCHEDULE)"
 id="status">
  ${status_codes[project.status]}
</div>
```

Creates a select box with project status codes (if the project isn't archived)

Displays status differently when it's behind schedule

As you can see, the `update_project` function is called whenever the status is changed. This same function is called whenever the description or project contact is updated, so let's take a closer look at it now:

```
function update_project() {
    var url = '/project/update_project';
    var params = {
        contact_id:  getElement('contact_id').value,
        status:      getElement('project_status').value,
        description: getElement('ta_description').value,
        tg_format:   'json',
        stamp:       new Date().getTime()
    };
    var data = queryString(params);

    function update_project_callback(result) {
        result = evalJSONRequest(result);
        if (result['success'] == true) {
            getElement('description_content').innerHTML = result['description'];
            getElement('contact_content').innerHTML = result['contact'];
            new Effect.Highlight('project_name');
        }
    }

    var req = getXMLHttpRequest();
    req.open('POST', url, true);
```

*Calls to this URL go to **update_project** in our project subcontroller*

*Sets up the request object, and tells it to call **update_project_callback** when it's done*

Turns the parameters into a query string to send to the server

Updates the description and contact values with new info

Creates a flashing yellow visual effect to signal that the update is complete

```
    req.setRequestHeader('Content-Type', 'application/x-www-form-urlencoded;
charset=utf-8;');
    sendXMLHttpRequest(req, data).addCallback(update_project_callback);
}
```

This little JavaScript function uses several MochiKit helpers to make the Ajax stuff easier. The most central is the `sendXMLHttpRequest` object, which abstracts away the various different `HTTPRequest` objects for IE-5, IE-6, and the more standards compliant browsers such as Firefox and Safari. Not only that, it handles the asyncronous part of Ajax for you, too. You just use the `addCallback` method on the `sendXMLHttpRequest` object to set up a function to handle the server response. This tells the browser which function to call when it receives a response from the server. If you didn't do this all asynchronously, the browser would just lock up until the server responded to the request.

In this case, the callback function is `update_project_callback`, which takes the JSON that is returned by the server, evaluates it, and updates the description and contact content using the `innerHTML` method discussed in Chapter 8. This is kind of an interesting hybrid approach. We mentioned earlier in this chapter that you can return plain XHTML or JSON, but in this case the server is returning two XHTML fragments wrapped in a JSON object. This allows WhatWhat Status to update the contact and description elements in a single request.

If you are particularly quick, you'll notice that the project status is updated on the server, but the status is not changed in the browser after that update is done. And if you're really quick, you've already figured out why: The status box is updated by the user, before this function is called, and will already match what was sent to the server.

Before we move on, let's take a quick look at the code on the server that is called by this little `update_project` JavaScript function.

```
    @tg.expose(allow_json=True)
    @tg.validate(validators=dict(contact_id=validators.Int(), status=validators.
Int(), description=validators.String()))
    def update_project(self, contact_id, status, description):
        contact = Person.get(contact_id)
        project = Project.get(self._active_project_id())
        project.set(status=int(status), contact=contact, description=description)
        contact_content = '<a href="mailto:%s">%s</a>' % (contact.emailAddress,
contact.displayName)
        desc = textile(description.encode('utf-8'), encoding='utf-8',
output='ascii')
        return dict(success=True, description=desc, contact=contact_content)
```

On the controller, the `update_project` method has two responsibilities. First, it has to take the updates sent in by our JavaScript and modify our model objects (and therefore our database) accordingly. And second, it has to return a JSON object containing three elements: a Boolean that tells the browser that the server update was successful, and two XHTML fragments that contain contact info, and the project description. Just like any HTTP Post, the values `contact_id`, `status`, and `description` are parsed out of the HTTP request by CherryPy and passed into the `update_project` method as parameters. The relevant project and contact objects are retrieved from their SQLObject classes, and the project is updated with the values sent in over the Ajax request.

When that's all done, the `contact` and `desc` XHTML fragments are set up, and the whole dictionary is returned as a JSON object. The `tg.expose(allow_json=True)` declares that it is okay for this function to return JSON, if that's what you ask for. And the way you ask is to send in a parameter `tg_format='json'`. This alerts the controller that what you want back is a JSON object, and it uses Bob Ippolito's `simple_json` package to turn the resulting dictionary into a JSON object. On its own, `simple_json` can handle native Python types; but if you include other objects in your dictionary, this might not work automatically for you. TurboGears makes extending `simple_json` easy, and even includes a file for your custom serialize in its standard quickstart. In this case, however, everything is standard, and it is automatically serialized.

There's a lot more code in the WhatWhat Status `project` template, but you should be able to work your way through all of it on your own.

9.4   Summary

- Ajax is a useful tool when used wisely. The authors of WhatWhat Status were able to ensure that everyone using the product would have a modern Ajax-capable browser, so they made extensive use of Ajax in the project's page to reduce the time their users wait for pages to reload and to make it easy to view or hide individual page elements dynamically according to what the user needs to see at the time.

- WhatWhat Status makes extensive use of JSON to pass data back to the client browser, where a simple `eval` turns the JSON string directly into JavaScript objects that can be used in JavaScript functions that update the page.

- The WhatWhat Status authors make use of the widely implemented `innerHTML` method to update various elements in the page. Even though `innerHTML` is not part of the standard, it is implemented on every modern browser, and it can be a lot easier to use than DOM manipulations.

- MochiKit adds the idea of callbacks to its request objects. You can use the `addCallback()` method to indicate what function should be run by the browser when a response is received back from the server.

- TurboGears includes `simple_json` that can automatically transform most native Python data types into JSON strings, so it is extraordinarily easy to create methods that return JSON to the browser.

PART IV
SQLObject and TurboGears Models

## Chapter 10

SQLObject Basics

In This Chapter

O ne of the first things you have to deal with when creating web applications is data persistence. You have data, and it needs to live somewhere, and you want to make it easy to find, edit, and delete. There are three main options: 1) store your data in simple files on the server; 2) store your objects using some kind of object database such as ZODB, Druis, or Axiom; or 3) use a relational database. By far, the most popular of these three to date is using a relational database. And so, TurboGears includes SQLObject to make storing your data in a relational database as easy as possible.

Nothing in TurboGears precludes using file-based storage, or a Python-based object database to store your data. For the vast majority of cases, however, using an object relational mapper (ORM) such as SQLObject makes using a relational database the easiest and best solution for your TurboGears application.

10.1   ORM Basics

An ORM is a software layer that maps data stored in a relational database to an object model in some object-oriented programming language.

You probably already know about relational databases. They are powerful tools to store data and to help ensure the integrity of that data. The theory behind relational databases was first explored by E. F. Codd in 1970, and in the years since then, various products that implement relational theory have grown up to become the dominant solution for storing and retrieving persistent data.

Relational databases can be accessed using the Structured Query Language (SQL), and every popular programming language has libraries that allow manipulating data in relational database management systems (RDBMSs) such as Postgres, MySQL, MSSQL Server, and Oracle.

Not long after relational algebra was invented and the first RDBMSs started appearing, another similar rise from obscurity to market dominance took place. Procedural programming began to give way to object-oriented programming, which allowed the bundling of data and actions into objects.

The problem we face is that when we write object-oriented applications, we want to manipulate the world through object models and not through the totally different paradigm of relational algebra. The ORM attempts to solve this problem by automatically mapping a particular DB schema to a corresponding object model in a specific language. For example, an employee table that contains columns such as `employee_id`, `department_id`, `name`, and `manager`, will be mapped to an Employee class and the columns will be mapped to properties/attributes.

> Note: There are also generic object-oriented application programming interfaces (APIs) for databases such as ADO.NET. These APIs enable the developer to access the database through objects and get objects as results of queries, but the level of abstraction is lower. The objects these APIs expose are tables, row/record sets, columns, and constraints.

10.1.1   Who Needs ORM?

It turns out that accessing data through object models (at least in object-oriented programming languages) is a popular approach. It removes the cognitive dissonance between totally different paradigms, it allows developers to think about everything in terms of objects, and in many cases, it abstracts away the particular database implementation so that it's easy to switch to another vendor. Many developers who don't use an ORM solution end up doing the mapping manually. Typically, such developers will have a data access layer in their code that accesses the DB through SQL or another API and constructs an object model based on the results. Developing this manual ORM layer is a tedious and error-prone job. Any change to the schema or the object model requires synchronization with the other component and in the code that performs the mapping. ORM is really an automated implementation of the Data Access Object (DAO) design pattern.

10.1.2   ORM Alternatives

You have several alternatives to ORM. First of all, you can just use SQL or some other non-object-oriented API and live with it. You can also generate the data access layer manually. Another option is to use object-oriented DB or XML. All of these are viable solutions and may be more suitable for certain situations. However, ORM is the mainstream approach these days.

10.1.3   ORM Negatives

ORM is not a silver bullet. The biggest problem with ORM is the impedance mismatch between the relational paradigm and the object-oriented paradigm. This means that sometimes there is not an easy way to map a relational schema to an object model. For example, inheritance is an object-oriented feature that doesn't have a counterpart in the relational paradigm.

There are ways to simulate inheritance, but they can introduce subtle issues. Another common mapping problem is how to handle the database NULL value for static languages. Microsoft solved this problem in the .NET 2.0 by introducing Nullable types. This means that objects of any type (such as an integer) can be NULL and not just object references. SQLObject simply uses Python's "None" to mean NULL. This is natural and doesn't require any kludge or extension to the language or a special SQLObject concept.

ORMs can also introduce subtle performance problems when you don't know what is happening under the covers. If you are working with huge data sets, or you find that data access is a bottleneck for your application, you might want to know what queries are being generated by the ORM.

SQLObject provides a debug mechanism for exactly this purpose, which can be turned on easily by appending `?debug=True` to the end of your database URI in the `dev.cfg` file. You will probably want to turn this on while you go through the examples in this chapter so that you can see exactly what SQL is being generated.

10.2   Basic SQLObject Features

SQLObject was designed from the bottom up to make you faster, stronger, and better looking. Okay, probably not stronger, and definitely not better looking, but it will make you more productive. It's up to you what you do with the time you get back in your life when you learn to let SQLObject save you from tedious and error-prone tasks. Perhaps you could write more unit tests, or perhaps you could ask the new marketing manager out for a date. The choice is yours.

The following sections describe some of the cool productivity-enhancing features, shortcuts, and ease-of-use tricks SQLObject provides.

The main goal of SQLObject is to translate SQL into objects. That means that what you used to do with SQL before, you can do now with a Python object. It's an implementation of the ActiveRecord design pattern. ActiveRecords have a one-to-one relationship between model classes and tables in the database.

As previously discussed, you can define classes that derive from the base SQLObject and represent tables in the database. Rows in the table are represented by instances of your SQLObject derived class.

When you set attributes on an instance, it updates column values in this row and updates the DB. Actually, you can defer updates to the DB for performance reasons, but we get back to that idea later.

When you set an attribute on the class itself, you operate on the entire table. That includes managing DB connections and creating your DB schema, indexes, constraints, default values for columns, relationships between tables, CRUD operations, and sophisticated queries. In addition, you can control the behavior and interaction of your model classes with the underlying database.

Here's a quick glance over the offerings of SQLObject. We'll go over the nuts and bolts in detail later.

10.2.1   Basic Connection Management

Every access to the database requires a DB connection. From the user's point of view, a connection is how you tell SQLObject to locate your database. It resembles a URI in the following format:

```
scheme://[user[:password]@]host[:port]/database[?parameters]
```

The connection is the only place where you specify the actual database you use. The rest of your data access code is totally DB-agnostic. Unfortunately, SQLObject doesn't provide a perfect abstraction; sometimes you need to consider the features of the underlying database you are using. Some databases don't support some features, or you might want to write a highly tuned query with database-specific features. With that said, SQLObject does a pretty darned good job, and you can write a large application using SQLite, and then switch to Postgres for production with no transition problems.

Here are a few sample database URLs:

```
mysql://user:pwd@/db
postgres://user:pwd@localhost:5432/db
sqlite:///full/path/to/db
sqlite:/C|full/path/to/db
sqlite:/:memory:
```

In TurboGears, you generally set this up in the `dev.cfg` file for your project, and it is then used by all the classes in your project. If you want more flexibility, however, there are multiple ways to specify the connection for a particular class. You can set the `_connection` class attribute, set the module's `_connection_` variable (so that all classes in this module can share the same connection), or pass a connection object to the `_init()` method of an instance (to control the connection in a granular way per record). Probably, the easiest way is to use the `sqlhub.processConnection` that controls the connection for all SQLObject, in the current process. You can also have a connection per thread or custom connections.

Here's how you manually set up a connection to a SQLite database on Windows:

```
from sqlobject import *

db_filename = os.path.abspath('test.db').replace(':\\', '|\\')
connection_uri = 'sqlite:/' + db_filename
connection = connectionForURI(connection_uri)
```

SQLite requires the full path to the database file, and on Windows you must replace the colon that follows the drive letter with a pipe (|). So, if your SQLite DB file is located in `c:\db_dir\db_file.db` the corresponding connection URI is `sqlite:/c|\db_dir\db_file.db` and in escaped form `sqlite:/c|\\db_dir\\db_file.db`. Note that this URI doesn't comply with URI format because there is only a single slash after the scheme. SQLite is a little different because it uses an actual filename for the connection. But don't let it distract you; other than the URI pointing to a file, the SQLite connection strings are exactly the same.

The `connectionForURI()` function creates a connection object. This connection object can now be used for declaring classes and accessing the DB. There are many ways to associate a connection with a model class. The simplest one is to assign one connection for the entire process. Every model class will automatically use this connection. Here is how it's done:

```
sqlhub.processConnection = connection
```

10.2.2   Automatic DB Schema Creation from SQLObject-Derived Classes

TurboGears provides a `tg-admin sql create` command, which we used to create the tables from the model class automatically.

But this is just a wrapper around functionality provided by SQLObject itself. This means that if you want to create tables programmatically from within your application, you can. Just define a class with some columns, call `createTable()`, and it will be created in the database. Here is how it's done:

```
class FighterRobot(SQLObject):
  name = StringCol()
  weapon_1 = StringCol()
  weapon_2 = StringCol()
  engine = StringCol(default='Basic engine')
  health = IntCol(default=100)


FighterRobot.dropTable(ifExists=True) # drop previous definition if exists
FighterRobot.createTable()
```

And here is the generated DB schema:

```
CREATE TABLE fighter_robot (
    id INTEGER PRIMARY KEY,
    name TEXT,
    weapon_1 TEXT,
    weapon_2 TEXT,
    engine TEXT,
    health INT
);
```

Note that the default values for engine and health didn't make it into the DB schema. SQLObject takes care of setting the values by itself, and whenever you create a new instance (insert a new row into the DB), it populates it properly.

Another important detail that you might notice is that the name of the class doesn't exactly match the name of the table that is created. SQLObject uses a special naming convention to translate Pythonic names to database names. That's why the `FighterRobot` class created a table called `fighter_robot`.

10.2.3   Fine Control on Behavior Using Metadata Class

Each model class has a nested class called `sqlmeta` that allows you to specify a plethora of interesting attributes such as caching and lazy updates, and a style object to control name translations. This is just a hint of what is to come. We discuss `lazyUpdate` thoroughly later on. Here is how to turn on lazy updates for the fighter robot:

```
class FighterRobot(SQLObject):
  class sqlmeta:
    lazyUpdate = True

  name = StringCol()
  weapon_1 = StringCol()
  weapon_2 = StringCol()
  engine = StringCol(default='Basic engine')
  health = IntCol(default=100)
```

10.2.4   Automatic Table Description from Existing DB Schema

This is the flip-side of automatic DB schema creation. If you already have an existing database, you don't have to labor through defining every column as an attribute of your model classes. You can just specify `_fromDatabase = True` and be done with it. Here is how it's done:

```
class FighterRobot(SQLObject):
    _fromDatabase = True
```

> Note: This system only works if the database itself and the Python drivers for that database provide the introspection capabilities that SQLObject needs. For example, this doesn't work for SQLite right now, but MySQL and Postgres work just fine. If you use one of the less commonly used SQLObject backends, your experience may vary.

Remember that your DB should have a table called `fighter_robot` to match the `FighterRobot` class name. This feature is useful if your DB is created and maintained by an external person or group. This way you are protected (to some degree) from DB schema changes. Of course, you must convert the data in the DB itself and change the parts of the code that relied on the old schema, but things such as adding a new column to a table or changing the name/type of a column you didn't access in your code should be transparent.

10.3   Simple Database Queries

SQLObject provides you many ways to access your data. You can get a single row by its ID, you can use `sqlbuilder` to construct SQL queries in a structured way, you can select a set of objects with some values using `selectBy()`, and you can just use plain SQL. In addition, SQLObject allows you to define one-to-many and many-to-many relationships between tables and access them as plain attributes.

SQLObject gives you three different ways to set up queries. The three query flavors are simple, structured, and raw. You've already seen raw queries in WhatWhat Status, and we cover how to use the query builder syntax to create complex, structured queries in Chapter 11, "Mastering SQLObject." For now, let's take a look at simple queries, which might just satisfy all your query needs. This is especially true if you are free to construct your DB schema in a way that fits your data access patterns. SQLObject tries hard (and succeeds) to make simple things simple and complex things possible.

10.3.1   Getting a Single Object by ID

It is useful sometimes to just get a single row by ID. I do it constantly during interactive development, and you might also find it useful in your program. The ID will usually be stored as a foreign key or as a result of a query. SQLObject makes it as easy as possible. Just call the `get()` method of your model class with the ID:

```
import os, sys
from sqlobject import *

db_filename = os.path.abspath('test.db').replace(':\\', '|\\')
sqlhub.processConnection = connectionForURI('sqlite:/' + db_filename)

class Highlander(SQLObject):
  name = StringCol()
  motto = StringCol()

Highlander.dropTable(ifExists=True)
Highlander.createTable()

Highlander(name='Connor Macleod', motto='There can be only one!')

o = Highlander.get(1)
print o.name, 'says:', o.motto
```

10.3.2   Getting an Entire Table

Getting all the objects in a table is common. Often, you need to display an entire table or export it to some other medium. SQLObject gives you the `select()` method. Just call it, and the contents of the entire table are at your fingertips:

```
class Something(SQLObject):
  name = StringCol()


Something.dropTable(ifExists=True)
Something.createTable()

for i in range(1,11):
  Something(name='Something #%d' % i)


sqlhub.processConnection.debug = 1
sqlhub.processConnection.debugOutput = 1

result = Something.select()
```

`select()` doesn't return a list of SQLObject instances that correspond to rows in your table as you might expect. Instead, it returns an instance of a special type called `SelectResults`. The idea is to allow you to work with large tables comfortably without hogging your memory. When `select()` returns, the DB has not been accessed yet. The DB will be accessed only when you try to retrieve something from the `SelectResults` object, and in the most efficient possible way. Here are a few access patterns and the corresponding SQL generated:

```
>>> result[4]
 1/QueryR  :   SELECT something.id, something.name FROM something WHERE 1 = 1 LIMIT
1 OFFSET 4
<Something 1 name='Something #1'>
>>>

>>> result.count()
 1/QueryR  :   SELECT COUNT(*) FROM something WHERE 1 = 1
10
>>>

>>> slice = result[3:5]
>>> slice
```

```
<SelectResults at ec15b0>
>>> list(slice)
 1/QueryR  :  SELECT something.id, something.name FROM something WHERE 1 = 1 LIMIT
2 OFFSET 3
[<Something 4 name='Something #4'>, <Something 5 name='Something #5'>]
>>>
```

SearchResults will query the DB for a single object when you access it by index, it will execute a COUNT(*) query if you call the count() method, and it will return a new SearchResults object when you slice an existing selectResults object. Note the slice [3:5] was actually extracted from the DB only when I called the list() factory function that actually creates a list of SQLObject instances. So, if you want to actually have an entire table for processing (for instance, for releasing the DB connection while you work on it), convert the selectResults to a list. SelectResults supports the for iteration syntax, too:

```
>>> for o in result[2:6]: print o
...
 1/QueryR  :  SELECT something.id, something.name FROM something WHERE 1 = 1 LIMIT
4 OFFSET 2

<Something 3 name='Something #3'>
<Something 4 name='Something #4'>
<Something 5 name='Something #5'>
<Something 6 name='Something #6'>
>>>
```

SelectResults emulates a sequence by implementing the special _getitem_ method. Note that it doesn't implement the _len_ special method that is called by Python when the len() function is invoked on an object. You must call count(). This is a little non-Pythonic because it breaks the illusion of selectResults being a regular Python sequence.

10.3.3 Selecting Rows by Column Values

Another common access pattern is to select rows from a table based on a specific column value or a combination of column values. SQLObject gives you the selectBy() method. Suppose you have a table of web frameworks in various programming languages and you want to select only the Python-based ones:

```
class WebFramework(SQLObject):
  name = StringCol()
  language = StringCol()

WebFramework.dropTable(ifExists=True)
WebFramework.createTable()

[WebFramework(name=f, language='Python') for f in ['TurboGears', 'DJango',
'Pylons']]

[WebFramework(name=f, language='Java') for f in ['Struts', 'Shale', 'WebWork',
'Spring MVC']]

[WebFramework(name=f, language='Ruby') for f in ['Ruby on Rails', 'ruby-waf']]

sqlhub.processConnection.debug = 1

result = WebFramework.selectBy(language='Python')

>>> for f in result:
...    print f.name
...
 1/QueryR  :  SELECT web_framework.id, web_framework.name, web_framework.language
FROM web_framework WHERE language = 'Python'

TurboGears
DJango
Pylons
```

You can use `selectBy()` with multiple values, too:

```
>> result = WebFramework.selectBy(name='Shale', language='Java')
>>> result[0]

 1/QueryR  :  SELECT web_framework.id, web_framework.name, web_framework.language
FROM web_framework WHERE name = 'Shale' AND language = 'Java' LIMIT 1
<WebFramework 5 name='Shale' language='Java'>
```

SQLObject will generate a WHERE clause with AND between all the column values you provide. `selectBy()` works best (fastest) if the relevant columns are indexed.

As you can see, SQLObject does a good job of providing a simple, yet efficient SQL-less query facility that may satisfy all your data access needs. If you need more, SQLObject is up to the challenge, as you will see in Chapters 11 and 12. Many of these features are explored in more depth, and you learn how to use SQLObject's query builder syntax—and much, much more.

10.4   Summary

- SQLObject implements the Active-Record pattern.
- Use `?debug=True` to have SQLObject print the SQL queries it generates to the console.
- SQLObject manages your database connections for you, and in TurboGears it gets the connection string from `dev.cfg` or `prod.cfg`.
- In addition to defining your classes first and generating you database tables from those classes the way we've been doing it in this book, you can also use `_fromDatabase=true`.
- SQLObject provides several different ways to define queries. The simplest of these is `get(ID)`, but `select()` is just about as easy.
- Only slightly more complex is the `selectBy()` method, which you can use to get records matching specific criteria.

Chapter 11

Mastering SQLObject

In This Chapter

SQLObject provides a simple object-oriented view of your tables, but if that were all it could do we'd still be in trouble. Sometimes you need to create one-to-many relationships, create complex queries, or handle very large datasets without bringing your server to its knees. Fortunately SQLObject has features that make all these tasks not only possible, but relatively easy.

Now that we know the basics of SQLObject, we can delve into a few of its more interesting capabilities. In this chapter, we look at how to set up relationships between tables, how to handle more complex database queries, and how to optimize queries for large or complex datasets.

We also take a deeper look at how `sqlobject` classes work, and how to modify the default behavior of SQLObjects using the `sqlmeta` class. Among other things, this is a critical piece of knowledge if you ever need to create model objects to match a "legacy" database.

11.1 Mapping Relationships

The most common of the advanced SQLObject features you'll need to understand if you need to get at the "relational" power of your database are "mapping relationships," which allow your objects to know how they are associated with other database tables. For those of you who aren't familiar with SQL and relational databases in general, the TurboGearsBook.com website contains links to several tutorials that might help you understand how all the underlying "relational" parts of relational databases work.

As you've seen, querying a single table is useful and can often get you quite a way to the functionality you want. But, even in our toy examples, we ended up needing some objects that contain information that reside in multiple tables. SQLObject enables you define one-to-many and many-to-many relationships between your tables and execute queries against them.

11.1.1 One-to-Many Relationships (MultipleJoin)

One-to-many relationships means that object A has or contains multiple objects of type B. For example, a Python module may contain multiple functions, but a function belongs to a single module. Let's represent this relationship with SQLObject classes:

```
class PythonFunction(SQLObject):
  name = StringCol()
  module_id = ForeignKey('PythonModule')

class PythonModule(SQLObject):
  name = StringCol()
  functions=MultipleJoin('PythonFunction', joinColumn='module_id')

for table in [PythonFunction, PythonModule]:
  table.dropTable(ifExists=True)
  table.createTable()
```

The `PythonFunction` class has a `module_id` attribute, which is a foreign key[1] of the `PythonModule` it belongs to. The `PythonModule` class has a `MultipleJoin` "functions" attribute. In SQLObject, `ForeignKey` indicates that there will be a one-to-one or one-to-many relationship with the other table.

If both tables use `ForeignKey`, the resulting relationship will be one to one. On the other hand if, as in the `PythonModule` case above, the other table has a `MultipleJoin` attribute rather than a `ForeignKey` attribute, the relationship between the tables is one to many.

If that sounds abstract, perhaps an example will help. In the following example, we create a `PythonModule` object. After the `PythonModule` has been created, we can then check to make sure it has no `functions` (yet):

```
m = PythonModule(name='xxx')
assert len(m.functions) == 0
```

Then we can create two `PythonFunction` objects for the module. The `functions` attribute of the module suddenly reflects the fact that it contains two functions:

```
f1 = PythonFunction(name='foo()', module_id=m.id)
f2 = PythonFunction(name='bar()', module_id=m.id)

assert len(m.functions) == 2
assert m.functions[0].name == 'foo()'
assert m.functions[1].name == 'bar()'
```

---

[1] A foreign key is a field in the database that refers to the primary key of another table in the database. The primary key uniquely identifies a particular record in a table. So, a foreign key creates a one-way mapping between its record and the record in the other table that it references.

In the preceding example, we used the ID field of the module object explicitly to create the mapping relationship we wanted. This makes sense because the foreign key field in the database contains that ID. But this takes extra typing and doesn't give us that nice object-oriented feeling. Fortunately, SQLObject provides a convenient feature that bypasses the need for all that. We can just pass a reference to the object itself, and SQLObject will figure out the right foreign key value to use for us. So, rather than using `m.id` when creating our new functions, we can write something like this:

```
f3 = PythonFunction(name='foo()', module_id=m)
```

As you can see, SQLObject makes using `ForeignKey` and `MultipleJoin` to add relationships between your tables easy.

`MultipleJoin` and `ForeignKey` create the necessary columns automatically, and they create attributes for the tables that make accessing the adjoining table data as easy and as object oriented as possible. So in the above example, the `PythonModule` object now has a `functions` attribute that contains a list of the functions in that module. This is accessible via standard Python list semantics, so you can get the first element of that list with a simple statement like this:

```
assert m.functions[0].name == 'foo()'
```

The default when creating joins using `ForeignKey` or `MultipleJoin` is to use the ID field of the adjoining table, but there are times when you want to join on another column, and SQLObject makes this easy by allowing you to override the default behavior easily by using the `joinColumn="module_id"` syntax. This gives you the flexibility to join on other key fields, or even to do what the SQL people call a recursive join against another column in the same table (as you saw in Chapter 6, "Exploring More Complex Models in WhatWhat Status").

11.1.2   Many-to-Many Relationships (RelatedJoin)

The one-to-many relationship can be used to describe a lot of the data you might have. Functions belong to one module. But sometimes you need to express relationships that don't have that "belong to" character. And that's where many-to-many relationships come in.

In dry academic terms, a many-to-many relationship means that object type A has or contains multiple objects of type B, and at the same time, object B has or contains multiple objects of type A. A real-life example is friends. You can have a whole bunch of friends, and all of those friends can have a whole bunch of other friends besides just you. Or, if you spend too much time programming to have friends, perhaps another example will work better: A Python module can contain multiple import statements, and a specific import statement may appear in any number of modules.

This many-to-many relationship can be represented by a set of SQLObject classes that looks like this:

```
class PythonImportStatement(SQLObject):
  statement = StringCol()
  modules = RelatedJoin('PythonModule')

class PythonModule(SQLObject):
  name = StringCol()
  imports=RelatedJoin('PythonImportStatement')

for table in [PythonImportStatement, PythonModule]:
  table.dropTable(ifExists=True)
  table.createTable()
```

SQLObject makes creating many-to-many relationships easy by providing the RelatedJoin column class. A RelatedJoin isn't like the other column classes, because it creates a whole intermediate table that contains a row for each pairing of the two objects. This table is created for you automatically, and is maintained by SQLObject using a number of useful methods.

The following code creates a bunch of PythonModule objects and PythonImportStatement objects. So far, they are not connected, so the imports attribute of each module is empty, and the modules attribute of each import statement is empty, too:

```
m1 = PythonModule(name='module_1')
m2 = PythonModule(name='module_2')
m3 = PythonModule(name='module_3')
for m in [m1, m2, m3]:
  assert len(m.imports) == 0

i1 = PythonImportStatement(statement='import os')
i2 = PythonImportStatement(statement='import sys')
i3 = PythonImportStatement(statement='import re')

for i in [i1, i2, i3]:
  assert len(i.modules) == 0
```

Here comes the magic . . . SQLObject automatically creates an `addPythonImport-Statement()` method for the `PythonModule` class, and an `addPythonModule()` method to the `PythonImportStatement` class. You can use either of these methods to create a new relationship between items in either class.

The code below uses the `addPythonImportStatement()` method several times on several modules and `addPythonModule()` on the i2 `PythonImportStatement`. The result of each of these calls is a link in the database between the `import` statements and the modules. As you can see in the assertions, the `imports` attribute of each `PythonModule` contains all the `PythonImportStatement` objects that were added using `addImportPythonStatement()`, and the `modules` attribute of each `PythonImportStatement` contains all the modules it was added to.

Where did the `addImportPythonStatement()` and `addPythonModule()` methods come from? They were created automatically by SQLObject via the "magic" of Python metaclasses. Fortunately, metaclasses aren't dark magic. If you're new to Python, you proably don't even need to know anything about metaclasses other than that they can be used to create custom classes, with special behavior. In this case, the metaclass is dynamically creating methods for your SQLObject class based on the presence and contents of a `RelatedJoin` column type.

But you don't need to know any of that to use these custom methods.

```
m1.addPythonImportStatement(i1)
m1.addPythonImportStatement(i2)
m2.addPythonImportStatement(i1)
m3.addPythonImportStatement(i1)
m3.addPythonImportStatement(i3)


i2.addPythonModule(m3)
```

After you've created the relationship, you get a list back whenever you access the `imports` attribute of a `module` or the `module` attribute of an `import`:

```
assert m1.imports == [i1, i2]
assert m2.imports == [i1]
assert m3.imports == [i1, i3, i2]
assert i1.modules == [m1, m2, m3]
assert i2.modules == [m1, m3]
assert i3.modules == [m3]
```

Under the covers, this works by the creation of an intermediate table that contains the ID values of the the `PythonModule` and `PythonImportStatements` objects that have been associated. In standard SQL, this table is called a join table.

11.2   Straight SQL Queries

But even when you have objects that express the full range of possible relationships, sometimes you still don't quite have what you want. You need to be able to select objects based on more-specific criteria. In standard SQL, you could just write a select query and get what you want. And you've already seen how you can pass a strait SQL query string into a SQLObject's `select()` statement (see Chapters 6 and 10). Sometimes you need something with a bit more flexibility.

There are some SQLObject-specific ways to handle this, which we cover in the next section. But sometimes you just need to get down and dirty and play with the database directly, which is why the SQLObject connection object has a `queryAll` method. This method lets you run raw SQL queries against the DB.

The following code creates a model class called `Digit` and populates it with the digits from 0 to 9:

```
names = ['Zero', 'One', 'Two', 'Three', 'Four',
         'Five', 'Six', 'Seven', 'Eight', 'Nine']

class Digit(SQLObject):
  name = EnumCol(enumValues=names)
  value = IntCol()

Digit.dropTable(ifExists=True)
Digit.createTable()

for i in range(0, len(names)):
  Digit(name=names[i], value=i)
```

And here is the DB schema:

```
CREATE TABLE digit (
    id INTEGER PRIMARY KEY,
    name VARCHAR(5) CHECK (name in ('Zero', 'One', 'Two', 'Three', 'Four', 'Five',
'Six', 'Seven', 'Eight', 'Nine')),
    value INT
);
```

Using the `queryAll()` method is different from using `select()` or `selectBy()`. You have to pass in an SQL query. The result is a list of tuples and not a `SearchResults` object. The database is accessed immediately and the entire result set is available immediately in memory. Another difference is that using `queryAll`, you can request only some of the columns of each row. Here's some code that extracts from the DB only the name and value (without the ID) of each `Digit` object whose value is greater than 5:

```
c = Digit._connection
results = c.queryAll('SELECT name, value FROM digit WHERE value > 5')
assert type(results) == list
print results
```

Output:

```
[(u'Six', 6), (u'Seven', 7), (u'Eight', 8), (u'Nine', 9)]
```

As you can see, you have to address the DB table name `digit` and not the class name `Digit`, and you have to compose the SQL query string properly. The pros of raw SQL are that you get absolute control on your query, and it's generally going to be faster. But there are some cons, too. Using `queryAll` means you lose access to all the reasons you chose to use SQLObject in the first place: DB-agnostic SQL, Pythonic API, encapsulated best practices, no string concatenation, automatic character escaping (which helps you avoid SQL injection attacks) and all the other general SQL maladies you'd rather avoid.

> **Note:** You can use `queryAll` to execute any SQL statement such as INSERT, DELETE, or even CREATE TABLE. Don't let the name `queryAll()` mislead you.

11.3   Smart Queries

So, perhaps you want to have the benefits of SQLObject without losing the flexibility to create complex queries against your database. Fortunately, the makers of SQLObject thought this, too, so they provide a couple of mechanisms that make it possible to create complex queries without the need to drop down to `queryAll`.

You've already seen a glimpse of how easy it is to query the DB using SQLObject `select()` and `selectBy()` methods. In this chapter, you'll see how to get the maximum out of your DB while still reaping the benefits of SQLObject. As always, there is a subtle balancing act between ease of use, level of control, and performance. Some object relational mappers (ORM) trap you into specific uses and prevent you from doing optimizations; other data access schemes push you to optimize your code for performance prematurely. But SQLObject gives you multiple ways to access your data with different mixes of these properties. Novices can stick to the simple API, and experts can dig deeper and find the right solution. The important thing is that SQLObject doesn't force you to do anything in a specific way. You can always tell it to stay out of your way.

11.3.1 `sqlbuilder`-Based Queries

SQLObject lets you have your cake and eat it, too. You can combine raw SQL power and easy object-oriented access with SQLObject. The key is the `SQLBuilder` module. This module defines a number of namespaces and classes that allow you to generate SQL expressions from objects. Suppose, for example, that you want to construct the following SQL query:

```
SELECT digit.name, digit.value

FROM digit

WHERE ((digit.value > 5) AND (digit.value < 9)):

from sqlobject.sqlbuilder import *

where_clause = AND(table.digit.value > 5, table.digit.value < 9)
columns = [Digit.q.name, Digit.q.value]
selectStatement = Select(columns, where_clause)
print selectStatement
```

To use the special `sqlbuilder` classes and operator, you must import names from `sqlobject.sqlbuilder`. They're not exported automatically from `sqlobject`. The `where` clause is an AND expression in this case. The columns to be selected are a list of objects accessible from the special `Digit.q` object. Each model class has a `q` member, which is a `sqlbuilder.SQLObjectTable` object. It is designed to allow `sqlbuilder` to work its magic on the columns and interact with the special `SQLExpression` objects. The `Select` instance accepts the column list and the `where` clause and generates the desired SQL query.

You can compose almost any SQL expression and use operators such as `OR`, `NOT`, `IN`, `LIKE`, `EXISTS`, `ENDWITH` and various joins.

If you want to select full rows from the DB, you can combine `sqlbuilder`-based `where` clauses with the `select()` method of model classes. Here is a complicated `where` clause that selects all the digits that have a name with more than four characters and a value greater than seven, or which have a name ending with ee (solution: three and eight):

```
whereClause = AND(func.length(Digit.q.name) > 4,
                  OR(Digit.q.value > 7, Digit.q.name.endswith('ee')))
print list(Digit.select(whereClause))

Output:

[<Digit 4 name=u'Three' value=3>, <Digit 9 name=u'Eight' value=8>]
```

The preceding code uses the `func.length` DB function to test the length of the name. The `func` namespace provides access to native DB functions. It also uses `endswith()` to test for names that end with ee. SQLObject provides `startswith()`, `endswith()`, and `contains()` as convenience methods that translate to STARTSWITH, ENDSWITH, and CONTAINS operators. Here is the generated SQL:

```
SELECT digit.id, digit.name, digit.value
FROM digit
WHERE ((length(digit.name) > 4)
AND ((digit.value > 7)
OR (digit.name LIKE '%ee')))
```

11.3.2 Selecting from Multiple Tables

SQLBuilder is cool and everything, but sometimes you still need more. You need to get a result set that contains columns from multiple tables. Of course, you could just use `MultipleJoin` and `RelatedJoin` to express these relationships and always use them to retrieve the related items of a single object. This is useful but potentially inefficient (talks a lot to the DB), and you don't always have control of the database to be able to add the relationships you want.

Once again, SQLObject has a solution. You can use SQLBuilder to create SQL join stantements for you. Let's take a look at a `Person` class and a `Book` class, where each book has an author who is a person:

```
class Person(SQLObject):
    firstName = StringCol()
    lastName = StringCol()

class Book(SQLObject):
    title = StringCol()
    author_id = ForeignKey('Person')
    genre = EnumCol('Fiction', 'Science', 'Science Fiction')
```

Let's add some authors and books:

```
for t in [Person, Book]:
    t.dropTable(ifExists=True)
    t.createTable()

# Authors
a1 = Person(firstName='Stephen', lastName='King')
a2 = Person(firstName='Donald', lastName='Knuth')
a3 = Person(firstName='Gigi', lastName='Sayfan') # bookless

# Books by Stephen King
Book(title='It', author_id=a1.id, genre='Fiction')
Book(title='The Shining', author_id=a1.id, genre='Fiction')
Book(title='Needful Things', author_id=a1.id, genre='Fiction')
# Books by Donald Knuth
Book(title='Concrete Mathmatics', author_id=a2.id, genre='Science')
Book(title='Literate Programming', author_id=a2.id, genre='Science')
Book(title='Surreal Numbers', author_id=a2.id, genre='Science')
```

Note that the preceding code *does not* define a MultipleJoin Books collection in the Person class, because not every person is an author, and this attribute doesn't make sense in a generic Person class. To list all the books and their authors, we can use the following code:

```
s = Select([Person.q.firstName, Person.q.lastName, Book.q.title], Person.q.id ==
Book.q.author_id)
result = c.queryAll(str(s))
for item in result:
    print item
```

Output:

```
('Stephen', 'King', 'It')
('Stephen', 'King', 'The Shining')
('Stephen', 'King', 'Needful Things')
('Donald', 'Knuth', 'Concrete Mathematics')
('Donald', 'Knuth', 'Literate Programming')
('Donald', 'Knuth', 'Surreal Numbers')
```

This constructs the query using `sqlbuilder`'s `Select` class and the `q` attribute of the `Person` and `Book` classes to specify the condition. Here is the generated SQL:

```
SELECT person.first_name, person.last_name, book.title FROM person, book WHERE
(person.id = book.author_id)
```

A similar result using `MultipleJoin` will require one query to get all the authors, and then going over his books and printing the title will generate another another query to the DB for *each* book.

11.3.3   Joins

You can also use various forms of `Join` expression with the `select()` method of model classes. The following code gets the list of authors (people who have published a book):

```
authors = Person.select(join=INNERJOINOn(Person, Book, Person.q.id == Book.
q.author_id), distinct=True)
for a in authors:
    print a
```

```
Output:

<Person 1 firstName='Stephen' lastName='King'>
<Person 2 firstName='Donald' lastName='Knuth'>
```

Here is the generated SQL:

```
SELECT DISTINCT person.id, person.first_name, person.last_name FROM person INNER
JOIN book ON (person.id = book.author_id) WHERE 1 = 1
```

Let's take it apart piece by piece. We pass two named arguments (`join` and `distinct`) to the `Person.select()` method. The `join` argument is an `INNERJOINOn` sqlbuilder expression. It expects the two tables to join and a condition. If the first table is `None`, it uses the primary table (`Person` in this case). The entire expression expands to this:

```
person INNER JOIN book ON (person.id = book.author_id)
```

The `distinct=True` argument is responsible for the `DISTINCT` keyword and to make sure we get every author just once and not once for every book. The other parts (`SELECT` keyword, column names, and the trivial `WHERE` clause) are generated by the `select()` method itself.

There is no book whose `author_id` points to Gigi Sayfan, so Gigi Sayfan is not listed. Because this is my first book, this is true at the time I'm writing this (now), but it will be false by the time you read this book (also now).

11.3.4   Nested Queries

Nested queries, or subselects, are often necessary to dissect complicated datasets or overcome some DB limitations. You can mix `Select` class instances in your `sqlbuilder` expressions to get nested queries. In general, any subselect can be written as a join, but not vice versa. Why should you even consider a subselect then? One reason is if you use the same subselect in multiple queries, you can use the results of the subquery without recomputing each time. Another reason is to break a complicated expression into multiple parts for clarity or debugging. The following code, using a subselect, will display the authors who published `Fiction` books:

```
subselect = Select(Book.q.author_id, where=AND(Outer(Person).q.id == Book.q.id,
Book.q.genre == 'Fiction')
authors = Person.select(IN(Person.q.id, subselect)))
```

What's going on? The `Person.select()` method selects only people who are in the results of the `IN` expression, which are all the IDs of people who have a book that is `Fiction`. The subselect is an instance of the `Select` class because I want to control the returned columns (just the ID).

11.4   Working with Large Result Sets

If you work with databases, you will end up working with large result sets, and you will need to think about performance. How large is large? It depends. Some applications need to access the DB frequently and touch every row or perform complex queries while inserting and deleting rows, so a few thousand rows can be considered a large dataset. Other applications access only a small part of the data in well-known patterns, so the DB can be optimized and even millions of rows will not present a problem.

There are several common performance gotchas:

1. Loading data you don't need
2. Loading too much data at a time into memory
3. Loading the same data multiple times

SQLObject is an abstraction layer that normally hides the gory details behind a magical thick veil. However, if you are responsible for the performance of your application and its efficient interaction with the DB, you must understand what's going on under the hood and be able to optimize when something is too slow. The following subsections discuss SQLObject-specific pitfalls, how they can cause one or more of the aforementioned gotchas, and some best practices.

11.4.1   Don't `list()` a Large Result Set. Use Slices.

Listing a large result set will bring it all to memory (or virtual memory). This is often not what you want: maybe you don't have enough memory, it takes longer to respond, and finally by the time you actually process some Nth row, it might already be stale. A much better approach is to use slices and process large result sets in manageable chunks. The following code demonstrates this:

```
class Bigwell(SQLObject):
    robot = StringCol()

Bigwell.dropTable(ifExists=True)
Bigwell.createTable()


for i in range (1, 101):
    Bigwell(robot='Robot #%d' % i)

# Getting the lazy SearchResults iterator (no DB access yet)
sr = Bigwell.select()


# List()ing the entire result set
robots = list(sr)
for r in list(sr):
    print r
```

```
# Processing in chunks
slice_size = 10
for i in range(0,sr.count() / slice_size):
    slice = sr[i * slice_size: (i+1) * slice_size]
    for r in slice:
        print r
```

Remember the *Robots* movie? The preceding code creates 100 Bigwell robot instances. Then it retrieves a lazy `SearchResults` iterator that doesn't access the DB, and
finally it prints all the robots in two ways. The first one is simple: just looping over
`list(sr)` and printing every robot in sight. Here is the generated SQL:

```
SELECT bigwell.id, bigwell.robot FROM bigwell WHERE 1 = 1
```

The result is that I access the DB once and get 100 robots in memory. If I insert
another billion and rerun the code, I'll have all of them in memory (if I'm lucky to have
that much memory). So, the code is simple but not very scalable.

The second approach is to slice the data and process it one slice at a time. The code
is much more complicated, involves a nested loop, and includes some nasty index manipulation. Here's the generated SQL for the first and fifth slices:

```
SELECT bigwell.id, bigwell.robot FROM bigwell WHERE 1 = 1 LIMIT 10
SELECT bigwell.id, bigwell.robot FROM bigwell WHERE 1 = 1 LIMIT 10 OFFSET 50
```

The result is that I have ten robots in memory (providing Python's garbage collec-
tor does its job) at any given moment. I can configure this number by changing the
slice size, and it is independent of the actual number of robots in the DB. The DB is
accessed again for every slice.

11.4.2   Don't Objectify a Large Result Set. Go with Straight SQL.

There's another problem that's specific to ORMs such as SQLObject when it comes
to large result sets. Every row in the DB incurs the overhead (time and memory) of
instantiating an object. In Python, instantiating a complicated object of an SQLOb-
ject-derived model class is especially painful. You pay this price even with slicing. If
you intend to process huge amounts in a read-only manner, it might be better to get
down and dirty and use the connection's `queryAll()` method and get a plain list of
tuples. Another benefit is that you can retrieve only a subset of the columns. Of course,

you will have to take care of the slicing yourself now. Finally, SQLObject caches every object that comes into existence (for example, when you insert a new object into the DB). Even if you don't refer to this object in your code, it will not be garbage collected because it's referenced in the internal cache. The bottom line is this: Objects don't go away unless you clean up the cache explicitly. You should be aware of this fact, especially if you have long-running processes. Here's some sample code that retrieves only the robot name from each row with proper slicing:

```
c = Bigwell._connection
chunk_size = 10
for i in range(0, Bigwell.select().count() / chunk_size):
    query = str(Select([Bigwell.q.robot]))
    query += ' WHERE 1=1 LIMIT %d' % chunk_size
    if i > 0:
        query += ' OFFSET ' + str(i*chunk_size)
    chunk = c.queryAll(query)
    for r in chunk:
        print r
```

I resorted to manual string concatenation to properly slice the result set. Note the ugly condition where the OFFSET is concatenated only if i > 0. The reason is that SQLite doesn't allow OFFSET 0. However, there is no overhead of getting fields we don't need from the DB (think tables that contain big blobs), and there is no instantiation of object per row. There's just a plain list of tuples that contain the robot value of each row.

Here is the SQL query and its results for the second iteration of the loop:

```
SELECT bigwell.robot FROM bigwell WHERE 1=1 LIMIT 10 OFFSET 10

[('Robot #11',), ('Robot #12',), ('Robot #13',), ('Robot #14',), ('Robot #15',),
('Robot #16',), ('Robot #17',), ('Robot #18',), ('Robot #19',), ('Robot #20',)]
```

11.4.3 Apply the Same Method to Bulk Inserts, Updates, or Deletes

If you have massive bulk inserts, updates, or deletes, you can take the raw SQL route, too. Remember that queryAll() executes any SQL statement. There is no point in instantiating a bazillion objects just to capitalize the last name when you could do the same thing with a single update statement.

11.4.4   Don't Go to the DB Multiple Times for the Same Objects

Another common performance problem you can run into when using SQLObject is redundant access to the DB. SQLObject caches object state by default. That means that if you access multiple attributes of the same object, SQLObject will not go to the DB for every access. However, if you access a particular object or slice of a `SearchResults` object, SQLObject will execute a query for each access. The following code sample demonstrates this point:

```
robots = Bigwell.select()

# Ten (5 x 2 )queries of 1 row
for i in range (0,5):
    id    = robots[i].id
    robot = robots[i].robot
    print id, robot

# One query of 5 rows
for r in robots[:5]:
    id    = r.id
    robot = r.robot
    print id, robot
```

Both code snippets print the `id` and `robot` columns of the first five rows in the Bigwell table. The first snippet accesses the robot's `SearchResult` object ten times (five iterations, two accesses per iteration) resulting in ten queries of one row. Each of the five rows is returned twice. Here is the SQL:

```
SELECT bigwell.id, bigwell.robot FROM bigwell WHERE 1 = 1 LIMIT 1
SELECT bigwell.id, bigwell.robot FROM bigwell WHERE 1 = 1 LIMIT 1

SELECT bigwell.id, bigwell.robot FROM bigwell WHERE 1 = 1 LIMIT 1 OFFSET 2
SELECT bigwell.id, bigwell.robot FROM bigwell WHERE 1 = 1 LIMIT 1 OFFSET 2

SELECT bigwell.id, bigwell.robot FROM bigwell WHERE 1 = 1 LIMIT 1 OFFSET 3
SELECT bigwell.id, bigwell.robot FROM bigwell WHERE 1 = 1 LIMIT 1 OFFSET 3

SELECT bigwell.id, bigwell.robot FROM bigwell WHERE 1 = 1 LIMIT 1 OFFSET 4
SELECT bigwell.id, bigwell.robot FROM bigwell WHERE 1 = 1 LIMIT 1 OFFSET 4

SELECT bigwell.id, bigwell.robot FROM bigwell WHERE 1 = 1 LIMIT 1 OFFSET 5
SELECT bigwell.id, bigwell.robot FROM bigwell WHERE 1 = 1 LIMIT 1 OFFSET 5
```

The second code snippet directly slices the `SearchResult` object and accesses in each iteration the `r` object. This is the right way to do it. The five rows are returned in a single query, and this query is not repeated. Here is the single query generated by this code:

```
SELECT bigwell.id, bigwell.robot FROM bigwell WHERE 1 = 1 LIMIT 5
```

11.5   Summary

- SQLObject's `ForeignKey`, `MultipleJoin`, and `RelatedJoin` column types make it easy to map database relationships to object relationships by creating attributes for your classes that return a list of related objects.

- Whenever you need to get around SQLObject's limitations and hack directly into your database, you can use the `queryAll` method that just executes raw SQL against the database.

- `queryAll` is nice when you need it, but it also means giving up all the good things that SQLObject brings to the table. Most important, you don't get automatic escaping, which means you should be careful whenever you use strings you got from a user into a SQL query.

- SQLObject's SQLBuilder syntax gives you a way to create powerful queries without dropping down to raw SQL. This is the easiest way to avoid SQL injection attacks.

- SQLBuilder lets you use standard Python comparisons to generate queries. But it also provides access to `startswith`, `endswith`, and other convenience functions to make creating joins easier.

- When working with large result sets, it pays to pay attention to how much data you're trying to keep in memory.

- You can use Python's slice syntax on an SQLObject iterator to get only a subset of your data at a time.

- When dealing with large datasets, you can save the cost of object instantiation by using `queryAll`, which doesn't turn your results into SQLObjects. If you have a billion records, this alone could mean a huge performance increase.

## Chapter 12

Customizing
SQLObject Behavior

In This Chapter

As you've already seen, SQLObject provides you with easy access to your database. You can handle large datasets, create relationships, and write complex queries using SQLBuilder. However, sometimes you need a little bit more power, or a little bit more flexibility. For example, you might need to map classes to existing database names that don't follow the SQLObject conventions, or you might need to write code that explicitly manages transactions to ensure data integrity.

Fortunately, SQLObject still has a few tricks up its sleeve: You can create custom behaviors for SQLObjects, customize the mapping between SQLObjects and the names of the tables they represent, and otherwise create flexible model classes.

This chapter explores the hooks that give you control of what happens when new instances are created, as well as the way SQLObject exposes your DBMS's transaction management system, and the ways that SQLObject helps you match classes built through inheritance with database records.

12.1 Customizing SQLObject Classes with `sqlmeta`

Sometimes the default behaviors of SQLObject get in your way, and tables aren't named the way you want them to be. Fortunately, SQLObject gives you a simple way to control that kind of thing.

You've already seen how to declare a model class that includes columns and corresponds to a DB table. But you haven't seen how to take control of this process to get what you want. SQLObject enables you to control many aspects of the way your model class behaves. This is done by setting attributes of a nested class called `sqlmeta`. Here is a quick example:

```
class Person(SQLObject):
  class sqlmeta:
    table='people'
  name = StringCol()
```

This code looks pretty simple, but why is the nested class necessary?

Well, it is not really necessary, and in previous versions of SQLObject the meta attributes were declared in the model class itself. (The attribute names were prefixed by an underscore.) The problem with this approach is that two different concepts, DB columns and metabehaviors, were specified using the same syntactical element in the same scope (class attributes). Adding the `sqlmeta` class provides a cleaner way to group together the meta attributes in their own namespace.

12.1.1   Inside the `sqlmeta` Class

`sqlmeta` is a class instance that is attached as a class attribute to every model class that's derived from SQLObject. This isn't exactly intuitive, but it is necessary because of the metaclass hocus-pocus SQLObject uses to transparently provide you with all these nice services. The bottom line is that metaclass tricks deal with classes, so things you might normally do in your code with objects, SQLObject has to do with classes.

`sqlmeta` stores the column information, joins, and indexes of its corresponding model class in addition to some control parameters. There are three types of meta attributes:

- Read-only (conceptually), which just provide meta information on the model class
- Writable, which you can set
- And one instance method that operates on a single instance, not on the entire class

Although there's nothing to stop you from modifying the read-only attributes, it is not recommended because elaborate work is necessary to create valid values.

12.1.2   Columns, Indexes, and Joins

The `sqlmeta` class contains a bunch of collections (lists and dictionaries) called `columns`, `columnList`, `columnDefinitions`, `joins`, `indexes`, `joinDefinitions`, and `indexDefinitions`. They must be kept in sync and shouldn't be modified by the user after they have been created. When you define your model class and specify column types and constraints, indexes, and joins, SQLObject calls methods such as `addColumn`, `addIndex`, and `addJoin` on the appropriate `sqlmeta` class.

Enough people have tried to change these things at run time, and have been bitten by database synchronization problems because they modified "the read-only attributes." So, to make a long story short, you really shouldn't mess with them after you've created your tables—unless you know exactly what you are doing.

Here are the column attributes, of a sample class:

```
class Metaful(SQLObject):
  name = StringCol()
  age = IntCol()
  lazy = ForeignKey('LazyBum')

print Metaful.sqlmeta.columns
print Metaful.sqlmeta.columnList
print Metaful.sqlmeta.columnDefinitions
```

Output:

```
{'age': <SOIntCol age>, 'lazyID': <SOForeignKey lazyID connected to LazyBum>,
'name': <SOStringCol name>}
[<SOStringCol name>, <SOIntCol age>, <SOForeignKey lazyID connected to LazyBum>]
{'age': <IntCol ecf950 age>, 'lazyID': <ForeignKey ecf9b0 lazy>, 'name': <String-
Col ecf970 name>}
```

12.1.3   Name Acrobatics

Names of class models and their attributes differ from the corresponding table names and column names in the DB. SQLObject uses a default naming scheme that basically generates a lowercase underscore-separated table name (for example, table_name) for a CamelCase class name (for example, TableName), so LazyBum becomes lazy_bum. You can override the naming scheme at different levels.

The following code for a Person model class results in a database table called person:

```
class Person(SQLObject):
  name = StringCol()

Person.createTable(ifNotExists=True)

CREATE TABLE person (
    id INTEGER PRIMARY KEY,
    name TEXT
);
```

If you want the table to be called `people` because you are sharing your database with a Rails application that creates pluralized names for your tables or because you are using some legacy database where the DB schema already has a people table, you can just use `table` attribute of `sqlmeta`:

```
class Person(SQLObject):
  class sqlmeta:
    table='people'
  name = StringCol()

Person.createTable(ifNotExists=True)

CREATE TABLE people (
    id INTEGER PRIMARY KEY,
    name TEXT
);
```

As you can see, SQLObject automatically created a primary key column called `id`. If your DB schema uses a different convention for the primary key, you can tell SQL-Object about it using the `idName` attribute:

```
class Person(SQLObject):
  class sqlmeta:
    idName='person_id'
    table='people'
  name = StringCol()

Person.createTable(ifNotExists=True)

CREATE TABLE people (
    person_id INTEGER PRIMARY KEY,
    name TEXT
);
```

Finally, you can completely change the naming style of tables and columns by setting the `style` attribute. There are three `style` classes:

- `Style` (the base class and the trivial no-translation style)
- `MixedCaseUnderscoreStyle` (the default style)
- `MixedCaseStyle` (leaves column names as mixed case)

You can use one of the other styles or derive your class from `style` and provide it to `sqlmeta`. You will have to override various methods such as `pythonAttrToDBColumn` and `pythonClassToDBTable`. Here is our `Person` table with the `MixedCaseStyle`:

```
class Person(SQLObject):
  class sqlmeta:
    style = MixedCaseStyle()

  name = StringCol()

Person.createTable(ifNotExists=True)

CREATE TABLE Person (
    id INTEGER PRIMARY KEY,
    Name TEXT
);
```

The SQLObject documentation claims that `MixedCaseStyle` creates mixed-case long IDs (for instance, `PersonID` rather than `id`), but this is not really the case (pun intended). If you want a long ID, you need to specify `longID=True` in the `style` constructor:

```
style = MixedCaseStyle(longID=True)
```

12.1.4 Lazy Updates and Caching

Let's keep up with the lazy bum and see the effects of the `lazyUpdate` and `cacheValues` settings. By default, SQLObject updates the DB every time you set a column attribute of an instance. This isn't what you want sometimes (for example, if you need to modify multiple attributes of the same instance). So, `lazyUpdate` tells SQLObject to wait with the update for an explicit `sync()` or `syncUpdate()` call. SQLObject also caches everything by default. If you set `lazyUpdate` to `True`, you will probably want to set `cacheValues` to `False` so that queries will return the actual state in the DB and not the partial update that might not satisfy the DB schema constraints. Well, this is one area where SQLObject can really confuse you. In the following code samples, all the asserts succeed, believe it or not (or try it yourself):

```
o = LazyBum(name='leave me alone...')
assert o.name == 'leave me alone...'
o.name = 'what do you want now?'
assert o.name == 'leave me alone...'
```

```
o.sync()
assert o.name == 'what do you want now?'
```

I create an instance (insert a row to the DB) of a `LazyBum` and assert that its name is indeed `leave me alone`.... Then, I set the name to `what do you want now?` but lo and behold the name is still `leave me alone`.... But, after the call to `sync()`, the name suddenly becomes `what do you want now?`.

What gives? SQLObject maintains an internal dictionary (called `_SO_createValues`) and a dirty flag for changed values under certain conditions such as lazy update and when inserting a new row. When you access an attribute for reading, it fetches it from the DB (because caching is turned off) and retrieves the original name even though you modified the instance.

Note that turning off caching is useful in other situations such as transaction management, which I cover later.

12.1.5   Expired Rows

When using caching, SQLObject retrieves a row just one time from the database and returns the cached result for subsequent query. Some situations require that some row be retrieved again from the DB without turning off caching for the entire table. For example, maybe there is a special row in a table that every process that modifies the table needs to update (perhaps for some internal bookkeeping purpose). SQLObject enables you to expire a particular instance, while the other rows of this table will remain cached (after the first time they are queried).

12.1.6   Default Order

The default order is the order expression that is passed to queries by default and used to order the query results.

12.2   More-Advanced SQLObject Customization

The `sqlmeta` class gives you quite a few opportunities to customize particular aspects of SQLObject's behavior. But `sqlmeta` has a limited and predefined set of behaviors for you to play with. Sometimes you want more.

You might also want to add additional attributes, or intercept attribute access and modify it in some way. As you will see in the next section, SQLObject provides helpers for these things, too.

12.2.1   Adding Magic Attributes

To gain the benefits of the model-viewer-controller (MVC) architecture, you can't go throwing business logic in your controller objects. Their job is to handle user actions. Wouldn't it be convenient if you could override attribute access in your model classes? That way you could keep your controller logic clean and keep your model logic together in one obvious place. Fortunately, SQLObject makes this easy, too.

Let's take a look at a simple example. Consider an Exam class that has simple arithmetic exercises and solutions to check against. One design is to have for each row an exercise column and a solution column. The problem with this approach is that you have to trust whoever populates this table to put in the right solutions. An elegant solution is to compute the solution on-the-fly when it is needed. This saves space because the table has only one column and also reduces traffic to the DB (could be important for remote DB). The question is where to calculate the solution. One obvious answer is to do it in the controller. However, if the computation is complicated and there are many applications that use the same SQLObject model classes, you can do it one time in the model class. Here is the code:

```
class Exam(SQLObject):
    exercise = StringCol()

    def _solve(self):
        return eval(self.exercise)

    solution = property(fget=_solve)


Exam.dropTable(ifExists=True)
Exam.createTable()

e = Exam(exercise='1+1')

print e.exercise, '=', e.solution
```

Output:

```
1+1 = 2
```

The solution attribute is a Python property that calls the _solve() method upon get access. The _solve() method solves the exercise by calling Python's eval function and returns the solution. Nice, simple, and uses standard Python features. SQLObject provides a shortcut. Instead of defining a full-fledged property, you can take advantage of a special prefix convention of _set_, _get_, _del_, and _doc_. If you have a method whose name starts with one of these prefixes, SQLObject will create a property for you. Here is the solution attribute with this shortcut:

```
def _get_solution(self):
    return eval(self.exercise)
```

It's just a little syntactic sugar. _get_solution magically creates the _solution attribute for you to get whenever you need it. In the same way, you could use _set_exercise to test the expression that is passed in to make sure it does not produce an error on eval before you save the exercise into the database.

12.2.2   Overriding Attribute Access

This is where the pedal really hits the metal. This is the holy grail of ORM because it enables you to massage the data before/after it gets into/out of the DB and provide useful services to the applications. Consider an account object with an encrypted credit card number field. If this object is being accessed from multiple applications, each application must know how and remember to encrypt/decrypt the credit card number on the way into and out of the DB. A better solution is to have the application provide the encryption key and have the model class do the encryption/decryption automatically upon access. In the following code, the application sets the encryption key as a regular Python class attribute called encryptionKey. The _get_ and _set_ property methods of the creditCard take care of encrypting/decrypting (using the super-secure xor algorithm) the credit card number before/after the actual DB access, which is done using the _so_get_ and _so_set_ special methods:

```
class Account(SQLObject):
    encryptionKey = 0
    name = StringCol()
    creditCard = IntCol()

    def _get_creditCard(self):
        value = self._SO_get_creditCard()
        print ('_get_creditCard() - encrypted credit ' + '
                'card # from DB:', value)
        return value ^ Account.encryptionKey
```

```
    def _set_creditCard(self, value):
        self._SO_set_creditCard(value ^ Account.encryptionKey)

Account.dropTable(ifExists=True)
Account.createTable()

Account.encryptionKey = 100334062
creditCard = 11111116
a = Account(name='Kozmo', creditCard=11111116)

assert a.creditCard == creditCard
print a
```

Output:

```
_get_creditCard() - encrypted credit card # from DB: 89355042
_get_creditCard() - encrypted credit card # from DB: 89355042
<Account 1 name='Kozmo' creditCard=11111116>
```

*DISCLAIMER: 11111116 is not really my credit card number.

> **Note:** _get_creditCard was called twice (once for the assert and once when printing a).
> This means that caching doesn't happen at the _get_ level, but in the _so_get level. If you
> are trying to monitor the actual DB activity, _get_ is not the right place.

12.3   SQLObject and Inheritance

Object-oriented programming languages provide many ways to represent relationships between objects: composition, containment, and inheritance. Relational databases can represent composition by reference as a row that has a foreign key column that points into another table. The DB can also represent containment with a reference table. However, there's no good way to represent inheritance through relational algebra.

Inheritance is often the best tool available to avoid code repetition, and SQLObject provides convenient methods to help you map the inheritance method to elements in the RDBMS. With that said, note that most problems can be resolved in multiple ways, and in some cases you might want to consider redefining your objects in terms of composition.

12.3.1 Python Objects, Inheritance, and Composition

Python is a fully object-oriented language. Every new-style class is derived from object, and it even supports multiple inheritance. Python also supports composition. Its flavor of composition is aggregation. This means that objects can hold references (or pointers) to other objects, but they don't own them. Ownership implies that the lifetime of the owned object is tied to its owner. Because Python is garbage collected and its garbage collection is based on reference counting, there's no object ownership in Python. If object A creates an object B and passes a reference to another object B, then B will stay alive as long as either A and C (or any other object) keeps reference to it. The fact that it was created by object A has no bearing at all.

12.3.2 Composition vs. Inheritance in Standard Python

Suppose you need to model a vehicle domain in your code. There are different kinds of vehicles, such as cars, airplanes, and submarines. There are many common attributes to all these vehicles (such as model, year, color, owner, and so on). But some attributes are relevant only for specific types of vehicles (such as number of doors for cars, wing span for airplanes, and max diving depth for submarines). You can represent this domain with the following composition-based design:

```python
class Vehicle(object):
    def __init__(self):
        self.make = ''
        self.model = ''
        self.year = ''
        self.color = ''
        self.owner = ''

class Car(object):
    def __init__(self):
        self.vehicle = Vehicle()
        self.doors = 0

class Airplane(object):
    def __init__(self):
        self.vehicle = Vehicle()
        self.wingSpan = 0

class Submarine(object):
    def __init__(self):
```

```
        self.vehicle = Vehicle()
        self.maxDivingDepth = 0

c = Car()
c.vehicle.make = 'Ford'
c.vehicle.model = 'Mustang'
c.vehicle.year = '1978'
c.vehicle.color = 'Red'
c.vehicle.owner = 'SpongeBob SquarePants'
c.doors = 3
```

The Car, Airplane, and Submarine classes have a common vehicle attribute that contains the model, year, color, and owner. Working with the common attributes is a little annoying because you have to go through one more level of indirection.

You can also represent the same domain with inheritance-based design. The Car, Airplane, and Submarine classes will inherit from the Vehicle base class instead of holding a reference to it:

```
class Car(Vehicle):
    def __init__(self):
        self.doors = 0

class Airplane(Vehicle):
    def __init__(self):
        self.wingSpan = 0

class Submarine(Vehicle):
    def __init__(self):
        self.maxDivingDepth = 0

c = Car()
c.make = 'Ford'
c.model = 'Mustang'
c.year = '1978'
c.color = 'Red'
c.owner = 'SpongeBob SquarePants'
c.doors = 3
```

As you can see, the code for inheritance-based design is more concise. However, the composition-based design allows more flexibility, such as dynamically attaching a new subtype of vehicle with extra attributes or methods to an existing car, airplane, or submarine. You can also share the same vehicle attribute between multiple instances.

Of course, you could use metaclasses and other dynamic tricks to achieve the same thing, but composition is often a lot cleaner and more obvious.

12.3.3   SQLObject Composition vs. Inheritance

SQLObject obviously supports composition out of the box. You can have a vehicle, Car, Airplane, and Submarine table. Every row in the Car, Airplane, and Submarine table will contain a foreign key column that will point to the vehicle table:

```
class Vehicle(SQLObject):
    model = StringCol()
    make = StringCol()
    year = StringCol()
    color = StringCol()
    owner = StringCol()

class Car(SQLObject):
    vehicle = ForeignKey('Vehicle')
    doors = IntCol()

v = Vehicle(make='Ford', model='Mustang', year='1978', color='Red',
owner='SpongeBob SquarePants')
c = Car(vehicle=v.id, doors=5)

print c
print c.vehicle.make, c.vehicle.model, c.vehicle.year, c.vehicle.color, c.vehicle.
owner, c.doors
```

Output:

```
Ford Mustang 1978 Red SpongeBob SquarePants 5
```

The problem with this approach is that you have to access the vehicle attributes via another indirection level, and you have to instantiate two objects to get a single conceptual object.

Because the ForeignKey column class makes the vehicle attributes available through the c instance, without requiring you to issue a special query, these limitations aren't serious. You can create nice interfaces using composition. But, you can do better (in this situation) with real inheritance. SQLObject supports it via a collection of classes called InheritableSQLObject, InheritableSQLMeta, and InheritableSelectResults that for the most part work like their noninheritable counterparts but let you specify inheritance relationships between SQLObject model classes:

```
from sqlobject.inheritance import InheritableSQLObject

class Vehicle(InheritableSQLObject):
    model = StringCol()
    make = StringCol()
    year = StringCol()
    color = StringCol()
    owner = StringCol()
class Car(Vehicle):
    doors = IntCol()


c = Car(make='Ford', model='Mustang', year='1978', color='Red', owner='SpongeBob
SquarePants', doors=5)
print c
```

Output:

```
<Car 1 doors=5 model='Mustang' make='Ford' year='1978' color='Red'
owner="'SpongeBob SquarePants'">
```

The syntax is so much sweeter now. You can really convey your intention in an object-oriented manner. You create a single object passing in the attributes of the "base class," too. It feels just like standard object-oriented Python. To make it all happen, you have to derive your base class (vehicle in this case) from InheritableSQLObject and your derived classes from the base class. The next question is to look inside the DB and see what SQLObject concocted there. Here is the DB schema:

```
CREATE TABLE car (
    id INTEGER PRIMARY KEY,
    child_name TEXT,
    doors INT
);
CREATE TABLE vehicle (
    id INTEGER PRIMARY KEY,
    child_name TEXT,
    model TEXT,
    make TEXT,
    year TEXT,
    color TEXT,
    owner TEXT
);
```

SQLObject transparently adds a `child_name` column to both tables. This column contains the name of the child table (if there is one). SQLObject uses this column to locate the linked table in order to aggregate the contents of corresponding rows in `car` and `vehicle` tables to a coherent `car` object:

```
connection.debug = True
connection.debugOutput = True

print Car.select()[0]
```

Output:

```
SELECT car.id, car.child_name, car.doors FROM car WHERE (car.id = 1) LIMIT 1

<Car 1 doors=5 model='Mustang' make='Ford' year='1978' color='Red'
owner="'SpongeBob SquarePants'">
```

SQLObject allows arbitrarily deep single-inheritance hierarchy. But for now at least, multiple inheritance isn't supported at all.

Here is an inheritance hierarchy with two levels. `Asset` is the base class, `Vehicle` inherits from `Asset`, and `car` inherits from `vehicle`. The `car` objects aggregate the attributes of all their base classes:

```
class Asset(InheritableSQLObject):
    price = StringCol()

class Vehicle(Asset):
    model = StringCol()
    make = StringCol()
    year = StringCol()
    color = StringCol()
    owner = StringCol()

class Car(Asset):
    doors = IntCol()

Car(make='Ford', model='Mustang', year='1978', color='Red', owner='SpongeBob
SquarePants', doors=5, price='$500')
```

> Note: SQLObject's debug facilities don't handle inheritable objects particularly well right now. You will get only the SQL statements on the derived class and not on the base class.

12.4　SQLObject and Transactions

A DB transaction is a series of basic operations that must all succeed or fail to preserve the integrity of the DB. The best example is moving an entity from one table to another. It requires deleting the object from one table and inserting it into the other table. If one of these operations fails, you end up with no object or with two objects. Most databases support transactions and provide a way to start transactions and roll back or commit a transaction.

12.4.1　Transactions and Connections

SQLObject relies on the underlying DB for transaction processing and provides a simple application programming interface (API) for transaction management. Before diving into the murky waters of the implementation, let's see transactions in action.

The background story is that you want to buy some groceries in the store. Your database contains two tables: store and Basket. The rows in both tables contain the name of the item and its quantity:

```
groceries = ['Apple', 'Bread', 'Milk', 'Enchilada']

class Store(SQLObject):
    class sqlmeta:
        cacheValues = False
    item = EnumCol(enumValues=groceries, unique=True)
    quantity = IntCol()

class Basket(SQLObject):
    class sqlmeta:
        cacheValues = False

    item = EnumCol(enumValues=groceries, unique=True)
    quantity = IntCol()
```

SQLObject transactions are objects that wrap a DB connection and can be used as a connection. To enable transaction processing, you must assign a transaction object to the connection attribute of the relevant tables. As you recall, there are many ways to set the connection attribute. Here is one way to do it:

```
# create a SQLite connection
db_filename = 'test.db'
db_filename = os.path.abspath('test.db').replace(':\\', '|\\')
```

```
db_filename = db_filename
connection_string = 'sqlite:/' + db_filename
connection = connectionForURI(connection_string)

# create a transaction object that wraps the connection
trans = connection.transaction()
# create the table and set their connection attribute
for t in [Store, Basket]:
    t.dropTable(ifExists=True)
    t.createTable()
    t._connection = trans
```

Buying some units of an item means decrementing the quantity of this item in the
store and adding it to the Basket with the purchase quantity. Interestingly, the item
column in both tables is unique. The following function performs the buy business
transaction:

```
def buy(item_name, quantity):
    print 'buy %d units of %s' % (quantity, item_name)

    try:
        product = Store.selectBy(item=item_name)[0]
        product.quantity -= quantity
        Basket(item=item_name, quantity=quantity)
        trans.commit()
    except Exception, e:
        print '[EXCEPTION]', e
        trans.rollback()
        trans.begin()
```

The function accepts as input an item name and a purchase quantity. It tries to get
a product with the name from the store and decrement its quantity. Then, it creates a
new object in the basket with the input name and purchase quantity. If all is well, the
transaction is committed and persists to the DB. If something goes wrong, it catches
the exception, rolls back the transaction, and starts a new transaction by calling trans.
begin(). The reason it's necessary to call begin() after rollback is that the transaction
enters an "obsolete" state, and further actions will fail unless begin() is called and the
transaction is reset.

You can purchase some groceries now by calling buy() and checking the status of
the store and your basket. The following code calls buy() four times. It tries to buy two

units of milk twice (the second one should fail), three units of bread, and two units of a nonexisting product (should fail, too). After the shopping frenzy subsides, it prints the status of the store and the basket:

```
buy('Milk',  2)
buy ('Milk', 2)
buy('Bread', 3)
buy ('No such product', 2)
def printTitle(title):
    print '\n%s\n' % title + len(title) * '-'

printTitle('store')
for x in Store.select():
    print x
printTitle('Basket')
for x in Basket.select():
    print x
```

Output:

```
buy 2 units of Milk
buy 2 units of Milk
[EXCEPTION] column item is not unique
buy 3 units of Bread
buy 2 units of No such product
[EXCEPTION] list index out of range

Store
-----
<Store 1 item=u'Apple' quantity=4>
<Store 2 item=u'Bread' quantity=1>
<Store 3 item=u'Milk' quantity=2>
<Store 4 item=u'Enchilada' quantity=4>

Basket
------
<Basket 1 item=u'Milk' quantity=2>
<Basket 2 item=u'Bread' quantity=3>
```

The failed transactions didn't hurt the data integrity of the DB. Without a transaction, the second milk purchase would decrement the quantity in the store to 0, but would fail to insert into the basket, and you would have lost two milk bottles. If you think of your code as a closed system, this might be considered a violation of the second law of thermodynamics.

12.4.2 `sqlhub` and Transactions

Remember `sqlhub`? It's the object that every model class uses as its connection if an explicit connection wasn't set directly in the class or using its module's __connection__ variable. Well, `sqlhub` can do transactions, too. The benefit is that if you have multiple classes that need to participate in a transaction, you can set it one time in `sqlhub`. The downside is that you have to manage it properly to make sure you don't keep transactions around too long. `sqlhub` has an attribute called `threadConnection` that you should set to your transaction. All the model classes will use this transaction when they access the DB from the current thread. The `threadConnection` is stored in the thread local storage, so each thread has its own. This guarantees that separate threads will not step on each other's toes and corrupt the transactions.

> **Note:** TurboGears adds a feature to SQLObject called the AutoConnectHub, which gets the database connection URI from your `dev.cfg` or `prod.cfg` file. But more important in this context, it wraps every CherryPy request in a transaction. So, if your controller methods comprise atomic units, all this transaction stuff is taken care of for you in the background. You can also append `:notrans` to your URI, to turn this feature off, and handle transactions on your own.

The following code demonstrates concurrent access to the DB by multiple threads. It builds on the `store` and `basket` classes: but instead of calling `buy()` from the main thread, it creates three buyer threads that take a short random nap and then call `buy()` to try to buy milk. The main thread starts the buyer threads and waits for them to complete:

```
import time
import threading
import random

class Buyer(threading.Thread):
    def __init__(self, name):
        threading.Thread.__init__(self)
        self.name = name
        sqlhub.threadConnection = sqlhub.getConnection().transaction()

    def run(self):
```

```
        self.nap()
        buy('Milk', 1)

    def nap(self):
        nap = random.randint(1,4)
        print self.name, 'is taking a nap for %d seconds' % nap
        for i in range(0, nap):
            print self.name, 'ZZZ...'
            time.sleep(1)

buyers = [Buyer('Buyer #%d' % i) for i in range (1,4)]

for b in buyers:
    b.start()

for b in buyers:
    b.join()
```

The important line is this:

```
sqlhub.threadConnection = sqlhub.getConnection().transaction()
```

You must set the `sqlhub.threadConnection` to a new transaction so that each thread will have its own connection.

12.4.3   Encapsulating Transactions Using a Wrapper Function

Writing code like the buy function is tedious, error prone, and mixes domain logic with the cross-cutting concern of transaction management. It would be much nicer to separate them. Ian Bicking, SQLObject's creator, had the same idea, and he suggested the following function as a solution:

```
def do_in_transaction(func, *args, **kw):
    old_conn = sqlhub.getConnection()
    conn = old_conn.transaction()
    sqlhub.threadConnection = conn
    try:
        try:
            value = func(*args, **kw)
        except:
            conn.rollback()
            raise
```

```
        else:
            conn.commit()
            return value
    finally:
        sqlhub.threadConnection = old_conn
```

You will call `do_in_transaction` and pass your function object and its arguments. (Functions are first-order citizens in Python.) Here is what it looks like (only the parts of the code that have changed):

```
for t in [Store, Basket]:
    t.dropTable(ifExists=True)
    t.createTable()
    #t._connection = trans

def buy(item_name, quantity):
        print 'buy %d units of %s' % (quantity, item_name)
        product = Store.selectBy(item=item_name)[0]
        product.quantity -= quantity
        Basket(item=item_name, quantity=quantity)

# call buy() Four times with do_in_transaction()
for x in [('Milk', 2), ('Milk', 2,), ('Bread', 3), ('No such product', 2)]:
    try:
        do_in_transaction(buy, x[0], x[1])
    except Exception, e:
        print '[EXCEPTION]', e
```

What's different? There is no need to assign a special transaction to the connection of each class or to `sqlhub`. The `buy` method is much simpler, and this is the real win if you have many similar operations. The code to invoke the `buy()` method is pretty ugly. You must pass your real function to `do_in_transaction()` with all its arguments.

It's not very readable and definitely looks alien.

12.4.4   Encapsulating Transactions Using a Decorator

Lucky for us, there is a solution. Instead of performing your domain actions through a wrapper function such as `do_in_transaction`, you can use a decorator instead. The syntax is sweet, and your intention is clear. The only downside is that decorators appeared in Python 2.4. The transaction decorator is similar to `do_in_transaction`; it sets the `sqlhub.threadConnection` attribute, intercepts exceptions, calls your function, and commits, or rolls back, if an exception occured. Finally, it restores the original `sqlhub` connection:

```
def transaction():
    def decorate(func):
        def decorated(*args, **kwargs):
            exception_raised = False
            conn = sqlhub.getConnection()
            t = sqlhub.threadConnection = conn.transaction()
            #t.debug = True
            t.autoCommit = False
            try:
                try:
                    return func(*args, **kwargs)
                except:
                    exception_raised = True
                    raise
            finally:
                if exception_raised:
                    t.rollback()
                else:
                    t.commit()
                    t._makeObsolete()
                sqlhub.threadConnection = conn
        return decorated
    return decorate

for x in [('Milk', 2),
          ('Milk', 2,),
          ('Bread', 3),
          ('No such product', 2)
          ]:
    try:
        buy(x[0], x[1])
    except Exception, e:
        print '[EXCEPTION]', e
```

As you can see, SQLObject tries to stay out of your way as much as possible when it comes to DB transactions. It provides a basic API that goes pretty much straight to the underlying DB implementation. You must understand the behavior of your DB to work effectively with transactions. Some DBs impose artificial constraints (cough, *SQlite*, cough), some DBs support nested transactions, and so forth.

12.5 Summary

- SQLObject provides special methods _set_, _get_, _del_, _doc_ that make it easy to create custom attributes. You can use these special methods to automatically perform some calculations before an object is created, or to have calculated values automatically created whenever you get an object.

- SQLObject provides a special _init (single underscore) method for you to use rather than the standard __init (double underscore) method to customize the initialization of your SQLObjects. Unlike SQLObject's __init method, _init is only called when your objects are created, not when they are retrieved from the database.

- As you've already seen, SQLObject supports object types created through composition, but you can use a special InheritableSQLObject to compose objects with inheritance, the same way you would in a standard Python program.

- You can control database connections using the begin, commit, and rollback methods on your connection object, to make managing transactions easier.

- TurboGears implicitly creates a transaction for you for every HTTP request, which is committed when the HTTP Response is processed. This avoids the need to write boilerplate code to wrap your controller object's data access in a transaction.

- If you want to write your own special transaction handlers, without the need for boilerplate code, you can encapsulate your functions, using standard Python function wrapping, or by using a decorator.

PART V

TurboGears View Technologies

Dynamic Templates with Kid

In This Chapter

Kid is designed to help you create XML documents safely and easily. The most common use for Kid is to create XHTML output for the browser, but as you've already seen, Kid can be used to create RSS. The possibilities don't stop there. You can create XML-RPC, SOAP, Atom, RelaxNG—really any kind of XML—safely and easily.

Don't let the simplicity of many of the examples in this book fool you. Kid has all the power you need to write powerful and dynamic templates that can handle any complexity you throw at them.

13.1 Creating Dynamic Templates with Kid

Python has been home to any number of HTML templating schemes. Some have been copies of other models:

PSP --> ASP/JSP

Velocity --> Velocity (Java)

Mighty --> Mason (Perl)

Others were developed in Python first:

DTML

Cheetah

ZPT

STAN

Even though Kid might be new to the block, it isn't unaware of the past, and it isn't afraid to borrow from other template systems.

With that said, Kid was not designed to be just another text-based HTML template system. It's designed to make creation of XML documents easier.

Some of its predecessors such as PSP and Cheetah are more like string templates than XML template systems, so they can't provide any guarantee that they'll produce well-formed XML.

Kid is more like ZPT than any of its other predecessors. In fact, the main difference is that instead of creating a whole new language around metal and macros, Kid
provides an easy way to embed full Python expressions in your XHTML.

This might seem like a small difference, but it makes the basics of Kid easy to learn
for people who already know XHTML and Python. And the more complex pieces are
actually easy to understand if you've ever had to do an XML transformation, and they
are a whole heck of a lot more fun than XSLT.

Kid has good online documentation available at http://kid-templating.org/ that
covers each of the language constructs in a lot more detail than we do here. But more
important, if you are using Kid outside of TurboGears, the online docs explain how to
use Kid's command-line tools to compile your templates, and do all the other things
that TurboGears does for you behind the scenes.

13.1.1   Python-Powered Processing Directives

As I said, Python expressions are one of the most important elements in Kid. They
enable you to import modules, classes, and functions into your template namespace.
They enable you to do anything you can normally do in Python right there in your
template. Some people think this is a bad idea, because they have used PHP, ASP, or
JSP and ended up with all their business logic in their templates. And it's true you
shouldn't do that—but Kid is designed around the premise that you are the one who
can make the best choices about what belongs in your template.

As you've already seen, all you have to do to embed Python directly into your template is to wrap it in `<?python ?>`. Then you can write something like this:

```
<?python
def some_function()
    pass
?>
```

One intentional limitation of the `<?python ?>` syntax can trip up users of PHP,
ASP, and JSP. The results of a Python expression evaluated inside of the `<?python ?>`
tag are *not* returned to the template output. You have to use Kid's content producing
constructs for that.

This might seem like an arbitrary constraint, but it makes Kid's internal workings
easier to understand. And even more important, it's just a good idea to keep whatever
program logic needs to be in your template separate from the presentation logic.

13.1.2   Content-Producing Expressions

At the heart of Kid are several mechanisms to move data from the Python side of the world into Kid output. The first is the `${}` syntax, which simply evaluates whatever Python expression is contained within `{}` and inserts the result into the template at that point. If you aren't using an expression, and just want to drop the value of a particular object into the template, you can even drop the curly brackets and just use a dollar sign before your object name like this: `$name`.

As mentioned before, this isn't particularly "designer friendly" when you use `${name}` in the text of your page. When a designer opens up a page like this in Dreamweaver, they'll see `${name}` directly, and it can be easy to accidentally enter a character where it doesn't belong and break the template. And whenever you're pulling longer items for insertion into the template, you rarely get a good picture of what the final output will look like by seeing `${story.text}` in the template.

So, Kid provides a number of other useful content-producing constructs that make it easy to avoid those problems and make your templates even more designer friendly. The `py:content="story.txt"` processing directive tells Kid to replace the contents of the tag that it is on with the value of `story.txt`.

```
<p py:content="story.txt">This is replaced by the txt attribute of the story
object</p>
```

One common Kid idiom is to use a `<span>` tag to hold some content you want placed into your template. The `<span>` tag allows you to have default text in the template when you preview it, and it doesn't impact the look of the final output. This is particularly useful for default content you want placed in the template you give to a designer, but which will be replaced programmatically in the final rendered output.

But sometimes you just don't want the `<span>` tag in the final output—in that case, you can add a `py:strip="True"` processing directive to the `<span>` tag, and it will be removed entirely from the final output. In this case, the content of the `<span>` tag is placed in the parent attribute.

In fact, the combination of `py:` and `py:strip` is so common that Kid provides a shortcut for it: `py:replace`. You can use the `<span py:replace="story.txt">some text</span>` to keep the processing directive hidden in a tag attribute (where it's less likely to be changed by a designer), you have default content in the template for better layout, and when the template is processed by Kid, the tag will be removed and replaced with the content's `story.txt`.

There's one last "content"-producing processing directive in Kid, which is used to add attributes rather than text nodes. If you pass some properly formatted object to the `py:attr` directive, those objects will automatically be turned into attributes for the tag element. You can pass a dictionary, a list of tuples in the form (name, value), or set of comma-separated keyword values in the form `"id=story.id', align='right'"`. All of these will be turned into attributes with the proper names and values.

> **Note:** All Kid files must be valid XML, which means that you always have to close your tags, and you have to escape any special characters. In particular, the < sign should always be substituted with `&lt` or `&#60`. Fortunately, Kid takes care of all that for you and escapes all the special characters that might be inserted into your template from the Python side of the world. So, your strings can all be blissfully unaware of the special needs of XML documents, and when you hand them off to Kid, everything will "just work."

13.1.3 Control Structures

Of course, no template system would be complete without conditional display and looping. Kid provides these through the `py:if`, and `py:for` processing directives. If you know Python, you already pretty much know how these work.

So, for example, the value of a `py:if` expression is false for all the same expressions where it would be false in Python. That is, `py:if="x"` is false if x is (1) an empty string, dictionary, or list; or (2) if x is 0, and 3 if x is the Boolean value `False`.

When a `py:if` statement evaluates to false, Kid removes the tag that it is an attribute of, along with all of its descendant elements.

In other words if the expression evaluates to anything false in Python, the tag *and all its children* will not be displayed.

The `py:for` works in much the same way, iterating over a list, and creating a new element for each value in the list. And just like `py:for`, any descendant elements are also reevaluated for each element. This makes it easy to turn a list of items into repeating page elements of any kind.

After you get the hang of this, it is easy to create highly involved layouts that iterate over complex data structures with a few simple Kid structures, as you saw with the WhatWhat Status projects page in Chapter 9, "Ajax and WhatWhat Status Projects."

When using `py:for` and `py:if`, however, you need to remember a couple of things. For one thing, the physical order you use for a set of `py:for` and `py:if` directives on the same tag matters. The `py:for` is always executed first. This is almost always what you want, because you are usually looping over a list of items and then checking some expression on each of the members of that list, to determine whether that particular list item ought to be displayed. If you really want a different execution order, just move the py:if to a <span> tag outside of the tag you will be iterating over, and you'll get what you want.

With what you know about Kid so far, you can solve every possible XML template problem, but it wouldn't necessarily be pretty. You would often have to repeat code within a page, as well as between pages. Lucky for us, Kid has a couple more processing directives that make code reuse a lot easier.

We'll get to see how to use Kid to reuse elements of another page in the next section, but let's take a look at py:def, which enables us to create reusable template functions.

When you add a py:def directive to a tag, you are creating a new function that encompasses that tag and all its member elements. Like a standard Python function, this new named template function can take any number of arguments (including *args and **kwargs style arguments).

When a tag has the py:def processing attribute, it is not rendered in the template where it appears—instead, it is rendered when it is called from a content-producing construct somewhere later in the template.

So, for example, we could use py:def to format the output of one of our bookmark objects from Part II. To do this, all you have to do is write something like this:

```
<p py:def="display_bookmark{bookmark}">
  The database contains a reference to ${bookmark.name} <br />
  at the web location ${bookmark.link}
</p>
```

And then you could tell Kid to display a single bookmark (passed in from the controller as current_bookmark) in our special format by calling the above template function like this:

```
${display_bookmark(current_bookmark)}
```

Or you could use the same function to display each of the bookmarks in the database like this:

```
<span py:for="bookmark in bookmarks">
  <p py:replace="display_bookmark(bookmark)">
    A list of all the bookmarks in the database will be printed here.
```

```
    </p>
</span>
```

`py:def` makes it possible to build large, complex XML documents based on reusable components. This isn't always critical for XHTML generation, but when you start creating larger XML documents, it's an absolutely necessary feature. And there are lots of places, even in XHTML, where you can use `py:def` to avoid code duplication and make your template code easier to read, understand, and maintain.

13.1.4   Kid's Built-In Functions

Before we move on to inter-template code reuse, let's take a look at the internal Kid functions that let you import XML content into your template. The first, and most often used, version is the `XML()` function, which allows you to pass an object containing properly formatted XML content into your template, bypassing the escaping mechanisms of Kid's standard content-producing constructs.

We saw the `XML()` function earlier in Chapter 8, "RSS, Cookies, and Dynamic Views in WhatWhat Status," because the WhatWhat project used Python's textile module to create XHTML markup from specially formatted strings.

But what if the XML you want isn't already inside some Python object? Perhaps it's sitting in a file on your system, or hanging out at some URL on the Internet. You could use a `<?python ?>` directive to get the XML from wherever it lives and package it up into a python object for you. But because this is a common need, Kid provides another shortcut function, `document()`. This can prove useful for all kinds of complex applications that pull XML from various places to put together a page. But you can also use it for simple things. For example, the Kid documentation provides us with this example:

```
<div py:content="document('header.html')"></div>
```

Kid's `document()` function resolves relative paths based on the location of the Kid template file.

13.2   Beyond the Basics: Keeping Your Templates DRY (Don't Repeat Yourself)

Most web applications have common headers, footers, sidebars, and other repeated page elements. Sometimes these are static, and sometimes they are dynamic. But unless your template system provides mechanisms for handling this kind of thing, you are going to end up with a lot of repeated code in various page templates. And repeated code makes future changes harder, turns finding all occurrences of a bug into a tedious and complex process, and can introduce subtle bugs.

You've already seen one of the mechanisms Kid provides for factoring similar template code out into named template functions. And if that's all there was, it would be enough to keep your code clean. But there is another more powerful, but also slightly more complicated function: `py:match`.

13.2.1 Transformations Using `py:match`

There are a number of advantages to the `py:match` approach, but perhaps the most important is that it takes only a single line of code per page to get headers, footers, sidebars, and other page elements inserted into your page.

You can use `py:match` to automatically add JavaScript or CSS references to all your pages, or even to add sidebars and other content to the body of all your pages. You can even use `py:match` to create custom tags like Java's taglibs.

Given all that power, it can take a while to work your mind around how `py:match` works. Conceptually it's simple: `py:match` searches through the rest of your template for matching elements and replaces them with the contents of the element to which the original `py:match` tag is connected.

For example, you could write something like this at the top of any page (for instance, the welcome page in a newly quickstarted project):

```
<h2 py:match="item.tag=='h2'">
        This replaces your other tag's content.
</h2>
```

This match template's match expression `item.tag=='h2'` will then be added to the list of match template filters. Every tag that is processed will be run through that match template filter. If one of your tags says `<h2>some random test here</h2>`, it will match the above tag and be replaced by the contents of the match tag. So, now rather than having a big heading on your page that says `some random text here`, you'll get a big heading that says `This replaces your other tag's content`. If you had a second `<h2>` tag, it too would be replaced with the contents of the mach tag, and you'd have another big `py:match test:This replaces your other tag's content` in your page.

Unfortunately, the preceding code won't work in a default TurboGears project because we declare a default XML namespace, which gets added to tag names before the match process happens. But simply appending the namespace to the tag name in the match expression solves that problem; and while we're at it, let's add a little something extra:

```
<h2 py:match="item.tag=='{http://www.w3.org/1999/xhtml}h2'">
        This will be added before your tag's original text! ${item.text}
</h2>
```

Notice that we put the namespace reference inside of curly braces right in front of the tag name. This will now match the tag, as it is represented in the `welcome.kid` file in a default quickstart. This is necessary because of the little `xmlns="http://www.w3.org/1999/xhtml"` at the top of the page that defines a default namespace.

But the real magic of `py:match` comes in the second line of our little sample template. `${item.text}` returns the text node of the matching `<h2>` element. This means that our `<h2>some random text here</h2>` element will now be replaced with this new combined element:

```
<h2>This will be added before your tag's original text! some random text here</h2>
```

When there is a match, the `item` variable contains the entire contents of the matching element as an ElementTree (http://effbot.org/zone/element-index.htm) element object. Element objects are designed to store hierarchical data sets, and much of Kid is built on top of ElementTree. To make scanning and manipulating the original contents of the matching tag as easy as possible, Kid exposes the ElementTree application programming interface (API) directly via the `item` object, which you can use to mix the match template body with elements from the body of the matching element from the original template.

In the preceding code, we are using the `text` attribute of an element to return its text node as a string that we can drop into our template text. But far more complex manipulations are possible at this point. This means that our template can produce output that is a combination of the original content along with whatever new information is provided by the match template.

As mentioned previously, `item` is an ElementTree element. It is the ability to take elements from the original page and mix them with the template code you write in the body of your `py:match` template that makes the `py:match` replacement structure so powerful. The possibilities are endless, and in a second we'll take a look at how to use this to create your own custom tag libraries.

But before we move on, let's take a quick look at some of the key features of the structure of an `element` object. The text method contains the first text node in the object. (Remember, if you have a sentence with `<b>some text</b>` in it, you have more than one text node, before the subelement `<b>`, and the text that comes after it.) The `item[]` object is a Python list that contains the child elements of the matching element. And that brings us to a common idiom for putting the entire contents of the matching tag inside the match template:

```
py:replace="[item.text]+item[:]"
```

This snippet of code places the first text node and any other remaining child elements of the matching tag into the body of the match template. So, you get the original tag and all its elements plus whatever your match template adds.

This means that there is a potential bug in the `py:match` template we used in our first example.

It works fine in the test case we had there. But what if we add a link, or even add an `<i>` tag around one of the words? Only the text before the first child element would be displayed.

So, if our page contains a tag such as `<h2> more <i>random</i> text</h2>`, we would have gotten this element in our output:

```
<h2> This will be added before your tag's original text! more</h2>
```

Notice how the italic text and everything after it was just dropped from the output. They were hanging out in the item list, but that was never used.

13.2.2   Creating Custom Tags with `py:match`

You aren't limited to matching existing tag names. You can use `py:match` to create your own custom tag libraries. This means you can add `py:match='item.tag == "sidebar"'` which automatically adds a sidebar to your page whenever the page has a `<sidebar>` tag.

In fact, there's nothing new to learn about how to create custom tags. You just use `py:match` in the same way we did before, but now you match against your own newly created tag name. Then, whenever you want that match template added to your page, just use the tag.

Because match templates have access to the matching element, you can easily define custom tag attributes that are processed by the match template to give you the custom tag behaviors. Because they are so flexible, you can use custom tags to do all kinds of interesting things. If you are familiar with Struts Tag Library concept, you can implement the same kind of thing in Kid—but your tag library can be specific to your application, and suffer from none of the limitations of the Struts Tag Library.

Just to whet your appetite for custom tag creation, and give you an idea of what you can do with a custom tag, let's look at a little sample page with an `<insult>` tag designed to deliver a random Monty Python-inspired taunt to everyone who views the page.

```
<!DOCTYPE html PUBLIC "-//W3C//DTD XHTML 1.0 Transitional//EN" "http://www.w3.org/
TR/xhtml1/DTD/xhtml1-transitional.dtd">

<?python
from random import randrange
def random_insult():
    """Get select 1 of 5 random insults"""
    insult_num = randrange(0,4)
    insult_options=["one", "two", "three", "four", "five"]
    return insult_options[insult_num]
?>

<html  xmlns:py="http://purl.org/kid/ns#"
    py:extends="'master.kid'">

  <b py:match="item.tag == 'insult'"
       py:content="item.get(random_insult())"> Random insult will go here!
  </b>
  <head>
    <title>Time of day demo</title>
  </head>
  <body>
    <p> Thanks for visiting our little page.
    <br /> Please leave now before we hurt you!
    <br /> By the way,
      <insult one="Your mother was a hamster!"
              two="Your father smelt of elderberries!"
                      three="Go and boil your bottoms, you son of a silly
person."
                      four="I fart in your general direction!"
                      five="You look like my mother!" />
```

```
    </p>
  </body>
</html>
```

1. This Python function just returns a text string, which will be looked up in our match template to determine which insult to use.

2. This is the match template. It looks up the attribute with matching the string returned by `random_insult`.

3. The `<insult>` tag defines the five possible insults, but says nothing about how they should be displayed. That's all handled in the match template.

13.2.3 Creating Parent Templates with `py:extends`

So, we have named template functions and match templates. If only we had a way to store these things outside of our template and have them automatically imported into our template, everything would be well with the world. We would then be able to create `py:match` and `py:def` directives and store them in a central file so that they could be reused wherever they were needed.

Kid provides exactly that functionality with another processing directive: `py:extends`. The `py:extends` directive can only be used at the root of a template. You set it equal to the template you want to extend. Here's the code from `welcome.kid` that tells it to extend the `master.kid` template:

```
py:extends="'master.kid'"
```

This means that all the named template functions in `master.kid` are now automatically available in the welcome template (but there aren't any yet—although you could easily add them). But more important, `py:extends` also imports match templates; any match expressions in `master.kid` will be checked against each tag in `welcome.kid`, and the appropriate match template substitutions will be made automatically.

13.3 Bringing It All Together

So, let's take a look at the `master.kid` file from a freshly created project. This contains a single match template that displays login information, Flash messages, and the TurboGears logo.

Chances are you'll want to keep something like this to have Flash and Identity messages automatically appear on your pages, but you'll likely want to edit the CSS references and add additional match templates:

```
<!DOCTYPE html PUBLIC "-//W3C//DTD XHTML 1.0 Transitional//EN" "http://www.w3.org/
TR/xhtml1/DTD/xhtml1-transitional.dtd">


<?python import sitetemplate ?>
<html xmlns="http://www.w3.org/1999/xhtml" xmlns:py="http://purl.org/kid/ns#" py:
extends="sitetemplate">


<head py:match="item.tag=='{http://www.w3.org/1999/xhtml}head'" py:attrs="item.
items()">
    <meta content="text/html; charset=UTF-8" http-equiv="content-type"
py:replace="''"/>
    <title py:replace="''">Your title goes here</title>
    <meta py:replace="item[:]"/>
    <style type="text/css">
        #pageLogin
        {
            font-size: 10px;
            font-family: verdana;
            text-align: right;
        }
    </style>
</head>


<body py:match="item.tag=='{http://www.w3.org/1999/xhtml}body'" py:attrs="item.
items()">
    <div py:if="tg.config('identity.on',False) and not 'logging_in' in locals()"
        id="pageLogin">
        <span py:if="tg.identity.anonymous">
            <a href="/login">Login</a>
        </span>
        <span py:if="not tg.identity.anonymous">
            Welcome ${tg.identity.user.display_name}.
            <a href="/logout">Logout</a>
        </span>
    </div>


    <div py:if="tg_flash" class="flash" py:content="tg_flash"></div>


    <div py:replace="[item.text]+item[:]"/>
```

```
    <p align="center"><img src="/static/images/tg_under_the_hood.png"
alt="TurboGears under the hood"/></p>
</body>

</html>
```

Here are a few things you might want to look for in the above code:

1. This `py:match` just provides sample headers, but ultimately passes the original headers through to the results of the match template untouched.

2. `py:attrs="item.items()` takes all the item attributes from the element object and uses Kid's `py:attrs` directive to put them into the template output.

3. The `py:match` expression matches the body element of all the pages that extend `master.kid`.

4. Adds a login link to the top of the page.

5. Display's login name if the user is logged in.

6. Displays the Flash content.

7. Puts the original body content back into the page.

8. Adds a "powered by TurboGears" logo to the bottom of the page.

The `master.kid` page is written so that it could be opened directly in your browser or image-editing tool without the need to preprocess it with Kid. This way, designers have something they can work with on the "master" template.

The first `py:match` element matches the header of the incoming page. But if you look inside it, all the tags use `py:replace` to replace themselves with empty strings. This is what makes it possible to view this page directly in a browser. And at the end, we have a `py:replace=item[:]` that takes all the head subelements from the original page, and puts them back into the match template's output page.

With a basic understanding of what is happening in this page, you should be able to modify it to add headers, footers, sidebars, or just about anything you need on every page of your TurboGears project.

13.4   Summary

- Kid always produces valid XML, so you don't have to worry about invalid output.

- Kid's `py:content`, `py:strip`, and `py:replace` are designed to enable you to add dynamic content to your page. You can also use the `${}` syntax to drop strings into your page.
- Kid provides the `py:if`, `py:for`, and `py:def` processing directives to control program flow and make reuse possible.
- The `py:match` processing directive makes it possible to add dynamic content to templates in an XML-specific way that allows for all kinds of powerful transformations.

- The `py:extends` directive allows you to keep reusable named template functions (`py:def`) and match templates in a central location to be "inherited" by multiple templates.

## Chapter 14

Creating Better JavaScript with MochiKit

In This Chapter

Leaving the comfortable and predictable world of Python for the wooly wilderness of in-browser JavaScript can be daunting. We've all heard horror stories of strange JavaScript idioms, weird behavior from browser to browser, and the pain of debugging anything in the browser that's used by more than 85 percent of Internet users. Many of us have lived to tell those tales.

Help has arrived, O wary Pythonista! MochiKit has a unique approach in the world of JavaScript libraries: It uses JavaScript the way the language is intended to work, but it also provides many of the functions that are familiar and useful to Python programmers.

14.1 How to Use This Chapter

MochiKit comes with very good documentation. But, it's *reference* documentation. It tells you what you need to know to use a specific function. That's certainly valuable, and this chapter doesn't try to reproduce that.

The goal of this chapter is to provide more background around the features of MochiKit with the perspective of Python programmers in mind.

The next section of the chapter covers `MochiKit.Base`, which are the lowest-level functions within MochiKit. We start off with the low-level functions and work our way up to the high-level ones, which tend to build on the low-level ones. If you want, you can jump on to the later sections of the chapter, but be aware that you may need to bounce back to pick up on functions that are used in those sections. Also, there are many useful functions in `MochiKit.Base` that can help you with your JavaScript tasks.

> Note: At the time of this writing, MochiKit 1.4 has not yet been released. Much of the development appears to have been done already, but it is possible that there will be some variation between the functions presented here and the final 1.4 version. This will be most true for `MochiKit.Style` and `MochiKit.Visual`.

14.1.1 MochiKit's Packaging

MochiKit is packaged up as a single, packed `MochiKit.js` file that contains all of the features. Note, however, that the features covered in "The Wow Factor" section of Chapter 15, "Effective Ajax with MochiKit," have not yet been packaged into a full `MochiKit.js`. You can use those modules separately now and you will still be able to do so after MochiKit 1.4 is released.

In addition to the single `.js` file format, you can use just the parts of MochiKit that you need. MochiKit's documentation provides a clear indication for each module of which modules are required, and MochiKit makes sure that the requirements are met. If you use `MochiKit.Iter` without including `MochiKit.Base`, for example, an exception is thrown.

The names of MochiKit's functions are put into their own namespaces for maximum compatibility. MochiKit's `Base.js` file, for example, places all of its functions into `MochiKit.Base`. When you use the `MochiKit.js` file in your project, the public functions are all put into the global JavaScript namespace. That is a nice convenience that saves on typing. (You can type `getElement` rather than `MochiKit.DOM.getElement`.)

MochiKit is expressly designed to work with JavaScript Archive Network (JSAN) and the Dojo Toolkit. Dojo's style is to namespace all the calls (for example, `dojo.io.bind`), and MochiKit sticks to that when used with Dojo's packaging system. Using MochiKit with Dojo means that you should use the full name (`MochiKit.DOM.getElement`) for functions that you access.

14.1.2 MochiKit's Interactive Shell

MochiKit provides an interactive shell demo that lets you interactively run JavaScript commands to do the same kind of ad-hoc testing and debugging you can do from the Python prompt. This is a great way to familiarize yourself with MochiKit and just play with the functions that it has to offer. Many of the examples given in this chapter are done from within the interactive interpreter.

The examples in this chapter can all work within the "mochiexamples" project that comes with this book (www.turbogearsbook.com). To try these examples, go into the mochiexamples directory and run the following:

```
./start-mochiexamples.py
```

You'll find the interactive interpreter at `http://localhost:8080/interpreter`.

14.2   Introduction to MochiKit and Its Interactive Shell

The TurboGears philosophy is to not shy away from JavaScript. After all, it *is* the language spoken by the browsers. Knowing a little JavaScript can help you tremendously when you need to work on something a little outside the features the framework gives you for free. As you can see in the examples in this chapter, MochiKit makes the move from Python to JavaScript a little more seamless, in addition to providing some high-level tools and cross-browser compatibility.

MochiKit is broken down into several modules:

- **Async**   For handling asynchronous things, such as Ajax.
- **Base**   Functional programming, comparisons, and other core functions.
- **DOM**   Manipulation of the Document Object Model (DOM), for doing things such as dynamically adding or updating the page.
- **Color**   Ability to work with colors and translate color values between different schemes.
- **DateTime**   Conveniences for working with (surprise!) dates and times.
- **DragAndDrop**   Functions for adding drag-and-drop behavior to your applications.
- **Format**   Functions for getting formatted strings.
- **Iter**   Python-style iteration for JavaScript.
- **Logging**   A better solution than `alert()` for debugging.
- **LoggingPane**   Interactive pane for viewing log messages.
- **Signal**   Universal event handling.
- **Sortable**   Provides drag-and-drop sorting of DOM elements.
- **Style**   Functions that help in working dynamically with CSS styles.
- **Visual**   Provides a way to create more advanced visual effects.

This chapter is not a JavaScript reference or tutorial. Many excellent books are available to help you learn the JavaScript language and the web browser programming environment.

14.3   Base Functions

The `MochiKit.Base` module provides a collection of functions to make basic programming tasks in JavaScript a bit more pleasant. `Base` helps out with comparison and representation of JavaScript objects, conversion to JavaScript Object Notation (JSON) format, array operations, and other useful tasks. If you use any other part of MochiKit, odds are that you'll need to use `Base`, too, because MochiKit relies heavily on the functions in `MochiKit.Base`.

MochiKit's interactive interpreter is really handy for trying out basic JavaScript language features. You'll probably want to fire it up for this section.

14.3.1   The Comparison Problem

JavaScript provides a typical set of comparison operators: `==`, `!=`, `<`, `>`, `<=`, `=>`. Starting by looking at just equality, JavaScript has two different ways to test equality: the standard `==` and the less-standard `===`. `==` will try to change the type of the objects being compared in an effort to see whether they match. For example, `"1" == 1` is true in JavaScript. The `===` is stricter: It doesn't do any kind of type conversion. So, `"1" === 1` is false.

JavaScript will also do type conversions for expressions such as `"1" < 2`. You might be thinking that JavaScript's comparison operators seem straightforward to use. And you'd be correct if you're only comparing some combination of numbers or strings. As soon as you get beyond that, JavaScript has no built-in facility to help you.

For example, the following expression *looks* true:

```
["burger", "fries"] == ["burger", "fries"]
```

But JavaScript will tell you that's false. MochiKit's `compare` function knows the truth, however:

```
compare(["burger", "fries"], ["burger", "fries"])
```

returns 0, which means that they're equal. `compare` gives you a negative number if the object on the left is less than the object on the right, and a positive number if the left is the greater one.

You can use `compare` for all of your comparisons:

```
compare("1", 1)
```

returns true, just as `"1" == 1` does.

14.3.2   More-Complicated Comparisons

The preceding examples show how JavaScript's operators handle comparisons of simple values and MochiKit's compare function handles simple values and arrays. What if you have something more complicated? Suppose, for example, that you have an object that represents a food order. Our order objects will have a hash of items with the quantity for each item:

```
Order = function(items) {
    this.items = items;
}
```

If you're entering this in MochiKit's interactive interpreter, be sure to end each line with // so that it knows that you've got more to type, or use the "Multiline input" box that is available in the "mochiexamples" version of the interpreter.

Ideally, you could do this

```
order1 = new Order(["burger", "fries"]);
order2 = new Order(["burger", "fries"]);
```

and be able to get true for order1 == order2. Sadly, it doesn't work that way. JavaScript sees that you've got two objects and just says, "Nope, not the same object," and returns false. Does MochiKit's magic compare function take care of it for us?

```
compare(order1, order2);
```

Nope. You get an exception stating that the objects cannot be compared. That's not the whole story, however. MochiKit can't compare them *now*, because we haven't told MochiKit how to compare them. We can tell MochiKit how to compare two orders by using the registerComparator function. As you saw in the preceding section, the compare function can handle two arrays just fine. A function that can compare two Orders to see whether they're the same is simple:

```
compareOrders = function(a, b) {
    return compare(a.items, b.items);
}
```

You can test this by running compareOrders(order1, order2) and see that it returns 0. Just having a function that can compare your objects is not quite enough for register-Comparator, however. registerComparator needs a way to know that compareOrders is the function is has to call to compare the objects that it has been handed. Let's make a function that will answer that question:

```
isOrder = function(obj) {
    if (obj.items) {
        return true;
    }
    return false;
}
```

With that function in hand, we can register a comparator:

```
registerComparator("Order", isOrder, compareOrders);
```

The first parameter is a name that we're giving to this comparator. After registering this comparator, our earlier desire to run

```
compare(order1, order2);
```

now works just as we'd expect and returns 0.

Other comparison functions available in `MochiKit.Base` are as follows:

- `objEqual(a, b)`   Returns true if `compare(a, b) == 0`.
- `objMax(obj[, ...])`   Use `compare` to find the maximum out of the list of arguments.
- `objMin(obj[, ...])`   Use `compare` to find the minimum out of the list of arguments.

14.3.3   A Word about Objects in JavaScript

You might have noticed that our `isOrder` function just checks that the object has items. What if there is some other object that has "items" on it? For the purposes of this script (and many JavaScripts on web pages), this is not a big concern. You don't have so many different objects floating around that you're likely to accidentally compare objects other than `orders` that happen to have items. However, if you do want to play it safer, it's important to know a bit about objects in JavaScript.

Python, like many object-oriented languages, has the notion of a class. A class represents a particular kind of object, and an instance is one example of that type of object. When you've got an instance in Python, you know what kind of thing it is. You just ask for its `__class__`, and Python will tell you what it is. You can also call `isinstance` to do a check to see whether a particular object is an instance of a given class. Unlike checking __class__, isinstance looks up the inheritance hierarchy to see whether the class you're looking for is anywhere up there.

In the example in the previous section, the Order object is declared as a function. No class is involved because JavaScript doesn't have classes. What it does have is a concept called a "prototype," which serves a similar purpose and can even be used to implement something more like the classes you're used to from Python.

Fundamentally, all objects in JavaScript "look the same" and are basically just hash tables where a string name points to a value that is an object or one of the basic types. Every object has a special "prototype" value set on it that you can access like any other attribute by looking at object.prototype. When you attempt to look up an attribute on an object, the object is checked first. If that name isn't found, the prototype is checked. And then the prototype's prototype is checked, and so on.

None of those objects have the special role of being a "class." They're all just objects. Any object you can get ahold of can be used as a prototype for inheritance purposes.

It turns out that even though there are no classes in JavaScript, you can still do the equivalent of an isinstance check. JavaScript's instanceof operator enables you to check whether two objects have the same prototype. When you use the code order instanceof Order, the JavaScript interpreter will compare the prototypes of your order instance against the Order function and see that they're the same and return a true value. instanceof will also search prototypes of prototypes, in the same way isinstance does in Python.

In Python, it's generally considered bad style to overuse isinstance. The preference goes to "duck typing": If it walks like a duck and quacks like a duck, it must be a duck. In other words, if the methods or attributes you're looking for are on the object, just go ahead and use them. The same is true of JavaScript. Type checks are more consistent with the thinking of statically typed languages such as Java. If you're working in Python or JavaScript, duck typing is a better way to go.

> **Note:** Douglas Crockford has written some excellent articles about the virtues of JavaScript's object model that are worth a read if you're interested in the topic: www.crockford.com/javascript/.

14.3.4 JavaScript and Python: Not So Different After All

There are some syntax differences and some object model differences, but the truth is that JavaScript and Python are more similar than they are different. These similarities are just increasing, and it's not a coincidence.

Brendan Eich, the creator of JavaScript, has written[1] about how JavaScript needs to solve some of the same problems Python does. Instead of treading over the same ground, he has chosen to take his inspiration directly from Python.

JavaScript 1.7 is evidence of this.[2] New features include generators, iterators, and array comprehensions that look *exactly* like their Python counterparts.

MochiKit makes it easier for Python programmers to cross the bridge into JavaScript programming, and JavaScript itself is evolving to make the transition even smoother!

14.3.5 Object Representation

Many object-oriented programming languages provide a facility to create a string representation of an object. In Java and JavaScript, for example, you can define a toString method to generate the string representation of an object. In Python, there are two different string methods: __zstr__ and __repr__. __str__ provides a string representation of the object that is suitable for users. _repr_ provides a representation for the programmers. The string returned by __repr__ ideally can be cut and pasted directly into the Python interpreter.

repr can prove very useful, especially when debugging. For this reason, MochiKit brings the repr function to JavaScript. Here's an example:

```
>>> animals = ["dog", "cat", "chinchilla"];
["dog", "cat", "chinchilla"]
>>> animals.toString()
"dog,cat,chinchilla"
>>> repr(animals)
"[\"dog\", \"cat\", \"chinchilla\"]"
```

The basic JavaScript toString for an array does a reasonable job in presenting the list of items. The repr for the array is useful, however, because you can paste it directly into a JavaScript program.

Previously, we created new Order objects to represent a food order. You may have noticed when creating an Order, the representation displayed was not amazingly useful:

```
>>> order1 = new Order(["Burger", "Fries"]);
[object Object]
```

1 "Python and JavaScript" from Brendan Eich's Roadmap Updates: http://weblogs.mozillazine.org/roadmap/archives/2006/02/js_and_python_news.html

2 New in JavaScript 1.7, from the Firefox 2 documentation: http://developer.mozilla.org/en/docs/New_in_JavaScript_1.7

That's because MochiKit doesn't know how to represent our custom objects. Using the `registerRepr` function, which works much like the `registerComparator` function, we can create a more useful representation:

```
orderRepr = function(order) {
    return "new Order(" + repr(order.items) + ")";
}


registerRepr("Order", isOrder, orderRepr);
```

As in `registerComparator`, we need to tell `registerRepr` how to identify that it has an `Order` object. Lucky for us, we can use the exact same `isOrder` function that we had defined previously. Now, if you type `order1` in the interactive shell, you'll see this:

```
>>> order1
new Order(["Burger", "Fries"])
```

And that's a lot easier to look at than `[object Object]`.

Creating a decent `repr` for your objects is a common enough task that MochiKit also provides a nicer way to do it. `registerRepr` is great when you're working with an object that is outside of your control. For your own objects, however, it is a lot nicer to just add a method to the object itself. MochiKit lets you do just that. If you define a `repr` or `__repr__` method on your object, that method will be called for the representation.

Let's try it out that way. The first thing we need to do is remove the `repr` implementation that we just added:

```
>>> reprRegistry.unregister("Order");
true
>>> order1
[object Object]
```

Now, create a prototype that uses the `repr` function we created previously:

```
Order.prototype.repr = function() {
    return "new Order(" + repr(this.items) + ")";
}
```

Let's see if that works:

```
>>> order1
new Order(["burger", "fries"])
```

Indeed it does!

14.3.6   JSON Serialization

The JavaScript Object Notation (JSON) format was discussed earlier in Chapter 9, "Ajax and WhatWhat Status Projects." TurboGears includes `simplejson` in Python to do conversions to and from JSON on the server. MochiKit enables you to do similar conversions on the browser side.

Converting from JSON to JavaScript is easy because JSON is, by definition, valid JavaScript. MochiKit includes an `evalJSON` function that simply wraps the JSON in parenthesis and runs `eval` on it.

MochiKit also includes a companion `serializeJSON` function to take JavaScript values and turn them into valid JSON. Many values work just as you'd expect:

```
>>> serializeJSON(1)
"1"
>>> serializeJSON("Hello")
"\"Hello\""
>>> serializeJSON([1,2,3])
"[1, 2, 3]"
```

How about objects, such as our `order` example?

```
>>> serializeJSON(order2);
"{\"items\":[\"Cheesy Beefwich\", \"Fizzy Beverage\"]}"
```

For primitive types (undefined, Boolean, string, number, null), `serializeJSON` is quite straightforward. For anything else, it gets trickier. But, when you think about it, JSON is just like `repr` but with a strict definition of what the representation needs to look like. `serializeJSON`, therefore, works a lot like `repr`. Here are the exact rules it follows:

1. Primitives are converted directly into their JSON representation.
2. If the object has a __json__ or json method, that is called to get the JSON representation. The result of the call to your json method is run through the JSON processing again. So, you can return an array of strings and be assured that the proper JSON will come out at the end.
3. Anything with a length property that is a number is assumed to be an array, and that is how it will be serialized.
4. You can register a JSON "simplifier" with the registerJSON function, which works just like the registration functions from the previous sections.
5. Failing all of that, MochiKit will take the object's properties and serialize them (using these same rules) as name:value pairs wherever it can. Some things, such as methods, won't be serialized because they can't be handled by any of these rules.

When we called serializeJSON on our order2 object, the object failed all of the tests until it got to the fifth rule. So, we ended up with a name:value pair. This serialization is not bad, but maybe what we really want is for the order to just be serialized as a list of items. Based on the preceding rules, we can get that easily:

```
>>> Order.prototype.json = function() { return this.items; }
function () { return this.items; }
>>> serializeJSON(order2)
"[\"Cheesy Beefwich\", \"Fizzy Beverage\"]"
```

We can also try it by registering a simplifier:

```
>>> delete Order.prototype.json
true
>>> orderItems = function(order) { return order.items; }
function (order) { return order.items; }
>>> registerJSON("Order", isOrder, orderItems);
>>> serializeJSON(order2)
"[\"Cheesy Beefwich\", \"Fizzy Beverage\"]"
```

MochiKit's JSON support makes it quite easy to ensure that your objects look the way they need to look for transporting to other systems. After the object has been converted to JSON, you can easily convert it back to a JavaScript object using evalJSON().

14.3.7   Working with Arrays

Python has a number of handy functions for working with lists that JavaScript doesn't. Mo-chiKit helps out with functions that work on "array-like" objects. The `isArrayLike` function returns true if the object has a `typeof` "object" and the object has a length property.

In Python, the `map` and `filter` functions have largely been replaced by list compre-hensions, and there is talk of deprecating those functions at some point years in the future. JavaScript doesn't offer list comprehensions yet, however. The `map` and `filter` functions can be amazingly useful and provide concise ways to do common operations with arrays. Here's an example of these in use:

```
>>> mylist = [1,2,3,4,5,6,7,8,9]
[1, 2, 3, 4, 5, 6, 7, 8, 9]
>>> filter(function(a) { return a % 2 == 0 }, mylist)
[2, 4, 6, 8]
>>> map(function(a) { return a*2 }, mylist)
[2, 4, 6, 8, 10, 12, 14, 16, 18]
```

`map` and `filter` both take a function as the first argument and an array as the second argument. `map` creates a new list by running the function on each element of the array in turn. `filter` creates a new list containing only the elements for which the function returns true.

`Base` also includes `xmap` and `xfilter` functions that use the extra arguments as the "ar-ray" instead of passing in an array explicitly. Here's the same odd/even example from above rewritten with `xfilter`:

```
>>> xfilter(function(a) { return a % 2 == 0 }, 1, 2, 3, 4, 5, 6, 7, 8, 9)
[2, 4, 6, 8]
```

Using these functions that take a function as the first argument, it is sometimes handy to be able to use JavaScript operators as if they were functions. `Base` includes a table of JavaScript's operators called `operator`. The functions contained in `operator` are found in Table 14.1:

TABLE 14.1 JavaScript Operators

Unary Logic Operators		
Function Name	**Implementation**	**Description**
`truth(a)`	`!!a`	Logical truth
`lognot(a)`	`!a`	Logical not
`identity(a)`	`a`	Logical identity

Unary Math Operators

`not(a)`	`~a`	Bitwise not
`neg(a)`	`-a`	Negation

Binary Operators

`add(a, b)`	`a + b`	Addition
`sub(a, b)`	`a - b`	Subtraction
`div(a, b)`	`a / b`	Division
`mod(a, b)`	`a % b`	Modulus
`mul(a, b)`	`a * b`	Multiplication
`and(a, b)`	`a & b`	Bitwise and
`or(a, b)`	`a	b`	Bitwise or
`xor(a, b)`	`a ^ b`	Bitwise exclusive or
`lshift(a, b)`	`a << b`	Bitwise left shift
`rshift(a, b)`	`a >> b`	Bitwise signed right shift
`zrshfit(a, b)`	`a >>> b`	Bitwise unsigned right shift

Built-In Comparators

`eq(a, b)`	`a == b`	Equals
`ne(a, b)`	`a != b`	Not equal
`gt(a, b)`	`a > b`	Greater than
`ge(a, b)`	`a >= b`	Greater than or equal to
`lt(a, b)`	`a < b`	Less than
`le(a, b)`	`a <= b`	Less than or equal to

Extended Comparators (Uses `compare`)

`ceq(a, b)`	`compare(a, b) == 0`	Equals
`cne(a, b)`	`compare(a, b) != 0`	Not equal
`cgt(a, b)`	`compare(a, b) == 1`	Greater than
`cge(a, b)`	`compare(a, b) != -1`	Greater than or equal to
`clt(a, b)`	`compare(a, b) == -1`	Less than
`cle(a, b)`	`compare(a, b) != 1`	Less than or equal to

Binary Logical Operators

`logand(a, b)`	`a && b`	Logical and
`logor(a, b)`	`a || b`	Logical or
`contains(a, b)`	`b in a`	Has property (note order)

The following functions are also included:

- `arrayEqual(a1, a2)`   Compares two arrays to see whether they're equal
- `concat(a1, a2, ...)`   Concatenates all of the array-like objects into a new array
- `extend(self, obj, skip=0)`   Adds elements from `obj` to `self`
- `findValue(lst, value, start=0, end=lst.length)`   Returns the index for the value in the list, using `compare()`
- `findIdentical(lst, value, start=0, end=lst.length)`   Returns the index for the value in the list, using `===`
- `flattenArguments(a1, a2, ...)`   Extends array-like arguments in place and returns a single, flat array
- `flattenArray(lst)`   Returns a new single-level array with all the elements of the arrays contained within `lst`
- `listMax(lst)`   Returns the largest element of the list
- `listMin(lst)`   Returns the smallest element of the list
- `listMinMax(which, lst)`   `which==1` is equivalent to `listMax`, `which==-1` is equivalent to `listMin`

14.3.8   Pythonic Version of `this`

In both Python and JavaScript, it's easy to pass around functions for use in other contexts. In Python, it's also easy to pass around a method that is bound to a specific object. Consider this example:

```
>>> class Pizza(object):
...     def _init_(self, toppings):
...         self.toppings = toppings
...
...     def eat(self):
...         print "You just ate a pizza with %s" % self.toppings
...
>>> def get_pepperoni_eater():
...     pizza = Pizza("pepperoni")
...     return pizza.eat
...
>>> func = get_pepperoni_eater()
>>> func()
You just ate a pizza with pepperoni
```

The get_pepperoni_eater function returns the eat method bound to the pizza object that was created.

We can do something similar in JavaScript, too, but you might notice that JavaScript is not quite like Python when it comes to methods. For example, try this in MochiKit's interactive interpreter:

```
Pizza = function (toppings) { this.toppings = toppings; }
Pizza.prototype = { 'eat' : function() {
                writeln("You just ate a pizza with " + this.toppings);
           } }
pizza = new Pizza("pepperoni");
pizza.eat();
[ You just ate a pizza with pepperoni ]
pizza2 = new Pizza("sausage");
pizza2.eat();
[ You just ate a pizza with sausage ]
func = pizza.eat;
func();
[ You just ate a pizza with undefined ]
func = pizza2.eat;
func();
[ You just ate a pizza with undefined ]
```

That last line *should* have said, "You just ate a pizza with sausage." That is, it should have said that *if we were using Python*. This is JavaScript, however. MochiKit provides functions to make this behave more like we're used to self behaving in Python:

```
func = bind(pizza2.eat, pizza2);
func()
[ You just ate a pizza with sausage ]
```

The bind function takes a function and an object and returns a new function that ensures that this is referring to that object. In the preceding example, we're certain that this will point to pizza2.

Of course, calling bind on every method would be a pain, so MochiKit includes a bindMethods function. Let's make a one-line change to the preceding example to see that this is bound properly:

```
Pizza = function (toppings) {
    this.toppings = toppings;
    bindMethods(this);
```

```
}
Pizza.prototype = { 'eat' : function() {
            writeln("You just ate a pizza with " + this.toppings);
        } }
pizza = new Pizza("pepperoni");
pizza.eat();
[ You just ate a pizza with pepperoni ]
pizza2 = new Pizza("sausage");
pizza2.eat();
[ You just ate a pizza with sausage ]
func = pizza.eat;
func();
[ You just ate a pizza with pepperoni ]
func = pizza2.eat;
func();
[ You just ate a pizza with sausage ]
```

`Base` also includes a function called `method` that is equivalent to `bind`, but the arguments are reversed.

14.3.9   Help with Calling Functions

`Base` also includes functions to help out with calling other functions a certain way when the time comes. For example, it's not uncommon for a function that you call to need a callback. Sometimes, those callbacks are required to take a certain number of arguments (often zero). You can use `partial` to fill in any arguments at the time the function is called:

```
partialmap = partial(xmap, function(a) { return a* 2 }, 0, 1, 2, 3);
partialmap();
[ [0, 2, 4, 6] ]
partialmap(4);
[ [0, 2, 4, 6, 8] ]
```

`partial` creates a new function that "bakes in" some arguments and then passes in any additional arguments that are passed in to the partial when it is called.

- `compose(f1, f2, ...)`   Creates a new function that is equivalent to `f1(f2(...))`
- `forwardCall(name)`   Returns a function that makes a method call to `this.name(...)`
- `methodCaller(name)`   Returns a function that calls the method `name` on its argument

14.3.10   Dictionary-Like Objects

In JavaScript, all objects act like dictionary or mapping objects. This example high-lights this:

```
>>> foo = new Object();
[object Object]
>>> foo.bar = "Hi";
"Hi"
>>> foo["bar"]
"Hi"
```

There is an exception to this dictionary-like behavior. Python dictionaries can have any object as keys. JavaScript objects coerce the keys to strings, which would almost certainly lead to behavior other than what you're looking for.

The ability to treat any object like a dictionary is handy, but JavaScript objects don't have some of the methods we have on Python dictionaries. `MochiKit.Base` provides `items(obj)` and `keys(obj)` to fill in some of the gaps.

Other functions for providing dictionary-like behavior to JavaScript objects include:

- `itemgetter(name)`   Returns a `function(obj)` that returns `obj[name]`
- `merge(obj[, ...])`   Creates a new object with every property from the given objects
- `setdefault(self, obj)`   Mutates `self` (and returns it), setting all properties from `obj` that are not already set on `self`
- `update(self, obj)`   Updates all the properties on self to match those in `obj`
- `updatetree(self, obj)`   Like `update` but will also recursively update where there is an object value in both `self` and `obj`

14.3.11   Working with Query Strings

Something that comes up fairly often in working on web pages is creating query strings for URLs or parsing a query string that you have in hand. `MochiKit.Base` provides a pair of functions that help out with this.

`parseQueryString(str, useArrays=false)` takes an encoded string and returns an ob-ject with either the values as strings or the values as lists. A couple of examples will make this clear:

```
>>> isp_info = parseQueryString("name=Hosty%20Most&city=South%20Barton")
[object Object]
>>> isp_info.name
"Hosty Most"
>>> isp_info.city
"South Barton"
```

In this example, you can see a URL encoded query string get converted into a convenient object. It's possible to also have multiple values for each parameter that is coming in, in which case you'll need arrays rather than individual values. Here's an example of this usage:

```
>>> isps = parseQueryString("name=Hosty%20Most&name=SBISP&name=BartonOnline",
true);
[object Object]
>>> isps.name
["Hosty Most", "SBISP", "BartonOnline"]
```

The flip side of parsing an existing query string is generating one. You can use the querystring function to generate query strings in a few different ways. Here is the inverse of the previous example:

```
>>> queryString(["name", "name", "name"], ["Hosty Most", "SBISP", "BartonOn-
line"]);
"name=Hosty%20Most&name=SBISP&name=BartonOnline"
```

In this form, queryString takes a list of parameter names and a matching list of parameter values. Note that queryString handles URL encoding for you.

If your page has a form on it, you can easily turn the form's values into a query string. You just pass the ID of the form DOM node as the only parameter to queryString.

Finally, you can pass an object (that is not a string or a DOM node) in to queryString:

```
>>> queryString({"name" : "Hosty Most", "city": "South Barton"})
"name=Hosty%20Most&city=South%20Barton"
```

One more function to help you with your URLs is urlEncode(un-encoded), which converts the unencoded string to a properly URL-encoded string.

14.3.12   Functions in `MochiKit.Base`

`MochiKit.Base` is also the home to other utility functions that don't more properly belong in a different module.

- `camelize(str)`   Converts a hyphenated string to `camelCase`
- `clone(obj)`   Returns a shallow clone of an object
- `counter(n=1)`   Returns a number that is one greater than the previous value, starting at `n`
- `isDateLike(obj[, ...])`   Returns true if all of the objects passed in have a `.getTime` method
- `isEmpty(obj[, ...])`   Returns true if `obj.length==0` for all objects passed in
- `isNotEmpty(obj[, ...])`   Returns true if `obj.length > 0` for all objects passed in
- `isNull(obj[, ...])`   Returns true if all arguments are null
- `isUndefinedOrNull(obj[, ...])`   Returns true if all arguments are undefined or null
- `keyComparator(key`   Returns a function that compares `a[key]` with `b[key]`, which is useful for sorting (see also `reverseKeyComparator`)
- `nameFunctions(namespace)`   Adds a `NAME` property to all the methods of namespace, based on the `NAME` property in namespace itself
- `noop()`   Equivalent to `function() {}`, which is sometimes used to avoid memory leaks in IE
- `nodeWalk(node, visitor)`   Nonrecursive breadth-first node walking function (the visitor returns a list of nodes to walk next)
- `reverseKeyComparator(key)`   Returns a function that compares `b[key]` with `a[key]` (the reverse order of `keyComparator`)
- `typeMatcher(typ[, ...])`   Returns a `function(obj[, ...])` that returns true if each object matches one of the types (listed as strings) passed in to `typeMatcher`

14.4   Iterators in JavaScript

Python's iteration protocol is very useful. It makes it possible to easily handle large data sets that get reduced down to results of a reasonable size. In addition, the `itertools` module provides a number of extremely convenient functions. If you haven't checked out `itertools` in Python, you definitely should.

Or, you can play around with MochiKit.Iter's extensive implementation of the same functions. To use iteration tools, however, you need to have iterators.

Just as in Python, an iterator in JavaScript will define a next() method that will throw a StopIteration exception when it is done processing. An iterable object will either define an iter() method or use registerIteratorFactory to tell MochiKit how to get an iterator for specific kinds of objects. MochiKit.Iter itself uses registerIterator-Factory to allow JavaScript arrays to participate in the iteration protocol.

For your own JavaScript code, you will likely just define iter on your prototype to return an iterator for your code. registerIteratorFactory is handy when you're trying to iterate over an object that is not directly in your control.

14.4.1   Making an Iterator

Here is a simple example that lets you iterate over the parameters in a query string:

```
queryObj = function(queryString) {
    this.qs = queryString;
}

queryObj.prototype = {
    "iter" : function() {
        return new queryIter(this.qs);
    }
}

queryIter = function(queryString) {
    this.items = queryString.split("&");
    this.current = 0;
}

queryIter.prototype = {
    "next" : function() {
        if (this.current == this.items.length) {
            throw StopIteration();
        }
        value = this.items[this.current++].split("=");
        value[0] = unescape(value[0]);
        value[1] = unescape(value[1]);
        return value;
    }
}
```

*Calling **iter(obj)** will call this function*

*When we've returned every item from the list, throw **StopIteration** to make it known*

Each item returned will be an array with 2 values: name and value of the parameter

Let's take a look at this in use:

```
>>> qs = new queryObj("name=Hosty%20Most&city=South%20Barton");
[object Object]
>>> i = iter(qs)
[object Object]
>>> i.next()
["name", "Hosty Most"]
>>> i.next()
["city", "South Barton"]
```

This is similar to how you define and use iterators in Python.

14.4.2   Functions from Itertools

MochiKit has faithful reproductions of all your favorites from Python's itertools.

The `groupby` function takes an iterable and a key function and returns an iterable where each item that comes out is a pair: the key, and an iterator for the values that match that key. The items are assumed to be sorted on that key in advance.

Here is an example that exercises `groupby`:

```
numbers = [2, 4, 6, 8, 10, 1, 3, 5, 7, 9];
i = groupby(numbers, function(val) {
    if (val % 2 == 0) {
        return "even";
    } else {
        return "odd";
    }
});
try {
    while (info = i.next()) {
        writeln("Group: " + info[0]);
        j = info[1];
        try {
            while (num = j.next()) {
                writeln(num);
            }
        } catch (e) {
            if (e != StopIteration) {
                throw e;
            }
        }
    }
```

```
    }
} catch (e) {
    if (e != StopIteration) {
        throw e;
    }
}
```

Here is the output you see when you run this in the interactive interpreter:

```
Group: even
2
4
6
8
10
Group: odd
1
3
5
7
9
```

MochiKit also has a version of this that is not found in itertools. `groupby_as_array` will return an array of arrays rather than an iterator of iterators.

Something that is found in Python, but not itertools specifically, is the `list` function. `MochiKit.Iter` implements this function for JavaScript. It returns a list (array) from an iterator.

Another function that is a Python built-in but is found in `MochiKit.Iter` is `reduce(func, i[, initial])`. `reduce` returns a single value by calling `func` with either the last returned value or the initial value and `i.next()`. This makes it easy to compute a result based on a lot of data that you iterate over.

The following functions are ones that `MochiKit.Iter` offers that are also in Python's itertools module or Python built-ins. These functions all return iterators, and the return values mentioned are what those iterators will return:

- `chain(i1, i2, ...)`   Returns elements from `i1`, then the elements from `i2`, and so on
- `count(n=0)`   Iterates incrementally starting at `n`
- `cycle(i)`   Saves each element returned and starts over from the beginning once `i` is exhausted

- `dropwhile(func, i)`   Starts returning elements from `i` once `func(i.next())` returns false
- `ifilter(func, i)`   Returns only the elements where `func(i.next())` is true
- `ifilterfalse(func, i)`   Returns only the elements where `func(i.next())` is false
- `imap(func, i1[, i2, ...])`   Returns `func(i1.next(), i2.next(), ...)`
- `islice(i, [start,] stop[, step])`   Returns the elements that fall within the slice (just as in Python's `[start:stop:step]` notation)
- `izip(i1[, i2, i3, ...])`   Like `zip`, aggregates the elements from each of the iterators
- `range([start,] stop[, step])`   Like `count`, but it returns a range of numbers
- `repeat(obj[, n])`   Keeps returning `obj`, or returns `obj` `n` times
- `reversed(i)`   Returns a reversed list from `i`
- `sorted(i[, cmp])`   Returns a sorted array from iterable, using the `cmp` function for comparison if provided
- `sum(i, start=0)`   Returns the sum of the elements starting at `start`
- `takewhile(func, i)`   Returns the elements from `i` while `func(i.next())` is true
- `tee(i, n=2)`   Splits `i` into `n` iterators that you can use independently (don't use the original after you call `tee`, however)

14.4.3   Functions Unique to `MochiKit.Iter`

As useful as Python's itertools module is, `MochiKit.Iter` adds some other functions, too.

- `applymap(func, seq[, self])`   Calls `func` with each element of `seq` (in the context of `self`, if supplied), returning a list of the return values from the calls to `func`
- `every(i, func)`   Returns true if `func(i.next())` is true for each item in the iterator
- `exhaust(i)`   Use up the iterable without saving the results anywhere
- `forEach(i, func[, self])`   Call `func` for each element of `i` without saving the return values
- `iextend(lst, i)`   Adds the elements from `i` to `lst`
- `some(i, func)`   Returns true if `func(i.next())` is true for at least one item

14.5 The Document Object Model

Web browsers maintain the state of the page that you're viewing in something called the Document Object Model (DOM). The DOM is such an important part of how browsers operate and are scripted that it is specified in an actual World Wide Web Consortium (W3C) standard.

Unfortunately, the DOM is not always easy to work with and, despite it being a standard, you're not always going to get the behavior you want when moving between browsers. The `MochiKit.DOM` and `MochiKit.Style` modules will help you deal with unruly DOMs.

As with the rest of JavaScript, plenty can be written about the DOM. This section focuses on working with the DOM using MochiKit, which is a far more pleasant experience than using the functions you get with the browser.

14.5.1 Retrieving Elements

Here's a simple example: One of the most common things you'll want to do is grab a specific element (sometimes called a node) from the document and do something to it. You'll typically do this by setting an `id` attribute on the node and then calling `document.getElementById(id_to_find)`. That wouldn't be so bad, except for the fact that you use that *all the time*.

MochiKit replaces that common idiom with the much simpler `getElement(id_to_find)` or, if you want to really reduce typing, `$(id_to_find)`. Even better, however, is that just about any function that takes a DOM node can take either a DOM node *or* a string with the ID of the node. In many cases, you won't need to use `getElement()` or `$()`!

Then MochiKit builds on even higher-level constructs such as: `getElementsByTag-AndClassName(tagName, className, parent=document)`. In one call, this hunts down all the elements that match the tag or CSS class you specify. You can pass in null for tag if you only care about the class and vice versa. This function can come in handy often and replaces more than just a few characters of work.

14.5.2 Working with Style

As you sit at your computer, wearing a tuxedo (or evening gown, as the case may be), sipping a martini, you may think to yourself, "Now I'm working with style." However, because this is a programming book, this section is not about fashion. It's about manipulating the styles that are applied to the objects in your web pages.

The most basic bit of style that you can apply to a DOM element is whether that element is visible. No need to worry about fonts if the user can't even see the element, right?

There are times when you need to hide an element and display it again when the user performs some action. This is common in web applications, and it's easy to do with MochiKit. hideElement(el[, e2, ...]) and showElement(el[, e2, ...]) toggle the display style of an element. As mentioned in the previous section, you can pass an element object in or pass in the ID of the element you want to change. Note, however, that these functions require that the element in question uses the "block" display style. showElement simply sets display: block on the element, so if it didn't start off with that display style, it will end up with it!

The MochiKit.style documentation provides another solution that works reliably in all cases:

```
<style type="text/css">
    .invisible { display: none; }
</style>

<script type="text/javascript">
    function toggleVisible(elem) {
        toggleElementClass("invisible", elem);
    }

    function makeVisible(elem) {
        removeElementClass(elem, "invisible");
    }

    function makeInvisible(elem) {
        addElementClass(elem, "invisible");
    }

    function isVisible(elem) {
        // you may also want to check for
        // getElement(elem).style.display == "none"
        return !hasElementClass(elem, "invisible");
    };
</script>
```

This solution requires the use of CSS, which is why MochiKit doesn't include these functions directly. Current browsers don't provide a reliable, portable mechanism for adding CSS rules to the document.

The four simple functions above introduce four more MochiKit functions: addElementClass, removeElementClass, toggleElementClass, and hasElementClass. These are used for setting and inspecting the CSS classes of an element. These functions might seem style related, but they are really just manipulating the DOM. With functions such as these, you don't need to remember exactly how objects in the DOM are set up, and it's easy to alter the appearance of an element as the page dynamics require. One other function that's available but not used here is swapElementClass(element, fromClass, toClass). If fromClass is set on element, it will be replaced with toClass.

If you want to get more granular in what you're looking up about an element, MochiKit has a function for getting one specific style property from an element: computedStyle(element, cssSelector). computedStyle('foo', 'font-size') will find out the current font size of the element with the ID of foo.

MochiKit.Style includes two object prototypes: Dimensions and Coordinates. Dimensions includes w and h attributes for the width and height, and Coordinates includes x and y attributes to represent the position of an element.

getElementDimensions(element) returns a Dimensions object with the inner width and height of an element, and setElementDimensions(element, dimensions, units='px') is used to set them. The default for units is px, but you can use any legal values from CSS (in, cm, and so on). You'll need to add in the padding, border, and margin to get the total amount of page space that is occupied by the element. As of this writing, there isn't a function to get that total value for you, but there may be by the time you read this.

getElementPosition(element[, relativeTo={'x':0, 'y':0}]) returns the absolute pixel position of the given element. relativeTo can be an element (or element ID) or a Coordinates object.

Here is a simple demo page to allow you to see these functions in action:

```
<!DOCTYPE html PUBLIC "-//W3C//DTD XHTML 1.0 Transitional//EN" "http://www.
w3.org/TR/xhtml1/DTD/xhtml1-transitional.dtd">
<html xmlns="http://www.w3.org/1999/xhtml" xmlns:py="http://purl.org/kid/ns#"
    py:extends="'master.kid'">

<head>
    <meta content="text/html; charset=UTF-8" http-equiv="content-type" py:
replace="'''"/>
    <title>MochiKit Examples</title>
    <style type="text/css">
        #thetestelem { border: 1px solid black; padding: 1em;
            background: lightblue; width: 8em;
```

```
                position: absolute;
                left: 350px; top: 50px;}
        .status { text-align: center; float: right;
                border: 1px dotted red;
                background: #cccccc; padding: 1em;}
    </style>
    <script src="static/javascript/style.js"/>

</head>

<body>
    <div class="status">Dimensions<br/>
        <span id="dimensions"></span><br/>
        Coordinates<br/>
        <span id="coordinates"></span>
    </div>

    <h1>MochiKit.Style Demo</h1>

    <p>View [<a href="${tg.url('/source', file='templates/style.kid')}" tar-
get="_blank">Kid source</a> | <a href="${tg.url('/source', file='static/javas-
cript/style.js')}" target="_blank">JavaScript source</a>]</p>

    <!-- This is our guinea testelem element -->
    <div id="thetestelem">This is the element we're going to manipulate.</div>

    <p><input id="hidebutton" type="button" value="Hide Element" onclick="hide
➥ TheTestElem()"/></p>

    <table>
        <tr>
            <td>Width</td><td><input type="text" id="width" size="4"/></td>
            <td rowspan="2"><input type="button" value="Set Dimensions"
                    onclick="setTestElemDimensions()"/></td>
        </tr>
        <tr>
            <td>Height</td><td><input type="text" id="height" size="4"/></td>
        </tr>
        <tr>
            <td>X</td><td><input type="text" id="x" size="4"/></td>
            <td rowspan="2">
                <input type="button" value="Set Position" onclick="setTestElem
➥Position()"/>
            </td>
        </tr>
```

```
<tr>
    <td>Y</td><td><input type="text" id="y" size="4"/></td>
</tr>
<tr><td>Opacity (0-1)</td>
    <td><input type="text" id="opacity" size="4" value="1"/></td>
    <td><input type="button" value="Set Opacity" onclick="setTestElemO
pacity()"/></td>
</tr>

<tr>
    <td><span id="testelemstyle"></span></td>
    <td>CSS property<br/>
        <input type="text" id="testelemprop" value="font-size"/>
    </td>
    <td><input type="button" value="Get Computed Style"
        onclick="getTestElemStyle()"/>
    </td>
</tr>
</table>

<script type="text/javascript">updateStatus();</script>
</body>
</html>
```

Figure 14.1 is a screenshot of this HTML page.

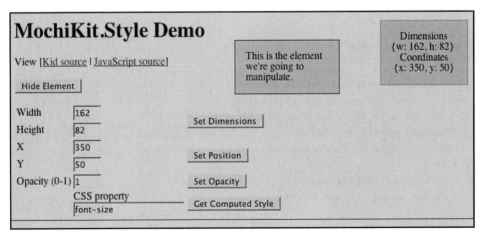

FIGURE 14.1 MochiKit.Style Demo

This page is a Kid template that is available with the code samples from this book and is part of the "mochiexamples" project. It can be used standalone by adding a script tag pointing to MochiKit.js in the <HEAD> section. The page provides a number of controls for manipulating a <DIV> element that is displayed, and it also shows a status display with the current coordinates and size of the element.

The page itself isn't where the MochiKit use shows up, however. We see that in the JavaScript:

```javascript
// getElementDimensions, getElementPosition
function updateStatus() {
    var e = getElement("thetestelem");

    var dim = getElementDimensions(e);
    var pos = getElementPosition(e);

    getElement("dimensions").innerHTML = repr(dim);
    getElement("coordinates").innerHTML = repr(pos);

    getElement("width").value = dim.w;
    getElement("height").value = dim.h;

    getElement("x").value = pos.x;
    getElement("y").value = pos.y;
}


// showElement and hideElement
function hideTheTestElem() {
    // Toggles our guinea testelem element
    var button = getElement("hidebutton");
    if (button.value == "Hide Element") {
        hideElement("thetestelem");
        button.value = "Show Element";
    } else {
        showElement("thetestelem");
        button.value = "Hide Element";
    }
    updateStatus();
}


// setElementDimensions
```

```
function setTestElemDimensions() {
    var e = getElement("thetestelem");
    var dim = new Dimensions(getElement("width").value,
                             getElement("height").value);
    setElementDimensions(e, dim);
    updateStatus();
}


// setElementPosition
function setTestElemPosition() {
    var e = getElement("thetestelem");
    var pos = new Coordinates(getElement("x").value,
                              getElement("y").value);
    setElementPosition(e, pos);
    updateStatus();
}


// setOpacity
function setTestElemOpacity() {
    setOpacity("thetestelem", getElement("opacity").value);
}


// computedStyle
function getTestElemStyle() {
    var prop = getElement("testelemprop").value;
    var style = computedStyle("thetestelem", prop);
    getElement("testelemstyle").innerHTML = style;
}
```

As you can see from the preceding example, it doesn't take much code to manipulate elements using `MochiKit.Style`'s functions.

Other functions available for working with DOM object styles are as follows:

- `setOpacity(element, opacity)`   Sets the opacity of an element (ranging from `0=invisible` to `1=opaque`)
- `setDisplayForElement(display, element[, ...])`   Typically called by `showElement` or `hideElement`
- `getViewportDimensions()`   Returns the width and height of the viewport as a `Style.Dimensions` object

14.5.3   Creating DOM Nodes

MochiKit.dom makes it easy to create new DOM nodes. One use of this is to make an Ajax request for some information that comes back in JSON format and then format the result completely within the browser. Doing this kind of formatting by creating DOM nodes without MochiKit would be painful indeed. With MochiKit, however, it's easy and very readable.

Dynamically creating DOM nodes for new content seems like a clean way to update the page, and it is. However, it's not the best performing way to do it. Setting innerHTML on a DOM node performs better than creating a bunch of nodes in Java-Script and attaching them to that node. If you are displaying a lot of information, you might want to use innerHTML.

That said, when you *are* working with a relatively small set of information, MochiKit. dom really helps out. Let's start with an example that you can run in the interpreter:

```
>>> writeln(DIV({"id" : "empty"}));
>>> row_display = function(num) {
    return TR(null, TD(null, num));
}
>>> new_contents = TABLE({"width" : "100"},
    TBODY(null, map(row_display, range(10))));
>>> replaceChildNodes("empty", new_contents);
```

When you go through these commands, you start off with an empty <DIV> that magically gets filled with a table of numbers at the end. There's a lot going on in this sample, so let's break it down:

```
>>> writeln(DIV({"id" : "empty"}));
```

writeln() is used to write to the interpreter window. It is able to write strings, but it is also able to write out new DOM nodes.

And that's exactly, what's happening. The DIV() function comes from MochiKit. dom. You probably won't be surprised to learn that it creates a new <div> element. The parameter we're passing in is a mapping of attributes. In this case, we're setting the id attribute to "empty."

```
>>> row_display = function(num) {
    return TR(null, TD(null, num));
}
```

This line creates a function that takes in a number, or anything for that matter, and puts it into a table row with a single table data cell. MochiKit provides functions for all the HTML DOM nodes you're likely to create. Note how the calls to `TR()` and `TD()` have `null` for the first parameter. That means that there are no attributes needed for those nodes.

The call to `TD()` has an additional parameter of `num`. All these functions that create DOM nodes have a signature like this: `TAG(attributes[, childNode1, childNode2, ...])`. In this case, we're passing `num` as a child node. That will just become the text of the table cell. Note also that the `<td>` that is created is a child node of the `<tr>`. This is easy and concise syntax for building up a tree of output.

`TD()` and the others are all partially applied forms of `createDOM(tag[, attrs[, node, ...]])`. If you find that there is a tag that you need that MochiKit hasn't covered, you can make the function yourself using `partial`. Or, it turns out, you can use the convenience function `createDOMFunc(tag[, attrs[, node, ...]])` to do that for you.

MochiKit will generally just do the right thing with the objects you throw at it when creating DOM nodes. Sometimes, however, you need to customize the behavior, and there are several ways to do that. Here are the rules that MochiKit uses when setting up the elements:

1. Functions are called with a `this` and first argument of the parent node and their return value is subject to the following rules (even this one).

2. `undefined` and `null` are ignored.

3. If `:mochiref:MochiKit.Iter` is loaded, iterables are flattened (as if they were passed in-line as nodes), and each return value is subject to these rules.

4. Values that look like DOM nodes (objects with a `.nodeType > 0`) are `.appendChild`'ed to the created DOM fragment.

5. Strings are wrapped up with `document.createTextNode`.

6. Objects that have a `.dom(node)` or `._dom_(node)` method are called with the parent node, and their result is coerced using these rules.

7. Objects that are not strings are run through the `domConverters:mochiref:MochiKit.Base.AdapterRegistry` (see:mochiref:`registerDOMConverter`). The adapted value is subject to these same rules. (For example, if the adapter returns a string, it will be coerced to a text node.)

8. If no adapter is available, `.toString()` is used to create a text node.

So, we created a function. Now we should use it somewhere:

```
>>> new_contents = TABLE({"width" : "100"},
    TBODY(null, map(row_display, range(10))));
```

By now, you can probably guess that this gives us a `<table>`. Note the use of TBODY(). Internet Explorer requires a `<tbody>` element when you're creating DOM nodes.

Then, we use the `map()` function described earlier in the chapter to call our `row_display` function for each number from 0 to 9.

With that, we have built our table of DOM nodes. But, we still need to display it:

```
>>> replaceChildNodes("empty", new_contents);
```

We introduce a new function now, `replaceChildNodes(element, childnode1 [, childnode2, ...])`. This call replaces everything inside of the `<div>` that we had created with the `id` of "empty," plugging our `new_contents` table in there.

Along those same lines, there is `appendChildNodes(element, childnode1[, childnode2, ...])`, which adds additional child nodes instead of replacing all of them.

14.5.4   Simple Events

MochiKit provides a complete and powerful event handling system in the MochiKit.Signal module. It also provides a few functions that you can use for simple, but common, event needs. Note, however, that the functions here are not compatible with MochiKit. Signal. When you start using signal, you'll need to switch over entirely. These functions predate signal and might not even exist had signal been there.

MochiKit provides three functions for simple event handling: addLoadEvent, focusOnLoad, and addToCallStack. These functions are easy to use, but their use is highly discouraged for new applications, given the superiority of the signal module. Rather than using addLoadEvent to take care of tasks when the page is done loading, you should use connect(window, "onload", <your function>). Check out Chapter 15 for more information about MochiKit.Signal.

14.5.5   Other DOM Functions

MochiKit provides the following useful additional functions for working with the DOM. These functions are straightforward to use and are not covered elsewhere in this chapter.

- `currentDocument()`   Returns the `document` object unless `withDocument` or `withWindow` is executing
- `currentWindow()`   Returns the `window` object unless `withWindow` is executing
- `escapeHTML(s)`   Make a string safe for inclusion in HTML
- `formContents(element)`   Returns a two-element array of names and values for every subelement of element that has `name` and `value` attributes
- `getNodeAttribute(node, attr)`   Gets the value of the given attribute for a DOM node, returning null if there's no match
- `removeElement(node)`   Removes and returns node from a DOM tree
- `scrapeText(node, asArray=false)`   Pulls out all the text from underneath the DOM node
- `setNodeAttribute(node, attr, value)`   Sets the value of a given attribute for a DOM node without raising exceptions
- `swapDOM(dest, src)`   Replaces `dest` with `src`, returning `src`
- `toHTML(node)`   Converts a DOM tree to an HTML string
- `updateNodeAttributes(node, attrs)`   Updates a hash of attributes on the node, with special support for IE names (see full MochiKit doc for details)
  - `withWindow(win, func)`   Calls `func` with the `window` variable set to `win`
  - `withDocument(doc, func)`   Calls `func` with the `document` variable set to `doc`

14.6 Using `MochiKit.Logging` to Debug

At this time, Firefox is the best web browser when it comes to debugging your JavaScript. Tools such as FireBug, the Web Developer extension, and the Venkman debugger provide many tools for tracking down problems with your JavaScript. But, odds are that you don't live in a Firefox-only world. Internet Explorer is still the dominant web browser, and a sizable percentage of Mac users use Safari. The cross-platform Opera browser also has a respectable following.

With all of these browsers to deal with, what is the tool that JavaScript programmers turn to? Generally, that tool is `alert(message)`. It's guaranteed to be available everywhere, but it's really annoying. Heaven forbid that you'd accidentally leave an `alert` call in your code, because that's always a sure way to drive customers away.

`MochiKit.Logging` provides a much more convenient way to add debugging instrumentation to your code. If you've used Python's logging module, you'll feel right at home with `MochiKit.Logging`. Even if you haven't, it's easy to use and ties in nicely with your browser's own native features.

14.6.1   Using Logging

The simplest way to use logging is with the `log(msg[, obj, ...])`. If you call `log("Hi there!")`, a logging message will appear.

You might be wondering *where* it will appear, particularly if you try that in the interactive interpreter and don't see any output. By default, it will appear in your browser's native console. Safari and Opera 9 both have the notion of a console they can print to. Firefox with the FireBug extension does, too. With Internet Explorer, `MochiKit.Logging` will interact with the Microsoft Script Debugger and the Atlas framework.

There is also a cross-browser way to view the logging output. You can add a bookmarklet that points to `javascript:MochiKit.Logging.logger.debuggingBookmarklet()`. Clicking that bookmarklet will display the logging output. The current version of MochiKit displays the log output in an alert box by default, but at least you only get one alert box instead of many.

MochiKit also includes a much nicer view of log messages that even includes filtering. By calling `createLoggingPane(inline)`, you'll get a DOM node for this nicer view that you can then put in a pop-up window or wherever you want. If you call that function with `inline=true`, you don't need to worry about where to put it: MochiKit automatically places the node at the bottom of your document.

Figure 14.2 at the end of this section is a screenshot that includes the logging pane.

14.6.2   Extended Logging

If you've used Python's logging module at all, you'd probably guess that there's more to `MochiKit.Logging` than just a `log` function. There is, indeed. For a great many applications, `log` (and some way to view the output) is all you need.

`MochiKit.Logging` supports different log levels, much like Python's logging module. There are five logging levels defined: DEBUG, INFO, WARNING, ERROR, and FATAL. You can call a `log<LEVEL>(msg)` function, such as `logDebug(msg)`, to log a message at a given level.

Logging levels can be helpful for visually identifying different kinds of messages as you're skimming the log output. But, they become most useful when combined with a listener that does something special.

A simple example is to display an alert if there is an ERROR or FATAL level log message. This can be done using built-in parts of MochiKit:

```
log.addListener("error_alert", "ERROR", alertListener);
logError("This will appear in an alert box");
```

Writing your own listener is easy enough: It's just a function. Listener functions take a single parameter: a `LogMessage` object that has `num`, `level`, `info`, and `timestamp` properties. `num` is a unique number identifying the message, `level` is the logging level for the message. `info` is an array of all the parameters passed to the `log` function. `timestamp` is a `Date` object reflecting when the message was logged.

With your own listener, and some of the techniques presented later in this chapter, you could save ERROR or FATAL log information on your server via Ajax, conveniently giving your app a built-in bug-reporting feature.

> **Note:** There are some other methods available on the logger object and some configuration flexibility such as the number of messages stored. These types of things are not commonly used, but you should consult the `MochiKit.Logging` documentation if you find that the module provides almost, but not quite, what you need for your application.

14.6.3   Simple Logging Demo

In this section, we show off a demo of `MochiKit.Logging`. With the demo page, pictured in Figure 14.2, you can enter a logging message with a log level and see the message appear in MochiKit's logging pane at the bottom of the screen.

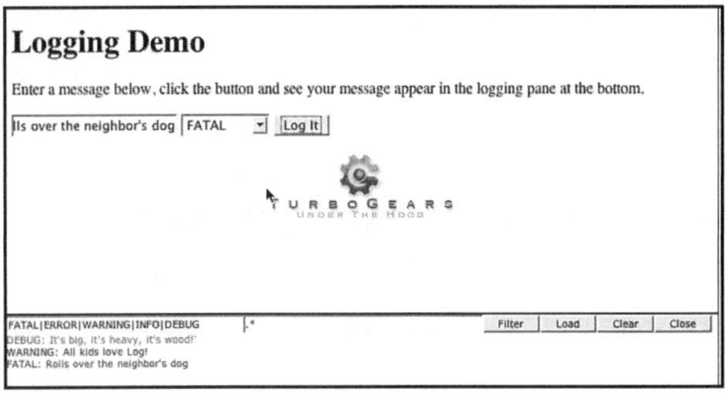

FIGURE 14.2 Logging Demo

Here is the code for the logging demo:

```
<!DOCTYPE html PUBLIC "-//W3C//DTD XHTML 1.0 Transitional//EN" "http://www.
w3.org/TR/xhtml1/DTD/xhtml1-transitional.dtd">


<html xmlns="http://www.w3.org/1999/xhtml" xmlns:py="http://purl.org/kid/ns#"
    py:extends="'master.kid'">


<head>
    <meta content="text/html; charset=UTF-8" http-equiv="content-type" py:
replace="''"/>
    <title>MochiKit Logging Example</title>


    <script type="text/javascript">
        function logUserMessage() {
            var msg = getElement("msg").value;
            var level = getElement("level").value
            // (1)
            logger.baseLog(level, msg);
        }
    </script>
</head>


<body>
    <h1>Logging Demo</h1>


    <p>Enter a message below, click the button and see your message appear in
the logging pane at the bottom.</p>


    <div>
        <input type="text" id="msg" value="It's big, it's heavy, it's
wood!'"/>
        <select id="level">
            <option>DEBUG</option>
            <option>INFO</option>
            <option>WARNING</option>
            <option>ERROR</option>
            <option>FATAL</option>
        </select>
        <input type="button" value="Log It" onclick="logUserMessage()"/>
    </div>


    <script type="text/javascript">
        // (2)
```

The baseLog method of a logger makes it easy to pass in a log level that was not known in advance. Usually you know what level you want to log something at.

```
            createLoggingPane(true);
        </script>
    </body>
    </html>
```

This one function call provides the nifty, filterable logging pane.

14.7   Working with Color

Color seems straightforward enough. You look up, and the sky is blue. You see a red car drive by. But, representing color with precision can be a tricky thing. MochiKit.Color is designed to help out with the different representations of color and also help with some common manipulations of color.

Colors can be represented by name (white), hue/saturation/lightness (0.0, 0.0, 1.0), red/green/blue (1.0, 1.0, 1.0), and as is common on the web, a hexadecimal representation of RGB (#ffffff). With all these different possible representations, MochiKit.Color provides a color object that represents these in an abstract form, allowing you to create a color based on what you know and get back a representation that you need.

14.7.1   The Demo

Typically, we think of color as a visual thing. When you work with color on the computer, there is also a computational component, which is where MochiKit's color conversions come in handy. We'll start by looking at the visual part of it.

This demo, pictured in Figure 14.3, features a big white-on-black block of text in the middle of the page. You can change the colors there in a variety of ways to explore how MochiKit.Color processes string representations of color.

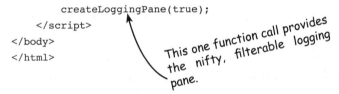

FIGURE 14.3 Color Example

The first control is a select box allowing you to tell the demo whether you're changing the foreground or background color.

After you've made a selection, you'll see the current color value in the text box. That will be in the form rgb(r,g,b), and it's what you get when you use a `color` object's `toString` method. When you click the Set Color button, the `color.fromString` function reads the value from that text box, which means that you're not limited to just rgb(r,g,b) as the format. Here are a few different things you can try:

- `red`
- `orange`
- `rgb(128,128,128)`
- `hsl(75%, 85%, 95%)`
- `#aabbcc`

`Color.fromString` provides a very natural interface for specifying a color using whatever format you may have available.

The Clone From Heading function uses a different technique to decide which color to use. MochiKit provides the functions `Color.fromBackground(elem)`, `Color.fromText(elem)`, and `Color.fromComputedStyle(elem, style)` to create a `color` object based on some element in your document. `fromBackground` and `fromText` are both shorthand for calls to `fromComputedStyle`. A good example of how to use `fromComputedStyle` is MochiKit's own definition of `fromBackground`:

```
c = Color.fromComputedStyle(
    elem, "backgroundColor", "background-color") || Color.whiteColor();
```

The code for the color demo is easy to follow. As in the style demo, this is a Kid template that could be made to work as a standalone web page:

```
<!DOCTYPE html PUBLIC "-//W3C//DTD XHTML 1.0 Transitional//EN" "http://www.
w3.org/TR/xhtml1/DTD/xhtml1-transitional.dtd">

<html xmlns="http://www.w3.org/1999/xhtml" xmlns:py="http://purl.org/kid/ns#"
    py:extends="'master.kid'">

<head>
    <meta content="text/html; charset=UTF-8" http-equiv="content-type" py:
replace="''"/>
    <title>MochiKit Color Example</title>
    <style type="text/css">
```

```
            #header { background-color: #AAAAAA; color: #CC1122; }
            #sample { background-color: black; color: white;
                      font-size: 18pt; padding: 1em;}
            #controls {padding-top: 1em; padding: 1em;}
        </style>
        <script src="static/javascript/color.js"/>
    </head>

    <body>
        <h1 id="header">Color Example</h1>


        <p>View [<a href="${tg.url('/source', file='templates/color.kid')}" tar-
get="_blank">Kid source</a> | <a href="${tg.url('/source', file='static/javas-
cript/color.js')}" target="_blank">JavaScript source</a>]</p>



        <div id="sample">This is the sample block that will change color
            based on your input.</div>


        <table id="controls" cellpadding="5px">
            <tr>
                <td>Which part of the sample do you want to change with the con-
trols below?</td>
                <td colspan="2"><select id="foreback" onchange="updateDisplay()">
                    <option>Foreground</option>
                    <option>Background</option>
                </select>
                </td>
            </tr>
            <tr>
                <td>Color String<br/>
                    <font size="-1">(try: red, orange, rgb(128,128,128), hsl(75%,
85%, 95%)</font>
                    </td>
                <td><input type="text" id="as_string" value="white"/></td>
                <td><input type="button" value="Set Color" onclick="setColor()"/>
                </td>
            </tr>
            <tr>
                <td colspan="3" align="center"><input type="button" value="Clone
From Heading" onclick="cloneColor()"/></td>
            </tr>
        </table>


    </body>
</html>
```

We set up the initial colors using standard CSS.

The color.js file is where the interesting stuff happens. That's up next.

Simple JavaScript events trigger the changes that you see.

Here is the source to `color.js`:

Everything hinges on whether Foreground or Background is selected in the select box, so there's a convenience function for getting that value.

```javascript
function getSelected() {
    return getElement("foreback").value;
}
```

We can show what the current state of our sample text is.

```javascript
function updateDisplay() {
    var textbox = getElement("as_string");
    var current = getSelected();

    if (current == "Foreground") {
        textbox.value = Color.fromText("sample").toString();
    } else {
        textbox.value = Color.fromBackground("sample").toString();
    }
}
function setSampleFromElement(elem, toSet) {
    var elem = getElement(elem);
    var samplediv = getElement("sample");

    var color = Color.fromString(elem.value);
    if (color == null) {
        alert("Unknown color string");
        return;
    }

    samplediv.style[toSet] = color;
    updateDisplay();
}
```

This is the line that's responsible for turning whatever you type in the box into a **Color** object. MochiKit's pretty lenient, but you can't type just anything into the box, so we check for null.

You can set a MochiKit **Color** object directly into the correct style property of an element (in Firefox, at least).

```javascript
function setColor() {
    var current = getSelected();
    if (current == "Foreground") {
        setSampleFromElement("as_string", "color");
    } else {
        setSampleFromElement("as_string", "background");
    }
}

function setForeground() {
    setSampleFromElement("foreground", "color");
}
```

```
function setBackground() {
    setSampleFromElement("background", "background");
}

function cloneColor() {
    var samplediv = getElement("sample");
    var current = getSelected();

    if (current == "Foreground") {
        samplediv.style.color = Color.fromText("header");
    } else {
        samplediv.style.background = Color.fromBackground("header");
    }

    updateDisplay();

}
```

Just as we pulled the current color from the sample, it's easy to clone another node's color using the same functions.

14.7.2   More Ways to Get a Color

In addition to the general `color.fromString`, you can directly call functions for each form of color specification. These functions are as follows:

- `Color.fromHexString(hexString)`

- `Color.fromHSL(hue, saturation, lightness, alpha=1.0)`

- `Color.fromHSLString(hslString)`

- `Color.fromHSV(hue, saturation, value, alpha=1.0)`

- `Color.fromName(name)` (W3C CSS3 color module name for the color. `transparent` is also accepted)

- `Color.fromRGB(red, green, blue, alpha=1.0)`

- `Color.fromRGBString(rgbString)`

MochiKit also has factories for a number of common colors:

- `Color.blackColor()`

- `Color.blueColor()`

- `Color.brownColor()`

- `Color.cyanColor()`

- `Color.darkGrayColor()`

- `Color.grayColor()`

- `Color.greenColor()`

- `Color.lightGrayColor()`

- `Color.magentaColor()`

- `Color.orangeColor()`

- `Color.purpleColor()`

- `Color.redColor()`

- `Color.whiteColor()`

- `Color.yellowColor()`

- `Color.transparentColor()`

Finally, you can get at MochiKit's master mapping of colors by calling `Color.namedColors()`. The object you get has properties with the color name in lowercase, and the value of each property is a string you can pass to `Color.fromString`.

14.7.3   Converting Colors

After you have a color specified in one format, you might need it in another, and MochiKit is ready and able to do the math for you. On a `color` object, you have the following methods:

- `toRGBString` -> rgb(r,g,b)

- `toHSLString` -> hsl(hue, saturation, lightness)

- `toHexString` -> #RRGGBB

You can also retrieve the individual color components, if you wish. Each of these functions returns an object with properties that vary between 0 and 1 for each component of the color:

- `asRGB` -> r, g, b, a

- `asHSL` -> h, s, l, a

- `asHSV` -> h, s, v, a

You can also do color conversions directly without creating a `color` object. These functions just return mappings with the appropriate set of color components:

- `hslToRGB(hue, saturation, lightness, alpha)`

- `hsvToRGB(hue, saturation, value, alpha)`

- `rgbToHSL(red, green, blue, alpha)`

- `rgbToHSV(red, green, blue, alpha)`

14.7.4   Modifying Colors

The last piece of functionality that you get from `MochiKit.Color` is the ability to change a color conveniently. You can use these methods on a `Color` object to create new `Color` objects that are variations on the original:

- `colorWithAlpha(alpha)`

- `colorWithHue(hue)`

- `colorWithSaturation(saturation)`

- `colorWithLightness(lightness)`

You can manipulate the color in other ways, too:

- `darkerColorWithLevel(level)`   Darker by the given level, between 0 and 1.
- `lighterColorWithLevel(level)`   Lighter by the given level, between 0 and 1.
- `blendedColor(other, fraction=0.5)`   The result is `other` * `fraction` plus (`1-fraction`) * this color.

Not sure if your color is bright enough? You can call the `isLight()` and `isDark()` methods of a color to see whether you've crossed the 0.5 mark.

14.8   String Conversions and Value Formatting

A common need in any software is to convert values between machine-maintained formats and human-understandable ones. MochiKit provides some of the most commonly required functions for working with dates and formatting numeric values as strings.

14.8.1   Working with Dates and Times

JavaScript has a handy `Date` object for keeping track of dates and times. Unfortunately, however, when you make an Ajax request to a server, that server isn't going to understand that `Date` object (even if you could find a way to directly send it!). And you're not going to get a JavaScript date back from the server. `MochiKit.DateTime` provides a set of functions for converting dates between JavaScript and the rest of the world.

To get a JavaScript `Date` object, use one of the following functions:

- `americanDate(str)` MM/DD/YYYY
- `isoDate(str)` ISO 8601 date (YYYY-MM-DD)
- `isoTimestamp(str)` ISO 8601 timestamp (YYYY-MM-DD hh:mm:ss or YYYY-MM-DDThh:mm:ssZ)

To convert a JavaScript `Date` object for use externally, use one of the following functions:

- `toISOTime(date)` Returns hh:mm:ss
- `toISOTimestamp(date, realISO=false)` Returns YYYY-MM-DD hh:mm:ss or, if realISO is true, YYYY-MM-DDThh:mm:ssZ
- `toISODate(date)` YYYY-MM-DD
- `toPaddedAmericanDate(date)` MM/DD/YYYY (for example, 04/05/2005)
- `toAmericanDate(date)` M/D/YYYY (for example, 4/5/2005)

14.8.2 Formatting Numbers

`MochiKit.Format` provides useful string formatting functions, including a powerful number formatter. No one likes to see a number such as 483483232 on a web page, although people in different countries might argue about what the proper way to display that number is. In the United States, we'd like that number to be formatted as 483,483,232. Here's how we do that with MochiKit:

```
>>> f = numberFormatter("#,###")
("#,###")
>>> f(483483232)
"483,483,232"
```

`numberFormatter(pattern, placeholder="", locale="default")` returns a function that will format a number according to the pattern. If you provide a placeholder and the value presented for formatting isn't a number, you'll get that placeholder back. The locale can be a known locale (`en_US`, `de_DE`, `fr_FR`, etc.) or an object with `separator` (the "thousands" separator), `decimal` (the decimal separator), and `percent` (the symbol for a percent).

The pattern, of course, is the most interesting part of the `numberFormatter` call. For displaying numbers, MochiKit uses the following special characters:

- `-` positions the minus sign for negative numbers.
- `#` a position for a number that is not zero padded.
- `0` a position for a number that will be zero padded.
- `,` the "thousands" separator. Only the first one applies.
- `.` the decimal separator.
- `%` a percent sign.

Note that you'll actually get the locale-specific characters rather than ",", "." and "%" in the final, formatted string. Here are some more examples to show off usage of the formatter:

```
>>> numberFormatter("USD $#,###.00")(15)

"USD $15.00"

>>> numberFormatter("#,### %")(0.75)

"1 %"

>>> numberFormatter("#,### %")(75)

"75 %"

>>> numberFormatter("#,###%")(75)

"7,500%"

>>> numberFormatter("0,000")(75)

"0,075"

>>> numberFormatter("##,##")(7534)

"75,34"
```

You can see from the middle examples that the position of the % sign makes a difference in whether MochiKit treats the number as a percentage.

14.8.3 Other String Formatting Functions

MochiKit includes the following additional simple functions for formatting values.

- `lstrip(str, chars="\s")`   Strips off the whitespace on the left of the string, or strips off any characters that match the `chars` regular expression
- `rstrip(str, chars="\s")`   Strips whitespace off of the right of the string
- `strip(str, chars="\s")`   Strips whitespace off of the right and left
- `roundToFixed(num, precision)`   Returns a string with `num` rounded to `precision` digits with trailing zeros (and works consistently across browsers)
- `truncToFixed(num, precision)`   Returns a string with `num` truncated to `precision` digits
- `twoDigitAverage(numerator, denominator)`   Returns `numerator/denominator` rounded to two digits, with the special feature that a 0 in the denominator will return 0.

14.9   Summary

- MochiKit includes an interactive interpreter demo that gives you an experience similar to what you get with Python's interactive interpreter.
- `MochiKit.Base` makes comparison and representation in JavaScript more flexible and useful.
- `Base` also provides a bunch of the functions that you know and love from Python such as map and filter.
- JavaScript 1.7 includes Python-style iterators, but it will be a while before we have universal browser support for that version of JavaScript. `MochiKit.Iter` gives you that capability now.
- `MochiKit.Logging` provides an easy way to debug your JavaScript that works in any browser.
- Creating and working with Document Object Model (DOM) nodes is simplified by `MochiKit.DOM`.
- `MochiKit.Color` knows how to convert between color representations so that you can get just the color you need to appear on the page.
- JavaScript includes a `Date` object, but doesn't help you convert from common external formats. `MochiKit.DateTime` includes functions for converting dates and times with the outside world.

## Chapter 15

Effective Ajax with MochiKit

In This Chapter

We've seen how MochiKit brings many good features that you can use for your applications today from Python into JavaScript. It also provides a number of functions that make different kinds of browser-specific programming tasks easier.

Users of web applications today demand quite a bit more from their applications than they did a few years ago. The functions that we learned about in the previous chapter help quite a bit, but there remains a large gap between those functions and the kinds of things that web applications need to do.

This chapter introduces MochiKit's functions for Ajax: timers, browser events, visual effects, and drag-and-drop. The functions on display here give your software the features and feel that they need with very little coding.

15.1 Handling Asynchronous Events—Including Ajax Requests

In the earliest days of the web, all we had were simple files that displayed in our web browsers. The next step was to dynamically generate on the server static information that displayed in the browser. The final step to making browser-based applications is to make it so that the information in the browser is no longer unchanging. Ajax is the name applied for using JavaScript to retrieve new information and update the page without a page refresh.

The `MochiKit.Async` package provides functions to help you do Ajax easily. In this section, you'll see how these work and take a look at a function that installs a timer on your page. How does a timer relate to Ajax? Timers and Ajax requests both represent functions that run asynchronously with results that show up at some point in the future.

15.1.1 Dealing with Results That Arrive Later

Web browsers provide an object called an `XMLHttpRequest` that is used for requesting additional information from the server. This object has two different ways of working: synchronous and asynchronous. Synchronous is how we'd *like* to be able to program this type of thing:

```
mypage = XMLHttpRequest(...);
doSomethingWithThatPage(mypage);
```

This style of programming is just like any other programming you do. Call a function, get a result back, and do something with it. It's very pleasant.

Unfortunately, the way XMLHttpRequest is implemented, doing things as in the preceding example will result in your user's browser becoming entirely unresponsive until the result comes back. If there's one sure-fire way to frustrate people, it's to give them a program that doesn't respond.

To get around this, XMLHttpRequest is generally used asynchronously. You create the request, and a function of yours gets called when the data is ready. The user's browser never locks up.

Support for Ajax in MochiKit is styled after the Twisted Network Programming Toolkit (Twisted) that's written in Python (www.twistedmatrix.com). This was a good choice, given that Twisted is all about asynchronous programming.

The way MochiKit handles Ajax requests is to hand you an object called a Deferred. A Deferred is like an IOU. It's a promise that later on you're either going to get a value back or an error. You can do some advanced things by creating your own Deferred functions, but most of the time you're just going to use the Deferred that is given to you by one of MochiKit.Async's functions.

15.1.2 Making a Request

Let's say that you're not out to do anything too fancy. You just want to run a simple XMLHttpRequest to get some more data from the server. Here's how you do that:

```
function showText(xmlhttp) {
    alert(xmlhttp.responseText);
}

d = doSimpleXMLHttpRequest("http://localhost:8080/yourcode");
d.addCallback(showText);
```

That's some easy Ajax.

doSimpleXMLHttpRequest returns a Deferred. By making the call, we know that the XMLHttpRequest was made, but we have no idea when it will return. We just have the promise that we will either get a result or an error condition after the browser has finished with the asynchronous request.

By calling `addCallback` on the `Deferred`, we tell MochiKit where in our JavaScript code the result of that Ajax call needs to go.

When that result arrives, our callback function is called with the `XMLHttpRequest` object as a parameter. In the preceding example, we put the exact text returned by the server into an alert box. The `XMLHttpRequest` has a few useful properties that we can look at, and these are enumerated in Table 15.1.

TABLE 15.1 Useful Properties of XMLHttpRequest

Property Name	Value
`responseText`	String data that came from the server
`responseXML`	A Document Object Model (DOM) representation of the data
`status`	The numeric status code returned from the server (for example, 200)
`statusText`	The string version of the status, as returned by the server (for example, "OK")

Most often, you won't need to refer to the status field because MochiKit automatically handles the values there for you. Statuses of 200 (OK) or 304 (Not Modified) are considered "success codes" and will result in your callback being called. If any other status code comes up, it's considered an error, which leads us to . . .

15.1.3 Handling Errors

If your Ajax call has an incorrect URL or some kind of error occurs on the server, your client-side code on the browser needs to be able to handle those cases. MochiKit `Deferred` objects differentiate between successful calls and failures. The `showText` function in the preceding example is only going to be called if the Ajax call was a success. What if it fails?

In our example, it would fail silently. The user wouldn't get a false indication of success, but he's probably not going to be happy about being given the silent treatment.

We can add to the example to provide a useful error message:

```
function showText(xmlhttp) {
    alert(xmlhttp.responseText);
}

function showError(err) {
    alert("An error occurred! The status was: " + err.number);
}

d = doSimpleXMLHttpRequest("http://localhost:8080/yourcode");
d.addCallbacks(showText, showError);
```

The `Deferred addCallbacks` method gives you one call to handle a common pattern: setting up callbacks for both success and error conditions. In this revised example, if the server yielded a 500 response, the error alert box would pop up telling you that. An alternative to `addCallbacks` is to call `addCallback` with your success callback and `addErrback` with the call that should be made in the event of an error. Another alternative that you can use if your function correctly handles both success and error cases is `addBoth`. In summary:

- `addCallback(callback)`   Adds a function to call on success
- `addErrback(errback)`   Adds a function to call on failure
- `addCallbacks(callback, errback)`   Adds functions to be called for success or failure
- `addBoth(callback)`   Adds a single function that will be called for both success or failure

The object passed to your error callback is an `XMLHttpRequestError` object. You can get at the original `XMLHttpRequest` object via the `req` property, and you can also get at the status via the `number` property, as seen previously.

15.1.4 Passing Parameters

Quite often, you want the server to return some specific data, so you need to pass parameters to tell the server what you're looking for. You could build up a string of the URL, properly encoding each part along the way. But, given that this is a common need, MochiKit provides a clean and neat way to do this:

```
d = doSimpleXMLHttpRequest("http://localhost:8080/order",
    {"size": size, "pepperoni" : pepp});
```

This ensures that the `size` and `pepp` variables are fit for passing in a URL. It's also much easier to build up a hash programmatically than it is to build up a properly formatted string.

15.1.5 Limitations of Ajax

The JavaScript security model prevents JavaScript code from making requests to servers other than the one the page originated on. A common desire today is to aggregate data that comes from different services. For example, if you have a business management application, you might want to pull census data for a specific city from another website.

One solution to this problem is to proxy the request through your application. The user's browser will make an Ajax call to your TurboGears application, which will then make its own HTTP request or requests to retrieve the data from the other server. This solution works, but you end up paying the bandwidth bill to pull the data down to your server and then pass it along to the user. In addition, this is likely to be slower for your users.

Some web services have started offering the ability to include a callback function name with your request. The script tag in HTML enables you to request a script from another domain. Combined with that callback parameter, you can retrieve and process data from services on other servers. For example, suppose your application needs to display the phone number of the nearest pizza delivery place, and pizzasforyou.com knows how to find that restaurant for you. You can write a function on your page that looks like this:

```
function showphone(result) {
    alert(result["phone"]);
}
```

Then, in your page, you include a script tag that looks like this:

```
<script src="http://www.pizzasforyou.com/search?phone=734-555-1212&format=json
&callback=showphone"></script>
```

That tag will make the call out to PizzasForYou, and the result would look something like:

```
showphone({"name":"Big Ed's Pizza Bistro","phone":"810-555-1212"});
```

This convenient workaround will result in your showphone function getting called when the result from PizzasForYou is ready. This approach is easy to implement on both the browser side (in your code) and on the server side (the code of the service provider). Unfortunately, it does require implementation on both sides, so you must check the documentation for any web service you connect to in order to determine whether this is supported.

15.1.6 Using JSON

In the preceding section, our request to PizzasForYou included a parameter `format=json`, and the result that came back included this:

```
{"name":"Big Ed's Pizza Bistro","phone":"810-555-1212"}
```

That looks suspiciously familiar to both JavaScript and Python programmers because that snippet is legal in both languages! This data is encoded in JavaScript Object Notation (JSON), a simple format that is also remarkably flexible. JSON allows you to nest JavaScript hashes and arrays that contain other hashes, arrays, and native types, letting you create a hierarchy of data with ease. In JavaScript, converting from JSON to native objects is as simple as `eval(json_value)`. MochiKit also provides functions for encoding JavaScript values into JSON. On the Python side, TurboGears uses `simplejson` to perform conversions to and from JSON.

Despite the fact that the x in Ajax stands for XML, JSON is an excellent format to use for your Ajax requests. It's fast, compatible with every browser, and made super simple by built-in features of TurboGears. When you know you're getting JSON back in MochiKit, you can use `loadJSONDoc` rather than `doSimpleXMLHttpRequest`. If you do, your result comes into your callback function directly as JavaScript objects rather than an `XMLHttpRequest` object that you need to inspect. `loadJSONDoc` is not a huge feature, but it's another one of those conveniences that makes MochiKit fun to use.

15.1.7 Working with Timers

Although this chapter is mostly about Ajax, it turns out that some of the same concepts apply to timers. The section on `Deferred`s talked about how a `Deferred` object is a promise for something that will happen later. By definition, when you put a timer on a web page, you're saying that you want something to happen later.

If PizzasForYou offers a 30-minute delivery guarantee, the order confirmation page can pop up an alert when the pizza should have arrived. Here's how to do that:

```
function pizzahere(pizza_description) {
    alert("Your " + pizza_description + " pizza should have arrived!");
}

// The following function would likely have been called from a button
// press that confirms the order
function orderpizza() {
```

```
    // Look up the element that's displaying the description
    // Which would look something like:
    // <div id="description">Large Pepperoni</div>
    pizza_description = $("description");

    halfhour = 60 * 30; // seconds * minutes
    d = wait(halfhour, pizza_description);
    d.addCallback(pizzahere);
}
```

The `wait()` function takes the length of time to delay (in seconds) and the result to pass in when the wait is over. It returns a `Deferred`, so it works just like the Ajax calls we've made previously. After 30 minutes, our `pizzahere` function will be called, displaying the description of the hot and tasty pizza that should have arrived. Woe unto the poor pizza delivery guy who didn't make it there before that alert pops up!

MochiKit also offers a `callLater` convenience function that can eliminate a line of code in the preceding example. Instead of separate calls to `wait` and `addCallback`, you can call `callLater(halfhour, pizzahere, pizza_description)`. `callLater` takes the length of the delay, the function to call, and the arguments to pass into that function. `call-Later` is also convenient, because you can pass multiple arguments into your callback function.

15.1.8 Canceling `Deferred`s

What if that large pepperoni pizza ordered in the preceding section has arrived? Do you still want the 30-minute timer alert box to pop up? Probably not.

`Deferred`s have a `cancel` method that allows you to cancel the `Deferred` before it has received a value. Both `wait` and `callLater` return a cancelable `Deferred`. If you hang on to the `Deferred` in a variable that's available to scripts on the whole page, you can create a "My Pizza Has Arrived" button that calls `d.cancel()` when the button is pushed.

15.1.9 Ajax, Timers, and Cancellation Combined

What if you want to apply a timeout to an Ajax call to gracefully handle the case where the user loses Internet connectivity or your server becomes otherwise unavailable? It becomes trivial if you combine the tools we've discussed in these last few segments:

```
d = loadJSONDoc("your_url");
callLater(30, d.cancel);
```

This adds a silent timeout. If you want an alert error message, you can just use JavaScript's closures to create a function that does the right thing:

```
d = loadJSONDoc("your_url");
callLater(30, function() {
    if (d.fired == -1) {
        alert("Unable to talk to the server!");
        d.cancel();
    }
});
```

This example checks the value of the fired attribute of the Deferred. fired starts at -1, which reflects that it has not yet called its callbacks or errbacks. Zero means that it has completed successfully, and 1 means that there was an error. If the JSON data has not been loaded in 30 seconds, this will display an alert message and cancel the JSON request.

15.1.10 More about Callbacks

Early in this chapter, you saw how easy it is to add a callback and an errback (a callback for errors) to your Deferreds. What we didn't talk about is what happens when you have more than one callback. Callbacks and errbacks are appended to a list, each element of which is called in order when the result arrives or the pending event occurs. Each callback gets the result of the previous callback as its parameter. This allows you to do useful transformations of the data that comes in.

For an example of this in action, we need look no further than MochiKit itself. We talked about using doSimpleXMLHttpRequest to perform an Ajax request. That function returns a Deferred that is later called back with the XMLHttpRequest object. loadJSONDoc effectively uses the chained callback feature of Deferred to return the JavaScript object rather than an XMLHttpRequest. Here's an approximation of what loadJSONDoc does:

```
var loadJSONDoc = function(url) {
    d = doSimpleXMLHttpRequest(url);
    d.addCallback(evalJSONRequest);
    return d;
}
```

The initial Ajax result arrives and gets post-processed by evalJSONRequest before your own callback sees the result, so you only need to worry about the JavaScript object that comes back.

15.2 Handling JavaScript Events with MochiKit.Signal

Event-driven programming is a handy model for making graphical user interfaces. The browser developers recognized this and created an event model that ties in to the browser's DOM. Unfortunately, they created slightly different models, and one browser that shall remain nameless (that one browser that lots of people use but is always a pain for developers) has some nasty memory leaks when using DOM events.

The popular Qt GUI library from Trolltech uses an event model called Signals and Slots. When some kind of event occurs, a "signal" is sent, and the signal is received by "slots." It's a simple model, and it's the one that's used by MochiKit.Signal.

Even better than choosing a nice, simple model, MochiKit.Signal provides a *consistent* model. Every browser serves up the same kinds of events, and none of the browsers will leak memory as a result of hooking in to browser events.

15.2.1 Getting Started with MochiKit.Signal

The first thing to do is to *not* use the native browser event application programming interfaces (APIs). This is straightforward: if you catch yourself adding onclick or some other on attribute to an element, stop what you're doing and call connect, which we talk about in a minute. The same goes for calls on the DOM nodes themselves (addEventListener) and so on. Finally, MochiKit's own addToCallStack and addLoadEvent functions are tied to traditional DOM events, so avoid those, too. In other words, to get the benefit of signal (and it's a big benefit, indeed!), you have to make a break from the past.

To get into using signal, we start with an example, pictured in Figure 15.1, that shows you what the signals themselves look like and how you can flexibly attach them to any DOM node.

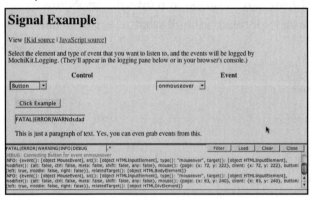

FIGURE 15.1 Signal Example

This demo lets you choose one of the DOM nodes defined on the page and then the kind of event you want to watch. As the events occur, you'll see output in the logging pane with the details of the event:

```
<!DOCTYPE html PUBLIC "-//W3C//DTD XHTML 1.0 Transitional//EN" "http://www.w3.org/
TR/xhtml1/DTD/xhtml1-transitional.dtd">
    <html xmlns="http://www.w3.org/1999/xhtml" xmlns:py="http://purl.org/kid/ns#"
        py:extends="'master.kid'">

    <head>
        <meta content="text/html; charset=UTF-8" http-equiv="content-type" py:
replace="'''"/>
        <title>MochiKit Signal Example</title>
        <script src="static/javascript/signal.js"/>
        <style>
            .control div { margin: 1em;}
        </style>

    </head>

    <body>
        <h1>Signal Example</h1>

        <p>View [<a href="${tg.url('/source', file='templates/signal.kid')}"
target="_blank">Kid source</a> | <a href="${tg.url('/source', file='static/
hjavascript/signal.js')}" target="_blank">JavaScript source</a>]</p>

        <p>Select the element and type of event that you want to listen to, and
the events will be logged by MochiKit.Logging. (They'll appear in the logging pane
below or in your browser's console.)</p>

        <table width="100%">
            <tr>
                <th>Control</th>
                <th>Event</th>
            </tr>
            <tr>
                <td width="50%">
                    <select id="elemselect">
                        <option>Button</option>
                        <option value="Textbox">Text Box</option>
                        <option value="paragraph">Paragraph</option>
                    </select>
                </td>
```

```
        <td width="50%">
            <select id="eventselect">
                <option>onclick</option>
                <option>onkeydown</option>
                <option>onkeypress</option>
                <option>onmouseover</option>
                <option>onmouseout</option>
                <option>onmousemove</option>
            </select>
        </td>
    </tr>
</table>

<div class="control">
    <div><input type="button" value="Click Example" id="Button"/></div>
    <div><input type="text" id="Textbox" value=""/></div>
    <div id="paragraph">This is just a paragraph of text. Yes, you can
even grab events from this.</div>
    </div>

<script type="text/javascript">
    createLoggingPane(true);

    changeSelected(null);

    connect("elemselect", "onchange", changeSelected);
    connect("eventselect", "onchange", changeSelected);
</script>
```

*There's more about the logging pane in the section on **MochiKit.Logging**.*

__changeSelected__ is where some of the interesting stuff happens and it appears in the JavaScript file that follows.

```
</body>
</html>
```

*These **connect** statements wire up the two **<select>** widgets so that **changeSelected** is called and we start listening to different DOM events.*

Here is the `signal.js` file:

```
var currentSelected = null;

function changeSelected(e) {
    if (currentSelected != null) {
        logDebug("Disconnecting " + currentSelected);
```

```
                disconnectAll(currentSelected);
        }

        var es = getElement("elemselect");
        currentSelected = es.value;
        var ev = getElement("eventselect").value;
        logDebug("Connecting " + currentSelected + " for event " + ev);


            connect(currentSelected, ev, log);
        }
```

*If we just keep calling **connect** without breaking connections, we'd eventually be listening to all of these events for these nodes!*

*After we've looked up which DOM node and event type we want to listen to, we just call connect passing in MochiKit's **log** function to display the event.*

This sample introduces two functions from `MochiKit.Signal`. The most important function available in `signal` is `connect`, because that's what activates the whole thing. Our use of `connect` here is about the simplest it could be. We're passing in a string with the ID of the DOM node we're interested in, the name of the event we're interested in, and a function. MochiKit hooks things up so that the event is passed neatly along to our function. You'll see more about `connect` in just a minute.

We also use `disconnectAll` here, passing in the ID of the node that was previously selected. That removes all signals that had previously been set up for that node. That might seem a little heavy-handed. What if you want to keep some signals? The answer to that starts with a deeper look at `connect`.

15.2.2 Connecting and Disconnecting

As mentioned previously, the form of `connect` we used looks like this: `connect(src, signal, func)`; and is about as simple as it gets. Lucky for us, `connect` never really gets much harder than that. The full signature is `connect(src, signal, dest, func)`. `src` can be a string that is the ID of a DOM node, or it can be any object that you want to get a signal from. `signal` is the name of the signal you're setting up.

`dest` is an object that you want to define the slot on. When you use the form of `connect` with a `dest` object, `func` can either be a string with the name of the function on the object or a function object itself. Either way, when the function is called, `this` will be bound to `dest`.

The `connect` function also returns a value that we didn't use in the example program. The value is an identifier that uniquely identifies that connection. You can call `disconnect(ident)` to remove that signal connection without disturbing any other connections.

15.2.3 Using MochiKit's Cross-Browser Event Objects

Over the years, browsers have become more standards compliant and just overall more compatible. However, there are still a number of areas in which you're likely to get bitten by compatibility issues. Events are one of those areas. If you're writing code that takes in a browser event object, you'll likely want to refer to Peter-Paul Koch's quirksmode.org site, which offers JavaScript Event Compatibility tables. Those tables are invaluable at figuring out which parts of the event object will tell you what you need to know for each browser.

Lucky for us, however, when you are using `MochiKit.Signal`, you're not using a browser event object. You're getting MochiKit's own event object. That object is designed to look the same to you, the JavaScript programmer, regardless of which browser the user is using. If you call the `event()` method on a MochiKit event object, you can get the browser's native event object. You should never have to do that, however.

Often, an event handler (slot) is hooked up to multiple signals. So, one of the first things you need to know is where that signal came from. It turns out that there are potentially two answers to this. Consider this case:

```
<table id="foo">
    <tr>
        <td>Here is some text in a table</td>
    </tr>
</table>
```

If you `connect` to the `"foo"` table, and click the `<td>` node in there, there are two interesting possibilities for the origination of the event: `"foo"`, where the signal was defined; and that `<td>`, where the actual click took place. Calling `src()` on the event will get you `"foo"` back, and `target()` will give you the `<td>` node where the click took place.

It turns out that there's actually a third element that you are interested in for some types of events: what element did the user move *to*? Specifically, for `onmouseout` and `onmouseover` events, you want to know about this third element, and the `relatedTarget()` method will give it to you.

A slot can also accept multiple kinds of signals, and the `type()` method on the event will tell you exactly which kind you're dealing with. Note that the return value of `type()` does not include the `on` prefix, so you'll have `click` instead of `onclick`, for example.

Next, you'll often want to know a bit more about the event. Questions you might want to ask an event object include these: What key was pressed? Where was the mouse when the button was clicked? Was it a Shift-click or a Ctrl-click?

The `modifier()` method returns an object with these properties: `shift`, `ctrl`, `meta`, `alt`, `any`. These will be true if the given modifier key was pressed, and `any` is true if any one of the modifier keys was pressed.

If you are listening for keyboard signals, you'll want to use the `key()` method on event. This method returns an object with two properties: `code` (a numeric code for the key) and `string` (a string representation of the key that was pressed). The value for `string` varies depending on whether you're listening for `onkeyup`/`onkeydown` or `onkeypress` events. You should use `onkeypress` for "printable" characters. When you do, you'll be rewarded with a `string` value that matches the character typed ("a" if the A key is pressed). However, special keys are not represented in `onkeypress`. If you're looking for function keys or other special keys, use `onkeyup` or `onkeydown`. The special keys are consistently named across browsers as `KEY_ESC`, `KEY_F1`, `KEY_ARROW_DOWN`, and so on, which is much easier to use than figuring out the character codes for the keys.

If you are listening for mouse signals, use the `mouse()` method on the event to get information about the mouse cursor position and the buttons that are pressed. The `page` and `client` properties are `MochiKit.Style.Coordinates` objects that tell you where in the HTML document and where within the browser window the cursor is located, respectively.

The `button` property returns an object with `left`, `right`, and `middle` properties that are true depending on which button was pressed.

In some browsers, IE and Firefox as of this writing, you can connect to the `onbeforeunload` event. If you do so, you can use the `confirmUnload(msg)` method to give the user a chance to stop navigating away from the page. This proves extremely useful with JavaScript and Ajax-powered applications, where the user could be halfway through a task and then lose a bunch of work if he navigates away.

> **Note:** As of this writing, the MochiKit documentation lists some browser bugs that impact the use of `mouse()`, so be sure to check the latest MochiKit documentation for up-to-date information.

Finally, there are methods to determine what happens *next* after your event handler. These are part of the DOM as defined by the W3C. `stopPropagation()` prevents the event from triggering any other event handlers connected to a parent or child node. preventDefault() allows the event to be passed along to other handlers, but stops the default behavior from happening if the event is cancelable. As an example, prevent-Default can stop characters from being added to a text area or a check box from being checked without preventing other event handlers from acting on the event. The preventDefault behavior is akin to the behavior you get if you return false in the old DOM event handling model.

15.2.4 Custom Events

If signals and slots are so useful a model for DOM events, why can't you use them for other things in your app? Short answer: You *can*. There's one more function in the Signal package that has not been discussed: signal(src, signal, ...). That function fires off a signal and passes all the additional parameters to the connected slots.

Here is something you can try in the interactive interpreter:

```
createLoggingPane(true);

orderManager = {};

new_order = function(order) {
    var d = callLater(5, signal, orderManager, "orderlate", order);
    var siginfo = {};



    var id = connect(order, "orderprocessed",
        partial(finished_order, siginfo, d));
    siginfo.id = id;

};

finished_order = function(siginfo, d, order) {
    signal(orderManager, "orderprocessed", order);
```

orderManager doesn't have data or behavior ... we just use it as an object to attach signals to.

You get 5 seconds when you create a new order to process it. After that, the orderlate signal goes out.

We listen for the order to announce that it has been processed. When it has, we clean up.

Based on the signal for a single order, a signal is sent to the orderManager for listeners that care about any order.

```
        disconnect(siginfo.id);
        d.cancel();
}
```

We clean up by disconnecting
the slot and canceling our alarm.

```
order_is_late = function(order) {
    alert(order + " is late!");
};
```

When a new order is
created, a signal is sent
via the **orderManager**
object.

```
ordernumber = 1;

Order = function() {
    bindMethods(this);
    this.ordernum = ordernumber;
    ordernumber += 1;



    signal(orderManager, "orderplaced", this);
};
```

The process method just lets all
of this order's slots know that
this order is complete.

```
Order.prototype = {
    "process" : function () { signal(this, "orderprocessed", this); },
    "toString" : function() { return "Order " + this.ordernum; }
};
```

This is where the behavior is wired up. Logging occurs at
every step, and an alert pops up when an order is late.

```
connect(orderManager, "orderplaced", new_order);
connect(orderManager, "orderplaced", partial(log, "New order: "));
connect(orderManager, "orderprocessed", partial(log, "Completed: "));
connect(orderManager, "orderlate", partial(log, "Late: "));
connect(orderManager, "orderlate", order_is_late);
```

   The signals and slots model provides an easy way to produce loosely coupled, event-driven scripts. This model works quite nicely for dealing with DOM events, and larger Ajax-style applications will likely benefit in their own code, too.

15.3 Visual Effects for That "Wow Factor"

Though people ultimately use software because of the things the software will do for them, how people perceive the software will have a big impact on how they feel about it. People learn better and work better when they're having fun. Visual effects don't add anything tangible to your product (you don't get to add an extra bullet point for them!), but they can make a huge difference in how your users feel about your product.

The `MochiKit.Visual` module provides a number of easy-to-use visual effects routines. `MochiKit.DragAndDrop` gives you a simple way to add drag-and-drop controls to part of your application. `MochiKit.Sortable` lets you give your users a way to sort a list with drag and drop with only a couple lines of code. Together, these three modules let you ratchet up the overall feel of your application by a couple of notches.

15.3.1 Rounded Corners

We start with the most humble feature in the package: rounded corners. Generally, if you want a rounded-off look for your application, you need to resort to images that you slice up just right to achieve the effect. The `visual` module lets you round the corners of an element (or collection of them) with a single call, no images required.

You can see the rounded-corners effect for yourself using MochiKit's interactive interpreter:

```
writeln(DIV({"class" : "rounded", "style" :
    "text-align:center; background:black; color: white"},
    "Square edge or round, you decide!"));
```

That command gives us a white-on-black `<DIV>` element, with the traditional squared-off corners. Now run this:

```
roundClass("div", "rounded");
```

Our `<DIV>` now looks rounded. That call said to make any `<DIV>` elements with the class `rounded` be rounded off. You can pass in `null` for either the tag or the class to match all tags or classes.

Some caveats apply to using the rounded elements feature: It only works properly on "block" nodes and can be thrown off by padding.

In addition to `roundClass`, there is also a `roundElement` function that lets you round a specific DOM node.

Both `roundClass` and `roundElement` have an optional additional parameter of an `options` object. The `options` available for rounding are found in Table 15.2.

This feature was ported from OpenRico to MochiKit, so you may be able to find additional information regarding rounded corners at the OpenRico site: http://openrico.org/.

TABLE 15.2 Corner Options

Option	Description
corners	Which corners should be rounded. This can be `all`, `top`, `bottom`, `tl` (top left), `bl` (bottom left), `tr` (top right), `br` (bottom right). The default is `all`.
color, bgColor	Determine whichh colors should be used for the border that is created. `color` defaults to `fromElement` and `bgColor` defaults to `fromParent`, and you can use any color specification that's valid in CSS.
blend	Should the color and background color be blended together to produce the border color? The default is true.
compact	Yields a smaller border with small rounded corners.

15.3.2 Getting Started with Effects

Visual lets you provide a nicer-looking experience right away. Give this a whirl in your interpreter. (Reload the page if you already had one open: otherwise, you'll have scrolling issues.)

```
writeln(DIV({"id" : "nowyouseeit"}, "Now you don't!"));
```

That puts a simple `<div>` up for you to play with. Let's make it disappear and then reappear, using functions we talked about earlier in the chapter:

```
hideElement("nowyouseeit");
showElement("nowyouseeit");
```

As expected, the element appears and then disappears, each transition happening in an instant. Compare that with this:

```
toggle("nowyouseeit");
toggle("nowyouseeit");
```

`toggle(element[, effect[, options]])` will do a nice, simple fade in/fade out by default. It's simple, but sometimes more pleasing than having an element abruptly disappear. `effect` can be one of `slide`, `blind`, `appear`, and `size`. Try those out, and you'll see that you can get pretty flashy without much fuss.

15.3.3 Effect Options

All the visual effects take an "options" parameter, which is an object that provides, you guessed it, options for the effects. There are a number of standard options, and their default values can be found in `MochiKit.Visual.DefaultOptions`.

The standard options and their default values are listed in Table 15.3.

TABLE 15.3 Standard Effect Options

Option	Default Value	Description
transition	MochiKit.Visual.Transitions.sinoidal	This is how the values for the transitions should be computed. Other transitions to try out in MochiKit.Visual.Transitions: flicker and pulse.
duration	1.0 (seconds)	Length of time for which the effect will run.
fps	25.0	This is how many frames per second the effect should use. In other words, how many values should the effect compute per second. The larger the number, the smoother the effect, but the more likely it is to slow down the user's computer, and the less you're likely able to do in parallel.
sync	false	By default, an effect will render its frames automatically. If `sync` is `false`, you can manually call the `render` method to control the timing of the effect. This is how the `Parallel` effect works.
from	0.0	Starting time for the effect, which is handy if you're coordinating multiple effects.
to	1.0	Ending time for the effect.
delay	0.0	Sets a fraction of the duration to wait before the effect actually kicks in. Set to 0.5, it will wait for half the duration and then start displaying the effect.
queue	`parallel`	By default, if you create multiple effects at once, they will all run at the same time (in parallel). You can also specify that you want a given effect to be at the `start` or `end` of the queue for the page, to easily allow effects to appear sequentially.

You can see the options in action for yourself with the `toggle` function we've already looked at:

```
toggle("nowyouseeit", "appear", MochiKit.Visual.Transitions.pulse);
```

If you have multiple interrelated elements, you can run the same effect on all of them in parallel:

```
>>> writeln(DIV({"id":"one"}, "The First Element"));
The First Element

>>> writeln(DIV({"id":"two"}, "The Second Element"));
The Second Element

>>> multiple(["one", "two"], fade);
```

15.3.4 The Core Effects

These effects are the building blocks for more-complicated effects. They are "classes," so you need to use `new` to use them. The general form used for all the effects, which we've already seen, is `effect(element[, options])`. For the core effects, you use `new Effect(element[, options])`, the one deviation from this in the standard set is `Scale` which also requires a `percent` parameter to be useful.

`Highlight` gives you the famous Yellow Fade technique. By default, a yellow background fades in and then disappears. Of course, you can change the color with the `startcolor` option.

The `Scale(element, percent[, options])` effect has several options and an extra parameter. The `percent` parameter specifies how much you would like the element to scale by. The other options offered for the `scale` effect are listed in Table 15.4.

Another class that is offered is `Parallel(effects[, options])`, which launches the provided effects in parallel.

The remaining core effects all have fewer options, as summarized here:

- `Opacity` Change the opacity of the element with `from` and `to` options that default to 0.0 and 1.0, respectively.

- `Move` Change the position of an element with `x` and `y` options that default to 0. There's also a `position` option (`relative`) to specify whether `x` and `y` are relative or absolute positions.

- `ScrollTo` Scrolls the window to the position of the given element, providing a smooth scrolling effect rather than an instantaneous repositioning.

TABLE 15.4 Options for the Scale Effect

Option	Default Value	Description
scaleX	true	Whether or not to scale on the X axis.
scaleY	true	Whether or not to scale on the Y axis.
scaleContent	true	Are you scaling just the box or the content as well?
scaleMode	`box`	By default, scaling is based on the visible area of the element. If you set scaleMode to contents, then the parts that are not in the visible area of the browser window will also be taken into account. If scaleMode is an object with originalHeight and originalWidth attributes, you can precisely define what the original size of the element was for use in the effect.
scaleFrom	100.0	What percentage of the size are you starting at?
scaleTo	`percent`	What percentage should the scaling end at.

15.3.5 Combination Effects

The "combination effects" build on the core effects to provide easy-to-use functions that have a polished and complete look. All of these functions have the signature effect(element[, options]). The combination effects are as follows:

- fade   Change the opacity of the element until it disappears with from and to options. from defaults to getOpacity(element) or 1.0 if that is not set. to defaults to 0.0.

- appear   The reverse of fade.

- puff   The element will double in size and then disappear.

- blindUp   The element's vertical size will shrink to 0, giving the effect of a blind rolling up.

- blindDown   The reverse of blindUp.

- switchOff   The element will shrink to nothing in the middle (reminiscent of a television set that shows a bright line in the middle of the screen before it turns off).

- dropOut   The element will fall straight down and fade.

- shake   The element shakes from left to right (but stays on the screen).

- slideDown   The element will slide down.

- slideUp   The element will slide up.

- squish   The element shrinks horizontally and vertically, starting with the upper-left corner, leaving nothing behind.

- `grow`   Restore the size of an element.
- `shrink`   The element slides to the right and shrinks to nothing as it goes.
- `pulsate`   The element appears and fades repeatedly. (The element remains visible at the end.)
- `fold`   Reduce the vertical size and then the horizontal size, leaving nothing behind.

15.3.6 Customizing Effect Behavior

The effect options described earlier in the chapter provide a number of ways you can customize the appearance of an effect, but they don't change the fundamental behavior of the effect. You can also change the behavior of an effect via options by setting callbacks for events that occur during an effect's lifetime. The events are as follows:

- `beforeStart`
- `beforeSetup`
- `beforeUpdate`
- `afterUpdate`
- `beforeFinish`
- `afterFinish`

A simple example will chain two effects:

```
writeln(DIV({"id" : "shaker"}, "Pulsate and shake!"));
pulsaste("shaker", {"afterFinish" : function() { shake("shaker"); } } )
```

You can also create your own, new effects based on the `MochiKit.Visual.Base` class. You can override the `setup`, `update`, and `finish` methods to design an effect that does whatever you want.

As an example of a completely custom effect, we'll make a "rolling sign" effect that roughly simulates those signs that keep changing letters around until they reach the final desired text. This is visually similar to that, but the intermediate letters that are chosen are completely random:

```
RollingSign = function(element, newstring, options) {
        this.__init__(element, newstring, options);
    }
```

This is a JavaScript function that acts as our "class." The idiom used for these classes is to have the real constructor be called __init__.

In this simulation of a class, you set a new Base object as your prototype.

```
RollingSign.prototype = new Base();

update(RollingSign.prototype, {

    __init__ : function(element, newstring, options) {
        this.element = getElement(element);
```

Set up default options that are overridden by new options that come in.

```
        options = update(
            {
                charSpaceSize: 26,
                startingChar: 65
            }, options || {});

        this.newstring = newstring;
        this.oldstring = this.element.innerHTML;
```

*Effects should call the **start** method once the constructor is done.*

```
        this.start(options);
    },
```

*The **update** function is called for each "position" of computation. The position is between 0 and 1 and represents how far through the effect you are.*

```
    update: function(position) {

        curchar = this.newstring.length * position;
        toMake = this.newstring.length - curchar;
```

Based on the position, we figure out how much of our new string we display and how much we generate randomly.

```
        ending = "";
        for (i = 0; i < toMake; i++) {
            ending += String.fromCharCode(
                Math.random() * this.options.charSpaceSize +
                this.options.startingChar);
        }
```

This generates our randomized end string.

Set the text to the beginning of our new string and the randomized ending.

```
        // (8)
        this.element.innerHTML = this.newstring.substr(0, curchar) +
            ending;
    },
```

*The **finish** method is called at the end. We set the new string to make sure that the final output is correct.*

```
    // (9)
    finish: function() {
        this.element.innerHTML = this.newstring;
    }
  }
);
```

You can try this code out easily in the interpreter after you've entered it:

```
writeln(DIV({id:"hiya"}, "Hey there!"));
new RollingSign("hiya", "That's all folks!");
```

You can also try tweaking standard options, such as `duration`, to see the effect they have.

Learning More about the Visual Effects

The visual effects in `MochiKit.Visual` were ported from Scriptaculous, which uses the Prototype JavaScript library as its basis. While you could just use Scriptaculous alongside of MochiKit, there have historically been compatibility problems between Prototype and other JavaScript libraries. MochiKit is designed to be very unobtrusive and compatible, and by porting Scriptaculous' effects to a MochiKit basis you gain that level of compatibility, plus you're able to work with MochiKit's other great features.

Scriptaculous is a popular package. The advantage to porting Scriptaculous rather than coming up with new APIs strictly for MochiKit is that many of the articles and add-on effects for Scriptaculous will readily apply for use with MochiKit.

You can find add-on effects and more information at http://script.aculo.us and web searches with "scriptaculous" for specific topics usually yield useful results.

15.3.7 An Effects Demo

Two more packages have also been ported from Scriptaculous: DragAndDrop and Sortable. Both of these let you provide a drag-and-drop (DND) user interface for your application with a minimum of fuss. DND is an important user interface feature because certain types of UI problems are not solved gracefully through any other means on the web.

One example of this is an "ordered list of items." Consider an election system where you don't just pick a single candidate, but instead need to put the candidates in order of preference. The "old-fashioned" way to do this in a web browser was a setup involving a "select multiple" control and up and down buttons. You'd select someone from the list and repeatedly click the up or down button until that person was in the right place. Then you'd painstakingly repeat the process until you were done, or until you just gave up and let the other guy win.

DND is much more natural for this. Just drag the person up to the spot where you want the person to be. Simple. Note that DND on the web is not likely to work with accessibility solutions for disabled users. You might still consider offering some kind of up and down buttons for that reason. Yahoo!'s My Yahoo service, for example, lets you drag and drop modules on your My Yahoo page, but also offers a separate, old-style page that is doubtless more accessible.

Ordered lists are such a common requirement that Scriptaculous/MochiKit offer something called a Sortable. A Sortable provides prepackaged, ready-to-run DND for ordered lists. As an example of this, we'll use an effects viewer that lets you view MochiKit's visual effects individually *or* create an ordered chain of effects that are run one after the other.

There are two things to note about this demo before we look at the code. As of this writing, `MochiKit.Visual` is not yet complete. The API is not likely to change much, but the packaging might change some. At present, the packed `MochiKit.js` distribution does not include `New.js`, `DragAndDrop.js`, or `Sortable.js`. This packaging issue will undoubtedly be resolved by the time MochiKit 1.4 ships. In addition, the Sortable name is not exported by the `Sortable.js` module. So, you'll note in the following code that we refer directly to `MochiKit.Sortable.Sortable`. That style of access will continue working later on, so feel free to use it. It's just a bit wordier.

And now, on to the Effects/Sortable/DND sample.

This demo program, pictured in Figure 15.2, enables you to watch a number of MochiKit's effects as they're applied to the header of the page. You can set the duration and then click a button to see the effect. You can also view the `RollingSign` effect implemented in the preceding section.

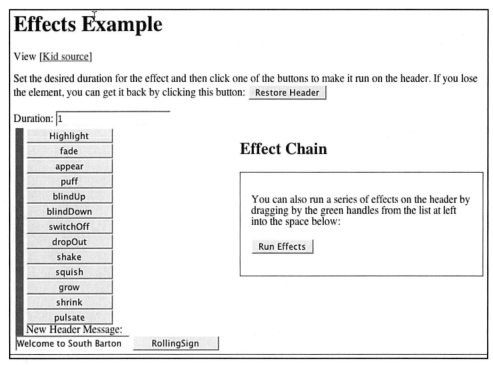

FIGURE 15.2 Effects Picture

Sortable comes in with the "effects chain" feature of the page. You can grab on to the green handles and drag effects from the left side of the page into the effects chain box. You can also change the ordering of the effects. That box will run the effects one after another in the same order in which the buttons appear on the page. It's a nifty bit of functionality, and you'll see that it's done with very little code:

```
<!DOCTYPE html PUBLIC "-//W3C//DTD XHTML 1.0 Transitional//EN" "http://www.w3.org/
TR/xhtml1/DTD/xhtml1-transitional.dtd">

    <html xmlns="http://www.w3.org/1999/xhtml" xmlns:py="http://purl.org/kid/ns#"
        py:extends="'master.kid'">

    <head>
        <meta content="text/html; charset=UTF-8" http-equiv="content-type" py:
replace="''"/>
        <title>MochiKit Effects Example</title>

        <style type="text/css">
            .handle { background: green; padding: 0.25em;}
            #effectlist input.effectbutton { width: 10em; }
```

```
</style>

<script type="text/javascript"><![CDATA[
        var nextInChain = [];

        // The RollingSign code from the previous section.
        RollingSign = function(element, newstring, options) {
            this.__init__(element, newstring, options);
        }

        RollingSign.prototype = new Base();

        update(RollingSign.prototype, {

            __init__ : function(element, newstring, options) {
                this.element = getElement(element);

                options = update(
                    {
                        charSpaceSize: 26,
                        startingChar: 65
                    }, options || {});

                this.newstring = newstring;
                this.oldstring = this.element.innerHTML;

                this.start(options);
            },

            update: function(position) {
                curchar = this.newstring.length * position;
                toMake = this.newstring.length - curchar;

                ending = "";
                for (i = 0; i < toMake; i++) {
                    ending += String.fromCharCode(
                        Math.random() * this.options.charSpaceSize +
                        this.options.startingChar);
                }

                this.element.innerHTML = this.newstring.substr(0, curchar) +
                    ending;
            },
```

```
            finish: function() {
                this.element.innerHTML = this.newstring;
            }
        }
    }
);

function restoreHeader() {
    replaceChildNodes("headenc",
        H1({id : "header"}, "Effects Example")));
}
```

Simple function to re-create the
header as it was originally, in case
the user has faded it away.

```
function opt() {
    var opts = {
        duration : getElement("duration").value
    };
```

Makes the options object for the effects.

Set the duration based on the text box.

```
    if (nextInChain.length > 0) {
        var next = nextInChain.shift();
        opts.afterFinish = partial(next.onclick, null);
    }

    return opts;
}
```

If we're running a chain, set **afterFinish**
up to call the **onclick** event handler with no
event. (We don't need one anyway!)

```
function showChain() {
```

Kicks off the effect chain.

```
    var chain = getElement("effectchain");
    nextInChain = getElementsByTagAndClassName("input",
                        "effectbutton", chain);

    if (nextInChain.length == 0) {
        return;
    }
```

Pull off the first effect and run it.
The additional effects in the chain
will be fired off automatically because of the **afterfinish** set in **opt()**.

```
    first = nextInChain.shift();
    first.onclick(null);
}
]]>
```

```
        </script>

    </head>

    <body>
        <!-- (8) -->
        <div id="headenc">
            <h1 id="header">Effects Example</h1>
        </div>
```

This is the header we're manipulating. The outer **‹div›** *is there so we can easily put the header back if needed.*

```
        <p>View [<a href="${tg.url('/source', file='templates/effects.kid')}" tar-
get="_blank">Kid source</a>]</p>

        <p>Set the desired duration for the effect and then click one of the but-
tons to make it run on the header. If you lose the element, you can get it back by
clicking this button: <input type="button" value="Restore Header" onclick="restore
Header()"/></p>

        <div>Duration: <input type="text" id="duration" value="1"/></div>

        <table width="95%">
            <tr>
                <td width="50%">
```

The effect list has all of the effects buttons in it. The onclick event of the button itself is responsible for firing off the event.

```
                    <div id="effectlist">

                        <div><span class="handle"> </span>
                            <input class="effectbutton" type="button"
                            onclick="new Highlight('header', opt())"
                            value="Highlight"/>
                        </div>

                        <div><span class="handle"> </span>
                            <input class="effectbutton" type="button"
                            onclick="fade('header', opt())"
                            value="fade"/>
                        </div>

                        <div><span class="handle"> </span>
                            <input class="effectbutton" type="button"
                            onclick="appear('header', opt())"
                            value="appear"/>
                        </div>

                        <div><span class="handle"> </span>
                            <input class="effectbutton" type="button"
```

```
              onclick="puff('header', opt())"
              value="puff"/>
    </div>

    <div><span class="handle"> </span>
        <input class="effectbutton" type="button"
         onclick="blindUp('header', opt())"
         value="blindUp"/>
    </div>

    <div><span class="handle"> </span>
        <input class="effectbutton" type="button"
         onclick="blindDown('header', opt())"
         value="blindDown"/>
    </div>

    <div><span class="handle"> </span>
        <input class="effectbutton" type="button"
         onclick="switchOff('header', opt())"
         value="switchOff"/>
    </div>

    <div><span class="handle"> </span>
        <input class="effectbutton" type="button"
         onclick="dropOut('header', opt())"
         value="dropOut"/>
    </div>

    <div><span class="handle"> </span>
        <input class="effectbutton" type="button"
         onclick="shake('header', opt())"
         value="shake"/>
    </div>

    <div><span class="handle"> </span>
        <input class="effectbutton"
         type="button" onclick="squish('header', opt())"
         value="squish"/>
    </div>

    <div><span class="handle"> </span>
        <input class="effectbutton"
         type="button" onclick="grow('header', opt())"
         value="grow"/>
    </div>
```

```
<div><span class="handle"> </span>
    <input class="effectbutton" type="button"
    onclick="shrink('header', opt())"
    value="shrink"/>
</div>

<div><span class="handle"> </span>
    <input class="effectbutton"
    type="button" onclick="pulsate('header', opt())"
    value="pulsate"/>
</div>

<div>
    <span class="handle"> </span> New Header Message:
    <input type="text"
    value="Welcome to South Barton"
    id="newtext"/>

    <input type="button" class="effectbutton"
    value="RollingSign"
onclick="new RollingSign('header', $('newtext').value, opt())"/>
        </div>
    </div>
</td>
<td width="50%" valign="top">
```

You'll note that there's nothing special in the HTML for doing our DND and sortable lists. We just set IDs on important nodes!

```
    <h2>Effect Chain</h2>

    <div id="effectchain"
    style="width:100%; border: 1px solid black; padding: 1em">
        <p>You can also run a series of effects on the header
          by dragging by the green handles from the list at
          left into the space below:</p>
        <p><input type="button" value="Run Effects"
            onclick="showChain()"/>
        </p>
    </div>
</td>
    </tr>
</table>
```

```
<script type="text/javascript">
```

First we create the main effect list Sortable. We've identified the effects with the **<div>**. The handle specifies a CSS class that represents the part the user should drag. We define a handle because we don't want to confuse clicks on the effects buttons with drags.

```
MochiKit.Sortable.Sortable.create("effectlist", {tag : "div", handle: "handle"});
MochiKit.Sortable.Sortable.create("effectchain", {dropOnEmpty: true, tag : div"});
</script>
```

```
</body>
</html>
```

The **effectchain** Sortable has the additional option of **dropOnEmpty**. That means that you can still drop things on the list even if there's nothing there to begin with.

15.3.8 Sortables and DragAndDrop

One call to `Sortable.create` packs a lot of power! `Sortable.create(element[, options])` takes an element (generally a `ul`) and a variety of options. Many of the options come straight from the DragAndDrop package, on which Sortable builds. Let's talk about the lower-level DND package before getting to the details of Sortable.

DND provides you with two kinds of objects: `Draggables` and `Droppables`. They have the familiar-looking signatures `new Draggable(element[, options])` and `new Droppable(element[, options])`. To allow an element to be picked up and dragged around the page is as simple as `new Draggable('elementid')`. However, you might want to change a number of options that affect the draggable's behavior. These options are listed in Table 15.5.

TABLE 15.5 Options for a Draggable Element

Option	Default Value	Description
handle	false	By default, the user can grab anywhere on the draggable element to start dragging it around. If you provide either a CSS class name or an element ID as the handle option, the user can grab the matching elements to drag them around.
starteffect	MochiKit.Visual. Opacity	When the drag is started, this callback is called with the element that is being dragged. Typically, this is an effect that you want to apply to the element.
revert	false	If true, the revert effect is called when the user releases the draggable somewhere other than an appropriate drop target.
revert-effect	MochiKit.Visual. Move	If you have the revert option set to true, this effect is called to return the draggable back to its original position.
endeffect	MochiKit.Visual. Opacity	Effect that will reverse the effect that was put on by the starteffect.

zindex	1000	CSS z-index for the element while it is being dragged. The default should put the element in front of every other element.
snap	false	Defines the behavior of the draggable while it's being dragged. It can be a function, a value, or an array of two values. As a function, it takes the (x,y) position as arguments and returns the position to draw in the browser. If it's a single value, it's used as a modulo for the x and y values. If it's a two-element array, a[0] is used as the modulo for the x-axis, and y[0] is used as the modulo for the y value.
selectclass	null	CSS class to be applied while the element is being dragged.
ghosting	false	If true, a "ghostlike" transparency will be applied to the element as it is dragged.
onchange	MochiKit.Base.noop	As the element is dragged, this function is called with the Sortable as its parameter.
scroll	false	Element in which the draggable can scroll around. For example, "window" will let it scroll around within the window.
scrollSen-sitivity	20	How quickly does the scroll speed increase as you get closer to the edges of the screen.
scrollSpeed	15	How fast does the scrolling move.
constraint	null	If set to horizontal or vertical, this will restrict the movement of this draggable to only the specified axis.

Wow! That's a lot of options! And that's just the draggable. It is, indeed, a lot of options. The DND module provides lower-level services and is set up to handle just about any drag-and-drop needs your application might have. It's quite easy to make an element draggable (new Draggable('elementid') is all it takes), but you'll likely spend a fair bit of time tweaking the behavior until it's exactly what you want it to be.

Let's take a look at the options available for a droppable, as listed in Table 15.6.

TABLE 15.6 Options for a Droppable Element

Option	Default	Description
greedy	true	MochiKit will stop looking for other droppables when a draggable is over this one.
hoverclass	null	The CSS class to apply when a draggable is hovering over this droppable.
hoverfunc	MochiKit.Base.noop	Called when a draggable starts or stops hovering over this droppable. The function is passed the draggable and true if the hovering has just started, false if the draggable has just been dragged off of the droppable.

accept	null	Array of CSS classes that `draggables` must have in order to be allowed to drop on this element. `null` means that no specific class is required.
active-class	null	CSS class applied.
onactive	MochiKit.Base.noop	When a `draggable` first comes over this `droppable`, this function will be called. This function is passed the `droppable` and the `draggable` as parameters.
containment	[ ]	This `droppable` will only accept a `draggable` that is either set as the value for `containment` or as one of the values in an array that is set as `containment`. Sortable uses this to control dragging behavior between Sortables.
onhover	MochiKit.Base.noop	This function is called as a `draggable` is moved over a `droppable`. It is passed three parameters: the `draggable`, the `droppable`, and a percentage of overlap.
ondrop	MochiKit.Base.noop	When a `draggable` is dropped, this function is called. It takes three arguments: the `draggable`, the `droppable`, and the event that resulted in the drop.

Using the `draggable` and `droppable` classes, you have a large amount of control over how the drag-and-drop experience looks (via CSS that is applied at various points) and acts (via the effects and callbacks). As you saw from the effects demo, the specific case of making a list of items that is sortable via DND has a high-level interface. Using Sortable, you don't need to worry about all the different event possibilities.

The options for Sortables can be found in Table 15.7.

TABLE 15.7 Options for Sortable Elements

Option	Default	Description
tag	"li"	Which tag your user can move around.
dropOnEmpty	false	Can you drop items on the list if there's nothing in the list?
overlap	"vertical"	The `draggable` needs to be overlapping by at least 50% in this direction in order to be `droppable`.
only	null	An element must have one of the CSS classes specified in `only` in order to be movable in the list.

format	`/^[^_]*_(.*)$/`	This regular expression is used for serialization based on the children's IDs. Using the default regular expression with ID values such as `foo_1`, `foo_2` and `foo_3`, you'll get back [1, 2, 3] as the values.
onChange	`MochiKit.Base.noop`	Called whenever the order of the sortable changes, even if the `draggable` isn't dropped into a new position.
onUpdate	`MochiKit.Base.noop`	Called after an element is dropped on the sortable.
tree	`false`	Makes a sortable tree. As of this writing, there is a warning in the MochiKit documentation that the speed of this feature becomes quickly unacceptable, so this is an experimental feature.

The features outlined in previous sections of this chapter enable you to craft powerful, interactive, web-based applications with far less effort than in years past. MochiKit's effects, combined with Sortable and DND functionality, can help put a serious shine on your application, giving it a modern look and feel that will delight your users. Have fun with it without overdoing it, and your users will love you for it.

15.4 Summary

- `MochiKit.Async` makes it trivial to retrieve data asynchronously from your Turbo-Gears server, providing your users with a responsive feel and up-to-date data.

- `Async` also lets you use exactly the same model for handling timed events within the browser.

- `MochiKit.Signal` gives you a consistent view and simple API for handling browser events, which is a key building block for sophisticated applications that perform actions based on user actions such as drag-and-drop or key presses.

- `MochiKit.Visual` gives your application a refined and fun appearance from simple features such as rounding the corners of your borders to complex animated transitions.

- In desktop applications, users take drag-and-drop for granted as a part of the experience. With `MochiKit.Sortable` and `MochiKit.DragAndDrop`, you can bring your web application up to the desktop-application standard with surprisingly little code.

## Chapter 16

TurboGears Widgets: Bringing CSS, XHTML, and JavaScript Together in Reusable Components

In This Chapter

If you develop web applications, there are a lot of things that you find yourself doing over and over and over again. If you are any good at your job, you don't want to write the same code over and over again with only small differences. Instead, you want to move that stuff out into separate functions, or even separate reusable packages. That's what TurboGears widgets are all about.

Widgets are particularly useful when you want to define reusable elements with complex display logic. Probably the most common web task that widgets are used for is form generation and display. So, the widgets package is integrated in with Form Encode, which helps validate form data and translate form data into valid Python objects.

16.1 Understanding Widgets

CherryPy, Kid, SQLObject, and MochiKit bring a lot to the table. TurboGears Widgets add another element which helps to complete the package. Other frameworks provide you mechanisms for reusing dynamic HTML snippets, and a couple even let you reuse chunks of JavaScript in your pages. But the `turbogears.widgets` package goes beyond all of that to make it easy to just call a widget in your template and have the HTML, CSS, and Javascript automatically added to your page—in the right places. But that's not all, widgets also help you to encode form results back into the right kind of Python objects, and handle any validation errors!

Widgets can be as simple as an HTML form element like the TextField or a MultipleSelect box, or they can be more complex Ajax-driven elements like the AutoCompleteField, Calender, Ajax Form, or the Lightbox Widgets.

As we mentioned in Chapter 5, "Enhancing Our Bookmark Application," you can safely send data into a widget in one of three ways:

- Assign a default at instantiation time
- Pass data in at render time
- Assign a callable at instantiation time which will return the required values—the callable will be executed at render time

About the only thing you shouldn't do is try to add data to your widget object outside of instantiation or render time. This is because widget objects are shared by *all* incoming requests. This means that changing attributes any time other than at instantiation or render time can lead to your data being used when answering another request.

16.1.1 Instantiation Time Customizations

One of the simplest and most common use cases for building your own widget is to create a form field with some of the customization points preselected. For example, say you want a text field widget with a particular default text to appear in several different forms. You could just write:

```
name = TextField(default="Enter your name here!")
```

You can then include this name widget in several forms, or render it on the page by itself, and it will always have the default text you want.

Perhaps this is overkill for something like default text, but it is very useful for slightly more complex widgets like the SelectField widget, which requires that you pass it a list of tuples defining the value and options for the widget to display.

```
domain_list = [(0, "google.com"), (1, "gmail.com"), (2, "blogger.com")
domain_selector = SingleSelectField(Options = domain_list, default=0)
```

You can also build a custom template for your widgets, and set up a new widget to always use that template:

```
name = TextField(default="Enter your name here!" template="bookmarker.templates.
namewidget)
```

In this case you'd also need to create a template file namewidget.kid, which might look something like this:

```
<input xmlns:py="http://purl.org/kid/ns#"
    type="text"
    name="${name}"
    class="${field_class}"
    id="${field_id}"
    value="${value}"
    py:attrs="attrs"
    size="30"
```

```
    maxlength="30"
/>
```

This template is the same as the standard TextField widget, except that we added the size and `maxlength` attributes. This means that our form will show a text field 30 characters wide, and not allow users to enter any more characters after that.

Of course, this is a trivial template modification. In fact the Widgets package even provides a shortcut for this kind of thing—but we'll get back to that in a second. For now it provides us with a simple example of how you can customize the template used to render a widget. If you wanted to you could create much more complex templates, with whatever HTML, JavaScript, or CSS you might need.

All widgets have the following attributes, any of which can be assigned at instantiation time:

TABLE 16.1 Default Widget Attributes

Attribute	Description
name	The name of the widget.
template	Kid template for the widget.
default	Default value for the widget.
css	List of CSSLinks and CSSSources for the widget. These will be automatically pulled and inserted in the page template that displays it.
javascript	List of JSLinks and JSSources for the widget. Same as css.
is_named	A property returning True if the widget has overridden its default name.
params	All parameter names listed here will be treated as special parameters. This list is updated by the metaclass and always contains *all* params from the widget itself and all its bases.
params_doc	A dictionary that contains each of the 'params' names and its associated docstring, which will be displayed in the Widget Browser

Some widgets have other attributes that you can use to customize their look or behavior. See section 16.2.2 for a complete listing of each of the standard TurboGears widgets and the attributes available for those widgets.

16.1.2 Render Time Attribute Assignment

Most of the time, if you want to set the value of a form widget that the user will see pre-populated in the form, you want to do it at render time, when you have the data from the database that you want to appear in the widget. We saw this in

Chapter 5, where we pulled the bookmark.link and other fields out of the database and assigned the defaults right at render time.

To do this, just drop the values you need into the form widget in your Kid template like this:

```
${my_form(value=values, action=action)}
```

Assuming you set up a dictionary of values with keys that match the names of the widgets on your forms, this whole thing will just work, and any missing values will either be given the default you defined at instantiation time or left empty if you didn't define a default.

There's actually one exception to this, which happens when you have form validation errors, but we'll come back to that in section 16.4 of this chapter, "Widgets and Validation."

16.1.3 Using Callables with Widgets

In Chapter 5, we saw how we could create a function (or really any callable), which we pass to our widget at initialization time. That function then calculates the list of options the widget needs every time the widget is rendered.

Our function grabbed the current list of categories from the database and returned them to the widget:

```
def get_category_options():
    categories = model.Categories.select()
    options = []
    for category in categories:
        options.append((category.id, category.categoryName))
    return options
```

We passed our callable into the widget in the same way we would the list of tuples it produces:

```
select_categories = widgets.MultipleSelectField(options=get_category_options)
```

This allows us to isolate the code necessary to create our options list in a function rather than repeating it in every form or controller that uses the widget. This is an incredibly useful idiom because it makes the widget capable of calculating its own options and helps keep our controllers and views clean and easy to understand.

16.2 Form Widgets

Form Widgets contain any number of form field elements. These elements are contained in a `WidgetsList` that contains all the form elements you want. A `WidgetsList` is like a Python list, so you can append new widgets to it dynamically, but remember this list will be rendered the same way for all incoming requests. So, in general, it's okay to create the `WidgetsList` pragmatically, but don't go around changing it after you've instantiated a form object with it, without thinking through the thread safety issues.

You might remember our widget example from Chapter 5:

```
class bookmark_fields(widgets.WidgetsList):
    bookmark_name = widgets.TextField(validator=validators.NotEmpty)
    link = widgets.TextField(validator=validators.URL)
    description = widgets.TextArea(validator=validators.NotEmpty)

bookmark_form = widgets.TableForm(fields=bookmark_fields(), submit_text="Save
Bookmark")
```

The first thing to notice here is that we create a simple `WidgetsList` that contains references to each of the fields we want in our form, along with whatever `validators` we want to use for that field. Then, we create a new `TableForm` widget instance called `bookmark_form` by passing in the list of fields to the form widget's `fields` param and setting the text we want to show up on the submit button.

If that's all you could do with `form` widgets, there would be a lot of cases where you might feel the need to write your forms by hand. Fortunately, widgets provide plenty of mechanisms for customization. So, unless your requirements are very strange, you should be able to get the form widget to do whatever you want.

16.2.1 Custom Form Layout

As we've already seen, it is easy to just take a list of form elements and build a `WidgetList`, pass it to your form and have everything automatically generated for you.

But, what do you do when you want to customize the layout of the resulting form?

Fortunately, TurboGears form widgets have a built mechanism that makes creating custom form templates easy.

If you have defined this form in your controller:

```
from turbogears import widgets

class MyForm(widgets.Form):
    template = "widgets.templates.wikiform"
    fields = [widgets.CalendarDateTimePicker("date"), widgets.
TinyMCEWidget("text")]
```

You can create a `wikiform.kid` template which lets you pick exactly where to render each of the widgets in your form.

```
<form xmlns:py="http://purl.org/kid/ns#"
    name="${name}"
    action="${action}"
    method="${method}"
    py:attrs="form_attrs">

  <h1> Choose the Date from the Calendar: </h1>
  ${display_field_for("date")}

  <h1> Enter some interesting text: >/h1>
  ${display_field_for("text")}
</form>
```

You can then render that form on any page, in the same way that you would render any other form. This provides you with total control of the way your form will be displayed on your final page. In this case you'll get two fields, both of which include some complex JavaScript stuff. The first provides a calendar pop-up for you to use to select the date you want. The second is a third-party widget that you can download from www.turbogears.org/cogbin, and it provides a nice WYSIWYG text editor.

16.2.2 Form Field Widgets

As we've already seen, TurboGears provides a number of interesting widgets for use in your forms. The basics are definitely covered with a matching widget for each of the HTML form element types. But, as we just saw, there are a few extra form filed widgets, which TurboGears provides to make creating dynamic web applications easier.

- `AutoComplete`—provides a list of possible selections that is dynamically updated as you type. The list of possible selections is provided by a search controller method that returns a JSONified list to the page. We'll explore this widget in more detail in section 16.7, "Anatomy of an Ajax Widget."

- `Button`—renders a generic button. It serves as a superclass for the SubmitButton, ResetButton, and ImageButton fields. You can subclass it to create your own custom button fields, too.

- `SubmitButton`—renders the submit button for a form.

- `ResetButton`—clears the data from the associated form.

- `ImageButton`—this button has an image on it.

- `CheckBox`—renders a simple checkbox field to your form.

- `CheckBoxList`—renders several checkboxes.

- `CalendarDateTimePicker`—renders a dynamic calender display that allows you to pick a date and time.

- `CalendarDatePicker`—just like the `CalendarDateTimePicker`, but only allows you to pick a date not the time.

- `HiddenField`—adds a hidden field to your form. Hidden fields can be an easy way to make sure data is passed back to the server with the form.

- `PasswordField`—displays a password type field where the characters the user types are not displayed.

- `RadioButtonList`—displays a radio button.

- `SingleSelectField`—displays a select field.

- `MultipleSelectField`—displays a select field that allows you to select multiple options.

- `TextArea`—displays a text area.

- `TextField`—displays a text field.

In the TurboGears ToolBox (which will be explored in depth in Chapter 19, "The TurboGears Toolbox and Other Tools") there's a Widget Browser tool that shows each of the installed widgets, along with descriptions, sample code, and the template code for that widget. You can use the Widget Browser to learn more about each of the above widgets, but there's another more important reason to check out the Widget Browser—it displays all installed widgets, not just the built in widgets mentioned here.

It's possible to package up a widget into a reusable component, and upload it to a central Python repository known as the Cheese Shop. These widgets are then automatically made available to you for easy_install. You can see a list of all the available thrid party widgets in the "CogBin" portion of the TurboGears website (www.turbogears.org/cogbin/).

Once you download and install a widget, it will automatically show up in the Widget Browser. So while we've provided brief descriptions of each of the form field widgets, the Widget Browser will provide descriptions for all kinds of other widgets, including all of the third-party widgets you've installed.

16.3 Compound Widgets

The form widget is made up of references to other widgets, and it's the most common case for one widget containing another, but there are lots of other cases where one widget contains another. We've already seen that the WhatWhat Status project has a NotesWidget that displays all the notes for a particular project, by calling the note_widget to display each individual project note.

So, rather than keeping all of the logic for maintaining Compound Widgets in the Form itself, the TurboGears widgets package maintains an abstract base class for Compound Widgets.

Having a CompoundWidget base class means that you can create your own Compound Widgets through subclassing. Here's the NotesWidget from the WhatWhat Status project:

```
class NotesWidget(CompoundWidget):
    template       = 'whatwhat.widgets.templates.notes'
    params         = ['notes', 'read_only']
    member_widgets = ['note_widget']
    note_widget    = note_widget
    read_only      = False
```

The member_widgets declaration is the key element that is specific to a CompoundWidget. The NotesWidget contains note_widgets.

In addition to the standard CompoundWidget, TurboGears also provides a CompoundFormField that can make your life easier when you want to create a set of form fields that are grouped together for some reason.

One popular example might be a form that allows you to type in the first portion of an email address and then select the remainder from a drop down list. If you don't understand the initialization setup, feel free to skip over it for the moment; we'll come back to it and explain what's happening in section 16.6, "Creating Custom Widgets."

```
class CompoundEmailField(CompoundFormField):
    member_widgets = ["usename", "domain"]

    template = """
    <div xmlns:py="http://purl.org/kid/ns#" class="${field_class}">
        ${display_field_for(username)}
        ${display_field_for(domain)}
    </div>
    """

    def __init__(self, tfield_params={}, sel_params={}, *args, **kw):

        # Call super to set params and bind them to the proper
        # widget instance
        super(CompoundEmailField, self).__init__(*args, **kw)

        # initialize the username and domain child widgets
        self.username = TextField("username", **tfield_params)
        sel_params.setdefault('validator', validators.Int())
        self.domain = SingleSelectField("domain",
                                        validator=validators.Int(),
                                        **sel_params)
```

As you can see, `CompoundFormField` templates can use the same `display_field_for` function that we used earlier when creating a custom form. This makes designing and styling compound form field widgets pretty easy. The above example is pretty simple, but you can easily see how it could be expanded to separate large forms, into separate reusable sub-forms.

If you aren't expecting to use your widgets in a form, you won't need all the validation bells and whistles of the `CompoundFormField`, so you'll be better off using the standard `CompoundFieldWidget`. And that brings us to our next topic—Validation.

16.4 Widgets and Validation

We briefly saw how validation works in Chapter 5, but there's a lot more power and flexibility in the validation library TurboGears uses than we've had a chance to cover.

Not only that, widgets have some special built-in features that help make form validation even easier and more painless.

Widget-based forms automatically handle validation errors, display error messages, and translate data from Python objects into the strings used in the form, and back again when the form is processed. We've already seen most of this in action in Chapter 5, so you probably have a general idea of what happens. But in the next few pages we're going to peel the covers back a bit and take a look at how all of this works and how you can customize things to get exactly the behavior you want from your forms.

16.4.1 How FormEncode Validators Integrate into Form Widgets

As we mentioned, nearly every web application is going to include forms and nearly every set of forms has required fields or other input validation associated with them. Not only that, nearly every form gets some data from the user that ought to be converted from a string (all form results come from the browser as strings) into a proper Python object. You want age to be an `int`, dates to be `datetime` objects, etc.

Coding all of this to work by hand isn't rocket science, but it's tedious and repetitive. So, TurboGears needed a way to get rid of all the repetitive stuff for you. Because the TurboGears philosophy is to use the best existing libraries wherever possible, it provides easy access to Ian Bicking's FormEncode package.

From day one TurboGears provided convenient access to Form Encode Validators via controller decorators (see Chapter 17, "CherryPy and TurboGears Decorators," for details). Widgets take this one step further and automate error display.

FormEncode is designed to convert and validate incoming data and produce validation error messages when necessary. The TurboGears validation mechanism ties directly into FormEncode to preprocess incoming form data so your controller objects get form data in the proper Python type.

If there are errors, the `error_handler` appends the validation error messages to the `cherrypy.request` object (more about all of this in Chapter 17, and sends the user to another controller method which can handle the errors.

Form widgets take this one step further, integrating FormEncode into the widget declaration/display process. This means that you can tell a form to act as its own `error_handler`, and it will take care of displaying validation errors for you.

We've already seen that widgets display `input_value` and validation error messages when their contents fail to validate, but let's take a quick look at how this all works.

The built-in form widgets know how to display their own errors. We didn't mention it earlier for the sake of keeping things simple, but TurboGears form widgets also check the `cherrypy.request` object to see if there are validation errors present and if errors are present, displays them next to the proper form element.

At the same time, `form` widgets know how to pull the `input_value` for each form element off the request object. The `input_value` contains whatever value was submitted by the user when she filled out the form. Because `TableForm` knows how to check `input_value` and `validation_errors` and display them properly, all you have to do is set `validators` on the field elements, and set up the save method's `error_handler` to point to a controller method that uses the same `form` widget to display validation errors.

16.4.2 More Validators

Sometimes you need more than an `Int()` validator. Fortunately, FormEncode provides a number of built-in validators that you can use. Not only that, it provides you with a simple mechanism for creating your own validators.

More often than not one of the built-in validators can give you what you need—the `regex` validator is particularly flexible. If you want to check that the user entered a valid number, a valid date, a valid URL, or a valid e-mail address, there are built-in validators to help you.

The most-up-to date list of built-in validators is available at www.turbogears.org/docs/api/formencode.validators-module.htm. Here's a list of the most commonly used validators:

- `Constant`—If you want to ignore the user's input, and always use a constant instead, this is the validator for you

- `CreditCardValidator`—Accepts only credit card numbers in a valid format (note it does not actually check that the card number is real)

- `DateConverter`—Converts a date mm/yy, dd/mm/yy, dd-mm-yy into a datetime object. `DateConverter` always assumes the second value is the month

- `DateValidator`—Checks that the user-entered date is within specified range (useful, for example, if you want to check that a user's birth date is over 18 years ago)

- `DictConverter`—Takes a list of key-value pairs, and matches user input against the keys to return a value

- `Email`—Checks the basic form of an email address

- **Empty**—Validates that the user didn't enter any value. (Fill in this textfield now or forever hold your peace...)
- **IndexListConverter**—Converts an index (which may be a string like "2") to the value in the given list
- **Int**—Converts a value to an integer
- **MaxLength**—Confirms that the string is shorter than the int you pass in
- **MinLength**—Confirms that the string is longer than the int you pass in
- **NotEmpty**—Confirms that the value is not empty (empty string, empty list, etc.)
- **Number**—Converts a value to a float or integer
- **OneOf**—Tests that the value is one of the members of a given list
- **PhoneNumber**—Validates, and converts to ###-###-####. It can even handle extensions (as ext.##...)
- **PlainText**—Confirms that the field contains only letters, numbers, underscore, and the hyphen—no special characters allowed. (This can be useful for security purposes, which we'll discuss in a bit more detail in Chapter 22, "TurboGears Identity and Security")
- **PostalCode**—Verifies that the number is a valid US Zip Code
- **Regex**—Checks the user input against a regular expression you provide
- **StateProvince**—Verifies that the user entered a valid two letter state or province code (US and Canada only)
- **String**—Converts data to string, but treats empty objects as the empty strings
- **TimeConverter**—Converts user entered times in the format: HH:MM:SSampm to a tuple in the format: (h, m, s)
- **URL** —Validates that the returned string is a structurally valid URL

Sometimes you want more than any one of these validators can give you. You want to assure that a form field is a valid URL, and it's at least 10 characters long. That's where compound validators come in—FormEncode provides the `any` and `all` validators, which do pretty much what they say. If you write:

```
mywidget=widgets.TextField(name = "int_or_plan_text",
                validator=validators.any(validators.PlainText(),
                                validators.Int())
```

The `mywidget` widget defined above will accept input as valid if either the value entered by the user is plain text, or an integer.

If, on the other hand, you wanted to check that the returned URL string didn't have any special characters, you can write something like this:

```
mywidget=widgets.TextTield(name= "URL_and_more_than_10_characters"),
                        validators.all(validators.plaintext(),
                                    validators.MinLength(15))
```

As we mentioned earlier, the `Regex` validator can handle most of your string validation needs. But, since the purpose of validators is not just to specify rules about the contents of user values, it is also to convert user entered values into usable Python objects, it is often advantageous to create your own validators. Fortunately that's actually pretty simple to do.

Creating your own validator is a three-to-four step process. Validators need to know how to convert Python object strings, how to convert strings to the right kind of Python object, and what kind of messages to display when something goes wrong. To create a new `validator` class:

1. Subclass `FancyValidator`.

2. Create an error `messages` dictionary.

3. Define a `_to_python` method that will convert the string returned by the browser into whatever Python object you want, and if necessary, create a `validate_python` method that will test the Python object in some way and raise an `Invalid` error when needed.

4. If necessary, define a `_from_python` method that will convert the Python object you have into a string for the browser.

Don't let the fact that this is a four-step process fool you into thinking that it's complicated. Here's the code for a simple validator:

```
class isWikiWord(validators.FancyValidator):
    wiki_regex = re.compile(r"\b([A-Z]\w+[A-Z]+\w+)")

    messages = {'non_wiki': 'Your Page Name must be a WikiWord'}

    def _to_python(self, value, state):
        return value.strip()

    def validate_python(self, value, state):
        if not self.wiki_regex.match(value):
```

```
        raise validators.Invalid(self.message("non_wiki"),
                        value, state)
```

If you have more than one failure mode, you just define the additional failure messages in your messages dictionary, and add additional raise Invalid exceptions to your _to_python or validate_python methods.

The FancyValidator class gives your validator several options which can be used when creating a new instance.

- **if_empty**—If set, this value will be returned if the input evaluates to false (empty list, empty string, None, etc.), but not the 0 or False objects. This only applies to **to_python**.

- **not_empty**—If True, then if an empty value is given raise an error. If validate_python true this will also check that the Python value is not empty, too.

- **strip**—If true and the input is a string, strip it (occurs before empty tests).

- **if_invalid**—If set, then when this validator raises Invalid during to_python, this value is returned instead.

- **if_invalid_python**—If set, when the Python value (converted with from_python) is invalid, this value will be returned.

- **accept_python**—If True then .validate_python and .validate_other will not be called when from_python is called.

16.4.3 Basics of Schema Validation

Sometimes you can't validate a piece of user input in isolation. Password verification fields are a common example. You want the data in each of those two fields to match. This is where schema validation comes in. Schemas are pretty simple as long as you don't have deeply nested compound widgets to match up with your schema.

If you have two password fields by themselves in the change_password form, you could create a schema that looks like this:

```
class UserFields(widgets.WidgetsDeclaration):
    passwd = widgets.PasswordField(validator=validators.NotEmpty())
    passwd2 = widgets.PasswordField(validator=validators.UnicodeString())

class UserSchema(formencode.schema.Schema):
    chained_validators = [validators.FieldsMatch('passwd', 'passwd2')]

form = TableForm(fields=UserFields(), validator=UserSchema)
```

The UserSchema class uses chained_validators, which are validators run on the dictionary of form responses after all the other validators are done. Since the schema is just another validator, you can create nested validation schemas, to do chain validation on nested dictionaries. In general you'll find your life is easier if you don't create too many nested dictionaries in need of validation (after all in Python "flat is better than nested").

There's another built-in validator designed especially for schema validation:

- **FieldsMatch**—Checks two fields to verify that they are identical.

16.5 CSS, JavaScript, and Widgets

Widgets are designed to have JavaScript behaviors and element IDs and classes built right into their template code. So, for simple JavaScript and CSS styling that may be all you need. But whenever you do anything slightly more complex, your widget may need access to JavaScript libraries, like MochiKit, Scriptaculous, or Dojo. Widgets provide a simple syntax to assure that the right script and CSS tags get added to your headers, and that they are only added once—even if multiple widgets ask for them.

The functions that do all of this are JSLink and CSSLink. When you display any widget on a page, its CSS and JavaScript links get thrown into a couple of set-like objects that contain only one of each CSS or JavaScript link. Then when the page is rendered, these links are conveniently placed in the headers of the page.

When you are using widgets, you don't need to worry about what JavaScript and CSS links need to be included, the widgets themselves know, and will do the right thing automatically.

You don't really need to deal with the JSLink or CSSLink functions unless you are creating your own widgets. But if you are creating or modifying a widget's CSS or JavaScript links, the code is very simple. Here's how the AutoComplete field defines the JavaScript and CSS that it requires in order to work properly.

```
javascript = [mochikit, JSLink(static,"autocompletefield.js")]
css = [CSSLink(static,"autocompletefield.css")]
```

We'll come back to the AutoComplete widget in section 16.7 where we'll go through each of its parts to show you how easy it is to create full-fledged Ajax-style widgets.

16.6 Creating Custom Widgets

We've already seen how the creators of the WhatWhat Status project used custom widgets to display and dynamically create editable forms for Project data. You may want to go back and take another look at Chapter 7, "Controllers, Views, and JavaScript in the WhatWhat Status," to go over those widgets in light of your new insight into how widgets work.

Rather than go over that same ground again in this chapter, we're going to look at how two very different widgets work.

First, let's take a look at how TableForm works to render errors, and form fields on the page, and how we could customize the `TableForm` widget.

Here's the original `TableForm` widget code.

```
class TableForm(Form):
    template = """
    <form xmlns:py="http://purl.org/kid/ns#"
        name="${name}"
        action="${action}"
        method="${method}"
        class="tableform"
        py:attrs="form_attrs"
    >
        <div py:for="field in hidden_fields"
            py:replace="field.display(value_for(field), **params_for(field))"
        />
        <table border="0" cellspacing="0" cellpadding="2" py:attrs="table_attrs">
            <tr py:for="i, field in enumerate(fields)"
                class="${i%2 and 'odd' or 'even'}"
            >
                <th>
                    <label class="fieldlabel"
                            for="${field.field_id}"
                            py:content="field.label" />
                </th>
                <td>
                    <span
                    py:replace="field.display(value_for(field), **params_for(field))"
                    />
                    <span py:if="error_for(field)"
                            class="fielderror"
                            py:content="error_for(field)" />
```

```
                <span py:if="field.help_text"
                        class="fieldhelp"
                        py:content="field.help_text" />
            </td>
        </tr>
        <tr>
            <td> </td>
            <td py:content="submit.display(submit_text)" />
        </tr>
    </table>
</form>
"""
params = ["table_attrs"]
params_doc = {'table_attrs' : 'Extra (X)HTML attributes for the Table tag'}
table_attrs = {}
```

As you can see, the bulk of the widget is the template code. You can either define your templates in a separate .kid file, and point to their location, or you can include them as a string right in the widget code itself as seen above.

You'll notice the error_for method is displayed just to the right of the field with an error. Some people prefer to see the errors formatted differently, or displayed above or before the form element. Fortunately, this kind of adjustment isn't hard at all. All you need to do is replace the widget's template with something more to your liking.

There are two ways we could go about doing this. We could create a CustomTableForm class very much like the TableForm, or we could just override the template attribute of the TableForm field whenever we instantiate a new TableForm object.

If the form is only being used once, it's probably easier to just override the template attribute at instantiation time. So, if we wanted to update the Bookmarker application that we built in Part 2, to use a custom form, we could change the bookmark_form instantiation to look like this:

```
bookmark_form = widgets.TableForm(template = "bookmarker.templates.custom_form",
                                  fields=bookmark_fields(),
                                  submit_text="Save Bookmark")
```

If, however, we wanted to use this new style form layout in several different places, or with several different forms, we can reduce code duplication by subclassing the TableWidget form like this:

```
class MyForm(widgets.TableWidget)
    template  = "bookmarker.templates.custom_form"
```

Of course, we are skipping something. We need to create the `custom_form.kid` file to be used in either case. This is a standard Kid template file.

```
<form xmlns:py="http://purl.org/kid/ns#"
    name="${name}"
    action="${action}"
    method="${method}"
    class="tableform"
    py:attrs="form_attrs"
>
    <div py:for="field in hidden_fields"
        py:replace="field.display(value_for(field), **params_for(field))"
    />
        <table border="0" cellspacing="0" cellpadding="2" py:attrs="table_attrs">
        <tr py:for="i, field in enumerate(fields)"
            class="${i%2 and 'odd' or 'even'}"
        >
            <th>
                <label class="fieldlabel"
                       for="${field.field_id}"
                       py:content="field.label" />
            </th>
            <td>
                <span py:if="error_for(field)"
                      class="fielderror" py:content="error_for(field)">
                    <br />
                </span>
                <span
                 py:replace="field.display(value_for(field), **params_for(field))"
                />
                <span py:if="field.help_text"
                      class="fieldhelp" py:content="field.help_text" />
            </td>
        </tr>
        <tr>
            <td> </td>
            <td py:content="submit.display(submit_text)" />
        </tr>
    </table>
</form>
```

The only difference between this and the standard `TableForm` widget is that we moved error reporting above the `value_for` insertion and included a break after the error message display. Because the template checks the existence of the error with `error_for(field)`, these will only be included in the table when there is an error.

Once you get the hang of it, widgets are infinitely customizable, and provide an excellent way to package up repeated code bits in highly customizable and reusable packages.

16.7 Anatomy of an Ajax Widget

Widgets are a part of the TurboGears view layer, so Ajax widgets need to work in cooperation with your application's controller methods to get data back from the server. The `AutoCompleteField` widget defines a couple of important `params` which are used to control not only how the widget works, but also which controller method should be called when the user starts typing.

There are two major parts of the auto-complete widget: the first is widget code presented here, and the second is the `autocomplete.js` file which contains all the Java-Script necessary to make everything work.

In many ways the `AutoCompleteField` is just like any other widget; it defines a template, and a couple of `params`. The template sets up a script tag and creates a new JavaScript Object called `AutoCompleteManagerX`, where X is replaced by the `field_id`. This keeps one `AutoCompleteManager` from stomping on another when you set up several `AutoCompleteFields` on the same page. The constructor for the JavaScript `AutoComplete` function takes several parameters, which are pulled from the widget's params, which we'll discuss after we take a closer look at the widget code itself.

There's a separate div class setup for the `autoCompleteResultsX` (again X will be replaced by the `field_id`). The `autoCompleteManager` based function does all the real work calling the server, parsing the results, and populating the `div` which displays possible matches.

Here's the widget code itself:

```
class AutoCompleteField(CompoundFormField):
    """Performs Ajax-style autocompletion by requesting search
    results from the server as the user types."""

    template = """
    <div xmlns:py="http://purl.org/kid/ns#">
```

```
<script language="JavaScript" type="text/JavaScript">
  AutoCompleteManager${field_id} = new AutoCompleteManager('${field_id}',
    '${text_field.field_id}', '${hidden_field.field_id}',
    '${search_controller}', '${search_param}',
    '${result_name}',${str(only_suggest).lower()},
    '${tg.url([tg.widgets, 'turbogears.widgets/spinner.gif'])}');

  addLoadEvent(AutoCompleteManager${field_id}.initialize);
</script>

${text_field.display(value_for(text_field), **params_for(text_field))}
<img name="autoCompleteSpinner${name}" id="autoCompleteSpinner${field_id}"
 src="${tg.url([tg.widgets, 'turbogears.widgets/spinnerstopped.png'])}"
 alt="" />


<div class="autoTextResults" id="autoCompleteResults${field_id}"/>
${hidden_field.display(value_for(hidden_field), **params_for(hidden_field))}
</div>
"""

javascript = [mochikit, JSLink(static,"autocompletefield.js")]
css = [CSSLink(static,"autocompletefield.css")]
member_widgets = ["text_field", "hidden_field"]
params = ["search_controller", "search_param",
                "result_name", "attrs", "only_suggest"]
text_field = TextField(name="text")
hidden_field = HiddenField(name="hidden")
attrs = {}
search_controller = ""
search_param = "searchString"
result_name = "textItems"
only_suggest = False
```

The `params` in this widget are all pretty important. But the single most important is the `search_controller` which tells the widget which URL on the server ought to be called to get a list of possible matches.

The `AutoCompleteManager` based function will call the `search_controller` URL with a single key-value pair—the key is whatever you've used as `search_param`, and the value is the current contents of the field.

The controller should return a JSON object, containing a key that matches the value of the `result_name` param. That `result_name` key should map to a list of strings that contain all the possible matches.

The last important `param` is `only_suggest`, which governs whether the `AutoComplete` field will accept strings that don't match the results received from the server. The default is False, which means that—unless you set `only_suggest` to True—the field will allow the user to enter a brand new value that does not match anything returned from the server.

All of this can seem a bit abstract, so lets's take a look at an example that uses the `AutoComplete` widget:

```
class DeleteUser(WidgetsList):
username = AutoCompleteField(search_controller = "/search_username",
                             search_param = "search",
                             result_name = "usernames")

task_form=TableForm(fields=DeleteUser())
```

Here's the `search_username` method:

```
@expose(allow_json=True)
def search_username(self, search):
  matching_users = User.select(User.q.username.startswith(search))
  usernames = [user.username for user in matching_users]
  return dict(usernames=usernames)
```

As you can see it's not hard to wrap an existing JavaScript funtion into a reusable Widget. Writing `autocomplete.js` would take considerably more time. The interface for using `AutoComplete` widgets is flexible and easy to use. Widgets make this all possible, and it's not hard to create your own widgets, or pick up new widgets from the CogBin.

16.8 Summary

- Widgets provide a way to Package HTML, CSS and JavaScript into reusable components.
- Widgets are shared between all incoming requests, so they should be stateless.

- Widget params can be given defaults at instantiation time, values at render time, or they can be assigned a callable which will be run automatically at render time to get the proper value.

- TurboGears provides a `form` widget which handles displaying its own validation errors.

- TurboGears form widgets integrate with FormEncode to handle validation.

- FormWidget makes it easy to create your own Validators by subclassing `FancyValidator.`

- The FormWidget is a special case of the more general CompoundWidget, which you can use to create nested widget structures of your own.

- `CSSLink` and `JSLink` provide a simple way to make sure that your pages only download the necessary files once, even if dozens or hundreds of widgets on your page include links to the same files.

- Widgets are customizable by overriding attributes, or by subclassing.

- The code for the AutoComplete widget shows how easy it is to integrate JavaScript, HTML, and CSS into a single reusable component.

- Widgets are view technology, so Ajax widgets interact with controller methods that handle user actions. The AutoComplete widget shows a simple example of how that works.

PART VI

CherryPy and TurboGears Controller Technologies

Chapter 17

CherryPy and TurboGears Decorators

In This Chapter

In this chapter, we cover the details of CherryPy and TurboGears controllers. As you have already seen, CherryPy converts URLs into calls to controller objects. In Chapter 8, "RSS, Cookies, and Dynamic Views in WhatWhat Status," you saw a foreshadowing of how CherryPy handles HTTP requests and responses, when we looked at `cherrypy.request.simple_cookie`. In this chapter, we take a deeper look into the details of how a user request is handled.

After we cover the basics of CherryPy, we turn to the TurboGears controller decorators. The `@expose` and `@validate` decorators make it easy to be flexible in the output that your controller gives. You can send out straight HTML, call a template to be rendered, create JSON to return to an Ajax call, or set up an XML interface to expose a web service.

Finally, we delve into REST and provide you with a simple recipe you can use with TurboGears to create RESTful interfaces for your model objects.

17.1   CherryPy URL Parsing

CherryPy has a special place in the TurboGears framework—it handles incoming requests and ultimately sends the response back to the user. The first thing CherryPy does is parse out the incoming request object into its component parts and stuffs them into the request object. It then takes the path of the incoming request and tries to match it up to the methods of your application's root class.

In practice, this is straightforward. But the underlying rules can seem a bit complex the first time through. So, we take care of those rules, and then look at some examples that will probably clear things up. Normally, CherryPy looks for the best match (the one that matches the highest number of path elements) and calls the last callable in the hierarchy that it matches. Any "leftover" path elements at the end of the path are turned into positional prarameters and passed into the object that gets called.

The last matching object can be a method, a function, or anything that implements the `_call_` method. In Python these objects are often referred to as a "callable" because they can be called with arguments, and they return a value of some kind.

On the surface, that sounds simple enough, but there are a couple of twists and turns that can cause you trouble if you aren't careful. In Python, a class is a callable, which returns an instance. But classes don't return values that can be published to the web when they are called; they return new instances. So, CherryPy introduces a special method index.

CherryPy calls index whenever the last matching object in the hierarchy has an index method—and there are no further path elements in the URL. So, when you have an object with an index method, CherryPy calls that index method rather than calling the object directly. This is roughly equivalent to the way that index.html is served up automatically when you go to a web directory without asking for a specific file. For example, in the Fast Track code, the root controller has a line:

```
dashboard = DashboardController()
```

After this has been defined, browsing to /dashboard or /dashboard/ will call the index method of the DashboardController class.

On the other hand, if the last callable object does not contain an index method, it is called directly.

But, wait, that's not all. The index method is *only* called when the URL maps directly to the last object with nothing "left over." The index method never receives positional parameters.

This brings us to the next "special" method—default. If you don't end up calling a class directly, but you didn't define a matching method or function attribute in that class, CherryPy looks for default and calls it if it exists. Unlike index, default gets all the remaining path elements as positional parameters.

17.2 CherryPy and the HTTP Request/Response Cycle

As you will see in Chapter 18, "TurboGears Deployment," you can run TurboGears applications directly on CherryPy, or behind ModPython, ModProxy, or behind any server that supports the Web Server Gateway Interface (WSGI) specification. But no matter how you configure the front end, CherryPy is still responsible for handling the incoming requests and creating the final responses to go out to the user.

The exact methods that CherryPy uses are probably not important, but it is often important that you know how to access the various request properties, and how to set response parameters. Luckily, the `cherrypy.request` and `cherrypy.response` objects provide easy access to each of these items.

For example, when extending the 20 Min Wiki (available on turbogearsbook. com), you might want to implement a common wiki feature that logs the IP address of every user who edits a page. This is extraordinarily easy: Just add a line such as `user_IP = cherrypy.request.remote_addr()`. You can then save `user_IP` into whatever log format you want.

Some people have complained about CherryPy because it doesn't differentiate between post and get requests. But this complaint is misdirected; you can create a simple controller object that determines the request method with a single call to `cherrypy.request.method` and use it to redirect you to objects that handle the specific request type that came in. And most of the time, the same object can handle both post and get requests, so less-common cases are easy, and the common case is absolutely trivial. In Table 17.1, you can see the attributes of the `request` object and what they return.

TABLE 17-1 `cherrypy.request` Object Attributes

Attribute	Type	Description
`request.remote_addr`	string	Contains the IP address of the client who made the request, or empty string (if remote address is unavailable).
`request.remote_port`	int	Contains the client port number, or -1 if the client port is not available.
`request.remote_host`	string	Contains the client host name if available
`request.headers`	dict	Contains a dictionary with the HTTP headers
`request.request_line`		The first line of the request, which will be something like `PUT /path/to/page HTTP/1.0`.
`request.simple_cookie`	simple_ cookie	Contains a `simple_cookie` object from the standard library's `cookie` module.
`request.rfile`	The un- processed request body (for post and put requests)	Contains the `rfile` attribute and is only available for post or put methods only when the `processRequestBody` value is set to `False`. If `processRequestBody` is `True`, the request body will be consumed and the results placed in `request.body` or turned into the parameters passed into the `controller` method.

`request.body`	the body of the request	Contains the contents of a put or post request that is not encoded as `application/x-www-form-urlencoded`
`request.processRequestBody`	boolean	This attribute doesn't contain data from the request—instead it controls whether the request body is processed by CherryPy or left in the `rfile` attribute for your controllers to process on their own.
`request.method`	string	Contains the HTTP request method (GET, POST, and so on).
`request.protocol`	string	Contains the version of the HTTP used for the request in the format `HTTP/1.1`.
`request.version`	num	Contains a numeric representation of the HTTP version used in the request.
`request.wsgi_environ`	dict	Contains the environment dictionary for use with Web Server Gateway Interface (WSGI) call (only available when you use a WSGI server).
`request.query_string`	string	The query string of the request (everything after the ?).
`request.path`	string	This contains the path portion of the URL from the request
`request.params`	dict	Contains all values from the query string and the values from the post body (if any).
`request.base`	string	Contains the base URL of the request.
`request.browser_url`	string	Contains the full URL from the browser, base + path + querystring.
`request.object_path`	string	Contains the object path of the exposed method that will be called for this request.
`request.original_path`	string	Contains the original path to the exposed method for this request—only useful if you have filters that might change the object path.
`request.original_params`	dict	Contains the original parameters in case they were modified by a filter on the way in.
`request.scheme`	string	"http" or "https" so you can tell whether the request came over a secure channel.

We've already mentioned that having the `remote_addr` and method information can be tremendously useful. We also saw `simple_cookie` used in Fast Track (Chapter 8). Many of the other attributes will only be used in unusual cases, but they are always there if you need them.

But, you can also store information specific to a particular request in the `cherrypy.request` object, and it will be automatically available anywhere you need it while processing that request. Table 17-2 lists each of the attributes of the `cherry.response` object. You can set these attributes to modify the response that will be sent to the user.

TABLE 17-2 `cherrypy.response` Object Attributes

Attribute	Type	Description
`cherrypy.response.headers`	dict	Just like `request.headers`, but contains the headers that will be included in the response.
`cherrypy.response.simple_cookie`	simple_cookie	Contains a simple cookie object that behaves like a Python dictionary.
`cherrypy.response.body`	string or itterable	Contains the response string of the cherrypy method, or a generator that will produce the final HTTP output.
`cherrypy.response.status`	int or string	The HTTP response string, or an int that corresponds to the nummeric value of the response code.
`cherrypy.response.version`	string	The HTTP version that should be used in the response.

17.3   CherryPy Filters

CherryPy also has hooks for running special functions called filters at several different points in the request cycle, before and after the published object is executed.

Filters allow for a lot of flexibility in the way requests are handled. CherryPy comes with several built-in filters to do caching, session management, compression, XML Remote Procedure Call (RPC) request processing, and to otherwise slice and dice the request object in interesting ways. But wait, that's not all. CherryPy also provides an easy-to-use mechanism for you to create your own custom filters, which are applied to whichever sections of your object hierarchy you choose.

But it's likely that future versions of TurboGears will use a somewhat different implementation of filters, so if you're using something more recent than 1.0 you may want to check the online documents.

17.3.1   Input Filters

The most logical place to start seeing what filters can do for you in CherryPy is to take a look at some of the built-in input filters. In Table 17-3 you will find a list of the built-in CherryPy input filters.

TABLE 17-3   CherryPy Input Filters

Filter	Description
`cache_filter`	Used for caching request responses to short-circuit the need for further evaluation.
`log_debug_info_filter`	The CherryPy filter that lists the request time.
`base_url_filter`	Automatically transform the `base_url` on the way in. We'll see this in use when we mount CherryPy behind Apache.
`virtual_host_filter`	This filter makes it easy to have independent sites that also appear as subdirectories of one main site.
`DecodingFilter`	Sets a default character encoding.
`SessionFilter`	Maintains session state for you. It sets a cookie, and turns that cookie into a link to session data that you can use while processing the request.
`SessionAuthenticateFilter`	This is a built-in CherryPyAuthentication filter, but Identity or TurboPeakSecurity are generally better choices for TurboGears projects.
`StaticFilter`	TurboGears uses this one by default to serve up static files for your application from the /static directory.
`NsgmlsFilter`	Process nsgml-formatted input.
`TidyFilter`	Validates HTML.
`XmlRpcFilter`	Handles XML requests for you by converting the posted data to a method name and parameters. See CherryPy's online documents for more detail.

These filters are contained in the `cherrypy.filter.input_order` list in the above order. You should be able to open that list and add your own filters; filters will be applied in the order they appear in the `input_order` list. Each item in this list should be a fully qualified package location. (This is already true for the built-in filters, but you want to follow the same convention for any filters you add!)

17.3.2   Output Filters

Just like the input filters, each of these output filters is contained in the `cherrypy.filters.output_filters` list, which defines the order of the filters that are run. You can configure any of these built-in filters by turning them on in the configuration `app.cfg` (which can be found in your project's config folder).

Here's a sample of how we turn on the static file filter for the /`static` directory:

```
[/static]
static_filter.on = True
static_filter.dir = "%(top_level_dir)s/static"
```

You can use the Output Filters described in Table 17-4 to compress the response before sending it back to the user, or even create XML-RPC output.

TABLE 17-4   Output Filters

Filter	Description
ResponseHeadersFilter	Creates custom headers.
XmlRpcFilter	Creates XML RPC on the way out.
EncodingFilter	Forces a particular encoding on the resultant response object.
TidyFilter	Validates/cleans outgoing HTML.
NsgmlsFilter	This filter provides XHTML validation using NSGMLS, which must also be installed.
LogDebugInfoFilter	Maintains session state for you.
GzipFilter	Compresses output using Gzip. If you are mounting TurboGears behind Apache, you will get better performance by doing this at the Apache layer.
SessionFilter	Injects the cookie necessary to maintain session state into the outgoing request.
CacheFilter	Provides access to update the CherryPy cache on the way out.

We talk more about CherryPy configuration in the next section. For now, all you need to know is that turning on the static_filter for the /static directory means that any files that you put in your TurboGears application's static folder will be returned without any further processing.

17.3.3   Creating Your Own Filters

If you want to create your own filters, all you have to do is to subclass BaseFilter from the cherrypy.filters.basefilter module:

```
class PrintMessageFilter(BaseFilter):
    def before_main(self):
        print "This happens before the main page handler is called"
```

If you define a new method with the name of one of CherryPy's predefined filter hook locations, that method will be called at that time in the request cycle.

But, it's probably not enough to define a new filter—you probably want to actually have it run on some set of your controller objects, too. Fortunately that's easy: You can just define a _cp_filters list containing all the custom filter classes that you want to run on objects in that controller class. So, if you want to run our PrintMessageFilter on every object in your whole hierarchy, you could write something like this:

```
class Root(controllers.RootController):
    _cp_filters = [PrintMessageFilter(),]
```

As mentioned earlier, there are several predefined hooks in CherrPy where filters can be run. Whenever the request/response cycle hooks occur, CherryPy runs any filters that are in `_cp_filters`, and which define a method with the name of the current hook. Not only that, but the filters are applied in the order they are found in the `_cp_filters` list as seen in Table 17-5.

TABLE 17-5 CherryPy Filter Hooks

Standard Request/Response Hooks	
`on_start_resource`	This occurs right at the beginning of the request cycle.
`before_request_body`	This occurs before CherryPy parses the request body.
`before_main`	This occurs before the controller method is called.
`before_finalize`	This occurs when the response object is about to be finalized and returned to the user.
`on_end_resource`	This occurs right at the end of the cycle, before the request object is recycled.
Filter Hooks for Errors	
`before_error_response`	This only occurs when there is an error, right before the error response is processed.
`after_error_response`	This only occurs when there is an error, right after the error is processed.

On the other hand, if you want to create a new filter and have it inserted into the CherryPy input or output filter lists, you can add your function to the `call_on_startup` list to register it to be run at startup, as follows:

```
from turbogears.startup import call_on_startup

def do_your_thing():
   call_on_startup.append(do_your_thing)
```

You can `do_your_thing` and insert filters into the CherryPy request phase or set up variables as needed.

17.4 CherryPy and TurboGears Configuration

TurboGears configuration files differ from standard CherryPy configuration files, but even though they are in different places, and split up in different ways, they share the same syntax for configuring CherryPy-specific elements.

TurboGears uses ConfigObj (www.voidspace.org.uk/python/modules.shtml#con figobj) to handle parsing the configuration files, and we cover ConfigObj in a bit more detail in Chapter 19, "The TurboGears Toolbox and Other Tools." And cover some of the best ways to configure CherryPy for production use in Chapter 18. But for now, let's take a look at where CherryPy-specific configuration information goes in a Turbo-Gears project, and how to set things up the way you want them.

A TurboGears project has three main configuration files, `dev.cfg` and `prod.cfg` in the top-level directory and `yourpackage/config/app.cfg`. The `dev.cfg` and `prod.cfg` files are deployment configs and contain the settings that apply for a given deployment scenario (development and production, respectively).

That means things such as the port to listen on and how your application may or may not be configured behind another production web server are going to be contained in the `dev.cfg` and `prod.cfg` files. And because most of the settings for static filters and things such as that are going to be stable in both, `app.cfg` is your application config and contains settings that apply regardless of where your application is deployed.

In the `dev.cfg` file, you'll find the following CherryPy-related settings:

```
# SERVER

# Some server parameters that you may want to tweak
# server.socket_port=8080

# Enable the debug output at the end on pages.
# log_debug_info_filter.on = False

server.environment="development"
autoreload.package="yourpackage"

# Set to True if you'd like to abort execution if a controller gets an
# unexpected parameter. False by default
tg.strict_parameters = True
```

Most of this is self-explanatory. You can set the port for CherryPy to listen on and which package to check for changes when deciding when to auto-reload. The `prod.cfg` has similar server settings. But you'll configure filters in `app.cfg` because they are a persistent part of your application that should work the same way in production as development.

We've already looked briefly at the static file filter and how it is configured. But let's take another quick look at how filter configuration works:

```
[/static]
static_filter.on = True
static_filter.dir = "%(top_level_dir)s/static"
```

The first line tells CherryPy which paths it should apply this filter to, the second which filter to use, and the third provides filter-specific configuration information (in this case, where the static file directory is located).

You can have as many of these filter configuration elements in your app.cfg file as you need.

17.5 Decorators

As you have already seen in the first few sections of the book, TurboGears makes extensive use of Python decorators to minimize boilerplate and promote the DRY (Don't Repeat Yourself) principle. And we've already covered the expose() and validate() decorators. But don't let the simplicity of their application programming interface (API) fool you. There's a lot going on under the hood, and it will be well worth our time to delve into some of their secrets because they can definitely help you create better and more flexible controller methods.

17.5.1 expose()

The TurboGears expose() decorator is an extension to CherryPy's expose decorator. It controls not only what methods should be accessible from the outside world but also how the output will be formatted. TurboGears uses the generic function mechanism from Philip Eby's RuleDispatch package. And much of the power and flexibility of the TurboGears implementation of the expose decorator is a result of the inherent flexibility of generic functions.

One of TurboGear's fundamental goals was to allow us to have a number of different "views" of the same controller method, just by adding additional expose decorators like this:

```
@expose("cheetah:mypackage.templates.text", as_format="text")
@expose("mypackage.templates.xml", accept_format="application/xml")
@expose("json")
@expose("mypackage.templates.view")
def view(self):
    pass
```

The first argument denotes how the output will be rendered, while `as_format` and `accept_format` help determine which rendering method will be used. Let's examine this declaration step by step:

```
@expose("cheetah:mypackage.templates.text", as_format="text")
```

This decorator tells TurboGears to use the Cheetah template engine ("cheetah:") to render a template named `text` located in `mypackage.templates` (a Python path is used when resolving) if the dictionary returned by the controller contains the key value pair ("tg_format":"text").

```
@expose("mypackage.templates.xml", accept_format="application/xml")
```

This second example uses `accept_format`, which checks the HTTP Headers to see if the browser (or other user agent) specified a preferred format. In this case it's checking to see if the requested format is "application/xml".

```
@expose("json")
```

After the default Kid template rendering, this is the second most common way that TurboGears controller methods are exposed to the web. So we've added a short-cut, so that a simple expose ('json') call will return results from the controller method serialised via JSON, if mapping "tg_format":"json" is returned by replacement in the controller method.

```
@expose("mypackage.templates.view")
```

If need be, the template to use can be set from within the controller method by returning a dictionary containing the key `tg_template`:

```
@expose()
def view(self):          return {"tg_template":"mypackage.templates.view"}
```

`expose()` also accepts the following (keyword) arguments:

`content_type`—content-type HTTP header.

`fragment`—is template only a fragment to be included into another page?

17.5.2   `validate()`

The `validate()` decorator validates input, and if it is valid, converts it into corresponding Python objects. These two steps can be performed on both the individual arguments to your controller methods and complete forms (see Chapter 16, "TurboGears Widgets," for more detail).

For individual arguments, you can easily set up validators for individual keyword arguments by setting up a dictionary where the keys are the names of the arguments, and the values are the validators you would like used on each argument. Here's a sample:

```
@validate(validators={"num":validators.Int(),
        "content":validators.NotEmpty()})
def page(self, num, content=None):
```

Note that validation is not limited to keyword arguments.

Validating forms is even simpler:

```
@validate(form=my_form)
def register(self, name=None, age=None, email=None):
```

Sometimes you need to get access to some "state" information outside of a request in order to validate your data. Fortunately enough, validators can have access to additional information to help them do their validation and that you can pass it along by providing a callable as state_factory.

Here's a brief example:

```
def state(state):
    while True:
        yield state
        state += 1
state = state(42).next

@validate(form=my_form, state_factory=state)
```

If validation fails, control is passed to the error-handling mechanism, which brings us to TurboGears error- and exception-handling mechanisms.

17.6   Error and Exception Handling

TurboGears maintains separate mechanisms for handling data validation errors and program exceptions. We start by covering errors and move on to exceptions.

17.6.1   Validation Errors

Every method decorated by `validate()` requires a corresponding error handler. The most straightforward way to do so is to declare a function an error handler for a given method via the `error_handler()` decorator:

```
@validate(form=my_form)
@error_handler(my_eh)
def register(self, name=None, age=None, email=None):
```

The function declared as an error handler can have an arbitrary signature, but you might want to declare a parameter `tg_errors` wherein a mapping of argument names to errors will be passed. If the same error handler is used for multiple methods, an argument `tg_source` mapped to the method that triggered the error can prove useful.

Other parameters of interest are any named the same as arguments being validated, allowing us to fully reconstruct the original call. Although not strictly necessary, it is considered good practice to provide default values for any such arguments:

```
def my_eh(self, tg_errors, tg_source, name=None, email=None):
```

A more general approach is to use `*identifier` and `**identifier`.

Of course, nothing prevents us from using an existing (exposed) method as an error handler.

A method can even be its own error handler when `error_handler` is applied without any arguments:

```
@error_handler()
```

Take care with this approach because it can introduce subtle bugs. In general, the order of your decorators doesn't matter, but `error_handler` changes program flow, so it can bypass other decorators. For the most part, this causes no problem because it's exactly what you want. But, if you place your `error_handler` decorator below `identity_require`, you're authorization check won't be performed when there's an error.

```
@validate(validators={"num":validators.Int(),
                      "content":validators.NotEmpty()})
@identity.require(in_group("editor"))
@error_handler()
def page(self, num, content=None):
```

You can be careful to always put `error_handler` above `identity_require`, or—alternatively—you can declare the parameter `tg_errors` in the method itself like this:

```
def page(self, num, content=None, tg_errors=None):
```

Be aware that `tg_errors` should be a keyword argument when used in this manner (because for valid input, the method will not get re-called as error handler, and therefore `tg_errors` will not get passed in).

If no applicable error handler is defined and validation fails, `NotImplementedError` exception (from the standard library) is raised.

17.6.2   Multiple Handlers

What if we want to handle certain validation errors differently than the rest? Fortunately, more than one `error_handler()` can be applied to a method. In such a scenario, the appropriate error handler is selected based on an arbitrary Python logical expression passed as a string via keyword argument rules. (Careful readers will note this is not unlike `expose()`; in fact, `error_handler()` is just an interface to an underlying generic function.)

```
@error_handler(pagenum_eh, "'num' in tg_errors")
@error_handler(content_eh)
```

The most specific applicable rule is selected, meaning if validation of `num` fails, `pagenum_eh` will be called regardless of the content's state; or in other words, `content_eh` will be called if and only if validation of content fails and `num` passes.

Because both arguments of `error_handler` are optional, specialization is possible even when the method is its own error handler:

```
@error_handler(rules="'num' in tg_errors")
```

(Recall that if the first argument is omitted, the method is declared its own error handler.)

17.6.3   Exception Handling

Analogous to `error_handler()` and `tg_errors`, TurboGears provides `exception_handler()` and `tg_exceptions` for handling program exceptions.

When no applicable exception handler is defined, the exception is passed to a lower layer (for example, CherryPy).

If having the same handler for both errors and exceptions is desired, you can use `errorhandling.register_handler`, which is similar to `error_handler` and `exception_handler` but without inherent specializations.

17.7   RESTful Resources in TurboGears

REST is an architectural style, or a way of thinking about application development, first described by Roy Fielding in 2000. Roy was one of the principal authors of HTTP, and REST is a distillation of why he thinks the web works so well in allowing people to create reusable resources.

Here are a few key principles of the REST way of thinking:

- There should be a universal locator syntax for published resources.
- Every request/response cycle should be truly atomic, no state memory allowed.
- The resource should have a set of well-defined operations that apply to every resource in the system.

In HTTP, the URL provides the universal resource identification syntax, Get and Post provide the initial set of well-defined operations, and there is no provision for stateful transactions.

So, to a certain extent, all web applications are built on a RESTful core—but it is easy to create URLs that don't represent particular resources, or that don't make it easy to define a limited set of actions. For example, you could have a URL for editing an existing bookmark that looks like this: http://localhost.com/bookmarker/edit_bookmark/form$id=15, which jumbles actions, values, configuration options, and miscellaneous information all into the URL in a pretty much random order.

The REST way of thinking is to make the URL into two sections: the resource locator, and the "verb" or action you want taken. So, the preceding URL would become /bookmark/15/edit, which indicates the resource you want is a bookmark, the particular one you want is 15, and the action you want to take is to edit that bookmark. This is certainly cleaner looking, but there are lots of other advantages because it is easier to understand and easier to program. You have specific elements that can be handled separately (for example, the resource location, and the choice of what action to take on that resource).

This way of thinking isn't a particularly natural way of working with CherryPy out of the box. CherryPy publishes objects that represent user actions, and these objects are passed parameters that tell CherryPy what resources that action ought to be taken on. Which is exactly the opposite way of thinking of REST.

Fortunately, creative use of the default method can make RESTful interfaces easy. For example, if you want to implement a simple interface for four actions—Create, Read, Update, or Delete (CRUD) on an item—you could write methods for each of those, and use them with this default method to give you a REST-style interface:

```
@expose
def default(self, *vpath, **params):
        if len(vpath==1):
                item=vpath[0]
                return read(item)
        if len(vpath)==2
                item, verb = vpath
                action = getattr(self, verb, None)
                return action(item, **params)

expose()
def read(self, item, **params):
   pass

expose()
def add(self, item, **params)
   pass

expose()
def update(self, item, **params):
   pass

expose()
def delete(self, item, **params):
   pass
```

The default method checks the number of positional parameters sent in; and if there's only one, it assumes that the read method should be called. If not, it calls the correct method for you, based on the value in the second positional parameter. The key to making this happen is hidden in the `action = getattr(self, verb, None)` line.

The `getattr` is a built-in function in Python that takes an object and any string and if that string matches any of the attributes of that object, returns a reference to that object. So, calling `getattr(self, "add")` is the same as `self.add`—both provide a reference to the add object, which can be assigned another name. This does not call the referenced object (which might not in fact be a callable—as you might guess from the name, the `getattr` function works on attributes, too).

In this case, `getattr` is used to find out whether the verb value (which, as you will remember, is a string pulled off of the end of the URL) matches any of the methods in this class. We can't call the add method directly because all we have is a string passed in from the URL; but with `getattr`, that's no problem.

The optional third parameter allows you to pick a default to return if the string does not match any attribute name. In this case, we are just returning None. You could skip this, but having a sane default makes handling malformed input easier.

Which brings us to a problem with our little default dispatcher: It doesn't handle invalid user input very well. It's also likely that you'll want to use something like this on more than one set of objects in your application. To help with both of those problems, the TurboGears wiki has described this nice little `content` class, which you can use as a base class for any number of controller classes:

```python
class content():
    @turbogears.expose()
    def default(self, *vpath, **params):
        if len(vpath) == 1:
            identifier = vpath[0]
            action = self.read
        elif len(vpath) == 2:
            identifier, verb = vpath
            verb = verb.replace('.', '_')
            action = getattr(self, verb, None)
            if not action:
                raise cherrypy.NotFound
            if not action.exposed:
                raise cherrypy.NotFound
        else:
            raise cherrypy.NotFound
        items = self.query(identifier)
```

```
    if items.count() == 0:
        raise cherrypy.NotFound
    else:
        return action(items[0], **params)
```

As you can see, this is pretty much the same thing as we did in our default method, but with better error handling. But, now we can get this default method in our class by including it in as one of the superclasses of our controller class, as follows:

```
class Root(controllers.RootController, content):
    @turbogears.expose(template='myapp.templates.show_thing')
    def read(self, thing):
        return dict(text=thing.text)
```

With this implementation, you could have any number of verbs available for this resource. And as long as you define the proper methods in your controller class, they will work automatically.

There is a whole world of reuse possibilities if you create resources that implement a consistent set of verbs. This is particularly true when you couple this API similarity with the ability to expose the same method in multiple ways (through a Kid Template, as a JSON struct, or via XML RPC, and so on). You could leave the default parameter out, but it's always a good idea to have a sane default when you're handling untrusted input.

17.8 Summary

- CherryPy maps URLs such as `http://ocalhost/cart/item/delete` to the object hierarchy of the "root" controller, so this URL would map to `root.cart.item.delete()`.

- CherryPy provides special routing for the `index` method, which is called (if it exists) whenever your URL maps to a class directly rather than one of its methods.

- CherryPy also allows you to define a `default` method for a class, which is called whenever the URL does not match any of the methods of that class.

- TurboGears has overloaded the `@expose()` decorator from CherryPy so it now controls not only which objects are published to the web, but also how the results of that object will be processed and returned to the user.

- The `@expose` decorator uses RuleDispatch's generic functon system to allow you to define multiple possible output formats for the same controller. The most specific matching rule will be chosen, and that's what will be sent back to the user.

- Multiformat outputs allow you to use the same controller method to provide HTML, XML RPC, JSON, and even SOAP output from the same controller. This makes creating web services easier, and also helps you create backward-compatible Ajax applications.

- The `@validate` decorator allows you to preprocess input to 1) validate its contents, and 2) convert the contents to the proper kind of Python object that you need.

- It's easy to create RESTful interfaces with CherryPy in a few lines of code. And if you have several different objects that will have the same style RESTful interface, you can create your own RESTful superclass to make your job even easier (and help you avoid repeating boilerplate code).

Chapter 18

TurboGears Deployment

In This Chapter

The Zen of Python says, "There should be one, and preferably only one, right way to do it." But, there are dozens of different TurboGears deployment options. It would certainly be nice to point everybody to one simple deployment scenario, but there's no way to do that without leaving some people out. The Zen of Python also tells us, "Practicality beats purity," so we've worked to support all the major deployment scenarios that you might need.

With all of that said, there are definitely some things to keep in mind, and some deployment configurations that perform better than others. This chapter outlines a couple of the most popular configurations and explains why you might want to choose one deployment configuration over another.

Much of this chapter was written by Remi Delon, a key force behind CherryPy. This intimate knowledge of CherryPy's inner workings, along with Remi's experience with TurboGears application deployment at WebFaction, means there's a lot of real-world experience behind the advice in this chapter.

WebFaction started in 2002 as a hosting provider specializing in Python. It has since grown into an all-around hosting company, offering a fast and reliable service for a reasonable price. But most of all, the team is a friendly group of Python experts, some of whom are CherryPy core developers. In our experience, this makes WebFaction a great choice if you are planning on hosting your TurboGears sites on a shared server at an ISP (www.webfaction.com).

18.1   Choosing Your Production Environment

So you've spent weeks or months developing your new application and now is the time to "go live." The first choice you have to make is determining which operating system you want to use on your production servers.

Here are the main decisions that you have to make and a few pointers to help you make these decisions. Of course, if you aren't working on your own web 2.0 start-up (and let's face it, most of us aren't), some of these choices might be imposed by your budget, your boss, or other outside forces.

18.1.1   Operating System of the Server(s): Linux, Mac OS, Windows?

The first choice you have to make is the operating system you plan to use for your upcoming deployment. The good news is that TurboGears runs equally well on all of these platforms, so it's really up to you to decide which one you want to use and support. So, you'll want to make this decision based on outside issues such as: your budget, familiarity with the operating system, your assessment of the stability/maintainability of the platform, corporate policy, and whatever other concerns are important to your particular situation. The good news is that no matter which of the major operating systems you choose, you'll be able to deploy your TurboGears application.

Of course, it's also possible that you made some choices in development that bind you to one operating system or another. For example, one of the authors deployed a TurboGears application to monitor, track, and manipulate windows services through a web interface. Because this required access to Active Directory, and Win32 services, the application as written could only be deployed on Windows.

With that said, most people find that Linux provides them with the best cost/benefit ratio for deployment. In this context, it's probably worth mentioning that unless you added OS-specific code as described above, there's nothing stopping you from using one operating system in development and another when you deploy.

18.1.2   Should I Run CherryPy behind Another Web Server?

CherryPy comes with a built-in HTTP server. This HTTP server is great for doing development, but can be limited for production websites:

- It doesn't support full HTTP/1.1.
- It doesn't have any support for Secure Sockets Layer (SSL).
- It can only listen to one port.
- It might not be very robust in handling buggy or nonstandard HTTP requests.
- It doesn't add or remove threads dynamically when the traffic increases or diminishes.

For these reasons, it is probably wise to run CherryPy behind another web server, such as Apache, IIS, or lighttpd. These web servers will provide you with several important benefits:

- You get HTTP/1.1 connections between the browser and the web client, which is where it matters the most.

- You can configure the web server to serve static data directly. This frees CherryPy from that task, and the web server will be faster than CherryPy for serving static data.

- You benefit from all the features from the web server, such as SSL support, GZip compression, and so on.

- Most web servers can handle "virtual hosting" (that is, multiple domains/ websites) and direct requests to one or more CherryPy servers accordingly.

So for any TurboGears site that is going to be exposed to the public Internet, you'll probably want to take advantage of Apache, IIS, lighttpd, or another dedicated web server.

18.1.3   The Basics of Configuring TurboGears for Production

But before we get into the specifics of how you configure the front-end server to work with TurboGears, it makes sense to look a bit more deeply at the way that TurboGears configuration works, and how to configure a TurboGears project for production.

TurboGears provides three files for configuration values: `dev.cfg`, `prod.cfg`, and `app.cfg`. You can probably already tell from the names what they are for:

- `dev.cfg` stores all the configuration information specific to your development environment.

- `prod.cfg` stores all the information specific to your production environment.

- `app.cfg` stores any configuration information for your application that isn't specific to the development or production environments.

Assuming for the moment that all you've modified in your `dev.cfg` file is the database URL (which is often all you need to do), all you need to get your `prod.cfg` file ready is to update the `prod.cfg` file with the location of your production database. But, how do you get TurboGears to pull the values from `prod.cfg` rather than `dev.cfg`? Fortunately it couldn't be easier—all you have to do is delete `dev.cfg`; TurboGears will automatically start using your production configuration.

18.2   Using `mod_rewrite` or `mod_proxy` to Connect to CherryPy

Because we don't have time to cover every possible configuration, we have to content ourselves with showing you how to set TurboGears up behind Apache. If for some reason you have to install behind another server, however, you can find good recipies at turbogears.org, and lots of helpful people on the mailing list.

We chose Apache because it *is* the most widely used web server in the world, it runs on Linux, Windows, and OSX; and if you are using shared hosting, it's almost certainly what's already installed.

When using `mod_rewrite` or `mod_proxy` to forward requests from the Apache front-end server to your TurboGears application, Apache uses the HTTP protocol to talk to CherryPy. Basically, whenever Apache gets a valid request that matches the criteria you set up, Apache forwards the HTTP request that it received from the browser to CherryPy, waits for a response from CherryPy, and then forwards that response right back down to the browser.

This is probably the easiest and most flexible way to run CherryPy behind a web server. The configuration details behind using `mod_rewrite` or `mod_proxy` are Apache specific, but this same technique is also likely to be your best choice when using other web servers such as IIS or lighttpd.

18.2.1   Advantages/Drawbacks of Using a Proxy in front of CherryPy

The advantages of this method are as follows:

- Easy to set up.
- You can still access your CherryPy directly (by using the port number), which is nice for debugging.
- It's fast. (Rough tests have shown that the overhead associated with forwarding the request/response can be as little as 1ms per request.)

The drawbacks of this method are as follows:

- You have to use special headers to get the actual `Host` header of the request and the IP address of the browser. This is because to CherryPy, requests will look like they come from the local Apache server rather than the remote browser. In the case of Apache, you get the original `Host` header in the `x-Forwarded-Host` header and the IP address of the browser in the `x-Forwarded-Host` header. Fortunately, there is an easy way to tell CherryPy to use these special headers (see 18.2.4).
- You are responsible for starting/stopping your CherryPy server and making sure that it restarts automatically in case it crashes. Again, this can be achieved using various techniques (see 18.2.5).

18.2.2   Configuring Apache with `mod_rewrite`

Let's assume that your CherryPy process is listening on port 80. All you have to do is tell Apache to forward requests to CherryPy. If you use `mod_rewrite`, this is done like this:

```
RewriteEngine on
RewriteRule ^(.*) http://127.0.0.1:8000$1 [P]
```

The equivalent with `mod_proxy` is this:

```
ProxyPass            /      http://localhost:2432/
ProxyPassReverse     /      http://localhost:2432/
```

For this to work, you have to make sure that the `mod_rewrite` or `mod_proxy` module is loaded (either dynamically, or statically linked when Apache was built). For more details about `mod_rewrite` or `mod_proxy`, refer to their documentation:

- `mod_rewrite` (http://httpd.apache.org/docs/2.0/misc/rewriteguide.html)
- `mod_proxy` (http://httpd.apache.org/docs/2.0/mod/mod_proxy.html)

18.2.3   Configuring Apache to Serve Static Content Directly

Chances are, your web server will be faster than CherryPy for serving static files. So, you should take advantage of this. Fortunately, it is trivial to achieve this with `mod_rewrite`:

```
RewriteEngine on
RewriteRule ^/static(.*) /home/myuser/static$1 [L]
RewriteRule ^(.*) http://127.0.0.1:8000$1 [P]
```

This way, if you have a static file `/home/myuser/static/foo.html`, it will be available at `http://<domain>/static/foo.html`.

18.2.4   Configuring CherryPy to Run Behind a Web Server

CherryPy doesn't really care whether it runs exposed or behind another web server. It works identically in both cases.

However, Apache modifies requests slightly before forwarding them to CherryPy:

- The `Host` header gets changed to `localhost`.
- The original host header gets put in `X-Forwarded-Host`.

- The request comes from Apache rather than the remote browser, so the IP address of the request will be that of the Apache server (127.0.0.1 if you run Apache locally) instead of being the actual IP address of the remote browser.
- The IP address of the remote browser gets put in `x-Forwarded-For`.

The remote IP address is not needed by CherryPy apart from logging purposes, but if you're logging the IP address inside your TurboGears application, make sure you use the `x-Forwarded-For` header from the request.

However, the `Host` header is needed when you need to generate "canonical" URLs (that is, URLs that include the full protocol and domain name). You might think that you can just use relative URLs everywhere in your app (such as: `/my/url`) and then you'll be fine. But this is only half true. Chances are you'll use some redirects (HTTP code 302 or 303) in your application, and the HTTP protocol specifies that you *must* include the canonical URL when you issue a redirect. And so, you really do need the full host path for your application.

Fortunately, we can use a CherryPy filter to make this easier. CherryPy's `base_url_filter` has an option to use the `x-Forwarded-For` value as the base URL, which gets used to generate full (canonical) URLs. All you have to do to get this automagical behavior is to add the following three lines to `prod.cfg`:

```
[/]
base_url_filter.on = True
base_url_filter.use_x_forwarded_host= True
```

Unfortunately the "X-. . ." headers are only there if you use Apache 2.0 or later. If you use Apache 1.3, the original `Host` and IP address are lost. In that case, you can still use `base_url_filters`, but you have to hard-wire the base URL into `base_url_filter` like this:

```
[/]
base_url_filter.on = True
base_url_filter.base_url = 'http://your.domain.com'
base_url_filter. use_x_forwarded_host= False
```

Of course, you will want to replace your.domain.com with your actual domain! This will set the `base_url` to a static value, which isn't quite as nice, but, hey, at least it works.

18.2.5   Making Sure That CherryPy Stays Up

When you run CherryPy behind your web server, you're responsible for making sure that your CherryPy server starts up when the machine boots and restarts if it ever crashes. This can be achieved using various techniques:

- Using a cronjob. (This is a crude way of doing it.) Set up a cronjob that checks every few minutes whether the process is still running. If it isn't, simply restart it. (If you're on Windows, you can set up a Scheduled Task to do the same thing.)

- Using a tool such as Supervisor (or FireDaemon on Windows). These tools can monitor other processes and restart them if the process ever goes down.

- Using Apache to start CherryPy. The trick is to use Apache's error-handling mechanism to start CherryPy. If Apache tries to forward the request to CherryPy but CherryPy isn't running, Apache will display an error message. This error message can be customized, and we can tell Apache to run a CGI script instead. We can then use the CGI script to start CherryPy.

There are advantages and disadvantages to the three techniques. Unfortunately, lots of shared hosting environments won't let you run cronjobs frequently, and they are very picky about what long running processes they'll allow. So, sometimes you're stuck with the CGI script hack. Lucky for us, it works well and is easy to set up. All you have to do is tell Apache to run a CGI script when an error occurs (along with the other `mod_rewrite` rules):

```
RewriteEngine on
ErrorDocument 502 /cgi-bin/autostart.cgi
RewriteRule ^/cgi-bin/(.*) /home/myuser/autostart.cgi [L]
RewriteRule ^/static(.*) /home/myuser/static$1 [L]
RewriteRule ^(.*) http://127.0.0.1:8000$1 [P]
```

The `autostart.cgi` file can be a simple Python script that starts CherryPy in the background:

```
#!/usr/local/bin/python
print "Content-type: text/html\r\n"
print """"""<html><head><META HTTP-EQUIV="Refresh" CONTENT="1; URL=/"></
head><body>Restarting site ...<a href="/">click here<a></body></html>"""

import os
os.setpgid(os.getpid(), 0)
os.system('/usr/local/bin/python2.4 cherrypy-site.py &')
```

> **Note:** We set the group ID of the process to 0. If you don't do that, Apache will kill the CGI process and its children (that is, the CherryPy process) after a while.

18.3 Running CherryPy on mod_python

Another popular deployment option is to use mod_python, which is basically a Python interpreter embedded in each of your web server processes.

18.3.1 Advantages/Drawbacks of Using mod_python

The advantages of this method are as follows:

- Slightly faster than mod_rewrite (because requests don't need to be forwarded)
- No need to start/stop your CherryPy process yourself (because it starts with Apache)

The drawbacks of this method are as follows:

- Apache starts multiple processes, so you can't use RAM-based sessions, for instance.
- A bit harder to configure than mod_rewrite.
- mod_python is not yet widespread among web hosting companies. (One current problem is that Apache needs to be restarted whenever you change something in your CherryPy code.)
- Might be less stable than mod_rewrite.

For some people who are using shared hosting, this might be your only option because your ISP will not allow long running processes.

18.3.2 Configuring Apache/CherryPy for mod_python

The recommended way to run CherryPy with mod_python is to use the mpcp module available from http://jamwt.com/. The following configuration example applies to Apache 2.0, mod_python 3, Python 2.4, and CherryPy 2.2. Here is how you configure Apache:

```
ServerName 'cherrypy.example.com'
PythonPath "['/path/to/project-root'] + sys.path"
<Location "/">
```

```
        SetHandler mod_python
        PythonHandler mpcp
        PythonOption cherrysetup control.main.root::mp_setup
</Location>
```

And here is sample code showing how to set up CherryPy for `mod_python`:

```python
import cherrypy

class CherryApp:
        @cherrypy.expose
        def index(self, **kwargs):
                return 'Hello, World!'

cherrypy.root = CherryApp()

if __name__ == '__main__':
        # CP server testing with autoreload, etc
        cherrypy.config.update({'global' : {'server.socket_port' : 8000}})
        cherrypy.server.start()

def mp_setup():
        """mod_python production setup"""
        cherrypy.config.update({'global' : {'server.environment' : 'production'}})
```

18.4   Other Ways of Running CherryPy behind a Web Server

We're not going to cover these options in depth, but it's worth mentioning that there are a number of other ways to run CherryPy behind a web server. Perhaps the most popular are FastCGI and WSGI.

- FastCGI or SCGI. These are other protocols (different from HTTP) that can be used to talk between the web server and CherryPy. They don't really add any benefit over HTTP (with `mod_rewrite`, for instance), but some web hosting companies support FastCGI but not `mod_rewrite`.

- WSGI. This is a relatively recent standard in the Python web world. Among other things, it separates the concept of a "WSGI application" from the concept of "WSGI server." Any application that respects the WSGI application programming interface (API) can be served by any web server that expects a WSGI application. CherryPy's applications can expose a WSGI interface, so they can run within any of the WSGI servers that already exist. (Unfortunately, none of these WSGI servers are up to the standard of Apache, lighttpd, or IIS yet.)

It's quite possible that WSGI will make Python web application hosting a lot easier in the future. But, for now, even if you are using WSGI, you are likely to want to throw an Apache server in front of your WSGI server and use `mod_rewrite`.

18.5 Scalability of Your Site

Scaling is the ability for your site to support more and more traffic by adding more resources (usually hardware) to it. Ideally, your site should be able to handle any amount of traffic just by adding enough servers.

This can be easily achieved by adding as many TurboGears application servers as necessary and throwing a load balancer in front. However, you have to be careful about one thing: A TurboGears process on one machine needs to be able to access all the data it needs. (That data can't be in a TurboGears process on another machine.)

If you avoided sessions and stored all your data in cookies or on the database, you're all set. Your application should "scale out" without any significant work at all.

18.5.1 Scaling Sessions

If you are using sessions, and you need to scale to multiple machines, fortunately all is not lost. If you're using sessions in your application, all you have to do is make sure that a user will keep getting session data across multiple requests. There are two basic ways to go about achieving that goal:

- Regardless of which machine the request goes to, the TurboGears process has access to the session data.
- The request for that user always goes to the same TurboGears process.

You can achieve the first option by storing the session data in a database. Then all you have to do is connect all your TurboGears processes to the same database. Alternatively, sessions can be stored in files and the filesystem could be shared by the various machines, but that is probably more complicated.

You can achieve the second option by using a "smart" load balancer that can extract the session ID from each request and direct the request to the corresponding Turbo-Gears process. That way you could still use RAM-based sessions, because the various TurboGears processes don't need to share the session data.

18.5.2 Scaling Your Application

You don't need to do anything special in your application to make sure it scales. All you have to do is store your data in a database. That way, you can add as many machines running TurboGears as you want, and they can all easily connect to the database to access the data.

If your database grows and your traffic increases, there might come a time when you have to start spreading your database itself over multiple machines, but then you benefit from years of research and development that went into making database engines scale. At the point where you need to scale your database, it is extraordinarily helpful if your data can be partitioned into seprate databases. If your customer data is all independent, for example, there is no reason you couldn't store each customer on its own database server.

If that's not possible, these days all the major database engines, such as Oracle, SQLServer, PostgreSQL, and MySQL, can be clustered on multiple machines. But database clustering is a topic for another book.

18.5.3 Scaling at a Lower Cost

Just because you can handle more traffic easily by adding more hardware doesn't mean that doing so is feasible in practice: All that hardware costs money to buy, and it also costs money to host it. For this reason, you probably want to make sure that you make the most out of your hardware (that is, handle as much traffic as possible with one machine).

To do this, be careful about how you program your application. You should measure how much time requests take to complete and identify the bottlenecks. Also, whenever possible, use caching techniques for your whole pages, or just part of your pages or database queries.

18.6 Summary

- Deployment, configuration, and testing are fast-moving targets. This chapter was written with the most stable deployment scenario in mind, but you can find a lot more about configuring and deploying you applications at www. turbogears.org, and www.turbogearsbook.com

- TurboGears `prod.cfg` contains all the production-specific configuration settings for your application. Often, all you have to do is edit this file to point to the proper location of your production database.

- The benefits of placing your TurboGears application behind Apache or IIS include HTTP 1.1 support, improved handling of buggy requests, and you can use "virtual hosting" to easily set up multiple TurboGears applications behind a single front-end web server.

- When you use `mod-proxy` or `mod-rewrite` you are responsible to monitor the Cherry-Py server to make sure that it gets started when the web server starts, and restarted if something should happen. We've included a little CGI script that starts your application whenever a user would otherwise have received a 502 error.

- The main advantage of `mod-python` is that everything runs in Apache, so you don't have to monitor another process. The main disadvantage is that Apache needs to be restarted whenever you change your application code (and on shared hosting, it's not likely you'll be allowed to start and stop Apache at will).

- TurboGears applications scale out to the extent that you use cookies and database storage rather than in-memory sessions.

PART VII

TurboGears
Extras

## Chapter 19

The TurboGears Toolbox and Other Tools

In This Chapter

TurboGears includes a number of nice features to make your life as a developer just a little bit easier. The TurboGears Toolbox provides tools for creating and charting your database model, adding data to your database with a web based GUI while you are still in development, debugging system problems, browsing all of the installed widgets, and internationalizing your application.

19.1 Toolbox Overview

The TurboGears Toolbox is started with the tg-admin toolbox command. Your browser should automatically pop up when you start the Toolbox, but if it doesn't you should still be able to browse to http://localhost:7654, where you'll see a web page with links for each of the tools in the toolbox (as seen in Figure 19.1).

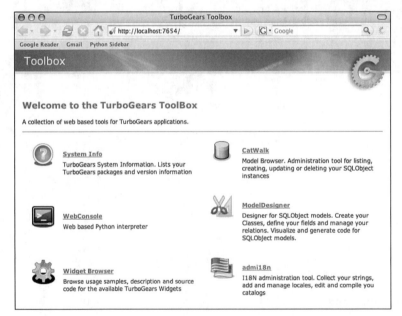

FIGURE 19.1 The TurboGears Toolbox home page

Each of the components in the Toolbox is also a TurboGears application, so you can also look at them as examples of how TurboGears applications are built.

Because there isn't anything in TurboGears that can't be done in code or from the command line, the use of the Toolbox is entirely optional.

19.2 ModelDesigner

The first tool we'll look at is the ModelDesigner. This tool is designed to help you create your SQLObject model classes. It provides a GUI interface that allows you to create new classes by filling out simple web forms. In Figure 19.2 you can see a Task class with several columns defined for it.

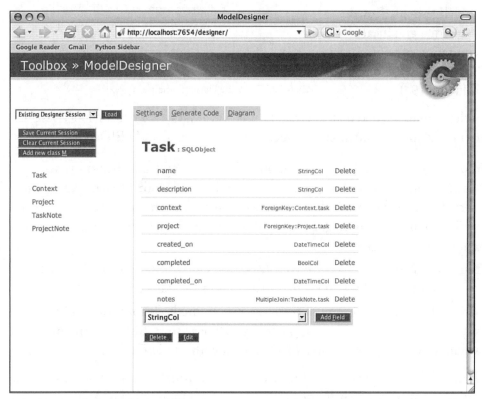

FIGURE 19.1 Default Widget Attributes

The main advantages of using the ModelDesigner are:

- You get a drop-down list of options for most fields so you don't have to remember things like all the possible column types.

- ModelDesigner gives you a form with all the `column` options so you don't have to remember those either.

- ModelDesigner creates both ends of joins at once so you don't have to make sure everything matchs up manually.

- ModelDesigner provides you with a graphical representation of your model "for free," as you can see in Figure 19.3.

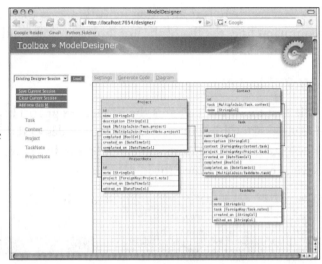

FIGURE 19.3 ModelDesigner diagram

All of that sounds so good that you might think you always want to use ModelDesigner, but there are a couple of limitations to remember when using the ModelDesigner:

- You can't start out defining your model classes by hand and then move to ModelDesigner when things get more complicated. ModelDesigner can write a new `Model.py` file, but it doesn't parse existing files. This also means you won't be able to use ModelDesigner with the automatically generated Identity tables that `tg-admin` can give you.

- You have to remember to save your ModelDesigner session or you'll have to start all over again if you need to add a column to a table.

- ModelDesigner has no way of tracking custom methods that you might add to your table classes, which means that you'll have to re-add those methods whenever you update your database schema with ModelDesigner.

With all of that said, using the ModelDesigner to rough out your schema at the beginning of the project can help you get started much more quickly. You can always move over to the old-fashioned method of defining your tables by hand whenever the limitations of ModelDesigner start feeling painful.

Using ModelDesigner is pretty simple, especially if you know how SQLObject works and have created a few tables by hand. About the only thing that trips people up is the load/save interface. You can save your project with whatever name you want, but it will always show up as "Existing TurboGears Session." Once you've defined your model, you can write it out to `model.py` from the "Generate Code" tab (as seen in Figure 19.4).

FIGURE 19.4 ModelDesigner "Generate Code" tab

19.3 CatWalk

Once you've created your database schema, you generally need at least a couple records worth of data in order to be able to start writing code and verifying that it works.

That's where CatWalk comes in. CatWalk provides an automatically generated GUI for editing sample data during development. The basic editing form, shown in Figure 19.5, is very easy to use for smaller data sets. If this database had a thousand projects in it, the drop-down list would be unmanageable. But, for adding a bit of data into your database during development, it couldn't get much easier than this.

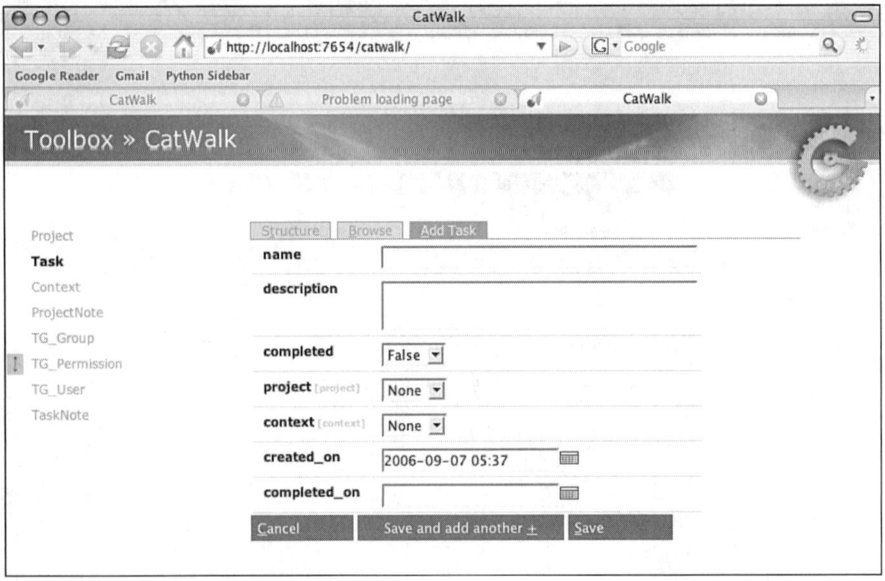

FIGURE 19.5 CatWalk editing

The one area that people sometimes get confused about with CatWalk is adding many-to-many join relationships. All you have to do is add the rows to the two tables, edit either of the rows you want to connect, and click the triangle next to the join "column." Then a selection form that lets you manage relationships will appear and you can set up new relationships to your heart's content.

In Figure 19.6, you can see another common use of the CatWalk tool—browsing data.

There are any number of ways you can customize CatWalk. You can have it display only some fields; you can change the way fields are ordered on your form; and you can even edit what appears in the drop-down lists so that you get actual project names rather than non-intuitive id values.

To do this all you have to do is click on the little edit icon in the browse view, and you'll get something like what appears in Figure 19.7. You can uncheck columns to have them not be displayed, or drag-and-drop them to change their order.

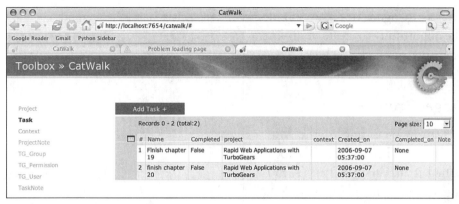

FIGURE 19.6 Browsing database data

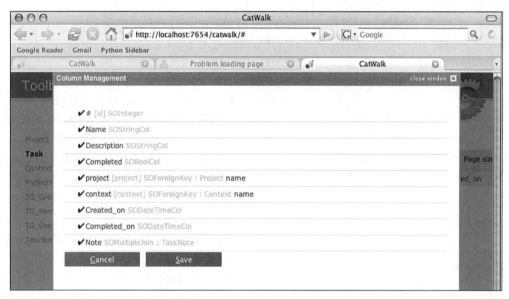

FIGURE 19.7 Customizing CatWalk

19.4 WebConsole

TurboGears also provides a web-based version of the interactive Python prompt. You can play with your model objects, add data, and even run adhoc tests from the WebConsole.

The Console also imports your model and sets up your database connection automatically so you can just get down to work. Admittedly, there's nothing you can do in the Console that you couldn't do from the `tg-admin` shell.

As you can see in Figure 19.8, the Console gives you the opportunity to create multi-line Python statements, or quick one liners.

19.5 Widget Browser

The Widget Browser is one of the most useful tools in the TurboGears Toolbox. We mentioned it in Chapter 16, "Turbo-Gears Widgets: Bringing CSS, XHTML, and JavaScript Together in Reusable Components;" let's take a little bit more time to look at it in depth here. The Widget Browser makes use of a special feature of setuptools, which allows eggs to define an

FIGURE 19.8 WebConsole

entry-point. Every widget package in the Cog Bin (www.turbogears.org/cogbin) has a specially-defined entry point. This allows the Widget Browser to dynamically grab information for every widget you have installed. The information is always up-to-date, and everything works.

There is one exception to this rule. Some third-party widgets do not define a widget description class and will not show up in the Widget Browser. If you're wondering what a widget description does, it isn't at all complicated. It defines a default instantiation of the widget, which is used to display the widget in the Toolbox.

As you can see in Figure 19.9, each widget is displayed with five tabs:

- A sample of what the widget looks like in use

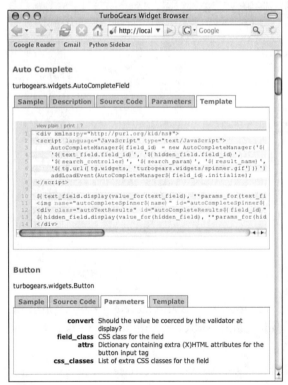

FIGURE 19.9 Widget Browser

- A description of the Widget (taken from the widget's `docstring`)

- A listing of the widget's source code, which is invaluable when you want to know exactly how something is done

- A listing of each of the widget's parameters and a brief description of what that parameter is for, which is taken from a `params_doc` dictionary in the widget itself so the description will always be up-to-date

FIGURE 19.10 Admi18n set up

- A listing of that particular widget's template code that can be cut and pasted by using the "view plain" link, allowing you to customize the way the widget is displayed

19.6 Admi18n and System Info

We'll cover the Admi18n tool (as seen in figure 19.10) for translation administration in depth in Chapter 20, "Internationalization." For now, we'll just mention that TurboGears includes a full-fledged tool for creating and maintaining translation files so that you can easily create multilingual TurboGears applications. For a few applications, where you don't have any strings coming from Python, you can actually just use this interface. For most applications, you're going to have to do a little bit of prep work before you can get started with translation. While it's not hard, there's enough going on under the covers that it's worth a whole chapter to explore.

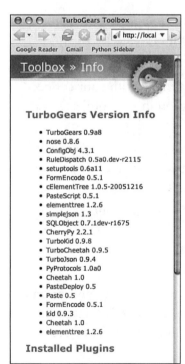

FIGURE 19.11 System Info

Unlike the rest of the Toolbox applications, there's not much to do with the System Info tool (as shown in Figure 19.11). It just displays a single dynamically-generated page that displays which version of TurboGears and all its associated dependencies are installed on your system. This information is very useful if you ever have to submit a bug report on the TurboGears bug tracker (trac.turbogears.org), or when asking for help with a framework problem on the TurboGears mailing list (groups.google.org/ group/turbogears).

19.7 The `tg-admin` Command

We've already seen the `tg-admin` command, but there's a lot more that it can do than just quickstart a new project, and even the `quickstart` option has some features we haven't touched upon yet. The core options of `tg-admin` are:

- `quickstart`—Creates a new directory based on the project and package names provided; has switches to use SQLAlchemy (-s) or use alternate project templates (`-t tgbig`)
- `shell`—Opens a new interactive shell with our model imported (When using SQLObject your database changes should autocommit)
- `i18n`—Internationalization is covered in depth in Chapter 20
- `sql`—Wraps around the SQLObject `sql-admin` command with your connection parameters pre-defined based on the information in your project's `config` file
- `toolbox`—Starts up the web-based Toolbox (You can use -n to not automatically open a browser window and -c to allow other specific IP addresses beyond the default localhost to connect to the Toolbox instance)
- `info`—Lists current versions of all installed TurboGears components

19.8 Other TurboGears Tools

TurboGears includes a number of optional tools for you to use if your application has specific requirements. There are also third-party tools like TurboMail. We can't cover all of these here, and new tools are popping up every day. But here's a list of a few tools that might save you some time if you need them:

- **Scheduler**—TurboGears includes support for a cron-like scheduler based on Kronos. You can find more information about the scheduler at http://docs.turbogears.org/1.0/Scheduler.
- **Configuration**—TurboGears uses ConfigObj to parse configuration files. You can find out more about how this works at http://docs.turbogears.org/1.0/Configuration.
- **logging**—TurboGears reuses the `logger` module from Python's standard library. You can learn more about TurboGears logging at http://docs.turbogears.org/The_Logging_system, and more about the logger at: http://docs.turbogears.org/The_Logging_system.
- **paginate**—When you need to paginate tabular results, TurboGears provides a simple decorator-based pagination mechanism that you can read more about at http://docs.turbogears.org/PaginateDecorator.

19.9 Summary

- TurboGears provides several graphical tools to help you get started more quickly, and to maximize your productivity.
- The ModelDesigner provides a quick and easy way to define your database structure—and it even gives you free database diagrams.
- CatWalk makes is easy to add sample data to your database before you start work on your user interface!
- The WebConsole and SystemInfo tools make it easy to test your application through a web interface, and get a list of the versions of all the libraries included in your TurboGears install.
- The Widget Browser gives you an up-to-date look at all the widgets installed on your system, along with descriptions, documentation, and sample code.
- The `tg-admin` command gives you access to a variety of features like quckstart, sql create, and shell, that we've been using throughout the book to start new projects, manipulate the database, and create database tables.

Chapter 20

Internationalization

In This Chapter

One of the first features to be submitted to TurboGears by a user was support for internationalization. Work on TurboGears, itself, is performed by a multinational team of developers, many (perhaps most) of whom are developing TurboGears applications in their native (non-English) languages. This leads to a high level of developer awareness of internationalization issues. When you couple this developer sensitivity with the full support for Unicode strings in Python, internationalization continues to be one of TurboGears's strongest assets.

20.1 Dealing with Unicode in Python

Even though TurboGears provides comprehensive support for internationalization, if you want your TurboGears application to be easily translatable, there are a few things you need to remember. Your application, like any Python program, requires some attention with respect to how you handle Unicode strings.

In the current version of Python there are strings and Unicode strings. The best piece of advice you can get if you are planning to internationalize your application is:

Always use Unicode strings everywhere!

Every string in your application should be a Unicode string. The only time you should ever convert to/from Unicode is at the IO boundaries of the application. So, if you receive a string from an email or other source, convert it to Unicode right away.

If you do this, it greatly reduces the chances that you'll get the infamous `UnicodeDecodeError`, which happens whenever Python tries to decode a Unicode string into an output format that can't handle all of the Unicode characters in that string.

The default string type in Python is ASCII (because ASCII works everywhere!). It's pretty likely that your Unicode string will contain some characters that can't be decoded into an ASCII output. This is easy to avoid as long as you use Unicode everywhere.

TurboGears libraries all use Unicode by default; but unfortunately, you still have to be careful when interfacing with third-party Python libraries. Many of them are still Unicode-ignorant and can pop up the `UnicodeDecodeError` you'll learn to hate.

The second most important rule of handling Unicode characters in your Turbo-Gears application is:

Always include strings with non-ASCII characters in your unit tests.

If you have appropriate tests, you'll be able to detect places in which Unicode strings get forced into ASCII right away. With the right tests, you'll find out that an imported library doesn't handle Unicode as soon as you attempt to use it. This is a lot better than finding out that something is broken when a user from Helsinki sends you an email telling you that your application doesn't work.

20.2 Dealing with Unicode in TurboGears

A lot of effort has gone into TurboGears to make sure it plays nicely with respect to Unicode. Rather than make you responsible for handling everything yourself, Turbo-Gears transparently encodes and decodes strings for you—most of the time.

For example, whenever you use `turbogears.flash()`, you pass a Unicode string to it that is correctly encoded to UTF-8 to set a cookie and then sent to the browser. When TurboGears receives the cookie back from the browser on a later request, it turns the cookie back into a Unicode string so that it can be processed in Python. Then, when it's returned to the browser for display, it's re-encoded in UTF-8 in order to display correctly to the user.

20.2.1 SQLObject and Unicode

SQLObject contains `_UnicodeCol_`, which provides transparent encoding/decoding of Unicode values. It's just like `_StringCol_` (in fact, it's a subclass of it) except that SQLObject encodes Python Unicode strings on the way to the database and decodes them on the way back. By default, UTF-8 encoding in the database table is assumed, which usually "just works."

If you have the following SQLObject declaration, you'll get a database column that holds Unicode strings in UTF-8 form:

```
class T1(SQLObject):
    name = UnicodeCol(length=40, alternateID=True)
```

The one caveat here is that your database of choice, and your database driver of choice, have to handle UTF-8. SQLObject helps you out where it can; but it can't get water from a stone or Unicode strings from an ASCII-only database!

Here's a sample usage:

```
>>> omega = T1(name=u'Greek \u03a9')
>>> omega
<T1 1 name=u'Greek \u03a9'>
>>> omega = T1.byName(u'Greek \u03a9')
>>> omega.name
u'Greek \u03a9'
```

As just noted, there is one important caveat to remember: transparent encoding/decoding breaks when you use custom SQL queries that you have built either with sqlbuilder or by hand. For example, if you submit the following query, you will get a `UnicodeEncodeError`.

```
>>> list(T1.select(T1.q.name==u'Greek \u03a9'))
Traceback (most recent call last):
...
UnicodeEncodeError: 'ascii' codec can't encode character u'\u03a9' in position 54:
ordinal not in range(128)
```

What happened? Well, the ASCII code used in the database driver can't handle all the Unicode characters you threw at it, and it blew up.

You can use Unicode in TurboGears with all of the DB-API drivers that support Unicode queries, but Unicode Columns break if you use a database driver that doesn't support Unicode. You will likely get a different error if your database doesn't support Unicode strings, so you might have to watch out for that, too.

The lack of helpful error messages when the Unicode support is missing from your database drivers, or your database itself, is a known problem and might be fixed by the time you read this; however, you'd better double-check. Right now you're likely to have trouble with Unicode and SQLite or the `psycopg` driver for `postgres`—but if you are using `postgres`, a simple switch to `psycopg2` will likely resolve your Unicode-related problems.

To work around this problem, you can encode your Unicode strings manually:

```
>>> list(T1.select(T1.q.name==u'Greek \u03a9'.encode('utf8')))
[<T1 1 name=u'Greek \u03a9'>]
```

20.2.2 Kid Templates

When you you use Unicode strings with Kid everything usually "just works."

TurboGears uses the _kid.encoding_ configuration option, which defaults to UTF-8 to automatically encode Kid HTML/XML output. The same option is used to set the "Content-Type" HTTP header so that the browser will display it correctly.

One pitfall to watch for is Kid file encoding. Just like any other XML file, the encoding is typically declared in the XML header line of your Kid file. Make sure that the declared encoding matches the actual file content. If the header line and file content don't match, you might get strange "input file not well-formed" error messages from Kid even though the file is okay, just saved with the wrong encoding.

Here's an example of a Kid template and usage:

Controller:
```
@expose(template="ch18.templates.welcome")
def index(self):
    names = [
        ('Cyrillic A', u'\u0410'),
        ('Cyrillic BE', u'\u0411'),
        ('Cyrillic VE', u'\u0412'),
    ]
    return dict(names=names)
```

Kid:
```
<p py:for="(title,s) in names"><em>${s}</em> &mdash; ${title}</p>
```

Browser displays:

А — Cyrillic A
Б — Cyrillic BE
В — Cyrillic VE

You will also want to check out the `kid.encoding` configuration option, which serves several different purposes.

First, if you want to compose your Kid templates using an encoding different from ASCII or UTF-8, say, latin1, you can set `kid.encoding` to specify that. Do not forget to put the corresponding XML declarations in the file itself.

```
<?xml version="1.0" encoding="iso-8859-1"?>
<!DOCTYPE html PUBLIC "-//W3C//DTD XHTML 1.0 Transitional//EN" "http://www.w3.org/
TR/xhtml1/DTD/xhtml1-transitional.dtd">
<html xmlns="http://www.w3.org/1999/xhtml" xmlns:py="http://purl.org/kid/ns#"
    py:extends="'master.kid'">
<body>
  ... Latin1 text goes here ...


</body>
</html>
```

The confuguration option `kid.encoding` is also used to guess the proper Content-Type to set when rendering the Kid template to the browser.

20.2.3 Unicode in CherryPy's Request/Response Cycle

In the default configuration, TurboGears converts all incoming parameters that are passed to your controller into Unicode strings. Here is a small test case:

```
@expose()
def process(self, name=None):
    return "Name is %r" % name
    # -> yields something like "Name is u'Smarty'"
```

Usually you would just keep it that way. If for some reason you disable this with the `decoding_filter` option, you might want to use `turbogears.validators.UnicodeString` to decode the selected parameters by hand:

```
@expose()
@turbogears.validate(validators={'name':validators.UnicodeString()})
def process(self, name=None, name2=None):
    return "Name is %r while name2 is %r" % name
    # -> yields something like "Name is u'Smarty' while name2 is 'Smarty'"
```

TurboGears also takes care of encoding Unicode on output:

```
@expose()
def process(self, name=None):
    return u'Smarty'
    # -> browser receives string "Smarty" encoded into utf-8 encoding
```

The same is true if you use Kid or some other templating engine—the output will be correctly encoded and the Content-Type header will be set correctly.

20.3 Translating Your Application

Now that you have a firm grasp on the basics of handling Unicode strings in Turbo-Gears, we can start delving into the process that TurboGears uses to create and maintain translation files.

There are several steps in the translation process, from marking what needs to be translated to creating catalogs of translated strings and making them available to the application. TurboGears uses the standard tool used in the GNU/Open Source world: GNUgettext.

There are several steps in the process:

1. Marking translatable strings in your source code (Python source, Kid/Cheetah templates, etc.)
2. Collecting these strings into so called "message catalog templates"
3. Creating or updating locale-specific message catalogs from the template file
4. Compiling message catalogs
5. Using run-time functions to set up the correct locale and read translations of the desired string

The message catalog is a set of text files that contains all the strings for translations and (usually) references the source file the string comes from. The reference makes it easier to track the changes down the road. The message catalog consists of two different types of files, the "master" catalog or template (with .pot extension) and "locale" catalog files (one per language). Each of these additional catalog files contains the translated strings for its language.

To translate your application's text, you edit each locale catalog file to provide all necessary translations. When you are done with the translations, you compile that locale into a binary representation for efficient run-time lookup.

As your source code evolves, you rerun the string collection process, update the locale catalog files, update translations, and recompile catalogs.

If you think this process sounds painful, you're right. Well, at least you would be right if you had to do it all by hand. While it may seem daunting to translate your application into a few dozen languages, TurboGears does everything it can to make the process as painless as possible by automating away the most tedious work.

20.3.1 Localization of Python Sources

Before we can set up the .pot files, we have to mark all of the translatable strings in our application. We also need to set up functions to return the right string for the user's locale whenever a string is generated that could go out to the user. Luckily for us, we do both of these things the same way!

There is a de facto standard for such things, and TurboGears follows that established standard rather than trying to invent something new. To mark a string for translation, you just use the"underscore" function—written as _(). Inside your TurboGears application, _() is a "built in" function, so you do not have to import anything in order to call it. The same is true for Python excerpts in Kid templates. Actually, Kid also has other even simpler localization options that we'll get back to shortly.

When using the _() function, also called the gettext function, sometimes you don't want to translate the text right away, instead you want to defer the results of its evaluation until later, when you know the user's locale. This is typical for declarative statements like the ones you use to define a widget or form:

```
signup_form = TableForm('signup', submit_text=_("Sign me Up"), fields=[...])
```

Here, gettext("Sign me Up") is called when the form is defined, not when it is actually rendered in a web page. This would give you a static message that may not be relevant for the user's locale because the same message is sent to all locales. Even worse, when the form was defined, no locale had yet been specified, so TurboGears would fallback to the default.

To overcome this issue, TurboGears uses a special flavor of the gettext function that is sometimes called lazy_gettext, which does not attempt to translate the string immediately, but instead returns a callable that knows which strings to return a translated value for and performs a translation only when needed. This "something" can be evaluated any number of times, and each time it will perform a new lookup for the message and locale specified.

Usually the lazy_gettext trick is transparent to you as a programmer. But, occasionally the trick can get you in trouble. As a result, it can be helpful to understand what is happening under the hood. When you want to control exactly what happens, TurboGears provides the plain_gettext and lazy_gettext functions, which work as you would expect: plain_gettext translates the message right away, while lazy_gettext returns the magic callable just described.

20.3.2 Localization of Kid Templates

As noted previously, you can use _() inside your Kid template. It requires some extra typing, but works fine, as illustrated below:

```
<p>${_('Welcome, %s!') % name}</p>
```

This is the only option if you need to have a parameterized string, as we do in the above example.

To translate static strings in your Kid template, there are some even simpler options.

You can have TurboGears translate all of your templates by using the i18n.run_template_filter = on configuration setting. This setting incurs small performance costs to process a template, but is very straightforward to set up and use.

For instance, in the following Kid excerpt :

```
<p>Welcome, <em>guest</em>!<br/>
Nice to see you again on my site.
</p>
```

The template filter would automatically extract these translatable strings:

```
'Welcome,'
'guest'
'!'
'Nice to see you again on my site.'
```

Note how the XHTML markup breaks the string and that whitespace is always stripped off.

If you don't want to translate everything, you can use more fine-grained control with the turbogears.i18n.translate helper function. To use it, you add the right py:match processing directive at the top of your Kid template and mark translatable text by adding lang attributes to corresponding nodes. Here is a fully functional example:

```
<!DOCTYPE html PUBLIC "-//W3C//DTD XHTML 1.0 Transitional//EN" "http://www.w3.org/
TR/xhtml1/DTD/xhtml1-transitional.dtd">
<?python from turbogears.i18n import translate ?>
<html xmlns="http://www.w3.org/1999/xhtml" xmlns:py="http://purl.org/kid/ns#"
    py:extends="'master.kid'">
  <translate py:match="item.attrib.has_key('lang')" py:replace="translate(item,
'lang')"/>
```

```
<body>
  <div lang="">
    <span>This message will be translated.</span>
    <span lang="en">And this one as well.</span>
  </div>
  <p>This is "normal" text that is not translated.</p>
</body>
```

An empty value in the `lang` attribute means "current user locale," which is what you want most of the time. You can override the selection of the current user locale by specifying a locale code "en" or "fi" instead. In this case, translation to this locale will be used, ignoring the current user locale (this may be useful, for example, for a site language selector UI).

The command-line version (`tg-admin i18n`) at least tries to support both approaches to translating Kid templates with—strict-kid-support/—loose-kid-support, while Toolbox `admi18n` simply grabs everything. Unfortunately, neither tool will automatically detect calling `gettext` (using the `_()` function) directly from Kid templates.

20.3.3 Auto-Detect User Language Preference

The `turbogears.i18n.get_locale()` function tries to guess the user's locale. It looks for locale information in several places: in the session, the HTTP Accept-Language header, and finally the `i18n.default_locale` configuration option. If none of these places contains a locale, TurboGears will fall back to a default locale of "en."

If the default lookup algorithm doesn't suit you (for instance, if you store locale information in the database), you can specify your own algorithm by assigning a lookup function to the `i18n.get_locale` configuration variable. The function is parameterless and returns a locale name.

Example:

```
def get_locale_from_db():
        user = identity.current.user
        if user and user.locale:
                return user.locale
        return turbogears.i18n.utils._get_locale() # fallback to default
```

If you store the user's locale information in session data, use `turbogears.i18n set_session_locale`. The default key is `locale`, but you can override that with the `i18n.session_key` variable. Make sure you have `session_filter.on` before using it.

20.3.4 Locale-Specific Objects

To localize an application completely, simply translating user interface messages often is not enough.

Different locales often use different representations for things like dates, numbers, currencies, and so forth. All locale-specific data resides in the `turbogears.i18n.format` module.

These functions also take an optional locale argument; if it is None, the current user locale is used.

These low-level functions might be of help if you are building your own locale libraries.

Higher-level functions solve more complete tasks:

- `format_number`—Formats a number using a locale-specific group separator symbol
- `format_decimal`—Like `format_number`, handles locale-specific separators, but also handles decimals with a specified precision (decimal symbol is read from the locale information)
- `format_currency`—Formats a number with a fixed precision (two digits)
- `parse_number`/`parse_decimal`—Counterparts of the `format_number`/`format_decimal` functions, reads locale-specific string representations of a number into Python long or float value
- `format_date`—Formats the `datetime` object to match one of the predefined locale-specific formats (full, long, medium, short) or a custom format template.

20.3.5 Admin i18n Interface

There are two tools in TurboGears that help you solve the mundane problems of dealing with i18n. One is web-based, the admi18n component of the Toolbox. The other tool is a command-line tool: the i18n subcommand of the `tg-admin` tool.

Both commands work in very much the same manner, so you can pick one based on your personal preferences. Generally speaking, the web interface is easier to use, while the command-line version provides some advanced options not found in the web version (not that these will be of interest to most folks).

20.3.5.1 Toolbox admi18n Tool

The tool includes built-in usage instructions so it should be straightforward to use.

20.3.5.2 `tg-admin i18n` Command-line Tool

The following sub-commands are available:

- `add`—Creates a message catalog for specified locale
- `collect`—Scans source files to gather translatable strings to a .pot file
- `merge`—Syncs message catalogs in different languages with the master .pot file
- `compile`—Compiles message catalogs (.po to .mo)
- `clean`—Deletes backups and compiled files

> Note: You'll need to run `tg-admin i18n collect` first to grab new strings from the source files. Once you've added new translations, run `tg-admin i18n compile` to actually see the changes.

The `tg-admin i18n collect` command processes a project's Python and Kid sources to find strings marked for translation. If a translation file exists, its content is updated with new data and a backup is made.

There are some options related to Kid template processing, run `tg-admin i18n -h` to get them.

To add another locale to your project, run `tg-admin i18n add` and supply an appropriate locale code, like es or uk_UA. This will create the locale's directory and the locale's message catalog file which contains translations.

The command `tg-admin i18n compile` compiles every locale's message catalog file into a machine efficient .mo file.

The command `tg-admin i18n merge` copies newly-added message strings from the master .pot file to each locale's message catalog, keeping existing translations intact.

20.4 Summary

- Unicode allows you to use a single encoding for every language, and Python's support for Unicode makes internationalization a lot easier.

- Not every Python library is Unicode aware, so if you use third party libraries, you should test them with Unicode strings.

- You can generally avoid Unicode decode errors by not mixing and matching Unicode and ASCII strings. In other words, just use Unicode all the time and you should be all set.

- SQLObject handles Unicode only as well as the underlying database/driver so you'll want to be careful which database and drivers you pick for your internationalized application.

- You can use the `gettext` and `lazy_gettext` functions anywhere in your Turbo-Gears project to get a localized string.

- The `i18n.run_template_filter = on` setting means that you can automatically populate your translation string files with the contents of your Kid file, and then automatically substitute translated strings into the output. No programming required!

- You can also use `format_number`, `format_curency`, `format_date`, and other similar functions to localize dates and numbers so that they will be displayed properly in various regional formats.

Chapter 21

Testing a TurboGears Application

Testing is a crucial part of the software development life cycle. Large-scale web application development is a serious endeavor that requires serious testing effort. There are different flavors of testing. Common wisdom suggests that you need to test your system at various levels of granularity using a combination of unit tests, integration tests, and functional tests. A respected TurboGears application has many components in different architectural layers and is distributed across at least two processes (the web server and the client's browser).

Different parts of the application should be tested using different tools and different testing strategies. In this chapter, we'll introduce some test tools and frameworks that are packaged with TurboGears or that can be used to test TurboGears applications.

Nose and `testutil` provide a great way to do unit and functional tests in development, Mechanize provides a good way to exercise your complete application stack and to run stress tests against your full production environment, and Selenium provides a great way to create tests that run right from within your browser—thus allowing you to test Ajax and other JavaScript.

21.1 Nose

Nose is a sophisticated and unobtrusive unit test framework for Python. It automatically discovers your tests (based on simple naming conventions), runs them, and reports the result. You can write simple test functions, unittest-based test cases or doctests. Nose will happily execute them all. Nose also knows how to intercept the standard Python assert, so you don't need to learn and depend on some Nose-specific mechanism in your test code. Nose is not TurboGears-specific, and you can (and should) use it to test all your Python code. Let's see Nose in action by testing a factorial function:

```
def factorial(n, recursive=True):
  """Computes the factorial of non-negative integers
  >>> factorial(0)
  1
```

```
>>> factorial(5)
120

>>> factorial(4, recursive=False)
24

"""
def recursive_fact(n):
  if n == 0:
    return 1
  return n * recursive_fact(n-1)

def iterative_fact(n):
  result = 1
  for i in xrange(1, n):
    result *= i
  return result

if not isinstance(n, int) or n < 0:
  raise ValueError('n must be a non-negative integer')
if recursive:
  return recursive_fact(n)
else:
  return iterative_fact(n)
```

This function is pretty sophisticated, as far as factorial functions go. It verifies that input is a non-negative integer and supports two algorithms for calculating the factorial: a recursive one and an iterative one. The algorithms are implemented as nested functions. The actual algorithm is selected by the value of the recursive named argument that defaults to True. Another interesting fact is that this function has a doc string that contains doctests. Doctests are interactive Python sessions that contain a command line and a response from the interpreter. The easiest way to write doctests is to copy and paste them from an interactive Python session. You can execute doctests with the doctest module, but why should you? Nose can do it for you. Okay, let's write some test code and put it in a file called test_factorial.py:

```
from factorial import factorial as f

def dummyNotCalled():
  assert False
```

```
def testAlwaysFails():
 assert False

def test_Success():
  assert f(0) == 1
  assert f(1) == 1
  assert f(2) == 2
  assert f(3) == 6
  assert f(4) == 28
  assert f(5) == 120
  assert f(6) == 720

def test_Exception():
  for x in (-1, 0.455, 'xxxx'):
    try:
      f(x)
      assert False # should never get here
    except ValueError:
      pass

def tesst_Iterative():
  for n, result in ((0,1), (1,1), (2,2), (3,6), (6,720)):
    assert f(n, recursive=False) == result
```

The filename and the names of the test functions are important. Nose discovers your tests by scanning the root directory (current directory, by default) recursively and executing all the functions and methods that match the test signature. This signature (a.k.a. `testMatch`) is, by default, the following regex: `(?:^|[b_.-])[Tt]est`. It means anything that starts with test or Test and anything that contains `_test`, `_Test`, `-test`, or `-Test`. This scheme covers most reasonable naming convention for tests. You can control many aspects of Nose execution by providing various switches. Let's launch Nose and tell it to execute doctests too:

```
nosetests --with-doctest

FFF.
======================================================================
FAIL: Doctest: factorial.factorial
----------------------------------------------------------------------
Traceback (most recent call last):
  File "/usr/local/lib/python2.4/doctest.py", line 2152, in runTest
    raise self.failureException(self.format_failure(new.getvalue()))
```

AssertionError: Failed doctest test for factorial.factorial
  File "/home/gsayfan/trunk/examples/example1/tutorial/nosedemo/factorial.py",
line 1, in factorial

File "/home/gsayfan/trunk/examples/example1/tutorial/nosedemo/factorial.py", line
6, in factorial.factorial
Failed example:
    factorial(5)
Expected:
    123
Got:
    120

File "/home/gsayfan/trunk/examples/example1/tutorial/nosedemo/factorial.py", line
9, in factorial.factorial
Failed example:
    factorial(4, recursive=False)
Expected:
    24
Got:
    6

==
FAIL: test_factorial.testAlwaysFails

Traceback (most recent call last):
  File "/home/gsayfan/nta/eng/linux64/lib/python2.4/site-packages/nose-0.9.0-
py2.4.egg/nose/case.py", line 52, in runTest
    self.testFunc()
  File "/home/gsayfan/trunk/examples/example1/tutorial/nosedemo/test_factorial.
py", line 7, in testAlwaysFails
    assert False
AssertionError

==
FAIL: test_factorial.test_Recursive

Traceback (most recent call last):
  File "/home/gsayfan/nta/eng/linux64/lib/python2.4/site-packages/nose-0.9.0-
py2.4.egg/nose/case.py", line 52, in runTest
    self.testFunc()
  File "/home/gsayfan/trunk/examples/example1/tutorial/nosedemo/test_factorial.
py", line 14, in test_Recursive
    assert f(4) == 28

```
AssertionError
```

```
----------------------------------------------------------------
Ran 4 tests in 0.010s
```

```
FAILED (failures=3)
```

Wow. Three failures out of four tests. That's impressive. This is one programmer that can really benefit from TDD (Test Driven Development). Nose gives a very nice and detailed report when a test fails. Let's go over the failures in reverse order. The `test_Recursive` function failed on the line `assert f(4) == 28`. Wait a minute, this is not right. 4! == 24. This a defective test. It happens. Let's fix it and move on. The next failure is `testAlwaysFails()`, which contains the statement, `assert False`, which, of course, always fails. This is easy to fix by simply commenting out this function. Note that `dummyNotCalled()`, which also contains `assert False` didn't cause a failure because the function name doesn't match the test signature and Nose just ignored it. Last, but not least, is the doctest failure. Note the friendly output. The problem here seems to be an actual bug in the code. The code that's executing is the iterative flavor of factorial, and it returns 6 for 4! instead of 24.

If you are factorially inclined you probably noticed that 6 is 3! and your nose tells you that an off by one error is involved. Indeed, the loop in `iterative_fact` stops one iteration short. The `xrange()` yields the half open range `(1, n)`. The fix is easy, just add 1 to range. Here is the correct function:

```
def iterative_fact(n):
    result = 1
    for i in xrange(1, n+1):
        result *= i
    return result
```

So, we fixed all the errors and bugs. Now we can run Nose again:

```
nosetests --with-doctest
```

```
...
----------------------------------------------------------------
Ran 3 tests in 0.009s
```

```
OK
```

That looks much better. Because the `testAlwaysFails()` function is gone, we ran three tests instead of four and they all passed. Nose practices the "silence is golden" principle and by default captures all standard output. Let's try it one more time with the -v switch:

```
nosetests --with-doctest -v

Doctest: factorial.factorial ... ok
test_factorial.test_Recursive ... ok
test_factorial.test_Exception ... ok


----------------------------------------------------------------------
Ran 3 tests in 0.008s

OK
```

Still okay. Unfortunately, we are missing a test. What happened to `test_Iterative`? It turns out that we misspelled it as: `tesst_Iterative`, so it didn't match the test signature and Nose ignored it. After fixing it, the output is finally what we expect:

```
nosetests --with-doctest -v

Doctest: factorial.factorial ... ok
test_factorial.test_Recursive ... ok
test_factorial.test_Iterative ... ok
test_factorial.test_Exception ... ok


----------------------------------------------------------------------
Ran 4 tests in 0.009s

OK
```

Nose intercepts unhandled exceptions and treats them as failures. If you have multiple asserts in a single test case, the first failure will abort the test case and continue to execute other tests. Nose boasts a plugin system that already includes a profiler (hotshot) and coverage report. We urge you to investigate Nose and put it to good use in your TurboGears applications and other Python projects.

21.2 TurboGears `testutil`

Nose is great, but TurboGears apps are complicated beasts, and it is sometimes not so trivial to test them properly. The `testutil` module of TurboGears provides lots of shortcuts and convenient classes and functions you can use. You will use the famous bookmarker as a test bed. If you recall in Chapter 4, "Creating a Simple Application," you already used `testutil` briefly to test your controllers and make sure they returned the proper data. The goal here is to make bookmarker a little more robust and to make sure that all bookmarks point to existing URLs (no 404 errors) and that there are no duplicate bookmarks (two bookmarks with the same name and/or same URL).

How do you test a TurboGears application? There are different test dimensions: you can test your DB to make sure it contains the right data; you can test your controller methods to make sure they return the right result; you can test your view to make sure it returns a properly formatted and styled page with the correct data; and you can test your Ajax code in the browsers (plural). All these tests are important; but, you usually don't have to write so many tests for every feature or bug fix. Usually you will have some generic mechanisms, like a Kid template, that know how to render a page given a list of records from your DB. Once you've tested this template on some record lists, you gain confidence that it works and you don't need to write additional view tests for new controller methods. It is enough to make sure that the new controller method returns a dictionary with the expected record list.

Let's start with the database and make sure that it doesn't allow you to store duplicate bookmarks. We'll start by getting the preliminaries out of the way. You need to import quite a few packages to conduct sophisticated tests. Besides your projects model and `controllers.Root`, you want TurboGears's `testutil` and `database`, as well as `cherrypy`.

By importing `testutil` you will get some enormous benefits. TurboGears creates a SQLite DB in memory. This is a wonderful feature of SQLite. You can't wreak havoc on your production DB, there is no need for admin rights, there aren't any permission issues or wrong filenames, and it's *fast*.

Of course, TurboGears supports you if you have to test with a different DB (e.g. your code uses nested transactions that SQLite doesn't support) or if you want to test on a real DB with lots of data. All you have to do is `set_db_uri` to point to whatever test database you want to use, and you are good to go.

You may also want to import the `with_setup` and `with_teardown` decorators from Nose. We use only `with_setup` in this code.

The next step is setting CherryPy's root to your Root controller. Once again, `turbogears.testutil` comes to the rescue and helps by setting a couple of useful configuration settings for you (new style logging, no autoreload) and starting the built-in CherryPy server so it will be ready for you.

```
import os, sys

from turbogears import (testutil,
                        database)
from bookmarker.controllers import Root
from bookmarker.model import (Bookmarks,
                        Categories)
import cherrypy

from nose import with_setup

cherrypy.root = Root()
```

It's time to define a test class. In the previous section, we showed how to write test functions. Nose supports test classes, too, and that's what we'll use now. The test class is called `BookmarkTest` and it subclasses `testutil.DBTest`. The base class provides fixture services `setUp`/`tearDown` to your test code. The `setUp` method is called before every test method and the `tearDown` method is called after each test. This allows great isolation of tests because you verify that every tests starts in pristine state. So, `DBTest` creates all your model's tables before every test and drops them after every test. It also rolls back your DB. I'm not sure how effective it is. If your code did something and committed it, the rollback won't help you. That is why it's a good idea to use the default memory database or another special testing database for your test class, rather than take the chance of corrupting your production database.

```
class BookmarkTest(testutil.DBTest):
    ...
```

Before we actually write some tests, let's define a helper class. The entire test class deals with saving new bookmarks to the DB so the `save_new_bookmark` will come in handy. It accepts a dictionary of parameters that match the `save_bookmark` method in your controller, prepares a url, and calls the `testutil.createRequest()` function (possibly multiple times).

```
def save_new_bookmark(self, params, times=1):
    pairs = ['%s=%s' % (k, params[k]) for k in params]
    url = '/save_bookmark/0?' + '&'.join(pairs)
    for i in range(times):
        testutil.createRequest(url)
```

`testutil` provides two ways to invoke your controller: the `call()` method and the `createRequest()` method. One simple tip can save you a lot of grief: Never invoke a redirected controller method (like `save_bookmark`) using `testutil.call()`. `testutil.call()` uses a `DummyRequest` class that works fine if the controller just returns a dictionary; but if a redirection is called for, the `DummyRequest` can't deliver the dictionary when it is accessed during processing. This is the reason that the `save_new_bookmark` helper uses `createRequest()`, which creates a full fledged CherryPy request object that can be redirected.

Finally, here is some actual test code. The following methods are very similar. They make sure that when you try to insert all kinds of bookmarks the DB doesn't allow duplicate links. `test_save_valid_bookmaek()` just puts in a single bookmark and verifies that it has been added. `test_duplicate_bookmark()` tries to insert the same bookmark twice. `test_duplicate_bookmark_name()` tries to insert two bookmarks with the same name and `test_duplicate_bookmark_url()` tries to inserts two bookmarks with the same URL.

```
def test_save_valid_bookmark(self):

    assert Bookmarks.select().count() == 0

    params={'link':'http://another_valid.com',
            'description':'good_one',
            'bookmarkName':'valid_bookmark'}
    self.save_new_bookmark(params)
    assert Bookmarks.select().count() == 1
    assert Bookmarks.get(1).link=='http://another_valid.com'

def test_duplicate_bookmark(self):
    assert Bookmarks.select().count() == 0

    params={'link':'http://another_valid.com',
            'description':'good_one',
            'bookmarkName':'valid_bookmark'}
    pairs = ['%s=%s' % (k, params[k]) for k in params]
```

```
    url = '/save_bookmark/0?' + '&'.join(pairs)

    # Will try to save the bookmark twice
    self.save_new_bookmark(params, times=2)

    assert Bookmarks.select().count() == 1
    assert Bookmarks.get(1).link=='http://another_valid.com'

def test_duplicate_bookmark_name(self):
    assert Bookmarks.select().count() == 0

    params={'link':'http://valid.com',
            'description':'good_one',
            'bookmarkName':'valid_bookmark'}
    self.save_new_bookmark(params)

    params['link'] = params['link'].replace('valid.com', 'different.com')
    self.save_new_bookmark(params)

    assert Bookmarks.select().count() == 1
    assert Bookmarks.get(1).link=='http://valid.com'

def test_duplicate_bookmark_url(self):
    assert Bookmarks.select().count() == 0

    params={'link':'http://valid.com',
            'description':'good_one',
            'bookmarkName':'valid_bookmark'}
    self.save_new_bookmark(params)

    params['name'] = params['name'].replace('valid_bookmark',
                                            'different_name')

    self.save_new_bookmark(params)

    assert Bookmarks.select().count() == 2
    assert Bookmarks.get(1).link=='http://valid.com'
```

If you run nosetests, you will get the following output:

```
======================================================================
FAIL: test_duplicate_bookmark_url (test_gigi.BookmarkTest)
----------------------------------------------------------------------
```

```
Traceback (most recent call last):
  File "/Users/gsayfan/Documents/docs/Publications/TG Book/svn/trunk/code/5/book-
marker/bookmarker/tests2/test_gigi.py", line 91, in test_duplicate_bookmark_url
    assert Bookmarks.select().count() == 1
AssertionError


----------------------------------------------------------------------
Ran 4 tests in 1.558s


FAILED (failures=1)
```

The `test_duplicate_bookmark_url()` failed. It is possible to enter two bookmarks with different names that have the same URL. Perhaps this is a bug, and perhaps it isn't. Feel free to decide either way and modify the bookmarker application or the test to match your decision.

21.3 Mechanize

We had some good fun testing our controllers and database application using Nose, and we've taken advantage of `testutil`. So far, all our tests took place directly on the server.

It's time to get out into the world. In real life, sometimes you also need to test your application from the client-side. This is necessary for several reasons, even if you pedantically hand-test the output from every controller method with every conceivable combination of application state and input arguments. You still need to test your deployment story and make sure that your application is available from a different machine or, better yet, from outside the firewall. You also want to make sure that the application spits out a proper mix of HTML/XML/CSS and JavaScript to satisfy every web browser (or web service client) that you want to support. It's probably a good idea to have some tests that run periodically against your production code to make sure that everything is working on your servers.

The good news is that Python has an easy-to-use solution to all these problems. Mechanize makes browser simulation testing in Python so easy, writing tests is almost fun.

Mechanize can impersonate a specific user agent and thus enable you to test the code generated for each browser. It operates just like any browser through HTTP, so if it works in Mechanize, it will work in the browser. Of course, Mechanize doesn't simulate browser rendering, so you still need to look at your pages in the various browsers you support and see if they look okay!

If you decide to use Mechanize, you'll need to install it, because it isn't part of TurboGears. We suggest you use the following command:

```
easy_install -Z mechanize
```

If you drop the -z, Mechanize will be installed as a zipped egg and you will not be able to debug it or browse its code. Mechanize depends on ClientForm, which allows you to process forms easily.

Let's see what Mechanize can do for you. Run the bookmarker application and execute the following code:

```
from mechanize import Browser

b = Browser()
b.open("http://localhost:8080/")

# Just get all bookmarks
r = b.follow_link(text=r"All Bookmarks")
assert b.viewing_html()

print r.geturl()
print r.info()  # headers
print r.read()  # body
```

You should see some metadata followed by the actual HTML page returned from the "All Bookmarks" link. Mechanize a wrapper around urllib2. If you are familiar with that module, you know that you can use most of its methods from within a Mechanize script.

The Browser class is a glorified urllib2.OpenerDirector wrapped in some thick layers of Mechanize code. This means that the urllib2 Request and Response objects are there (not to be confused with the CherryPy Request and Response objects), and that the entire API is very urllib2 like. Having said that, you'll likely run into some trouble if you mix plain urllib2 objects with mechanize objects.

Mechanize provides very fine-grained ways to navigate your application using regular expressions to follow links and analyze the responses. You can reload the current page, go back, set and control proxies, handle cookies, and logging levels of specific operations like redirects and refreshes.

Let's see how Mechanize can handle forms. The following test function is trying to add a new bookmark using the bookmark/add form. First, it verifies that the `All book-marks` page doesn't contain the word `'Mechanize'`. Then it navigates to the bookmark/add page, gets the form object, populates the object with proper value, and submits it. Then it verifies that 'Mechanize' appears in the new response and even validates that the actual URL appears in the links. Note that we use a regular expression to locate the link, which is one of the amenities that Mechanize offers. The code feels very natural and Python-like.

```python
from mechanize import Browser
import ClientForm

def test_add_link():
    # Just get all bookmarks
    b = Browser()
    b.open("http://localhost:8080/")
    # follow link to All bookmarks page
    r = b.follow_link(text=r"All Bookmarks")
    assert b.viewing_html()
    assert not 'Mechanize' in r.read()

    # Open the add bookmark page
    b.open("http://localhost:8080/bookmark/add")

    # get the form
    forms = ClientForm.ParseResponse(b.response(), backwards_compat=False)
    form = forms[0]

    # Fill the form
    form["bookmarkName"] = "Mechanize"
    form["link"] = "http://wwwsearch.sourceforge.net/"
    form["description"] = "The best browser simulator ever!!!"

    # Submit the form
    r = b.open(form.click())

    # Make sure it's in there
    assert 'Mechanize' in r.read()
    links = list(b.links(url_regex=".*wwwsearch.*"))
    assert len(links) == 1
    assert links[0].url == 'http://wwwsearch.sourceforge.net/'
```

Mechanize and its `clientForm` sidekick have a lot to offer, but unfortunately the documentation (on the site and on the web) is somewhat scant. If you really want to utilize Mechanize be prepared to dig into the source.

Another option to make writing mechanized-based testing easier is the fantastic twill library, which offers an easy-to-use layer on top of mechanizing to write tests from Python, or in a domain specific browser emulation language. Twill is well documented, and available at: http://twill.idyll.org/.

21.4 Selenium

Mechanize is great but sometimes you need to be able to see the test with your own eyes to make sure everything is correct and placed in the right place. Selenium is a great tool that helps you run tests inside the browser. You install Selenium into your web server. We recommend `/static/selenium` in your TurboGears project. Make sure that the following section is in your `config/app.cfg`. It should be included by default:

```
[/static]
static_filter.on = True
static_filter.dir = "%(top_level_dir)s/static"
```

Selenium works by injecting JavaScript code into your application that executes in the browser on the client side. The benefit is that Selenium's code can interact very intimately with the HTML DOM of your application. You write Selenium tests in regular HTML files that contain HTML tables with some commands in a special language called Selenese. Don't worry, you can learn it in 40 seconds. These tables are loaded and the commands are executed by Selenium's `TestRunner` in your browser. Here is a simple test for the bookmarker application:

```
<html>
<head>
<meta http-equiv="Content-Type" content="text/html; charset=UTF-8">
<title>New Test</title>
</head>
<body>
<table cellpadding="1" cellspacing="1" border="1">
<thead>
<tr><td rowspan="1" colspan="3">New Test</td></tr>
</thead><tbody>
<tr>
```

```
        <td>open</td>
        <td>../../</td>
        <td></td>
</tr>
<tr>
        <td>clickAndWait</td>
        <td>link=All Bookmarks</td>
        <td></td>
</tr>
<tr>
        <td>verifyTextPresent</td>
        <td>-- Main TurboGears website </td>
        <td></td>
</tr>

</tbody></table>
</body>
</html>
```

Let's clean it up a little and concentrate on the actual content:

...

```
<td>open</td>
<td>../../</td>

<td>clickAndWait</td>
<td>link=All Bookmarks</td>


<td>verifyTextPresent</td>
<td>-- Main TurboGears website </td>
```

...

Each row in the table contains a command with arguments. The first row opens the ../../ url, which happens to be the root of bookmarker, because the test is located in /static/selenium/SeleniumTestList.html. The second row clicks the All bookmarks link and waits for it to show up. The third row verifies that the text "-- Main TurboGears website" appears on the new page. This is a complete test that starts from the browser, moves through the network into CherryPy via the bookmarker controller code, accesses the database, and sends the information all the way back to the browser.

Selenium supports practically all browsers in common use. We tested it on modern versions of Firefox, Safari, and Opera on OSX, Firefox on Ubuntu, and even IE 6 on Windows XP. It worked perfectly on all of them.

Let's see another example. Suppose you want to add a new link. You will have to fill up a form and submit it:

```
<html>
<head>
<meta http-equiv="Content-Type" content="text/html; charset=UTF-8">
<title>New Test</title>
</head>
<body>
<table cellpadding="1" cellspacing="1" border="1">
<thead>
<tr><td rowspan="1" colspan="3">New Test</td></tr>
</thead><tbody>
<tr>
        <td>open</td>
        <td>../../</td>
        <td></td>
</tr>
<tr>
        <td>clickAndWait</td>
        <td>link=Add New Link</td>
        <td></td>
</tr>
<tr>
        <td>type</td>
        <td>bookmarkName</td>
        <td>abcd</td>
</tr>
<tr>
        <td>type</td>
        <td>link</td>
        <td>http://222.com</td>
</tr>
<tr>
        <td>type</td>
        <td>description</td>
        <td>great site.really</td>
</tr>
<tr>
        <td>clickAndWait</td>
        <td>//input[@value='Save Bookmark']</td>
```

```
        <td></td>
</tr>
<tr>
        <td>verifyTextPresent</td>
        <td>abcd -- great site.really </td>
        <td></td>
</tr>
</tbody></table>
</body>
</html>
```

Note that the submit button is specified using an XPath expression this time. This is important if you have elements without ID or name that you want to locate. The 'type' command, which you haven't seen before, is used for populating form fields.

Now that you have written a couple of tests, it is time to run them. The best way to run them is to write a test suite. A test suite is another simple HTML file:

```
<html>
<head>
    <title>Test Suite</title>
</head>

<body>
    <table id="suiteTable"     cellpadding="1"
            cellspacing="1"
            border="1"
            class="selenium">
        <tbody>
            <tr><td><b>Test Suite</b></td></tr>

            <tr><td><a href="./SeleniumTestList.html">TestList</a></td></tr>
            <tr><td><a href="./SeleniumTestAddLink.html">TestAddLink</a></td></tr>
        </tbody>
    </table>
</body>
</html>
```

You can put your tests and TestSuite.html file anywhere in the /static directory.

Once you've put your tests in the static directory, you can browse to http://local-host:8080/static/selenium/TestRunner.html. You will see a nice web-based Selenium GUI that allows you to select a test suite file. Use a relative path from /static/selenium to locate your TestSuite.html file. The TestRunner will display your tests. You can select one of them, and you will see the commands in the middle pane. You can run a selected test or all the tests, walk through the tests, or even debug them (including breakpoints). It is really a very rich test environment considering that everything happens inside the browser. When you run your tests, the TestRunner will color successful commands in green and failed ones in red (and stop).

There is, of course, a lot more to Selenium. Once you understand the basics and how Selenium works, it is easy to expand your knowledge and explore further.

Now, we have something to confess. We didn't write these Selenium tests.

We used a wonderful Firefox extension called Selenium-IDE. This extension allows you to capture tests in a GUI fashion just by navigating through your site, clicking links, and filling out forms. You can even run your tests there. The tests that are captured are cross-platform, and you can run them on other browsers. The only limitation, and it's awfully small, is if you do any browser sniffing and generate different markup for different browsers, tests generated on one browser may break when run in a different browser.

The Selenium IDE is a great time-saver and makes the entire experience of writing web GUI tests fun, or at least tolerable.

Finally, there is another project called Selenium4Gears, which requires you to write some glue code in your application but provides automated tests based on your controller methods.

21.5 Summary

- The Nose testing framework makes it easy to define test functions, test classes, and even doctests and run them every time you make a change.

- TurboGears provides a number of utilities that make unit and functional testing with Nose even easier. `testutil` and the `DBTest` class make it easy to run tests against an in-memory SQLite database or any other test database you've got set up.

- Python's Mechanize module makes it easy to script a simulated browser session. This is helpful to make sure that everything is working or that CherryPy filters are being applied correctly. You can also use Mechanize to run scripted tests against your production server that will tell you if anything bad is happening.

- Selenium allows you to run tests against your TurboGears application directly from your browser. This is great because it lets you test JavaScript and Ajax features, and because it lets you see your tests in action.
- You can use the Selenium IDE for Firefox to automatically generate test scripts for you as you browse through your application.

## Chapter 22

TurboGears Identity and Security

In This Chapter

There are two major segments to creating a "secure" web application. You need to write code to manage user authentication and authorization to assure that you grant access only to the right people. Then you need to make sure that you don't write application code that opens you up to potentially malicious behavior.

For the first set of issues, TurboGears provides the Identity framework, which can handle user authentication for you, and provides a very user-friendly API for adding authorization logic into your application.

For the second set, TurboGears provides a number of "automatic" mechanisms to help you avoid cross-site scripting and SQL injection attacks. TurboGears is designed around the philosophy that it should feel easy and natural to do the right thing when it comes to writing secure code. Of course, that doesn't mean you can ignore the potential security problems you might face. In this chapter we'll go over the major types of vulnerabilities so you'll be able to avoid them.

22.1 Basic Authentication/Authorization with Identity

The TurboGears Identity framework defaults to using your application's database to store usernames, privilege information, and passwords. For most stand-alone web applications this is what you want; but it isn't at all hard to validate against an external provider.

As we saw briefly in the WhatWhat Status application, Identity provides a simple API for defining access restrictions to individual pages, page sections, or whole "directory trees." While you can go back in later and add Identity to an existing project, it's easier to install Identity when you create the project by answering Yes when `tg-admin quickstart` asks if you want Identity. This automatically generates the model classes you need and adds them to your fresh `model.py` file. Not only does it add everything you need for a login page, it also adds `login` and `logout` methods to `controller.py` and a `login.kid` file to your templates directory.

Once you have a project with Identity up and running, you can decorate any controller with the `require` decorator, adding whatever restrictions you need. So, to restrict access to the `DashboardController` `index` method to only logged-in users, you could write something like this:

```
@tg.expose(template="securesite.admin")
@require(identity.in_group("admin"))
def siteadmin(self):
    pass
```

As we saw in Chapter 7, "Controllers, Views, and JavaScript in the WhatWhat Status," you can also secure a whole directory tree by creating a controller class that inherits from `SecureResources`. You can then override the `SecureResources` `require` method with whatever restrictions you need. We'll explore the details of Identity's `require` syntax in Section 22.2, "Validating User Access with Identity." First let's take a look at the autogenerated code.

We created a new project called `securesite`, with the `tg-admin` command, and included Identity. Let's take a quick look at some of the code it generates, before we get started creating secure page. Here's the `login` method from a freshly quickstarted site:

```
@expose(template="securesite.templates.login")
def login(self, forward_url=None, previous_url=None, *args, **kw):

    if not identity.current.anonymous \
        and identity.was_login_attempted() \
        and not identity.get_identity_errors():
        raise redirect(forward_url)

    forward_url=None
    previous_url= cherrypy.request.path

    if identity.was_login_attempted():
        msg=_("The credentials you supplied were not correct or "
            "did not grant access to this resource.")
    elif identity.get_identity_errors():
        msg=_("You must provide your credentials before accessing "
            "this resource.")
    else:
        msg=_("Please log in.")
        forward_url= cherrypy.request.headers.get("Referer", "/")
    cherrypy.response.status=403
    return dict(message=msg, previous_url=previous_url, logging_in=True,
            original_parameters=cherrypy.request.params,
            forward_url=forward_url)
```

There's quite a bit going on here. This page will be called whenever a user who is not logged in tries to access a secured resource. Because we want to forward the user back to the page they were trying to access originally, the default `login` controller does quite a bit of work to grab the URL from `cherrypy.request.headers`, and store it in `forward_url`.

If you want to rename the login page, you can do it easily by editing this method's name, going to `app.cfg`, and updating this line of code, to match your new method name.

```
identity.failure_url="/login"
```

Other than that, the login controller should be pretty self-explanatory. It checks to see if you are logged in and forwards you to the correct place if you are logged in and there are no errors. If there are any errors, it sends you out to the form with an appropriate message.

The `login.kid` form is found in `login.kid` and can be customized to your heart's content. It includes some CSS, which is not shown here, to create a nicer appearance, and you will very likely want to update that code so the login form matches the overall look and feel of your site:

```html
<body>
    <div id="loginBox">
        <h1>Login</h1>
        <p>${message}</p>
        <form action="${previous_url}" method="POST">
            <table>
                <tr>
                    <td class="label">
                        <label for="user_name">User Name:</label>
                    </td>
                    <td class="field">
                        <input type="text" id="user_name" name="user_name"/>
                    </td>
                </tr>
                <tr>
                    <td class="label">
                        <label for="password">Password:</label>
                    </td>
                    <td class="field">
                        <input type="password" id="password" name="password"/>
```

```
                    </td>
                </tr>
                <tr>
                    <td colspan="2" class="buttons">
                        <input type="submit" name="login" value="Login"/>
                    </td>
                </tr>
            </table>

            <input py:if="forward_url" type="hidden" name="forward_url"
                value="${forward_url}"/>

            <input py:for="name,value in original_parameters.items()"
                type="hidden" name="${name}" value="${value}"/>
        </form>
    </div>
</body>
```

As you can see there's nothing new in `login.kid`. It's just a manually-generated form that will be submitted back to the page that originally created the identity verification request. The `require` decorator will handle verifying the login and either grant or deny authorization for the login.

It's not nearly as interesting, but the default quickstarted project also includes a logout controller class, which logs the current user out and redirects to the index page.

```python
@expose()
def logout(self):
    identity.current.logout()
    raise redirect("/")
```

With the default Identity setup, all of your user and permission information will be stored in the database. To this end there are five model classes added to the database.

In `model.py` we find:

```python
class Visit(SQLObject):
    class sqlmeta:
        table="visit"

    visit_key= StringCol( length=40, alternateID=True,
                          alternateMethodName="by_visit_key" )
    created= DateTimeCol( default=datetime.now )
    expiry= DateTimeCol()
```

```
def lookup_visit( cls, visit_key ):
    try:
        return cls.by_visit_key( visit_key )
    except SQLObjectNotFound:
        return None
lookup_visit= classmethod(lookup_visit)

class VisitIdentity(SQLObject):
    visit_key = StringCol(length=40, alternateID=True,
                          alternateMethodName="by_visit_key")
    user_id = IntCol()
```

visit maintains information on a special "visit" cookie that connects the user to a particular server context. The cookie is used by Identity to keep track of which user is making a particular request. The visit_key is a unique hash that is stored in a cookie and is then connected to the user_id in the user class in VisitIdentity.

That brings us to the most important and complex of the Identity related classes in model.py, the User class:

```
class User(SQLObject):
    """
    Reasonably basic User definition. Probably would want additional attributes.
    """
    # names like "Group", "Order" and "User" are reserved words in SQL
    # so we set the name to something safe for SQL
    class sqlmeta:
        table="tg_user"

    user_name = UnicodeCol(length=16, alternateID=True,
                           alternateMethodName="by_user_name")
    email_address = UnicodeCol(length=255, alternateID=True,
                               alternateMethodName="by_email_address")
    display_name = UnicodeCol(length=255)
    password = UnicodeCol(length=40)
    created = DateTimeCol(default=datetime.now)

    # groups this user belongs to
    groups = RelatedJoin("Group", intermediateTable="user_group",
                         joinColumn="user_id", otherColumn="group_id")

    def _get_permissions(self):
        perms = set()
```

```
    for g in self.groups:
        perms = perms | set(g.permissions)
    return perms

def _set_password(self, cleartext_password):
    "Runs cleartext_password through the hash algorithm before saving."
    hash = identity.encrypt_password(cleartext_password)
    self._SO_set_password(hash)

def set_password_raw(self, password):
    "Saves the password as-is to the database."
    self._SO_set_password(password)
```

The `User` class uses the special `_get` and `_set` tricks SQLObject provides to allow you to override attribute access and creation. We looked at the `_get` and `_set` techniques in depth in Chapter 12, "Customizing SQLObject Behavior." Basically, whenever you set the `password` attribute, `_set_password()` will be called instead. Likewise when you access the permissions attribute, which is magically created by SQLObject, you'll get all the permissions for all of the groups of which a particular user is a member.

You can easily add attributes to your `User` class. For example, you may want to store the user's email address or first and last name. However, the Identity module relies on the existing attributes and methods, so you'll have to be careful when modifying pre-existing attributes.

Part of the permissions model built into Identity is that `Users` can belong to any number of `Groups`. In many cases this is all you need to secure your application. You can just check if a user is a member of the "admin" or "editor" or "superhero" groups and grant them access to the proper resources appropriately.

Here's the code for the `Group` class:

```
class Group(SQLObject):
    """
    An ultra-simple group definition.
    """

    # names like "Group", "Order" and "User" are reserved words in SQL
    # so we set the name to something safe for SQL
    class sqlmeta:
        table="tg_group"

    group_name = UnicodeCol(length=16, alternateID=True,
```

```
                              alternateMethodName="by_group_name")
    display_name = UnicodeCol(length=255)
    created = DateTimeCol(default=datetime.now)

    # collection of all users belonging to this group
    users = RelatedJoin("User", intermediateTable="user_group",
                        joinColumn="group_id", otherColumn="user_id")

    # collection of all permissions for this group
    permissions = RelatedJoin("Permission", joinColumn="group_id",
                              intermediateTable="group_permission",
                              otherColumn="permission_id")
```

The `Group` class has a many-to-many relationship with both `Users` and `Permissions`. This allows you to create more fine-grained access control. You can say that the `"can_add_user"` permission is available to members of the `"admin"` group, as well as to the `"hr_manager"` group. Again, if you want to store some group-related table, there's no problem. Just add columns to your table as you need them.

That leaves the `Permission` class:

```
class Permission(SQLObject):
    permission_name = UnicodeCol(length=16, alternateID=True,
                                 alternateMethodName="by_permission_name")
    description = UnicodeCol(length=255)

    groups = RelatedJoin("Group",
                         intermediateTable="group_permission",
                         joinColumn="permission_id",
                         otherColumn="group_id")
```

You can define users, groups, and passwords using standard SQLObject syntax or by using CatWalk. Passwords are automatically hashed before they go into the database by the `_set_password` method. So, administering Users, Groups, and Permissions is as painless as updating any other table in your database.

22.2 Validating User Access with Identity

The Identity package includes several features that you can use to create more complex validation logic. The validation method names are self-explanatory; however, you should remember that the values you are checking against are strings from the database. If you wanted to verify that a user was in the admin group you'd write:

```
@require(identity.in_group("admin")
```

Here's a list of the methods you can use to validate that a user has permission to access a resource.

- `not_anonymous`
- `in_group`
- `in_all_groups`
- `in_any_group`
- `has_permission`
- `has_all_permissions`
- `has_any_permission`
- `from_host`
- `from_any_host`

There are also two special methods, `Any` and `All`, which allow you to combine any number of the above checks into more complex logical groupings:

```
@require(identity.All(identity.in_group("superhero"),
                      identity.has_permission("access_hall_of_justice"))
```

as

You can use this validation logic in the `@require` decorator before any controller method to block access to the whole method. Or, as we saw in Chapter 7, you can subclass `SecureResource` in one of your controllers and run permission checks using any of the above functions by overriding the `require` attribute of the `SecureResource` class.

You can also use identity checks within your controller method. This, too, requires that your controller subclass `SecureResource`, so that the Identity exceptions you throw will be caught and handled appropriately.

```
class MyController(controllers.Controller, identity.SecureResource):

    @turbogears.expose(html="mytemplate")
    def myFunction(self):
```

```
if not ("admin" in identity.current.groups or
    "super" in identity.current.groups):
    raise identity.GroupMembershipRequiredException(("admin", "super"))
```

You can also use `tg.identity` as an automatically-imported alias for `turbogears.identity.current`. That will allow you to use standard `py:if` statements to display or hide various page elements based on user permissions:

```
<a py:if="'superhero' in tg.identity.groups" href="/display_powers">
  List possible superpowers
</a>
```

22.3 Avoiding Common Security Pitfalls

There are three common security problems in web applications: buffer overruns, Cross-Site Scripting (XSS) attacks, and SQL injection attacks. Because TurboGears applications are written in Python, your potential exposure to buffer overuns is minimal.

That leaves XSS and SQL injection attacks. XSS is made possible when user input is rendered to HTML without being escaped. Fortunately Kid escapes everything you insert into your template for you automatically. As a result, the only time you need to think about XSS attacks is when you are using Kid's XML function to bypass escaping.

In addition, SQLObject automatically escapes any strings you pass into it; so, unless you are constructing SQL by hand, you don't have to worry about SQL injection attacks.

Both SQL injection attacks and XSS attacks are subclasses of the same problem. User data is executed rather than processed as data. It's possible to do this in Python too; you want to be very careful when using the `exec` statement anywhere even remotely near user-entered data.

22.4 Summary

- The TurboGears Identity module makes it easy to add authentication/authorization logic to your project.
- You can modify the identity classes in `model.py` to add new features; however you shouldn't remove columns or you could break your identity code.

- Identity provides mechanisms to restrict access to particular controller methods via the `@require` decorator.

- You can use `SecureResource` to restrict access to an entire class (and therefore an entire web directory).

- You can use Identity checks from within your Kid templates, to custom generate pages based on user permissions.

- TurboGears makes escaping text that goes into your HTML the default, so you have to do a little bit of work to write code that could expose a cross site scripting attack.

- TurboGears automatically escapes data that you are sending to your database, making SQL injection attacks that much harder

- You can still write insecure applications with TurboGears if you bypass automatic escaping mechanisms or execute user data in any way. TurboGears isn't designed to prevent you from writing insecure code, but it is designed to make doing things the right way easier.

PART VIII
Appendix

Appendix

SQLAlchemy

SQLAlchemy is a powerful database-independent SQL layer and object-relational mapper library. It is newer than SQLObject and doesn't have as many tools within TurboGears, but TurboGears supports SQLAlchemy to handle those cases where SQLObject is not enough. This appendix includes a guide for migrating your SQLObject application to SQLAlchemy.

A.1 A Quick Tour of SQLAlchemy

SQLAlchemy, which was first announced in October 2005, is a newer object relational mapper (ORM) than SQLObject. SQLAlchemy is influenced by Hibernate, SQLObject, and others; and can handle a number of cases that are difficult or impossible for SQLObject.

SQLAlchemy's power comes from a few different aspects of its design:

1. It has an explicit, separate database-independent SQL generation layer.
2. Its ORM is built with the Data Mapper pattern (we'll talk more about Data Mapper in section A.3).
3. Its "unit-of-work" approach makes its basic object caching clear.

In addition, SQLAlchemy has some features that SQLObject lacks. It offers Oracle support and better support for compound and noninteger primary keys.

Here is a quick sample to show you what SQLAlchemy feels like. It's a data model for a simple wiki that allows tags to be applied to pages:

```
from sqlalchemy import *
from turbogears.database import metadata

page_table = Table("page", metadata,
    Column("page_id", Integer, primary_key=True),
    Column("pagename", String(30), unique=True),
    Column("data", String)
)

tag_table = Table("tag", metadata,
    Column("tag_id", Integer, primary_key=True),
    Column("tagname", String(20), unique=True)
```

```
)

page_tag_table = Table("page_tag", metadata,
    Column("tag_id", Integer, ForeignKey("tag.tag_id"), primary_key=True),
    Column("page_id", Integer, ForeignKey("page.page_id"), primary_key=True)
)

class Page(object):
    pass

class Tag(object):
    pass

tag_map = mapper(Tag, tag_table)

page_map = mapper(Page, page_table, properties=dict(
    tags = relation(Tag, secondary=page_tag_table, lazy = False,
                    backref=backref("pages"))
))
```

Mappers manage the connection between tables and Python classes.

Mappers automatically handle simple column-to-property mappings, and will manage table relationships with little work.

After running `tg-admin sql create` to build the database, we can play with it in an interactive session with `tg-admin shell` (the sample below was done with IPython installed):

```
In [1]:metadata.engine.echo = True
In [2]:page = Page()
In [3]:page.pagename = "FrontPage"
In [4]:page.data = "Hi!"
In [5]:tag = Tag()
In [6]:tag.tagname = "intro"
In [7]:page.tags.append(tag)
In [8]:session.save(page)
In [9]:session.flush()
[2006-07-21 13:20:42,411] [engine]: BEGIN

[2006-07-21 13:20:42,420] [engine]: INSERT INTO tag (tagname) VALUES (?)
[2006-07-21 13:20:42,421] [engine]: ['intro']
[2006-07-21 13:20:42,430] [engine]: INSERT INTO page (pagename, data) VALUES
(?, ?)
[2006-07-21 13:20:42,432] [engine]: ['FrontPage', 'Hi!']
[2006-07-21 13:20:42,440] [engine]: INSERT INTO page_tag (tag_id, page_id)
VALUES (?, ?)
[2006-07-21 13:20:42,441] [engine]: [1, 1]
[2006-07-21 13:20:42,444] [engine]: COMMIT
```

This lets us see the queries as they run.

session.save is how we tell SQLAlchemy about a new object.

Unlike SQLObject, which runs queries immediately, SQLAlchemy runs all the queries when you flush.

We only called **session.save** on the page object, but SQLAlchemy also saved the tag for us by following the connection we had defined in the mapper.

SQLAlchemy knows how to fill in the many-to-many join table (**page_tag**) automatically.

This appendix introduces you to SQLAlchemy and its use within TurboGears. It is not a comprehensive reference or guide to SQLAlchemy. You can find excellent documentation at the official website, www.sqlalchemy.org.

In addition to covering the use of SQLAlchemy in TurboGears, this appendix provides some documentation for the ActiveMapper extension and a guide for migrating an application from SQLObject to SQLAlchemy.

A.2   SQLAlchemy in TurboGears

TurboGears 1.0 uses SQLObject as its default database layer. This is partly due to SQLAlchemy's release status, because it remains a fairly recently released package with a low version number. More importantly, as of this writing, TurboGears tools such as CatWalk and Model Designer do not yet support SQLAlchemy.

However, everything you need to use SQLAlchemy in a TurboGears project is available, and quite a few significant projects are already using SQLAlchemy in production. Support for SQLAlchemy is readily available on the mailing list should you run into problems. If SQLAlchemy fits your project, you can feel confident that it is a good solution that delivers on its promises.

TurboGears support for SQLAlchemy includes the following:

- Quickstart can generate an SQLAlchemy-based project. Your project will have all the proper imports and configuration to use SQLAlchemy.
- The Identity package includes an identity provider for SQLAlchemy.
- TurboGears provides implicit database transactions around your requests.
- The `tg-admin sql` command supports SQLAlchemy.

When you quickstart a new project, you can specify that it is an SQLAlchemy project by adding the `-s` parameter. For example:

```
tg-admin quickstart -s ProjectName
```

> Note: TurboGears does not let you mix SQLAlchemy and SQLObject in the same project.

When you do this, the generated configuration files will be correct for SQLAlchemy, and your `model.py` file will be all set up to use SQLAlchemy.

When working with your SQLAlchemy project, you will find two objects in `turbogears.database` that will prove useful to you: `session` and `metadata`.

When defining SQLAlchemy `Table` objects, be sure to define the tables in the `turbogears.database.metadata` if you want commands such as `tg-admin sql create` to work properly.

TurboGears provides implicit transactions around each request. This includes a `session.flush()` and also includes `session.clear()` at appropriate points in the request cycle. If you create a new object that needs to be stored in the database, you should use `session.save(new_object)` on the session located in `turbogears.database`.

A.3   Data Mapper and Active Record

As discussed initially in Chapter 8, "RSS, Cookies, and Dynamic Views in WhatWhat Status," SQLObject follows the Active Record design pattern. In short, this pattern says that each table in your database is represented by a Python class. Instances of those objects directly represent rows in the database table.

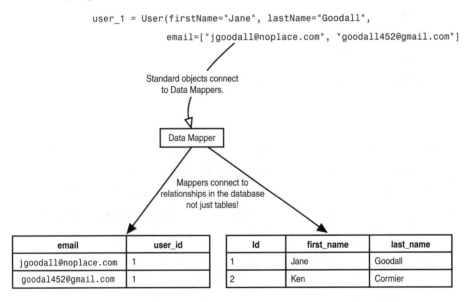

The Data Mapper pattern adds an extra layer. There are classes that represent the tables in the database, but there are also objects that separately map from database tables to your classes. The Data Mapper pattern has some advantages over Active Record:

1. Your classes are not tied to the database. They can freely be used in other contexts, such as tests, without worrying about database setup.

2. Any "relation," in relational database management system (RDBMS) terms, can be mapped. This means that the results of arbitrary queries can be mapped to Python objects.

3. Python objects can be composed of data from different tables.

The drawback to the Data Mapper pattern is that it requires more setup. Instead of setting up one class, you now have two to worry about. It turns out, though, that the Data Mapper pattern is a superset of Active Record. There is an extension included with SQLAlchemy called ActiveMapper. When your Python class subclasses ActiveMapper, ActiveMapper creates `Table` and `Mapper` objects behind the scenes, giving you the same ease-of-use that you get from an Active Record-based library such as SQLObject.

Choosing to use ActiveMapper at the beginning of the project does not mean you lose any of SQLAlchemy's power. You can still access a class's `Table` object by looking up the `table` class property:

```
class Plate(ActiveMapper):
    class mapping:
        size = column(Integer)


print type(Plate.table)
<class 'sqlalchemy.schema.Table'>
```

A.4 More about ActiveMapper

The SQLAlchemy documentation covers SQLAlchemy's features in detail, but it does not cover the "extensions," and ActiveMapper is an extension. Luckily, there is not much you need to know about ActiveMapper. In SQLAlchemy, when you define a table, you typically do something like this:

```
products = Table("products", metadata,
    Column("product_id", Integer, primary_key=True),
    Column("product_code", String(20), unique=True),
    Column("description", String))
```

You can easily tell SQLAlchemy to map a class to that table:

```
class Product(object):
    pass


pmap = mapper(Product, products)
```

At that point, `pmap` offers methods for retrieving `Product` objects from the database. Here is the equivalent table and class created with ActiveMapper:

```
class Product(ActiveMapper):
    class mapping:
        product_id = column(Integer, primary_key=True)
        product_code = column(String(20), unique=True)
        description = column(String)
```

All of the methods (`get_by`, `select`, and so on) that are typically found on the `pmap` object in the first example are available directly on the `Product` class in the second example.

The mapper is available via `Product.mapper` and the table object is available via `Product.table`, if you need to work directly with those objects.

Not much actual difference exists between the two examples, and that is part of the idea. ActiveMapper does not try to reinvent any of SQLAlchemy's core object-relational mapping features. It just provides a more concise syntax for times when the Active Record pattern works well.

One useful behavior to note about ActiveMapper: ActiveMapper will automatically `save()` new objects that you create into the session located at `turbogears.database.session`. This behavior differs from what you get using plain SQLAlchemy, but it is equivalent to what you get with SQLObject.

A.5   How Objects Are Cached in SQLAlchemy

SQLObject includes some options (`lazyUpdate` and `cacheValues`) to control how SQLObject caches values. Most people don't use these options, and SQLAlchemy doesn't offer the equivalent options because its caching is simpler.

SQLAlchemy is built around a "unit-of-work" pattern, as described by Martin Fowler in *Patterns of Enterprise Application Architecture*. This means that you typically work with various objects while accomplishing a specific task. In SQLAlchemy, you have `session` objects that hang on to all the objects you're working with in a unit of work. TurboGears maintains one for you as `turbogears.database.session`. When an object needs to be retrieved from the database, its primary key is first looked up in the session. If it's already present in the session, the existing object is returned directly:

```
>>> page1 = Page.get(1)
>>> page2 = Page.get(1)
```

```
>>> page1 is page2
True
```

SQLAlchemy does not issue *any* database update commands until the session is told to "flush." Objects loaded from the database will stick around until `clear` is called on the session. TurboGears automatically flushes the session, commits the database transaction, and clears the session at the end of the request.

If you are working with many objects or need to explicitly refresh an object from the database, you can call methods on the session to flush and clear objects as needed.

When using SQLObject with TurboGears, you are already following a pattern similar to SQLAlchemy's unit of work because of how TurboGears handles transactions.

A.6   Should I Use SQLAlchemy or SQLObject?

Philosophically, we try to present one way to do common tasks with TurboGears. But, there are two places where we need to deviate from that:

1. There are some less-common needs that need to be accommodated.
2. A new "best" approach is discovered.

SQLAlchemy is supported in TurboGears for both of these reasons.

If you are connecting TurboGears to a legacy database, you will find that SQLAlchemy can handle a much wider variety of potential schemas. If you have specific performance constraints, SQLAlchemy also makes it easier to optimize the SQL that is produced while still maintaining database independence and a Python feel.

We think that SQLAlchemy is maturing into the best database access layer available for Python. For many applications, we would opt for SQLAlchemy rather than SQLObject. However, because TurboGears provides many more tools for working with SQLObject databases, SQLObject might be a better choice for newcomers to TurboGears and Python.

As with any choice in software, the choice you make almost always depends on the application at hand and the people involved.

We hope to eventually have a compatibility layer that makes migration from SQLObject to SQLAlchemy easy. For now, the following section will help you make the move if you start with SQLObject and later decide that you need specific features offered by SQLAlchemy.

A.7   Migrating a Project to SQLAlchemy

Using ActiveMapper, it is not too difficult to migrate a typical project from SQL-Object to SQLAlchemy. Some transformations are required to move from SQLObject to SQLAlchemy:

1. Database configuration in the deployment config file

2. Identity configuration in the application config file

3. Class definitions in your project's `model.py` file

4. Calls to `bySomeColumn(SomeValue)` need to change to `get_by(SomeColumn=SomeValue)`

5. Changes to your queries

This section is not an exhaustive guide to migrating a project to SQLAlchemy, but it should help you along the way. All the most common SQLObject features are represented. It might seem like there are many steps to go through in the coming sections, but the translation is fairly mechanical and straightforward.

A.8   Deployment Configuration

When you create a project, you get two deployment configuration files: `dev.cfg` and `sample-prod.cfg`. If you look in these files, you'll find `sqlobject.dburi` options. Change this parameter to `sqlalchemy.dburi`. SQLAlchemy's database URI syntax is similar to that of SQLObject, and you will likely not have to change anything other than the name of the configuration parameter. Note that you will also need to change your production configuration file when you are deploying your code into production for the first time.

A.9   Application Configuration

If your project does not use identity, you don't need to make any changes in your application configuration.

Your main application configuration is stored in `yourproject/yourpackage/config/app.cfg`. This file contains your application's identity configuration. Turbo-Gears includes identity providers for both SQLObject and SQLAlchemy. There are three changes to be made in this file:

1. Replace all occurrences of "soprovider" with "saprovider".

2. Set `visit.manager="sqlalchemy"`

3. Set `identity.provider="sqlalchemy"`

A.10 Class Definitions

The most direct path you can use to migrate your model definition is to use Active-Mapper. This section outlines the basic steps required to migrate from SQLObject to SQLAlchemy with ActiveMapper. Before getting into the detailed steps of doing a conversion, you can get a feel for the differences by looking at some code in both SQLAlchemy and SQLObject. We'll go through the TurboGears Identity model class by class, showing the SQLObject version and then the SQLAlchemy with ActiveMapper version.

The `visit` class for handling anonymous and authenticated site visitors is as follows:

```
class Visit(SQLObject):
 class sqlmeta:
     table="visit"

 visit_key= StringCol( length=40, alternateID=True,
                       alternateMethodName="by_visit_key" )
 created= DateTimeCol( default=datetime.now )
 expiry= DateTimeCol()

 def lookup_visit( cls, visit_key ):
     try:
         return cls.by_visit_key( visit_key )
     except SQLObjectNotFound:
         return None
 lookup_visit= classmethod(lookup_visit)
```

To convert this over to ActiveMapper, we need to turn the column definitions inside out, declaring `column` objects and specifying their types rather than declaring columns of specific types. Other than that, the two look quite similar:

```
class Visit(ActiveMapper):
    class mapping:
        __table__ = "visit"
        visit_key = column(String(40), primary_key=True)
        created = column(DateTime, nullable = False, default=datetime.now)
        expiry = column(DateTime)
```

```
    def lookup_visit(cls, visit_key):
        return Visit.get( visit_key );
    lookup_visit= classmethod(lookup_visit)
```

The `VisitIdentity` class maps from a visit to the identity of a known user:

```
class VisitIdentity(SQLObject):
    visit_key = StringCol(length=40, alternateID=True,
                          alternateMethodName="by_visit_key")
    user_id = IntCol()
```

This conversion follows the same pattern as the last:

```
class VisitIdentity(ActiveMapper):
    class mapping:
        __table__="visit_identity"
        visit_key = column(String, # foreign_key="visit.visit_key",
                           primary_key=True)
        user_id = column(Integer, foreign_key="tg_user.user_id", index=True)
```

A `Group` collects up a bunch of users so that they can all be granted a set of permissions at one time. Here is the SQLObject definition for a `Group`:

```
class Group(SQLObject):
    """
    An ultra-simple group definition.
    """

    # names like "Group", "Order" and "User" are reserved words in SQL
    # so we set the name to something safe for SQL
    class sqlmeta:
        table="tg_group"

    group_name = UnicodeCol(length=16, alternateID=True,
                            alternateMethodName="by_group_name")
    display_name = UnicodeCol(length=255)
    created = DateTimeCol(default=datetime.now)

    # collection of all users belonging to this group
    users = RelatedJoin("User", intermediateTable="user_group",
                        joinColumn="group_id", otherColumn="user_id")

    # collection of all permissions for this group
    permissions = RelatedJoin("Permission", joinColumn="group_id",
                              intermediateTable="group_permission",
                              otherColumn="permission_id")
```

This is one case where ActiveMapper has not yet caught up with SQLObject's simplicity. `Group` has two many-to-many relationships. SQLObject automatically defines the join tables for those relationships, whereas ActiveMapper does not. The definitions are straightforward:

```
# tables for SQLAlchemy identity
user_group = Table("user_group", metadata,
                   Column("user_id", Integer,
                          ForeignKey("tg_user.user_id"),
                          primary_key=True),
                   Column("group_id", Integer,
                          ForeignKey("tg_group.group_id"),
                          primary_key=True))

group_permission = Table("group_permission", metadata,
                         Column("group_id", Integer,
                                ForeignKey("tg_group.group_id"),
                                primary_key=True),
                         Column("permission_id", Integer,
                                ForeignKey("permission.permission_id"),
                                primary_key=True))
```

With those two tables in hand, we can define the SQLAlchemy version of `Group` following the pattern we've used for the other tables:

```
class Group(ActiveMapper):
    """

    An ultra-simple group definition.
    """

    class mapping:
        __table__="tg_group"
        group_id = column(Integer, primary_key=True)
        group_name = column(Unicode(16), unique=True)
        display_name = column(Unicode(255))
        created = column(DateTime, default=datetime.now)

        users = many_to_many("User", user_group, backref="groups")
        permissions = many_to_many("Permission", group_permission,
                                   backref="groups")
```

The definition of the `User` class is a little more involved than the previous classes. It has a handful of fields on it, a special setter for encrypting the password, and a getter to retrieve all of the permissions that the user has been granted:

```
class User(SQLObject):
    """
```

```
    Reasonably basic User definition. Probably would want additional
attributes.
    """
    # names like "Group", "Order" and "User" are reserved words in SQL
    # so we set the name to something safe for SQL

    class sqlmeta:
        table="tg_user"

    user_name = UnicodeCol(length=16, alternateID=True,
                           alternateMethodName="by_user_name")
    email_address = UnicodeCol(length=255, alternateID=True,
                               alternateMethodName="by_email_address")
    display_name = UnicodeCol(length=255)
    password = UnicodeCol(length=40)
    created = DateTimeCol(default=datetime.now)

    # groups this user belongs to
    groups = RelatedJoin("Group", intermediateTable="user_group",
                         joinColumn="user_id", otherColumn="group_id")

    def _get_permissions(self):
        perms = set()
        for g in self.groups:
            perms = perms | set(g.permissions)
        return perms

    def _set_password(self, cleartext_password):
        "Runs cleartext_password through the hash algorithm before saving."
        hash = identity.encrypt_password(cleartext_password)
        self._SO_set_password(hash)

    def set_password_raw(self, password):
        "Saves the password as-is to the database."
        self._SO_set_password(password)
```

The ActiveMapper User class defines the getter method for the permissions attribute, but does it in the standard Python form with a call to property. The current version of the SQLAlchemy Identity model does not include the encryption feature:

```
class User(ActiveMapper):
    """
    Reasonably basic User definition. Probably would want additional
attributes.
    """
```

```
class mapping:
    __table__="tg_user"
    user_id = column(Integer, primary_key=True)
    user_name = column(Unicode(16), unique=True)
    email_address = column(Unicode(255), unique=True)
    display_name = column(Unicode(255))
    password = column(Unicode(40))
    created = column(DateTime, default=datetime.now)

    groups = many_to_many("Group", user_group, backref="users")

def permissions(self):
    perms = set()
    for g in self.groups:
        perms = perms | set(g.permissions)
    return perms
permissions = property(permissions)
```

Finally, we come to the definition of a `Permission`. This one just uses features that we've seen in previous classes:

```
class Permission(SQLObject):
    permission_name = UnicodeCol(length=16, alternateID=True,
                                 alternateMethodName="by_permission_name")
    description = UnicodeCol(length=255)

    groups = RelatedJoin("Group",
                         intermediateTable="group_permission",
                         joinColumn="permission_id",
                         otherColumn="group_id")
```

The ActiveMapper version is basically the same, and we're able to reuse the many-to-many join table definition that we created earlier:

```
class Permission(ActiveMapper):
    class mapping:
        __table__="permission"
        permission_id = column(Integer, primary_key=True)
        permission_name = column(Unicode(16), unique=True)
        description = column(Unicode(255))

        groups = many_to_many("Group", group_permission,
                              backref="permissions")
```

Here are the basic steps required to migrate your database model using
ActiveMapper:

1. Change the imports.

   a. Remove the `SQLObject` import line.

   b. Add the `SQLAlchemy` imports:

      ```
      from sqlalchemy import *

      from sqlalchemy.ext.activemapper import ActiveMapper, column, \

      one_to_many, one_to_one, many_to_many
      ```

   c. Remove the lines related to the `PackageHub`, which is part of TurboGears's
      SQLObject support.

   d. Add `from turbogears.database import metadata`.

2. Change the base class for your model class from SQLObject to ActiveMapper.

3. Create a new inner class named `mapping` and indent all the column definitions
   to be a part of that class.

4. Update your column definitions to use `column` from ActiveMapper (see Table
   A-1).

5. Migrate `sqlmeta` parameters into your mapping class. `table` in `sqlmeta` becomes
   `_table_` in mapping.

6. Use Python's `property` built-in function to create properties
   from your `_get_*` and `_set_*` methods. For example, if you have
   `_get_password` and `_set_password` you should add a line that says
   `password = property(_get_password, _set_password)`.

7. Create many-to-many join tables. As of this writing, SQLAlchemy does not
   create many-to-many join tables for you. You have to create these `Table` objects
   yourself (see below for an example).

8. Be sure to provide column and table names based on SQLObject's "style." By
   default, SQLObject converts mixedCaseNames to names that contain under-
   scores when you create the database. If you have a table that is named something like TableName, the name of the table in the database with SQLObject
   will be `table_name`. You can tell SQLAlchemy/ActiveMapper to make this
   translation by setting `_table_ = table_name` in your mapping class. If you
   have a column called columnName, it will be translated by SQLObject to
   `column_name` in the database. You can do the same with ActiveMapper by passing `colname=column_name` in your `column()` call.

9. Create a primary key column for each table. SQLObject automatically creates a primary key column called `id` for your tables. ActiveMapper can automatically create an ID column for you, too, but it does not use the same naming convention. You just need to add something like this to your mapping class:

```
id = column(Integer, primary_key=True).
```

Table A-1 Column Type Conversions

SQLObject	SQLAlchemy
SQLObject	SQLAlchemy/ActiveMapper
StringCol()	column(String)
	column(String(40))
UnicodeCol()	column(Unicode)
IntCol()	column(Integer)
FloatCol()	column(Float)
DecimalCol()	column(Numeric)
DateTimeCol()	column(Datetime)
DateCol()	column(Date)
TimeCol()	column(Time)
BLOBCol()	column(Blob)
BoolCol()	column(Boolean)
PickleCol()	column(PickleType)
	one_to_many('Class')

Table A-2 Column Options

SQLObject	SQLAlchemy
SQLObject	SQLAlchemy
notNone	nullable
unique	unique
alternateID	unique

As of this writing, ActiveMapper does not automatically create join tables for you for a many-to-many mapping (`RelatedJoin` in SQLObject). Luckily, they are easy to define:

```
join_table = Table("join_table_name", metadata,
                   Column("class1_id", Integer,
                          ForeignKey("table1name.id"),
                          primary_key=True),
                   Column("class2_id", Integer,
                          ForeignKey("table2name.id"),
                          primary_key=True))
```

You should define this table object *before* the first class that is part of the many-to-many relationship.

A.11 Changing Calls to `byName` Methods

SQLObject defines a number of useful methods on your classes such as `select`, to retrieve many objects based on query parameters, and `get`, to retrieve a single object based on its primary key. SQLAlchemy gives you those class methods.

For every column that you declare as an "alternateID" in SQLObject, SQLObject creates a class method called `byColumnName`. The idiom used in SQLAlchemy is different: There is a class method called `get_by` and you pass in a keyword parameter to retrieve a specific instance by that alternate ID. You have two options:

1. You can change all the calls to `byColumnName`. In SQLObject you say
   `obj = YourClass.byColumnName(value_to_find)`. In SQLAlchemy, you say
   `obj = YourClass.get_by(columnName = value_to_find)`.

2. You can add a `byColumnName` method to your class:

```
class Products(ActiveMapper):
    class mapping:
        productCode = column(String(20), unique=True)

    @classmethod
    def byProductCode(cls, code):
        return cls.get_by(productCode=code)
```

A.12 Updating Queries

Part of the reason that migration from SQLObject to SQLAlchemy is not too onerous is that SQLAlchemy has largely adopted SQLObject's query style.

The first change you need to be aware of is that SQLObject's `q` object for referring to columns has been named `c` in SQLAlchemy. Consider the case of a wiki:

```
class Page(ActiveMapper):
    class mapping:
        pagename = Column(String(40), unique=True)
        data = Column(String)
```

In the equivalent SQLObject definition, if you want to query on `pagename` you do something like this: `Page.select(Page.q.pagename > 'F')`. In SQLAlchemy, you would do this: `Page.select(Page.c.pagename > 'F')`. The only difference between those two is that `Page.q` has been replaced by `Page.c`!

The operator handling is similar between the two packages. One difference is that SQLObject uses functions called AND, OR, and NOT. SQLAlchemy uses `and`, `or`, and `not_` (with the trailing underscore being the PEP 8 listed style for naming a function the same as a Python keyword). If you use the & and | operators, those work the same between SQLObject and SQLAlchemy.

Both packages support `startswith` and `endswith` and both use `func` to refer to database engine functions.

One important difference to note: In SQLObject, `select()` returns an iterable `SelectResults` object. SQLAlchemy's `select()` call, on the other hand, returns a list directly. In SQLObject, you can say `Page.select().count()` to get a count of the pages. To do the same in SQLAlchemy, you run `Page.count()`. SQLObject lets you place limits on a query by using Python's slice ([x:y]) notation; for example, `Page.select()[0:10]`. In SQLAlchemy, you add the limits more explicitly before running the query as part of the select call `Page.select(limit=10, offset=1).execute()`.

A.13   Final Thoughts

SQLAlchemy's application programming interfaces (APIs) are well thought out and generally stable, but it is likely that there will still be some fluctuation. The code itself is solid and has an extensive set of tests. If you are willing to accept the need to make minor changes to your code from time to time as SQLAlchemy evolves, you will find that it is an incredibly powerful and yet easy-to-use object relational mapper and database-independent SQL generator.

Index

G

BOOKS ONLINE

ENABLED

THIS BOOK IS SAFARI ENABLED

INCLUDES FREE 45-DAY ACCESS TO THE ONLINE EDITION

The Safari® Enabled icon on the cover of your favorite technology book means the book is available through Safari Bookshelf. When you buy this book, you get free access to the online edition for 45 days.

Safari Bookshelf is an electronic reference library that lets you easily search thousands of technical books, find code samples, download chapters, and access technical information whenever and wherever you need it.

TO GAIN 45-DAY SAFARI ENABLED ACCESS TO THIS BOOK:

- Go to **http://www.prenhallprofessional.com/safarienabled**

- Complete the brief registration form

- Enter the coupon code found in the front of this book on the "Copyright" page

If you have difficulty registering on Safari Bookshelf or accessing the online edition, please e-mail customer-service@safaribooksonline.com.

PRENTICE HALL

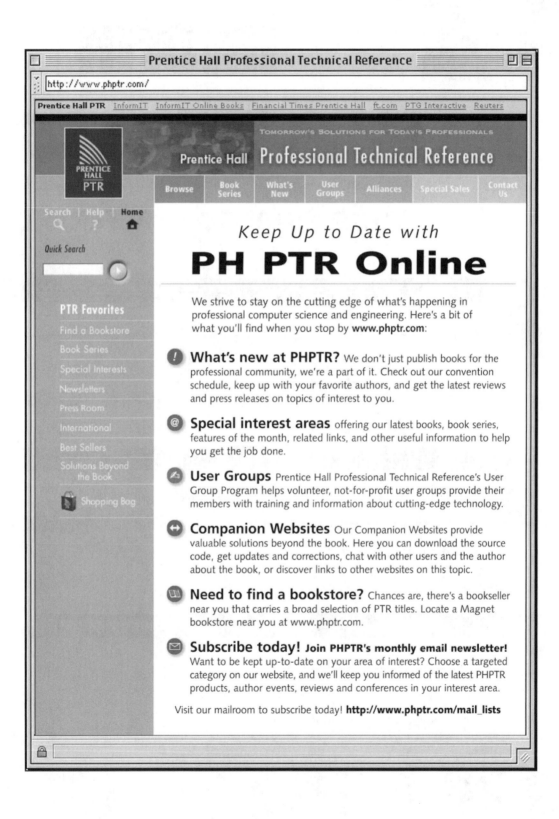